THE COMPREHENSIVE NCLEX®-RN REVIEW
Fifteenth Edition

Fundamentals for Nursing

Adult Medical-Surgical Nursing

Mental Health Nursing

Maternal Newborn Nursing

Nursing Care of Children

Pharmacology for Nursing

Nursing Leadership and Management

Community Health Nursing

The Comprehensive NCLEX®-RN Review
Your Guide to Preparing for the NCLEX-RN Exam
Fifteenth Edition

Editors

Cherralene L. Peer, MSN, RN, CLNC
Heather H. Stranger, MSN, RN, CNE
Kathryn A. Meglitsch-Tate, MSN, RN
Teresa M. LaFave, NP, MSN, RN

Associate Editor

Brant L. Stacy, BS Journalism, BA English

IMPORTANT NOTICE TO THE READER

Assessment Technologies Institute®, LLC is the publisher of this publication. The publisher reserves the right to modify, change, or update the content of this publication at any time. The content of this publication, such as text, graphics, images, information obtained from the publisher's licensors, and other material contained in this publication are for informational purposes only. The content is not providing medical advice and is not intended to be a substitute for professional medical advice, diagnosis, or treatment. Always seek the advice of your primary care provider or other qualified health provider for any questions you may have regarding a medical condition. Never disregard professional medical advice or delay in seeking it because of something you have read in this publication. If you think you may have a medical emergency, go to your local emergency department or call 911 immediately.

The publisher does not recommend or endorse any specific tests, primary care providers, products, procedures, processes, opinions, or other information that may be mentioned in this publication. Reliance on any information provided by the publisher, the publisher's employees, or others contributing to the content at the invitation of the publisher is solely at your own risk. Health care professionals need to use their own clinical judgment in interpreting the content of this publication, and details such as medications, dosages, and laboratory tests and results should always be confirmed with other resources.

This publication may contain health- or medical-related materials that are sexually explicit. If you find these materials offensive, you may not want to use this publication.

The publishers, editors, advisors, and reviewers make no representations or warranties of any kind or nature, including, but not limited to, the accuracy, reliability, completeness, currentness, timeliness, or the warranties of fitness for a particular purpose or merchantability, nor are any such representations implied with respect to the content herein (with such content to include text and graphics), and the publishers, editors, advisors, and reviewers take no responsibility with respect to such content. The publishers, editors, advisors, and reviewers shall not be liable for any actual, incidental, special, consequential, punitive, or exemplary damages (or any other type of damages) resulting, in whole or in part, from the reader's use of, or reliance upon, such content.

USER'S GUIDE AND ORGANIZATION

Congratulations graduate! You have successfully completed your program of nursing studies and are now eligible to take the licensing exam created by the National Council of State Boards of Nursing (NCSBN®).

Understanding the organizational format of this review book will help guide you through a focused review in preparation for NCLEX. Each unit focuses on a specific area of nursing care. Unit 1 offers practical information about the exam, including how to prepare and test-taking strategies. The next eight units review essential content for the exam:

- Fundamentals for Nursing
- Adult Medical-Surgical Nursing
- Mental Health Nursing
- Maternal Newborn Nursing
- Nursing Care of Children
- Pharmacology for Nursing
- Nursing Leadership and Management
- Community Health Nursing

Tables and graphics are provided throughout to simplify more challenging content.

The content provided in this book is organized by body systems and focuses on manifestations, diagnostics, and nursing interventions expected of a graduate nurse. The information is presented in a manner that promotes analysis and application of knowledge and reinforces priority of care when managing client care.

Nursing interventions are noted throughout the book with a stethoscope icon.

A bolded exclamation point icon designates key points to remember such as safety issues and the Airway, Breathing, and Circulation (ABC) principle.

Feedback is always welcome. Therefore, please send suggestions for improvement, any noted errors, and personal testimonials of effectiveness to comments@atitesting.com.

UNIT ONE

REVIEW OF TEST-TAKING STRATEGIES FOR THE NCLEX-RN EXAM

SECTION 1

INFORMATION ABOUT THE EXAM

What to Know About the NCLEX-RN Exam

- General Information
  - The purpose of the exam is to determine that a candidate is prepared to safely practice entry-level nursing.
  - The exam is designed to test essential nursing knowledge and a candidate's ability to apply that knowledge to clinical situations.
  - The new test plan will bring the exam in line with current nursing behaviors (the nursing process and decision making).
  - The exam is pass/fail, and no other score is given.
- Computerized Adaptive Testing
  - The computer program continuously scores answers and selects questions suitable for each candidate's competency level for a more precise measurement of competency.
  - Use the mouse to move the cursor on the screen to a desired location.
  - Single-click the mouse to select an option as the answer.
  - A drop-down calculator is also featured. Double-click the mouse on the calculator icon, and the drop-down calculator will appear.
  - After confirming the selection, click on "next" to input the answer and proceed to the next screen.
  - You cannot go back to a previous question to change your answer.
  - The exam includes 15 unmarked experimental questions that do not impact the final score.
- Exam Schedule
  - The exam is given all year long.
  - The exam can only be repeated every 45 days.

- Number of Questions and Time Allowed
  - There is not a minimum amount of time for the exam; however, a candidate must answer a minimum of 75 test questions. The maximum time is 6 hr, with a maximum of 265 test questions.
  - The computer will automatically stop as soon as one of the following occurs:
    - The candidate's measure of competency is determined to be above or below the passing standard.
    - The candidate has answered all 265 test questions.
    - The maximum amount of time (6 hr) has expired.

SECTION 2

NCLEX AND ITEM FORMATS

Exam Breakdown

- NCLEX questions are distributed and weighted according to the following client need categories in the test plan blueprint:
  - Safe and Effective Care Environment
    - Management of Care 16 to 22%
    - Safety and Infection Control 8 to 14%
  - Health Promotion and Maintenance 6 to 12%
  - Psychosocial Integrity 6 to 12%
  - Physiological Integrity
    - Basic Care and Comfort 6 to 12%
    - Pharmacological and Parenteral Therapies 13 to 19%
    - Reduction of Risk Potential 10 to 16%
    - Physiological Adaptation 11 to 17%
- *Information provided courtesy of the National Council of State Boards of Nursing, Inc., Test Plan April 2010*

NOTES

Exam Procedure

- Look for the BEST answer to each question.
- It is not possible to skip questions or return to previous questions.
- Breaks are optional and the clock will continue to run when a break is taken.
- A dry erase board is provided for calculations.

NCLEX Item Types

- Standard Multiple-Choice Question
  - Traditional NCLEX question
  - Most common type of question on the exam
  - Has four options, only one of which is correct
- As of April 2003, the NCLEX started including items other than standard multiple-choice questions. These items are known as alternate test items.

 Point to Remember

- The candidate should allow more time for answering alternate test items.

- Fill-In-The-Blank
  - Fill-in-the-blank items are primarily calculation problems. The question may ask for an answer in a specific unit amount or a rounded decimal.
  - To answer these questions, a number should be typed into the answer box on the screen.

 Points to Remember

- Solve for the correct unit value.
- Write out the calculations on material provided.
- Bring up the drop-down calculator.
- Double-check work.

- Drag and Drop/Ordered Response
  - Drag-and-drop/ordered response items list steps that must be placed in a correct sequence as indicated by the prompt.
  - To answer these questions, drag options in the left-hand column into the appropriate order of performance in the right-hand column.
  - There is only one correct sequence to maintain the client's safety at each step in the care continuum.

- Multiple Response
  - Multiple-response items require test takers to choose more than one answer. Any number of the options may be correct. Although, not all the options in a question can be correct.
  - To answer these questions, click on all the answers that apply.
  - Credit will only be given for completely correct answers. No partial credit is given.

 Point to Remember

- Consider each response as a true-false question.

- Hot Spot
  - Hot spot items use a "point and click" method that requires a test taker to choose the correct anatomical location on a figure.
  - Click on the area that constitutes the landmark to correctly answer the item.
  - Read the question carefully, then analyze the image.
  - The exam will allow the test taker to reclick on the image as many times as necessary.

 Point to Remember

- It is very important to remember that the screen is NOT a mirror image. If the question asks for an answer on the right or left side of the body, make sure to click on the appropriate side.

- Chart/Exhibit
  - Standard multiple-choice questions may also include chart exhibits that must be analyzed and understood to correctly answer the question. The chart/exhibit question cannot be answered without obtaining further information; this is where the chart comes in to play. On-screen tabs, similar to the tabs either in a client's chart or computerized medical record, will allow the test taker to select various client documents. For example, one tab may say "Medication Administration Record," another may be labeled "Vital Signs," or "Laboratory Results." These documents will contain information that the test taker must analyze to correctly answer the question.

NOTES

- First, read the question carefully. Then, analyze the charts or exhibit. Use the mouse to click on each tab to open the document. When the tab is clicked, a separate window will open to display the data contained in the selected section of the client's chart. Analysis of the data in each of these documents provides the information necessary to answer the question.

- Graphic Option
  - These items display images for each answer option.
  - The answers to these items are preceded by circles. So, be sure to click on the circle to select the answer.

- Audio
  - Audio items may test knowledge of audible breath and heart sounds, or examples of change-of-shift client reports or unit-transfer reports.
  - When an audio item is presented on NCLEX, the candidate is prompted to apply headphones. Ear phones will be provided to accurately identify the audio sound. The volume of the audio may be adjusted and replayed as often as needed.

SECTION 3

PREPARING FOR AND ANSWERING QUESTIONS ON THE EXAM

- New nursing graduates should review content and questions daily until they take the exam. Adequate review depends on scores obtained on practice assessments, and NCLEX preparation after a live review may take anywhere from 2 to 8 weeks.

- For content review, use this NCLEX-RN review book that outlines content. Use other nursing reference materials for more detailed information.

- Begin with areas that are most difficult or least familiar.

- When studying body systems and the associated diseases:
  - Define the disease in terms of the pathophysiological process that is occurring.
  - Identify the client's early and late manifestations.
  - Identify the most important or life-threatening complications.

- Review the medical treatment.
- Identify and prioritize the nursing interventions associated with early and late manifestations.
- Identify the teaching that the nurse should provide to the client/family to prevent or adapt to the disease.

- Study Time
  - The practice assessment score reports will identify and help direct review of content.
  - Take one assessment at a time and then review the content and topics missed on the score report.
  - The assessments are timed and may only be taken once.

Interpreting ATI Assessment Scores

- Complete the ATI assessments to identify areas of weakness. Achieving an assessment score of 60% or greater suggests success in mastering comprehension of the content.
  - If you answer less than 60% correctly on an exam, or in a sub-content area within a practice exam, this is a signal that additional time needs to be spent reviewing content in this area.

SECTION 4

ANSWERING NCLEX QUESTIONS

Identify the Issue in the Question

- The issue in a question is the problem that is being asked about.
- The issue may be a:
  - Medication – digoxin (Lanoxin), furosemide (Lasix)
  - Nursing problem – a client who is at risk for infection or is in pain.
  - Behavior – restlessness, agitation.
  - Disorder – diabetes mellitus, ulcerative colitis.
  - Procedure – glucose-tolerance test, cardiac catheterization.

NOTES

Identify the Client in the Question

- The client in the question usually has a health problem.
- The client may be a relative, significant other, or another member of the health care team with whom the nurse is interacting.
- The correct answer to the question must relate to the client in the question.

Look for Key Words

- Key words focus attention on important details.
- Examples
  - During the early period, which of the following nursing procedures is best?
  - The nurse should expect to find which of the following characteristics in an adult who has diabetes mellitus?
  - Which of the following nursing actions is vital?
  - Which of the following nursing actions should the nurse take first?

Identify What the Stem is Asking

- Understand what the stem is asking before viewing the options.
- If the question is not clear, rephrase it.
- Determine whether the question has a true-response, a false-response, or a priority stem.

True-Response Stems

- Requires an answer that is a true statement.
  - Examples
    - Which of the following tasks should the nurse assign to an assistive personnel?
    - Which of the following manifestations should the nurse expect to assess?
    - Which of the following is a therapeutic response by the nurse?
    - The nurse evaluates that the client has a positive response to the medication when the client exhibits

False-Response Stems

- Requires an answer that is a false statement.
  - Examples
    - Which of the following nursing actions is inappropriate?
    - Which of the following statements by the client indicates a need for further instruction?
    - Which of the following describes incorrect placement of the hands during CPR?
    - Which of the following actions will place the client at risk?

Eliminating Incorrect Options

- Most questions on the NCLEX are standard multiple-choice questions that have four options. The correct answer is the BEST answer. The other three options are distractors. Distractors are options made to look like correct answers. They are intended to distract you from answering correctly.
- As you read each of the four options, make a decision about it.
  - This option is true (+)
  - This option is false (–)
  - I am not sure about this option (?)
- If the stem is a true-response stem:
  - An option that is true (+) may be the correct answer.
  - An option that is false (–) is a distractor.
    - Eliminate this option.
  - An option that you are not sure about (?) may be a correct answer.
- If the stem is a false-response stem:
  - An option that is true (+) is a distractor.
    - Eliminate this option.
  - An option that is false (–) may be the correct answer.
  - An option that you are not sure about (?) may be the correct answer.
- Avoid returning to options that have been eliminated.
- If one option is left, that is the answer.

NOTES

- If one option is (+) and another (?), select the (+) option as the answer.
- If two (+) options remain, use strategies to select the best answer.

Answering Communication Questions

- The NCLEX includes many communication questions, because the ability to communicate therapeutically is essential for safe practice.
- Identify the critical elements in all questions. Pay particular attention to identification of the client in the question. Remember that the answer must relate to the client.
- Learn to identify communication tools that enhance communication.
  - Being silent – nonverbal communication
  - Offering self – "Let me sit with you."
  - Showing empathy – "You are upset."
  - Focusing – "You say that..."
  - Restatement – "You feel anxious?"
  - Validation/clarification – "What you are saying is...?"
  - Giving information–"Your room is 423."
- Learn to identify nontherapeutic communication blocks.
  - Giving advice – "If I were you, I would..."
  - Showing approval/disapproval – "You did the right thing."
  - Using clichés and false reassurances – "Don't worry. It will be all right."
  - Requesting an explanation – "Why did you do that?"
  - Belittling feelings – "Everyone feels that way."
  - Being defensive – "Every nurse on this unit is exceptional."
  - Focusing on inappropriate issues or persons – "Have I said something wrong?"
  - Placing the client's issues on hold – "Talk to your doctor about that."
- When answering communication questions, select an option that illustrates a therapeutic communication tool. Eliminate options that illustrate nontherapeutic communication blocks.

Answering Questions That Focus on Priorities

- Priority-setting questions ask the test taker to identify either what comes first, is most important, or gets the highest priority.
- Examples
  - What is the nurse's initial response?
  - The nurse should give immediate consideration to which of the following?
  - Which of the following nursing actions should receive the highest priority?
  - Which of the following actions should the nurse take first?
- Use guidelines to answer priority-setting questions
  - Maslow's Hierarchy of Needs indicates that physiological needs come first.
  - The hierarchy indicates that when no physiological need is identified, safety should come first.
  - The nursing process indicates that assessment is a priority.
  - The communication theory indicates the need to focus on encouraging the client to verbalize feelings.
  - The teaching/learning theory emphasizes the importance of client motivation as the criteria for success.

SECTION 5

EXAM DAY

Plan for Everything

- Everything needed for the exam should be assembled the night before.
  - Identification – When candidates arrive at the test center, they will be required to present one form of acceptable identification and their valid authorization to test form. The name on the ID must match, exactly, the name on the application sent to the Board of Registered Nursing. Please visit the NCSBN Web site for acceptable forms of ID – www.ncsbn.org.
- Plan to arrive at the test site early.
  - Verify the route to the exam site, and take a test drive several days prior.

NOTES

- o Determine how long it will take to get there.
- o Be sure to have enough change for a parking meter.
- Pay close attention to your physiological needs.
  - o Dress in layers.
  - o Get a good night's sleep the night before the exam.
  - o Eat a nourishing meal that includes long-acting carbohydrates.
  - o Avoid stimulants and depressants.
  - o Use the bathroom just before the exam.
- During the exam:
  - o Listen to and carefully read the instructions.
  - o Pace yourself; don't spend too long on any one question.
  - o Don't let yourself become distracted. Focus attention on answering one question at a time.
  - o Go with your first choice. Use test-taking strategies only when you cannot decide between close options.
  - o Think positive.

Manage Anxiety Level

- Mild levels of anxiety increase effectiveness.
- Avoid cramming the night before the exam.
- Do something enjoyable and relaxing the night before the exam.
- Learn and practice measures to manage your anxiety level during the exam, as needed.
  - o Take a few deep breaths.
  - o Tense and relax muscles.
  - o Think positively.
  - o Visualize a peaceful scene.
  - o Visualize your success.

NOTES

UNIT TWO

FUNDAMENTALS FOR NURSING

SECTION 1

CLIENT SAFETY AND INFECTION

- The content of the NCLEX-RN test is organized into four major Client-Need categories. One of the four categories is Safe and Effective Care Environment, which is divided into two subcategories – Management of Care and Safety and Infection Control.

 Point to Remember – Providing for and maintaining client safety is a collaborative goal that requires a committed effort from all members of the health care team and the client.

SECTION 2

ENVIRONMENTAL SAFETY

- Falls account for 90% of all reported facility accidents.
- Equipment-related accidents result from malfunction, disrepair, or misuse of equipment.
- Equipment should be used only after a safety inspection and only by individuals who have been instructed on its use.
- Use restraints as a last resort. The nurse should consult with the health care provider and obtain an order detailing the purpose of the restraints and length of use.
- All health care workers must be aware of:
  - Safety procedures.
  - Response(s) to dangerous situations.
  - Security protocols.
  - Implementation of protocols.
  - Documentation of incidents and responses per facility policy.
- The nurse is responsible for assessing, reporting, and documenting all client allergies, and she should notify the health care provider of her findings.

- Falls
  - Falls are significantly higher in older adult clients due to decreased strength, endurance limitations, impaired mobility and balance, cognitive dysfunction, sensory impairment, decreased visual acuity, and bowel and bladder dysfunction.
  - Contributing medical factors include orthostatic hypotension, dementias, cardiovascular and neurological disease processes, and side effects of medications.

  - Nursing Interventions
    - Complete a fall-risk assessment upon the client's admission and at regular intervals.
    - Document all identified risks in the client's health care record and discuss them with the client/family. Notify the provider if the client has any specific needs.
    - Provide the client with nonskid footwear.
    - Keep the floor free of clutter and maintain an unobstructed path to the bathroom.
    - Instruct a client who is unsteady to ring the call bell for assistance before ambulating.
    - Provide adequate lighting (a night light for necessary trips to the bathroom).
    - Orient the client to the setting (grab bars, call bell) including how to use and locate all necessary items.
    - Keep assistive devices within reach. Determine the client's ability to use such devices (glasses, walkers, transfer devices).
    - Report and document all incidents per the facility's policy.
    - Answer call lights promptly to prevent clients who are at risk from trying to ambulate independently.
    - Use chair or bed sensors for clients who are at risk.
    - Lock wheels on beds, wheelchairs, and gurneys to prevent rolling during transfers or stops.
    - Assign clients at risk for falls to a room close to the nurses' station.

NOTES

- Keep the bed rails up and the bed in a low position for clients who are sedated, unconscious, or high risk.
- Complete home safety surveys prior to discharge of the client to identify and correct any safety issues in the home.
- Provide instruction to client/family/caregivers as needed to maintain safety.

- Seizures
  - Seizures may have a sudden onset and include violent tonic-clonic movements that may result in injury (head injury, aspiration, and falls).
  - Implementing seizure precautions for clients who are at risk
  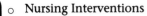 Nursing Interventions
    - Assess the client's seizure history, noting frequency, presence of auras, and sequence of events.
    - Identify triggers/conditions that may exacerbate or lead to seizures.
    - Review the client's medication history.
    - Place rescue equipment at the client's bedside, including oxygen, an oral airway, and suction equipment.
    - Establish IV or saline lock access.
    - Inspect the client's environment for items that may cause injury in the event of a seizure. Remove any unnecessary items from the immediate environment.
    - At the onset of a seizure, position the client for safety.
    - If the client is sitting or standing, ease him to the floor. Protect the client's head. If the client is in bed, raise the side rails and pad for safety.
    - Roll the client to the side with his head flexed slightly forward.
    - Do not put anything in the client's mouth.
    - Accurately document the event, including timing, precipitating behaviors or events, and a description of the event (movements, any injuries, mention of aura, postictal state).
    - Report the seizure to the provider.

- Restraints
  - Restraints can be human, mechanical, or physical devices that restrict freedom of movement or diminish the client's access to parts of the body.
  - Nurses must understand and follow federal/state laws and facility policies that govern the use of restraints.
  - Restraints are used as a last resort in consultation with the provider.
   Nursing Interventions
    - Try nonpharmacological methods prior to the use of chemical or physical restraints, such as positioning, back rubs, music, or diversional activities.
    - Prior to using restraints, the nurse should review the manufacturer's instructions for correct application of the device.
    - Remove and replace restraints every 2 hr to assess the client's circulation to the area and allow for full range of motion to the limb(s) that are restricted.
    - Pad bony prominences and perform neurosensory checks every 2 hr to identify any neurological or circulatory deficits in the client.
    - Always tie the restraint to the bed frame with a slip knot that is easily removed.
    - Verify that the ties cannot tighten when the bed is adjusted.
    - Explain the purpose of restraint use to the client and family.
    - Regularly assess and document the client's need for continuation of the restraints.
    - Do not leave the client unattended while the restraint is removed for range of motion or circulatory checks.
    - Restraints should:
      - Never interfere with treatment.
      - Restrict movement only enough to ensure client safety.
      - Never be used because of short staffing or staff convenience.

NOTES

- ☐ Fit properly according to manufacturer's guidelines.
- ☐ Be easily removable by staff to decrease the potential for injury and to provide for the highest level of dignity.
  - ■ Documentation of restraint use should be completed every 2 hr, precisely detailed, and include:
    - ☐ Client behaviors and rationale for use.
    - ☐ Interventions attempted prior to placement of restraints.
    - ☐ The client's level of consciousness.
    - ☐ The type of restraint used and location.
    - ☐ Education/explanations to the client and family.
    - ☐ Exact time of application and removal.
    - ☐ Client's behavior while restrained.
    - ☐ Time discontinued and the client's status at that time.

- Chemical Restraints
  - o Medications used to modify a client's behavior places the client at risk for injury.
  - o Chemical restraints should be used as a last resort.
  - o Use of chemical restraints without an order is considered false imprisonment and is illegal.

- Electrical Safety
  - o Electrical equipment must be grounded (three-pronged plug and grounded outlet) to decrease the risk for electrical shock.
  - o Use outlet covers in environments where clients are at risk for sticking items into outlets.
  - o Unplug equipment by grasping the plug to prevent bending the plug prongs and increasing the risk for electrical shock.
  - o Never pull the plug out by the cord.
  - o Do not overcrowd outlets. The use of extension cords is not permitted in any client care areas.
  - o Disconnect all electrical equipment prior to cleaning.
  - o IV pumps must have free-flow protection to prevent the overdose of fluids or medications.

- o Only use equipment for its intended use to prevent injury.
- o Do not adjust equipment while touching the client, as this can create an electric circuit that could result in a shock to the client.
- o If the client receives a shock, turn off the electricity before touching the client.

- Fire Safety
  - o All staff must be instructed in fire response procedures.
    - ■ Keep emergency numbers near or on the phone at all times.
    - ■ Know the facility's fire drill and evacuation plan.
    - ■ Know the location of all fire alarms, extinguishers, and exits, including oxygen shut-off valves.
    - ■ Follow the fire response sequence in the facility (RACE):
      - ☐ Rescue – Protect and evacuate clients in immediate danger.
      - ☐ Alarm – Report the fire.
      - ☐ Contain – Close doors or windows.
      - ☐ Extinguish – Use approved fire extinguishers to eliminate the fire.
    - ■ The correct fire extinguisher must be used to promptly and safely extinguish a fire.
      - ☐ Class A – paper, wood, upholstery, rags, or trash
      - ☐ Class B – flammable liquids and gases
      - ☐ Class C – for electrical fires
  - o Point to Remember – Nurses who work in the home setting should teach clients and families to have a plan of action in the event of a fire, including a route of exit and a location where family members will meet.

- Bioterrorist Attack
  - o The use of biological agents is considered to be the most likely form of a terrorist attack.
  - o Health care officials express concern about anthrax, bubonic plague, smallpox, and botulism.

NOTES

- o Nursing Interventions
  - ▪ Health care facilities should be prepared to treat mass casualties.
  - ▪ Nurses should be aware of emergency management plans through training and education by the facility.
- Poisons in the Home
  - o Toddlers, preschoolers, school-age children, and older adults are at high risk for accidental poisoning.
  - o In older adults, diminished eyesight and impaired memory can result in an accidental overdose of prescribed medications.

- o Nursing Interventions
  - ▪ Recommend the use of medication organizers that can be filled weekly.
  - ▪ Instruct parents to use child-resistant caps and to place medications or hazardous materials out of the reach of children.
  - ▪ Instruct clients/families that the Poison Control Center phone number should be posted or saved on home/mobile telephones.
  - ▪ Accidental ingestion
    - ▫ Identify the type and amount of substance that the client has ingested.
    - ▫ Before initiating any home remedies, immediately call the Poison Control Center.
    - ▫ Save the client's vomitus and deliver to the Poison Control Center or laboratory for analysis.
    - ▫ Never induce vomiting following ingestion of caustic substances, such as lye, grease, petroleum products, or household cleaners.

SECTION 3

TRANSMISSION OF PATHOGENS

- Transmission Precautions for Infectious Agents
  - o Standard precautions
    - ▪ Standard precautions apply to the care of all clients in health care settings, regardless of the suspected or confirmed presence of an infectious agent.
    - ▪ Standard precautions are based on the principle that all blood, body fluids, secretions, excretions, nonintact skin, and mucous membranes may contain transmissible infectious agents.

    - ▪ Point to Remember – Implementation of standard precautions for all clients as well as hand hygiene represents the primary strategies for the prevention of transmitting infectious agents among clients and health care personnel.
    - ▪ Centers for Disease Control and Prevention, elements of standard precautions
      - ▫ Respiratory hygiene/cough etiquette
        - ‣ Implement infection control measures at the first point of encounter within a health care setting (reception and triage areas in the emergency departments, outpatient clinics, and health care providers' offices).
        - ‣ Target clients, family members, and friends who have suspected respiratory infections. This applies to symptoms present when entering a health care facility including coughing, rhinorrhea, or increased productions of respiratory secretions.
    - ▪ Safe injection practices
      - ▫ Adhere to basic principles of aseptic technique for the preparation and administration of parenteral medications.

NOTES

- Follow the principles of using a sterile, single-use disposable needle and syringe for each injection. Also, prevent contamination of injection equipment or medication.
- Whenever possible, use single-dose vials, especially when medications will be administered to multiple clients.
- Infection control practices for a lumbar puncture
  - Use a face mask for the individual placing of the catheter or when injecting material into the spinal/epidural space.

 o Nursing Interventions
- Provide education to health care staff, clients, and visitors. Post instructional signs for clients/families/visitors in the language that is appropriate to the population served.
- Ensure that all health care workers understand and adhere to the recommended practices of the facility.
- Handle all blood and body fluids as if they are contaminated.
- Follow standard hand hygiene guidelines.
- Wear a gown and gloves when touching blood or body fluids, nonintact skin, mucous membranes, or contaminated materials.
- Wear masks and face and eye protection when anticipating splashing of contaminated fluids.
- Clean equipment according to the facility's policy.
- Discard all needles and sharps in the appropriate containers; do not recap.
- Place contaminated linens in the appropriate receptacles per the facility's policy.
- Clean spills with a solution of bleach and water (1:10 dilution) or according to the facility's policy.
- A private room is not necessary unless the client's diagnosis places others at risk for contamination.

o Transmission-based precautions
- Transmission-based precautions are used for clients who are known or suspected to be infected or colonized with infectious agents, which include certain epidemiologically important pathogens that require additional control measures to effectively prevent transmission.
- Since the infecting agent may not be known at the time of admission, transmission-based precautions are used according to the suspected disease process and modified when the pathogen is identified or ruled out.
- Transmission-based precautions are used when the route of transmission is not completely interrupted using standard precautions.
- Three categories – contact, droplet, and airborne precautions
  - Contact precautions (includes enteric-precautions) – Prevents transmission of infectious agents that are spread by direct or indirect contact with the client or the client's environment. These precautions are applied in the presence of wound drainage, fecal incontinence, or other bodily discharges that suggest an increased potential for environmental contamination and risk of transmission.

 ▶ Nursing Interventions
      ▷ When a private room is unavailable for a client, consultation with infection control personnel is recommended to assess the risks associated with other client placement options.
      ▷ There should be a 3-foot separation between beds to reduce the opportunity for sharing of items between the client who is infected/colonized and another client.
      ▷ Health care personnel should wear a gown and gloves when entering a client's room and for all interactions that involve contact with the client or potentially contaminated areas in the environment.

NOTES

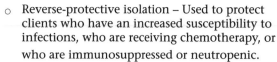

- ☐ Droplet precautions – Prevents the transmission of pathogens spread through close contact with mucous membranes or respiratory secretions.
  - ▸ Nursing Interventions
    - ▷ When a private room is unavailable for a client, consultation with infection control personnel is recommended to assess the risks associated with other client placement options.
    - ▷ Spatial separation of greater than 3 feet and drawing the curtain between the beds is important for clients sharing rooms.
- ☐ Airborne precautions – Prevent the transmission of infectious agents that remain infectious over long distances when suspended in the air.
  - ▸ Nursing Interventions
    - ▷ Preferred placement is an airborne isolation room, previously referred to as a negative-pressure room.
    - ▷ A respiratory protection program for staff is required in any facility with an airborne infection isolation room. Instruction about respirators (also referred to as a small particulate mask), fit-testing, and user-seal checks is required.
    - ▷ Health care personnel who are caring for clients receiving airborne precautions must wear a mask or respirator, depending on disease-specific recommendations. If the client needs to leave the room, it will be necessary to apply a small, particulate mask to that client.
- ○ Barrier precautions
  - ▪ Private room preferred
  - ▪ A mask is generally donned before entering the room
  - ▪ If contact with oral secretions is anticipated (feeding an infant), a gown may be needed
  - ▪ A mask should be placed on the client if absolutely necessary to leave the room.

- ○ Reverse-protective isolation – Used to protect clients who have an increased susceptibility to infections, who are receiving chemotherapy, or who are immunosuppressed or neutropenic.
  - ▪ Nursing Interventions
    - ☐ Ensure that there is minimal dust, dirt and moisture in the client's room.
    - ☐ Follow hand hygiene before entering the client's room.
    - ☐ Wear sterile gloves, a gown and/or masks when in contact with the client; discard after treatment.
    - ☐ Institute maximum protection, which includes the use of sterile linens, food and other supplies; may be required for clients who are immunosuppressed, but is not necessary for clients who have eczema.
    - ☐ Maximum protective isolation requires the use of a ventilated or positive pressure room.
    - ☐ If visitors are admitted to the isolation room, provide detailed instructions about all isolation procedures.
    - ☐ The nurse should clean the bell of a personal stethoscope with an alcohol swab between clients, even if special precautions are not ordered.
- ○ Hand hygiene
  - ▪ Wash hands with an antimicrobial soap and water when hands are visibly soiled.
  - ▪ If hands are not visibly soiled, use an alcohol-based, waterless antiseptic agent to decontaminate the hands.
  - ▪ Follow hand hygiene:
    - ☐ Before and after direct contact with clients.
    - ☐ After contact with blood, body fluids or excretions, mucous membranes, nonintact skin, or wound dressings.
    - ☐ After contact with a client's skin (when taking a pulse, blood pressure, or lifting a client).
    - ☐ Before moving hands from a contaminated body site to a clean body site during care.

NOTES

- After contact with inanimate objects in the immediate vicinity of the client (including medical equipment).
- After removing gloves.
  - Avoid wearing artificial fingernails or extenders if duties include direct contact with clients.
- Application of personal protection equipment
  - Personal protection equipment must be worn when in contact with potentially infectious materials.
  - The type of personal protection equipment used will depend on the level of contact and type of infection or disease process suspected/identified.
  - Always work from a sterile or clean area toward a dirty area.
  - If gloves become torn or heavily contaminated, change immediately.
  - Order of application
    - Gown – The gown must cover everything from the bottom of the neck down to the knees and wrists. Fasten it securely behind the neck and at the waist.
    - Mask – The mask should be secured with ties or elastic. Pinch the flexible bridge to secure it to the nose. It must extend below and under the chin.
    - Goggles/face shield – Apply the goggles/face shield and verify that they fit securely to prevent them from slipping off.
    - Gloves – Make sure that gloves are correctly sized for a snug fit. They should extend upward to completely cover the wrist of the gown.

- Point to Remember – Personal protection equipment must be disposed of in the room in which it was used, using the specifically designated waste receptacle.
- Removal of personal protection equipment
  - Personal protection equipment must be removed in a specific manner to avoid contact with any contaminated materials.

- After removing the equipment, the nurse should wash her hands immediately before touching her face or mouth.
- Order of removal
  - Gloves – Extend arms away from the face and slowly peel one glove downward, turning it inside out. With the ungloved hand, slide a finger under the inside portion of the remaining glove, turn it inside out, and discard.
  - Goggles/face shield – Grasp the ear pieces or headband only to remove, as the lens and outer parts are contaminated.
  - Gown – Unfasten neck, then waist ties, and pull forward away from the body, folding it inside out and rolling it into a bundle to dispose.
  - Mask – Only remove it by its ties. Take care not to touch the front of the mask. Dispose of it immediately.
- Point to Remember – When a client requires isolation in a private room, a sense of loneliness may develop, which can be psychologically harmful, especially for children. A nurse must act to reduce these feelings, as an altered emotional state can interfere with the client's healing.

LABORATORY TESTS TO SCREEN FOR INFECTION		
Laboratory Value	Normal (adult) Values	Indication of Infection
WBC count	4,800 to 10,800/mm³	• Increased in acute infection • Decreased in certain viral or overwhelming infections
Erythrocyte sedimentation rate	• Men – 0 to 15 mm/hr • Women – 0 to 20 mm/hr	• Elevated in the presence of an inflammatory process (autoimmune and infectious process)

NOTES

PRECAUTIONS REQUIRED FOR SPECIFIC DISEASE PROCESS

Disease/Infectious Agent	Precautions	Duration	Reservoir	Nursing Considerations
AIDS/HIV	Standard/contact precautions	Duration of illness	Blood and body fluids including breast milk	Hand hygiene; personal protective equipment if in contact with potentially contaminated materials
Cytomegalovirus	Standard precautions	None	Urine and respiratory secretions Breast milk	Staff who are pregnant require special instructions
Clostridium difficile	Standard/contact precautions	Duration of illness	Feces	Hand hygiene; personal protective equipment (enteric precautions) if in contact with potentially contaminated materials
Rotavirus	Standard precautions	Duration of illness	Feces	Contact precautions used, particularly for children who are wearing diapers or incontinent; < 6 years old for duration of illness
Salmonella	Standard/contact precautions	Duration of illness	Feces	Contact precautions used, particularly for children who are wearing diapers or incontinent; < 6 years old for duration of illness
Shigellosis (dysentery)	Standard/contact precautions	Duration of illness	Feces	Contact precautions used, particularly for children who are wearing diapers or incontinent; < 6 years old for duration of illness
Hepatitis A	Standard/contact precautions	Until 7 days after onset of jaundice	Feces	Contact precautions used, particularly for clients wearing diapers or who are incontinent; minimum of 1 week, depending on the client's age
Hepatitis B	Standard/contact precautions	Duration of illness	Blood and body fluids	Contact precautions for blood and body fluids; hand hygiene
Hepatitis C	Standard/contact precautions	Duration of illness	Blood and body fluids	Hand hygiene

PRECAUTIONS REQUIRED FOR SPECIFIC DISEASE PROCESS

Disease/Infectious Agent	Precautions	Duration	Reservoir	Nursing Considerations
Herpes simplex (recurrent oral, skin, genital)	Standard/contact precautions	Until lesions crust	Fluid from lesions	Horizontal transmission from contact with skin, saliva, and secretions; vertical transmission from mother to child in utero or childbirth
Herpes zoster (shingles) disseminated or localized in clients who are immnocompromised	Standard/airborne/ contact precautions	Duration of illness or with visible lesions	Lesions	Persons who have not had chickenpox or the vaccine should not provide care
Chickenpox (varicella)	Standard/airborne/ contact precautions	Until lesions are crusted over	Lesions, respiratory secretions	Persons who have not had chickenpox or the vaccine should not care for the client
Methicillin-resistant Staphylococcus aureus (MRSA)	Standard/contact precautions	Duration of illness	Body fluids and sites contaminated with MRSA	Gloves; personal protective equipment including a gown/ mask if in contact with site of infection
Staphylococcus aureus (infection or colonization)	Standard/contact precautions	Duration of illness	Body fluids and sites contaminated with MRSA	Gloves; personal protective equipment including gown/mask if in contact with site of infection
Respiratory syncytial virus	Standard/airborne/ contact precautions	Duration of illness	Respiratory secretions	Contact/droplet precautions; follow established guidelines for administration of Ribovirin
Tuberculosis (TB) (pulmonary)	Standard/airborne precautions	Until three sputum smears are negative or TB is ruled out	Airborne respiratory droplet nuclei	Special particulate mask; client wears surgical mask when transported outside of negative-airflow room
Vancomycin-resistant enterococci (VRE) (infection or colonization)	Standard/contact precautions	Until three negative cultures from infectious site (1 week apart)	Stool, body sites from which VRE is isolated	Hand hygiene and gloves; gowns if in contact with contaminated material

POSITIONING CLIENTS

Position	Description	Indications
Semi-Fowler's	Head of bed elevated to 30°	Head injury, postoperative cranial surgery, respiratory illness with dyspnea, postoperative cataract removal, increased intracranial pressure
Fowler's	Head of bed elevated to 45°	Head injury, postoperative cranial surgery, postoperative abdominal surgery, respiratory illness with dyspnea, cardiac problems with dyspnea, bleeding esophageal varices, postoperative thyroidectomy, postoperative cataract removal, increased intracranial pressure
High-Fowler's	Head of bed elevated to 90°	Respiratory illness with dyspnea: emphysema, status asthmaticus, pneumothorax, cardiac problems with dyspnea, feeding, meal times, hiatal hernia, during and after meals
Supine (dorsal recumbent)	Lying on back, head, and shoulders; slightly elevated with a small pillow	Spinal cord injury (no pillow), urinary catheterization
Prone	Lying on abdomen, legs extended, and head turned to the side	Client who is immobilized, is unconscious, postlumbar puncture 6 to 12 hr, postmyelogram 12 to 24 hr (oil-based dye), postoperative tonsillectomy and adenoidectomy
Lateral (side-lying)	Lying on side with most of the body weight borne by the lateral aspect of the lower ilium	Postabdominal surgery, client who is unconscious, seizures (head to side), postoperative tonsillectomy and adenoidectomy, postoperative pyloric stenosis of the lower scapula and the lateral (right side), postliver biopsy (right side), rectal irrigations
Sims' (semi-prone)	Lying on left side with most of the body weight borne by the anterior aspect of the ilium, humerus, and clavicle	Client who is unconscious, enemas
Lithotomy	Lying on the back with hips and knees flexed at right angles and feet in stirrups	Perineal procedures, rectal procedures, vaginal procedures
Trendelenburg	Head and body are lowered while feet are elevated	Shock
Reverse Trendelenburg	Head elevated while feet are lowered	Cervical traction; also used to feed clients restricted to supine position, such as postcardiac catherization
Elevate one or more extremities	Elevate legs/feet or arms/hands by adjusting or supporting with pillows	Thrombophlebitis, application of cast, edema, postoperative surgical procedure on extremity

SECTION 4

STAGES OF ILLNESS/SYMPTOMS

- Course of Infection by Stage
  - Incubation period – The interval between the entrance of a pathogen into the body and the appearance of symptoms (chickenpox, 10 to 21 days after exposure).
  - Prodromal stage – The interval between the onset of nonspecific symptoms and more defined symptoms.
  - Illness stage – The interval when symptoms are specific to the type of infection (mumps, high fever, and parotid and salivary gland swelling).
  - Convalescence – The interval when acute symptoms of infection disappear; may take several days or months.
- Nonspecific Body System Defenses
  - Skin – intact
  - Mouth – intact; saliva
  - Respiratory tract – cilia; cough reflex
  - Urinary tract - intact; urine flowing
  - Gastrointestinal tract – acidity, peristalsis
  - Vagina – normal flora causes low pH
  - Normal flora – large intestine, mouth, pharynx
  - Inflammation – primary body response to infection, irritation or injury
    - Key features
      - Swelling
      - Decreased function
      - Pain
      - Redness
      - Warmth

SECTION 5

ERGONOMIC POSITIONING

- General Guidelines to Prevent Injury
  - Use assistive devices such as slides and mechanical lifts whenever possible.
  - Obtain assistance from staff members.
  - Use correct body mechanics.
    - Face equipment or the client when moving.
    - Bend at the knees, not the waist.
    - Turn by pivoting the body. Do not twist at the waist.
    - Ensure that the object being moved is close to the body.
    - Push instead of pull.
    - Have a wide base of support; feet should be shoulder width apart.
    - Move using smooth, even motion.
    - Do not lift if able to slide.
  - Transferring clients from bed to chair or chair to bed
    - Instruct the client how to assist during the procedure.
    - Lower the bed to the lowest setting.
    - Position the bed or chair so that the client is moving toward her strong side.
    - Assist the client to stand, then pivot.
  - Repositioning clients in bed
    - Raise the bed to waist level.
    - Lower side rails.
    - Use slide boards or draw sheets.
    - Have the client fold his arms across his chest while lifting his head. Proceed in one smooth movement.
    - Use other staff members for help.
  - Working at a computer
    - Align body in a neutral position.
    - Keep hands, wrists, and forearms parallel to the ground.
    - Adjust computer screen so that eyes look straight ahead.
    - Keep elbows close to the body and bend them 90° to 120°.
    - Support back.
    - Adjust position at least every 15 min.

NOTES

- o Assisting during surgery
  - Raise the table to waist level.
  - Prevent reaching by standing on stools.
  - Adjust position at least every 15 min.
  - Position trays at a level between the waist and shoulders.
  - Elevate one foot when standing.

SECTION 6

IV ACCESS

- IV Access – peripheral insertion of an IV catheter into a vein to establish access for administration of fluids.
  - o Contributing factors
    - May be used for fluid replacement
    - Infusion of supplemental nutrients
    - Administration of blood or blood products
    - Dispensing medications
    - Accessible site for emergency treatment
  - o Tubing administration sets
    - Macro set
      - □ Available with or without filter
      - □ Drop factor varies from 10 gtts/mL to 15 gtts/mL
      - □ Used for rapid infusion of fluids, such as trauma or shock
    - Micro set
      - □ Used with IV pump
      - □ Drop factor is 50 gtts/mL or 60 gtts/mL
      - □ Used for keep vein open (KVO) rates
  - o Peripheral IV catheters
    - Over the needle catheter
    - Through the needle catheter
    - Butterfly needle (also called scalp vein needle)
    - Follow facility policy for changing tubing, dressing, and IV site rotation
      - □ Length and diameter of catheter is determined by the purpose of IV, (intermittent or continuous), flow rate, and type of solution ordered.

- □ Large bore for blood (18 gauge or greater) or irritating substances (potassium)
- o Peripheral-venous sites
  - Contributing factors
    - □ Client's age and condition of veins
    - □ Duration of IV use
    - □ Mobility of area
    - □ Right or left handedness
    - □ Clients on anticoagulation therapy
    - □ Obese or dehydrated clients
  - Primary sites (upper extremities)
    - □ Dorsal hand – cephalic, basilic, or dorsal metacarpal vein
    - □ Anterior forearm – cephalic, basilic, or accessory cephalic vein
    - □ Posterior forearm – cephalic, median ante brachial, accessory cephalic, or basilic vein

  - Nursing Interventions
    - □ Verify the order (type of IV and rate of infusion).
    - □ Check the client for allergies to latex (tourniquet) or Betadine (prepping solution).
    - □ Follow facility policy for insertion of IV catheter.
    - □ Enter the skin with the needle bevel up at a 30° angle. Then, immediately lower the angle to 10 to 15° to enter the vein.
    - □ Document date, time started, size and site location of catheter, type of fluid and rate, number of failed attempts, client's response, and nurse's initials.

- Complications of IV Therapy
  - o Infiltration – Leakage of infusion fluid from the vein into the surrounding tissue due to catheter displacement or puncture of vein wall.
    - Manifestations
      - □ Edema at or surrounding the insertion site
      - □ Pain, discomfort, or tightness of skin at site
      - □ Lack of return blood flow in catheter
      - □ Coolness of skin at insertion site
      - □ Slowing of infusion

NOTES

- Nursing Interventions
  - Assess site every shift for manifestations of complications (every 2 hr for a continuous infusion).
  - Instruct the client to report any pain or swelling immediately.
  - If infiltration occurs, remove IV cannula and initiate a new site.
  - Apply a warm compress to the site once cannula is removed.
- Thrombophlebitis – An inflammation or irritation of the vein caused by injury during catheter insertion, infusion of a caustic solution, or clot formation secondary to excessively slow IV.
  - Manifestations
    - Pain or redness at the insertion site
    - Swelling that may extend along length of the vein
    - Sluggish IV infusion or high pressure alarm
    - Vein may feel hard to the touch
  - Nursing Interventions
    - Remove cannula and initiate a new site.
    - Apply warm compresses to the area.
    - Never attempt to force fluid through the line to irrigate the insertion site, as this may dislodge a clot.
- Insertion site infection – Contamination of IV site or surrounding tissues by bacteria secondary to poor aseptic technique or lack of proper site care; in cases of older adult or clients who are immunocompromised, bacteria may enter the blood stream resulting in sepsis.
  - Manifestations
    - Swelling at insertion site
    - Purulent or foul-smelling discharge
    - Redness, warmth, pain at site

- Nursing Interventions
  - Remove cannula immediately.
  - Obtain an order to culture drainage; cleanse site thoroughly and cover with sterile dressing.
  - Monitor the client's vital signs for indications of sepsis.
- Catheter embolus (life-threatening) – A piece of cannula breaks off within the vein and travels to the lungs, usually as the result of forcefully irrigating the IV, attempting to reinsert stylus into the needle, or the client moving during insertion.
  - Manifestations
    - Weak, thready pulse with hypotension
    - Altered level of consciousness
    - Respiratory distress, dyspnea
    - Noted cyanosis

  - Nursing Interventions
    - Provide cardiovascular support for the client.
    - Apply tourniquet high above the insertion site to block progressive movement of foreign body.
    - Notify the health care provider immediately.
    - X-ray may be ordered to verify cannula remnant.
- Speed shock – Development of shock secondary to too rapid of an infusion or improper administration of bolus fluid.
  - Manifestations
    - Flushed face and headache
    - Chest tightness with irregular pulse
    - Dizziness, hypotension
    - May result in cardiac arrest

  - Nursing Interventions
    - Stop the infusion immediately.
    - Provide cardiovascular support to the client.
    - Initiate dextrose 5% in water at KVO rate for emergency treatment.
    - Notify the provider immediately.

NOTES

- ○ Circulatory overload – excess amount of fluid infused into the body, resulting in failure of the system to maintain function
  - ■ Manifestation
    - □ Tachycardia and hypertension
    - □ Tachypnea with moist cough
    - □ Distended neck veins
    - □ Crackles in lung fields
  - ■ Nursing interventions
    - □ Slow infusion to KVO.
    - □ Place client in high-Fowler's position.
    - □ Administer oxygen to the client.
    - □ Obtain the client's vital signs.
    - □ Notify the health care provider.
    - □ Monitor I&O.
- ○ Nerve damage – compression or damage to a nerve, resulting from an improper cannulation technique or incorrect vein location; may be temporary or permanent, if the nerve was completed transected
  - ■ Manifestations
    - □ Sudden or severe pain accompanied by a tingling sensation
    - □ Numbness or paresthesia below the insertion site
  - ■ Nursing interventions
    - □ Immediately stop insertion and remove the catheter.
    - □ Assess the client's pain level or symptoms.
    - □ Avoid using the wrist area, if possible, particularly the inner and lateral wrist.
    - □ If cannula is near a joint, support with armboard to minimize movement.
- ○ Points to Remember
  - □ Select the most distal site available in the upper extremities, using the smallest needle appropriate for the prescribed therapy.
  - □ Do not use lower extremities due to risk of thrombus (most facilities require an order to insert an IV into a lower extremity).

- □ Do not use extremities with fistulas, burns, sclerotic veins, areas of recent infiltration, or any side of the body affected by a cerebrovascular accident or mastectomy.
- • Injection Site Landmarks for Adults
  - ○ Deltoid – Locate the lower edge of the acromial process and a point on the lateral upper arm in line with the axilla. The injection site is located 1 to 2 fingerbreadths (approximately 1 to 2 inches) below the acromial process at a 90° angle (maximum amount of fluid should be 0.5 to 2 mL).
  - ○ Ventrogluteal – Place the heel of the hand on the greater trochanter of the femur, with fingers upright and thumb pointing toward the groin. Spread the index and middle fingers from the anterior superior iliac spine, extending as far as can be reached along the iliac crest. The injection site is located between the first two fingers at a 90° angle (maximum amount of fluid should be 1 to 5 mL).
  - ○ Dorsogluteal – Facing the buttocks, mentally divide into four quadrants, using the coccyx as the center axis. The injection site is located in the upper outer quadrant, 2 to 3 inches below the iliac crest (maximum amount of fluid should be 1 to 5 mL). This site is not recommended unless absolutely necessary because of the potential for injury to the sciatic nerve. It is still the recommended site for medications requiring Z-track administration.
  - ○ Vastus Lateralis – Using the lateral quadriceps muscle of the thigh, measure one hand's width below the greater trochanter and one hand's width above the knee. The injection site is in the middle third of the muscle (maximum amount of fluid should be 1 to 5 mL; for infants that amount should be 1 to 3 mL).

NOTES

UNIT THREE

ADULT MEDICAL-SURGICAL NURSING

SECTION 1

FLUIDS AND ELECTROLYTES, ACID-BASE BALANCE

Fluids and Electrolytes

- Body Fluids
  - Adults
    - Women – 50 to 55% body weight is water
    - Men – 60 to 70% body weight is water
    - Older adults – 47% body weight is water
  - Infants – 75 to 80% body weight is water
  - Intracellular – 80% of total body water
  - Extracellular – 20% of total body water
- Electrolytes
  - Extracellular
    - Na^+ 135 to 145 mEq/L
    - Ca^{++} 8.5 to 10 mg/dL
    - Cl^- 85 to 115 mEq/L
    - HCO_3^- 22 to 26 mEq/L
  - Intracellular
    - K^+ 3.5 to 5.0 mEq/L
    - PO_4 2.5 to 4.5 mg/dL
    - Mg^+ 1.8 to 3.0 mEq/L
- Function
  - Promote neuromuscular excitability.
  - Maintain fluid volume.
  - Distribute water between fluid compartments.
  - Maintain cardiac stability.
  - Regulate acid-base balance.
- Types of Solutions
  - Isotonic – The same concentration as plasma, which prevents shifting between cells.
    - 0.9% sodium chloride, D_5W, lactated Ringer's solution
  - Hypotonic – Less concentrated than extracellular, so that fluid moves into cells.
    - 0.45% sodium chloride, dextrose 5% in water
  - Hypertonic – More concentrated than extracellular, so fluid is pulled from cells.
    - 3% sodium chloride, dextrose 50% sodium chloride

Fluids and Electrolyte Balance/Imbalance

- Fluid-Volume Deficit – Water and electrolytes are lower than normal body levels; blood and urine become concentrated.
  - Contributing factors
    - Fever
    - Vomiting and diarrhea
    - Excessive urinary output
  - Manifestations
    - Weight loss/poor skin turgor
    - Dry mucus membranes
    - Increased heart rate and respirations
    - Dark urine, odorous with decreased volume
    - Hct hemoconcentrated
  - Nursing Interventions
    - Weigh the client daily.
    - Monitor I&O.
    - Replace fluids orally or start IV.
    - Assess urine-specific gravity (normal range is 1.010 to 1.030).
- Fluid Volume Excess – Water and electrolytes greater than normal body levels; blood and urine are diluted.
  - Contributing factors
    - Excessive IV fluids
    - Body systems malfunction (cardiac, renal, or liver)
    - Excessive sodium levels
  - Manifestations
    - Cough, dyspnea, crackles
    - Increased blood pressure, pulse, and respirations
    - Hemodilution of Hct
    - Headache

NOTES

- Weight gain (1 L of water = 1 kg of weight)
- Late signs include jugular vein distention, tachycardia, and pitting edema.

 o Nursing Interventions
- Administer diuretics as prescribed.
- Restrict fluids and monitor I&O.
- Weigh the client daily.
- Provide frequent skin care.
- Use semi-Fowler's position.
- Maintain a low sodium diet.

 Points to Remember
  - o Clients who have low sodium levels display confusion, leading to an increased risk of falls in older adult clients.
  - o Never give potassium to a client who is not voiding (no "P", no "K").
  - o Calcium and phosphorus have an inverse relationship (calcium UP, phosphorus DOWN).

Metabolic/Respiratory Imbalance – Acidosis Alkalosis

- Acid-Base Normal Values
  - o Normal value is 7.35 to 7.45
  - o CO_2 is 35 to 45
  - o HCO_3^- is 22 to 26
    - Lungs control carbon dioxide levels.
    - Kidneys regulate sodium bicarbonate levels.
- Metabolic Acidosis – Sodium bicarbonate levels below 22
  - o Contributing factors
    - Diarrhea
    - Renal failure
    - Systemic infections
    - Diabetic ketoacidosis
    - Starvation, malnutrition, anorexia nervosa
    - Ketogenic (high-fat) diet
  - o Manifestations
    - Headache, confusion
    - Stupor, loss of consciousness
    - pH below 7.35, HCO_3^- below 22

- Tachypnea or Kussmaul breathing

 o Nursing Interventions
  - Promote good air exchange.
  - Monitor potassium levels.
- Metabolic Alkalosis – Sodium bicarbonate levels above 26
  - o Contributing factors
    - Vomiting
    - Long-term diuretic therapy
    - Gastric suction
    - Alkali ingestion (baking soda)
  - o Manifestations
    - CNS symptoms – confusion, irritability, coma, agitation
    - Shallow respirations
    - Muscle cramps
    - pH above 7.45 and HCO_3^- above 26

 o Nursing Interventions
  - Monitor potassium levels.
  - Evaluate for signs of tetany.
  - Promote the intake of potassium-rich foods.
- Respiratory Acidosis – Excess carbon dioxide in the blood (can be acute or chronic)
  - o Contributing factors
    - Acute – respiratory suppression or obstruction due to pulmonary edema, over-sedation, or pneumonia
    - Chronic – chronic airflow limitation or COPD
  - o Manifestations
    - Acute
    - Confusion, restlessness, coma
    - Weakness, headache
    - pH below 7.35 and CO_2 above 4.5
    - Chronic (classic signs of COPD)
    - $PaCO_2$ above 4.5 mm Hg
    - Tachypnea with dyspnea
    - Weight loss

NOTES

---

o Nursing Interventions

- Promote good respiratory exchange.
- Administer bronchodilators as prescribed.
- Monitor ABGs.

- Respiratory Alkalosis – Deficit of carbon dioxide in the blood.
  - o Contributing factors
    - Hyperventilation
    - Decreased O_2 (pulmonary edema or pneumonia)
    - Salicylate poisoning
  - o Manifestations
    - Circumoral numbness
    - Loss of consciousness
    - $PaCO_2$ below 35 mm Hg

 o Nursing Interventions
    - Assist the client to breathe into a paper bag or cupped hands.
    - Provide oxygen if hypoxic.

- Blood Gases
  - o ABGs
    - Most accurate method of assessing respiratory function
    - Drawn into heparinized syringe
    - Keep on ice and transport to laboratory immediately
    - Document amount and method of oxygen delivered for accurate results
    - Pressure applied at the site for 5 to 10 min

 Points to Remember
    - If the acid/base imbalance has a respiratory origin, the pCO_2 is inversely related to the pH, and compensation originates in the metabolic system.
    - If the acid/base imbalance has a metabolic origin, the HCO_3^- is directly related to the pH, and compensation originates in the respiratory system.
    - In relation to the pH, apply "Rome" – Respiratory – Opposite, Metabolic – Equal.

ACID-BASE IMBALANCE			
	PH	PCO_2	HCO_3^-
Respiratory Acidosis	↓	↑	Normal or ↓
Respiratory Alkalosis	↑	↓	Normal or ↑
Metabolic Acidosis	↓	↓	↓
Metabolic Alkalosis	↑	↑	↑

SECTION 2

RESPIRATORY SYSTEM DISORDERS

- Anatomy of the Lungs
  - o Right – 3 lobes, 10 segments
  - o Left – 2 lobes, 8 segments
  - o Alveoli – Tiny distal air sacs where gas exchange takes place; produces surfactant, a phospholipid secretion (Type II cells), to reduce surface tension of fluid lining the alveoli, allowing expansion to take place; without surfactant, the lungs would collapse. Oxygen is required for surfactant production.
  - o Diffusion – Exchange of gases (oxygen and carbon dioxide) at the alveolar/capillary membrane.
- Diagnostic Tests
  - o Chest x-ray (CXR) – Noninvasive procedure with no special preparation; use a lead shield for adults of child-bearing age.
  - o Mantoux Test – Diagnostic test that indicates exposure to TB; not solely diagnostic for active TB; diagnosis confirmed with acid-fast bacillus (AFB) sputum culture and CXR.
  - o Administration
    - Given intradermally in the upper $\frac{1}{3}$ inner surface of the forearm
    - Insert needle bevel up
    - Inject 0.1 mL of purified protein derivative.
    - Must read in 48 to 72 hr

NOTES

MAJOR ELECTROLYTES – IMBALANCE/INTERVENTIONS

Electrolyte	Potassium (K⁺)	Sodium (Na⁺)	Calcium (Ca⁺⁺)	Magnesium (mg⁺⁺)
Normal Value	3.5 to 5.0 mEq/L	135 to 145 mEq/L	8.5 to 10 mg/dL	1.8 to 3.0 mEq/L
Sources	• Fruits ○ Bananas, peaches, melons, raisins, dried fruits, black licorice • Juices – tomato, orange, grape • Nuts • Vegetables	Table salt, processed foods, baking soda, MSG	Milk, cheese, sardines, salmon, tofu, soy nuts, yogurt	Fruit, peas, beans, nuts, pumpkin seeds, sunflower seeds, spinach, salmon, halibut, black beans, navy beans
Etiology – Deficiency	• Hypokalemia ○ Associated with renal loss, diuretics, burns, massive trauma, colitis, uncontrolled diabetes mellitus, diarrhea, excessive perspiration, decreased intake, vomiting, gastric suction	Hyponatremia, increased perspiration, drinking water, gastrointestinal suction, irrigation of tube with plain water, adrenal insufficiency, potent diuretics	Hypocalcemia, massive infection, burns, administration of citrated blood, hypoparathyroidism, surgical removal of parathyroid gland	• Hypomagnesemia • Vomiting, diarrhea, chronic alcoholism, impaired gastrointestinal absorption, enterostomy drainage, use of diuretics
Manifestations	Muscle cramping, muscle weakness, weak pulse, dyspnea, mental changes, hallucinations, depression, ECG changes (sensitivity to digitalis), respiratory arrest	Lethargy, hypotension, cramps, vomiting, oliguria, apprehension, muscular weakness, headache, convulsions	Tetany, tingling, numbness, hyperactive reflexes, cardiac arrhythmias, Chvostek's sign, Trousseau's sign	Disorientation, convulsion, hyperactive deep tendon reflexes, tremors, arrhythmias, headaches, increased blood pressure
Nursing Interventions	• Maintain I&O. • Observe for ECG changes • Potassium supplements: ○ Never give by IV push. ○ Assess renal function before giving. ○ Dilute and mix well before administering; not greater than 40 mEq/L.	• Use 0.9% sodium chloride (no distilled water) for irrigation. • Avoid tap-water enemas. • Drink juices and bouillon.	• Teach proper use of antacids/laxatives and the importance of adequate milk intake. • Keep 10% calcium gluconate on hand for use, start after thyroid surgery.	• Encourage tap water and foods high in Mg++; bananas, seafood, dark green vegetables, nuts, grains, oranges, chocolate. • Monitor respiratory/cardiac systems
Etiology – Excess	Hyperkalemia, renal failure, cell damage, Addison's disease, acidosis	Hypernatremia, decreased water intake, diarrhea, impaired renal function, acute tracheobronchitis, unconsciousness	Hypercalcemia, excessive vitamin D milk ingestion, hyperparathyroid, multiple myeloma, prolonged bed rest, renal disease	• Hypermagnesemia, hypotension, respiratory paralysis • Associated with renal failure, diabetes mellitus, dehydration

MAJOR ELECTROLYTES – IMBALANCE/INTERVENTIONS

Electrolyte	Potassium (K⁺)	Sodium (Na⁺)	Calcium (Ca⁺⁺)	Magnesium (mg⁺⁺)
Manifestations	Listlessness, weakness, flaccid paralysis, abdominal cramps, arrhythmias, muscle weakness	Edema, hypertonicity, dry sticky mucous membranes, elevated temperature, flushed skin, thirst	Renal calculi, nausea, anorexia, weight loss, deep bone pain, flank pain, lethargy, anorexia, muscle weakness, pathological fractures	• Contraindicated to administer antacids containing magnesium to clients with renal failure. • Excessive magnesium depresses the CNS system, resulting in decreased respirations and diminished reflexes.
Nursing Interventions	• Administer IV glucose and insulin (promote entry of K+ into cells). • Give fluids to increase urinary output, Kayexalate exchanges Na+ for K+ ion.	• Administer D₅W. • Give water between tube feedings. • Older adult clients drink up to 10 glasses.	• Increase mobility. • Avoid large doses of vitamin D supplementation. • Provide adequate hydration.	Monitor deep tendon reflexes in clients who are receiving magnesium IV.

NOTES

- Induration (area of elevation) – 10 mm or greater indicates a positive reading; with HIV or clients who are immunosuppressed, indurations of 5 mm or greater is considered positive.

○ Sputum examination

- First morning specimen is preferable, approximately 15 mL required

- Obtain sputum sample prior to initiating antibiotics

- Instruct the client to rinse his mouth before collecting specimen, as this decreases oral flora and improves accuracy of results

○ Thoracentesis – Aspiration of fluid and/or air from the pleural space.

- Ensure that informed consent has been obtained.

- Obtain baseline vital signs.

- Position client sitting on side of bed with feet supported on stool, leaning over bedside table.

- Postprocedure

  □ Apply pressure to the puncture site and assess for breath sounds/crepitus.

  □ Place in semi-Fowler's position.

  □ Monitor for complications (shock, hemorrhage, pneumothorax, respiratory arrest, subcutaneous emphysema).

○ Bronchoscopy – Direct examination of the tracheobronchial tree using a bronchoscope.

- Preparation of client

  □ Ensure that informed consent has been obtained.

  □ The client must be NPO after midnight.

  □ Obtain baseline vital signs.

- Postprocedure

  □ Keep NPO till gag reflux returns to prevent aspiration.

  □ The first liquids must be water.

  □ Monitor vital signs until stable.

  □ Assess for respiratory distress and fever.

  □ Place in semi-Fowler's position.

□ Assure the client it is normal to expectorate some blood-tinged mucus.

□ Monitor for increased amount of bloody mucus.

Management of Clients with Respiratory Disorders

- COPD (may also be referred to as Chronic Airflow Limitation) – A group of chronic lung diseases that include pulmonary emphysema, chronic bronchitis, and bronchial asthma.

- Pulmonary Emphysema – Destruction of alveoli, narrowing of bronchioles, and trapping of air; resulting in loss of lung elasticity.

  ○ Contributing factors

    - Cigarette smoking is the chief cause of respiratory problems.

  ○ Manifestations

    - Dyspnea with productive cough

    - Difficult exhalation, use of pursed lip breathing

    - Wheezing, crackles

    - Barrel chest with clubbed fingernails

    - Shallow, rapid respirations

    - Respiratory acidosis with hypoxia

    - Anorexia, weight loss

   ○ Nursing Interventions

    - Position the client upright and leaning forward.

    - Provide frequent pulmonary toilet.

      □ Bronchodilator medication via nebulizer as prescribed

      □ Chest physiotherapy/pulmonary drainage

      □ Check breath sounds and pulse oximetry routinely

    - Schedule activities to allow for frequent rest periods.

    - Administer oxygen at lowest flow rate for the client's comfort (a maximum of 3 L).

    - Encourage fluids of 3,000 mL/day unless contraindicated.

    - Decrease carbohydrates and increase calories and protein to meet energy requirements.

NOTES

- Provide emotional support.
- Teaching
  - Avoid crowds.
  - Encourage diaphragmatic and pursed-lip breathing.
  - Immediately report signs of upper respiratory infection.
  - Avoid allergens such as dust, pollen, and odors.
- Chronic Bronchitis – Chronic cough with excessive mucus secretions in the airways.
  - Contributing factors
    - Heavy cigarette smoking or infection
    - Pollution
  - Manifestations
    - Cough (copious amounts of sputum)
    - Dyspnea on exertion or at rest
    - Hypoxemia resulting in polycythemia (ruddy look to skin)
    - Crackles, rhonchi
    - Pulmonary hypertension leading to Cor pulmonale and right-sided heart failure
  - Nursing Interventions
    - Identify and avoid irritants.
    - Increase room humidity to 70%.
    - Relieve bronchospasms with deep breathing and medications.
    - Provide chest physiotherapy/pulmonary drainage.
- Asthma – Air trapping within the lungs, with secondary hyper-reactivity to allergens or triggers.
  - Contributing factors
    - Extrinsic – antigen-antibody reaction triggered by food, medications, or inhaled substances
    - Intrinsic – pathophysiological abnormalities within the respiratory tract
  - Manifestations
    - Sudden, severe dyspnea with use of accessory muscles
    - Sitting up, leaning forward

- Diaphoresis and anxiety
- Wheezing, gasping
- Cyanosis (late sign)
- Nursing Interventions
  - Remain with the client during the attack.
  - Use the high-Fowler's position.
  - Monitor lung sounds and pulse oximetry.
  - Administer epinephrine hydrochloride (Adrenalin) subcutaneously; evaluate effectiveness.
  - May need to administer aminophylline (Theophylline) IV.
  - Monitor medication levels to prevent toxicity. Therapeutic level is 10 to 20 mcg/mL.
  - Observe for side effects of medications (nausea, vomiting, or seizures).
  - Give bronchodilators via nebulizer and metered-dose inhalers.
  - Monitor oxygen therapy.
  - Administer corticosteroids to decrease airway inflammation.
  - Point to Remember – An improvement in wheezing with no improvement in the client's condition may actually indicate deterioration secondary to the tightening of the airways and decreased airflow.
- Status asthmatics – Life-threatening episode of airway obstruction, which is nonresponsive to therapy; a medical emergency.
  - Nursing Interventions
    - Place in high-Fowler's position.
    - Monitor continuous pulse oximetry or ABGs.
    - Monitor respiratory status for signs of hypoxia.
    - Administer bronchodilators, IV steroids, or epinephrine.
    - Provide emotional support.
    - Prepare for emergency intubation.

___

NOTES

- Complications of COPD (Cor Pulmonale) – Right ventricular hypertrophy and right-sided heart failure secondary to lung
  - Disease of pulmonary vessels or chest walls
  - Increased resistance of pulmonary capillary bed
  - Manifestations
    - Signs of right-sided heart failure, followed by left-sided heart failure (See cardiac content on heart failure.)
    - Shunting of unaerated blood across the collapsed alveoli

  - Nursing Interventions
    - Give diuretics, occasionally nitrates.
    - Ensure the client rests frequently.
    - Monitor oxygen therapy and pulse oximetry.
    - Maintain a low sodium diet.
    - Monitor for signs of digoxin toxicity (nausea, vomiting, anorexia).
- Carbon dioxide toxicity – Near comatose state secondary to increased CO_2 from chronic retention.
  - Contributing factors
    - Carbon dioxide retention
    - Excessive oxygen delivery
  - Manifestations
    - Drowsiness, irritability
    - Hallucinations
    - Convulsions and coma
    - Tachycardia with arrhythmias

  - Nursing Interventions
    - Avoid excessive concentrations of oxygen.
    - Keep below 3 L/min (no more than 70% oxygen delivered). Cannula 40%, mask 60%, nonrebreather 100%.
    - Monitor blood gases and pulse oximetry.

- Pneumothorax – Collection of air or fluid in the pleural space; can be spontaneous or tension.
  - Contributing factors
    - Trauma (gunshot, stabbing)
    - Thoracic surgery (excessive or prolonged)
    - Positive pressure ventilation
  - Manifestations (spontaneous)
    - Sudden, sharp chest pain
    - Severe shortness of breath with violent attempts to breathe
    - Hypotension, tachycardia
    - Hyper-resonance and decreased breath sounds over the affected lung area
    - Anxiety, diaphoresis, restlessness
  - Manifestations (tension)
    - Subcutaneous emphysema (crepitus)
    - Acute chest pain
    - Tympany on percussion
    - Mediastinal shift – Contents of mediastinum pushed toward unaffected side (heart/lungs, esophagus, trachea, and great vessels).

  - Nursing Interventions
    - Remain with the client.
    - Place in high-Fowler's position.
    - Assess vital signs, continuous pulse oximetry, breath sounds, and observe for shock.
    - Prepare thoracentesis tray for insertion of chest tubes.
      - Assist health care provider with insertion (may be bedside, operating room, or emergency room).
      - Placement of a chest tube in the lower lung is used for evacuation of fluid.
      - Placement of chest tube in the upper lung is used for evacuation of air.
      - Obtain chest x-ray immediately following insertion.

NOTES

- Closed-Chest Drainage System – A three-chamber, self-contained, disposable container used to remove air or fluid from the pleural space; attempts to re-establish normal negative pressure in the pleural space.
  - Components
    - The suction control chamber is connected directly to the wall suction, and should continuously bubble.
    - The water seal is the middle chamber, and should bubble intermittently with respirations (tidaling).
    - The drainage chamber connects directly to the client and should not bubble.
    - The drainage amount and color is recorded each shift and should decrease over time.
  - Nursing Interventions
    - Assess respiratory status and pulse oximetry.
    - Observe for bubbling in the suction control chamber.
    - Observe for tidaling in the water seal chamber.
    - The client should turn, cough, and deep breathe every 2 hr.
    - Calculate and record the amount of drainage at the end of each shift.
    - Check tubing for kinks or dependent loops; keep the tubing coiled on the bed.
    - The closed chest drainage system must always be below the level of the client's heart.
    - Do not strip or milk chest tubes.
  - Points to Remember
    - Problem – There is continuous, rapid bubbling in water seal bottle chamber.
      - Solution – Start at the chest and move down the tubing to locate the leak; repair or replace the segment.
    - Problem – There is no tidaling in the water seal chamber.
      - Solution – Check for kinks in the tubing; also assess for breath sounds (lungs may have re-expanded).

- Problem – There is no bubbling in the suction-control chamber.
  - Solution – Turn up the wall suction until gentle, continuous bubbling is noted; also verify that the tubing is correctly attached and that water is filled to the prescribed amount.
- Problem – The chest tube is disconnected from the system.
  - Solution – Insert the open end of the chest tube into sterile water until the system can be replaced.
- Problem – The tube was accidentally pulled out of the insertion site.
  - Solution – Cover the insertion site with an occlusive sterile dressing (securing only three sides), and call the primary care provider immediately.

Infectious Pulmonary Diseases

- Tuberculosis (TB) – Infectious, communicable pulmonary disease that can spread to any part of the body.
  - Must be reported to state health authorities
  - Etiology
    - Mycobacterium tuberculosis; nuclei droplets spread by laughing, coughing, sneezing
    - Miliary TB spreads to all parts of the body and can lay dormant for years, reinfecting the client later
  - Contributing factors
    - Overcrowding and poor living conditions
    - Poor nutritional status, immunocompromised
    - Lack of screening or treatment
    - Close contact with infected person
    - Long-term care facilities, prisons
  - Manifestations
    - Productive cough with hemoptysis
    - Night sweats, low-grade fever
    - Dyspnea
    - Malaise, pallor
    - Anorexia, vomiting, weight loss

NOTES

- o Diagnostic tests
  - Mantoux test/CXR
  - Sputum for acid-fast bacillus (specimen obtained each morning for 3 days)
  - History and physical exam
- o Antituberculin medications (given long-term in multiple combinations)
  - Ethambutol (Myambutol) – contraindicated in children due to optic neuritis
  - Rifampin (Rifadin) – orange discoloration of all body fluids; gastrointestinal distress, shock, acute renal failure, and thrombocytopenia
  - Isoniazid (INH) – must avoid tyramine-rich foods; peripheral neuritis, give supplemental vitamin B_6, possible seizures
  - Streptomycin sulfate – aminoglycoside used with antitubercular therapy; monitor for ototoxicity and nephrotoxicity

- o Nursing Interventions
  - Obtain sputum sample before initiating medication.
  - Medications should be taken in combination and on an empty stomach at the same time every day.
  - Medications should be taken for 6 to 12 months, as directed.
  - Maintain adequate nutritional status.
  - Teach the client to avoid foods containing tyramine.
  - Instruct the client to watch for signs and symptoms of hepatotoxicity, to notify a primary care provider of signs of nephrotoxicity, and visual changes.
  - Teaching
    - ☐ Encourage the client to practice good hand hygiene and to always cover his nose and mouth when sneezing or coughing.
    - ☐ The nurse should wear a particulate mask when entering the client's room.
    - ☐ Isolate the client in a negative pressure room.

 Point to Remember – With tuberculosis, long-term medication therapy is necessary to prevent the development of resistant organisms. Medication therapy is continued for 6 to 12 months, even if the x-ray is within normal limits. Medication is given in a single dose daily. The client should avoid using alcohol and liver function tests must be monitored due to the risk of hepatotoxicity.

- Pneumonia – Inflammation of the lung parenchyma caused by infectious agents
  - o Contributing factors
    - Classified as community acquired or facility acquired (nosocomial)
  - o High-risk population
    - Older adults or infants
    - Substance abusers and smokers
    - Postoperative clients or those on prolonged bed rest
    - Clients with chronic illnesses such as COPD/CAL
    - Clients who are immunosuppressed
  - o Manifestations
    - Sudden onset of chills, fever, flushing
    - Cough is dry and painful initially, and later produces a yellow- to green-colored sputum
    - Dyspnea, pleuritic pain with respiration
    - Tachypnea, tachycardia

  - o Nursing interventions
    - Assess the client's respiratory status frequently.
    - Assess the thickness and color of the client's sputum.
    - Administer oxygen to maintain oxygen saturations greater than 95%.
    - Administer cough suppressants, bronchodilators, metered-dose inhalers and antibiotics as prescribed.
    - Administer mild analgesic as needed to decrease pain with breathing.
    - Encourage small, frequent meals and increase fluid intake.

NOTES

- Provide pulmonary toilet and frequent mouth care.
- Encourage ambulation, as tolerated.

 Points to Remember

o Most occurrences of pneumonia have a sudden onset.

o Penicillin remains the medication of choice for pneumonococcal pneumonias (unless the client is allergic).

o If the client is allergic to penicillin, cephalosporins can not be administered.

o Antibiotics must be given to the client on time to maintain blood levels.

o Watch for side effects of antibiotic therapy, particularly allergies.

- Cancer of the Lung – Primary or secondary (metastatic from a primary site) malignant tumor located in the lung or bronchi.

o Contributing factors

- Primary smoking and exposure to asbestos or other carcinogens (coal dust, uranium, and nickel).

o Manifestations

- Asymptomatic in the early stages
- Later stages
  - Coughing with hemoptysis
  - Dyspnea, hoarseness
  - Anorexia and weight loss
  - Chest pain, weakness

o Pneumonectomy (removal of lung)

- Position the client in a dorsal recumbent or semi-Fowler's position, on the affected side.
- Encourage range of motion to the affected shoulder.
- No closed chest drainage system is required; serum fluid accumulates in the empty thoracic cavity and consolidates, therefore preventing a mediastinal shift.

o Lobectomy (removal of a single lobe) – Chest tube(s) is required postoperatively.

 o Nursing Interventions

- Encourage the client to turn, cough, and deep breathe.

- Assess the client's incision for approximation and potential infection.
- Administer oxygen as prescribed.
- Provide pain medication as needed.
- Promote fluids to thin respiratory secretions.
- Place needed items on the client's surgical side to encourage use of the affected arm.
- Teaching
  - Splint the chest incision when coughing.
  - Exercise the arm on the affected side.

o Complications of Pulmonary Disease

- Pleural effusion – An accumulation of fluid in the pleural cavity secondary to respiratory disease.
  - May occur with pneumonia, lymphomas, pulmonary edema, or cirrhosis.
  - Occasionally occurs following cardiac or pulmonary surgery.
- Empyema – Accumulation of exudate in the pleural cavity.
  - Could cause lung infection, complications of pneumonia, TB, abscess, or bronchiectasis.
  - May need a chest tube and antibiotics.

Pulmonary Therapies

- Chest Physiotherapy – Using cupped hands to perform percussion and vibration over the thorax to loosen secretions in the lungs.

 o Nursing Interventions

- Perform the procedure in the morning upon rising, 1 hr before meals, or 2 to 3 hr after meals.
- The nurse should keep a layer of material between her hands and the client's skin.
- Instruct the client to continue to cough and take deep breaths during the procedure.
- After completion, follow with oral hygiene.
- Stop if pain occurs.

NOTES

- o Contraindications
  - If bronchospasms occur
  - History of pathological fractures, obesity, or osteoporosis
  - New incision in the chest area or upper abdominal area
- Postural Drainage – The use of gravity to drain secretions from segments of the lung; often combined with other chest physiotherapy.

 o Nursing Interventions
  - Position the client such that the lung segment to be drained is uppermost.
  - Perform upon rising in morning, 1 hr before meals or 2 to 3 hr after meals.
  - Provide mouth care following the procedure.
  - Maintain this position for 5 to 20 min, or as tolerated.
  - o Contraindications
    - Unstable vital signs
    - Increased intracranial pressure
    - Cyanosis or exhaustion
- Pulmonary Toilet – Physiological procedures that assist the client to clear excessive secretions from lung fields.
  - o Components
    - Turn, cough, and deep breathing
    - Chest physiotherapy
    - Incentive spirometry
    - Early ambulation
- Inhalers and Nebulizer Treatments
  - o Inhalation therapy
    - Doses may vary; standard dose is 2 puffs, with no more than 12 puffs administered in 24 hr. For maximum effectiveness, administer bronchodilators or nebulizer treatments prior to ordered pulmonary therapies such as postural drainage.
  - o Types of inhalers
    - Bronchodilators relax airways to decrease airway resistance.

- Side effects
  - Tachycardia, palpitations, dysrhythmias
  - Restlessness, tremors, anxiety
  - Anorexia, nausea, vomiting
  - Hyperglycemia, mouth dryness
  - Headaches, dizziness
- Types of medications
  - Albuterol (Proventil) – rapid acting
  - Ipratropium bromide (Atrovent, Combivent) – moderate acting
  - Salmeterol xinafoate (Serevent, Advair) – for long-term asthma control and prevention of bronchospasms; not for acute attacks
- Cromolyn sodium (Intal) – nonsteroidal antiallergy agent; inhibits mast cell release
  - Can cause coughing bronchospasms
  - Do not discontinue abruptly, as rebound attacks can occur.
- Steroids – A medication used to decrease inflammation and swelling of the airways.
  - o Side effects
    - May cause oral superinfection (thrush); always follow with oral care
    - May mask signs of infection
    - Decreases strength of the immune system
    - When administering inhalers, always give the steroid last.
  - o Types
    - Triamcinolone acetonide (Azmacort)
    - Fluticasone propionate (Flovent)
- Ventilators – A mechanical device used to provide respiratory support for clients who are unable to breathe or maintain their airway independently.
  - o Types
    - Assist control ventilation – Programmed with a preset tidal volume and rate; if the client does not initiate a breath, one is delivered by the ventilator. This is the most common mode, since it requires little effort from the client.

NOTES

- Synchronized intermittent mandatory vent – Although the tidal volume and rate are preset, the client can establish his own rate and volume to override system. This is useful in weaning.

- Bilevel positive airway pressure – Noninvasive pressure support that is mainly used by clients with sleep apnea. Forced breaths are delivered via a mask, to support respiratory efforts when the client is unable to maintain oxygenation during rest.

- Positive end-expiratory pressure – Pressure given during the expiratory phase of mechanical ventilation, to prevent atelectasis and improve gas exchange. Settings are determined by the health care provider. The most common complication is pneumothorax, secondary to constant pressure to lungs.

  o Ventilator alarms – Indicates mechanical or respiratory complications, preventing the client from receiving designated respiratory support. The nurse must investigate immediately.

    - Low pressure alarm – Indicates that the appropriate volume or rate is not being delivered, due to a disconnection of the ventilator circuitry. Check all tubing connections and see if there is a leak of endotracheal cuff/balloon.

    - High pressure alarm – Indicates that excessive pressure is needed to deliver breaths to the client; may be due to buildup of secretions or mucus plug within the airway or endotracheal tube. Can also be caused by client biting on endotracheal tube or extreme client anxiety, which is often referred to as "fighting the vent."

- Suctioning – Assisting the client to remove excessive airway secretions when she is unable to cough or expectorate mucus.

  - If suctioned orally, the procedure is not sterile.

  - If suctioned via endotracheal tube or through tracheostomy, the procedure is sterile.

  o Nursing Interventions for Tracheal Suctioning

    - Use standard precautions based on the client's status.

- Prelubricate the suction catheter with sterile saline before insertion.

- Preoxygenate the client and apply gloves if sterile.

- Advance the catheter without suction during inspiration.

- While applying intermittent suction, withdraw the catheter, rotating between thumb and index finger for a maximum of 10 to 15 seconds.

- Oxygenate the client.

- Discard the catheter and gloves.

- Document the client's response to the procedure, lung sounds, volume and appearance of sputum, and oxygen saturation levels.

  o Adverse effects

    - Hypoxia

    - Cardiac dysrhythmias

    - Bronchospasms

    - Infection

SECTION 3

PREOPERATIVE AND POSTOPERATIVE CARE

- Preoperative Care – Procedures or teaching completed prior to a surgical procedure to reduce potential complications, reduce postoperative discomfort, relieve client anxiety, and increase client participation.

  o Preoperative teaching

    - Perform frequent pulmonary toilet.

    - Turn, position, and perform early ambulation, including leg exercises.

    - Use analgesics and pain control.

    - Prepare the client for routine and expected postoperative care (dressings, IVs, drains, or NG tube).

  o Preoperative procedures

    - Check for informed consent (a nurse may witness only).

    - Assess for Latex allergy.

    - Obtain baseline vitals.

NOTES

COMMON POSTOPERATIVE COMPLICATIONS

Complication	Manifestations	Common Causes	Occurence	Nursing Interventions
Atelectasis	Increased pulse and respirations, decreasing saturation levels	Shallow respirations	First 48 hr	Turn, cough, and deep breathe frequently, and encourage/assist with early ambulation.
Pneumonia	• Fever, increased pulse and respiration • Crackles and rhonchi	Shallow respirations	48 hr	Turn, cough, and deep breathe frequently, and encourage/assist with early ambulation.
Hypoxia	Confusion, increased blood pressure and pulse, dyspnea	Depressed respirations secondary to anesthesia	48 hr	• Cough and deep breathe. • Ambulation and turning.
Nausea	Nausea, gastrointestinal distress and anorexia	Response to anesthesia or narcotics	48 hr	Advance diet as tolerated
Shock	• Decreased blood pressure and urinary output, increased pulse • Cold, clammy, pale skin • Change in level of consciousness	• Loss of fluids and electrolytes • Hemorrhaging	48 hr	• Assess for change in vital signs. • Monitor for bleeding.
Urinary retention	Inability to void, restlessness, bladder distention	• Anesthesia or narcotics • Local edema	48 to 72 hr	• Stand upright to void (male). • May need to catheterize to empty bladder. • Monitor I&O.
Wound hemorrhage	• Signs of shock • Bleeding from tubes or surgical site	Wound dehiscence	First 48 hr and until wound is closed	Assess incision frequently for approximation.
Thrombophlebitis	Redness, warmth, pain and swelling	Venous stasis, use of IV therapy in the lower extremities, pressure to legs	7 to 14 days	Encourage leg exercises, antiembolism stockings, pneumatic stockings.
Wound infection	Redness, pain, and edema at the incision site; increase in the amount or character of drainage; may be yellow, green, or purulent	Poor aseptic technique, debilitated obesity or comorbidities	3 to 5 days	• Maintain nutritional status. • Maintain aseptic technique for dressing changes. • Maintain standard or appropriate precautions.

COMMON POSTOPERATIVE COMPLICATIONS

Complication	Manifestations	Common Causes	Occurence	Nursing Interventions
Wound dehiscence and evisceration	• Incision or sutures open, inner contents spill out • Intervention: place sterile saline-soaked gauze over the site and place in recumbent position	Comorbidities, obesity, muscle weakness, incorrect suture technique, long-term use of corticosteroids	4 to 15 days	• Teach client to splint incision when coughing or moving. • If evisceration occurs, cover area with sterile saline-soaked gauze; notify surgeon immediately.
Urinary tract infection	Dysuria, hematuria, urgency, frequency	Indwelling urinary catheter, postanesthesia urinary retention	4 to 7 days	• Maintain sterility of catheter, increase fluids. • Remove catheter as soon as possible.

NOTES

- Verify NPO status.
- Complete preoperative check list, including any ordered operative preparation.
- Administer prescribed antibiotic or sedation.
    o Preoperative medications
        - Purpose – To reduce anxiety, decrease secretions, control nausea and vomiting, and reduce the amount of anesthesia required.
        - Types
            □ Meperidine (Demerol) – narcotic
            □ Hydroxyzine (Vistaril) – antihistamine
            □ Odansetron (Zofran) – antiemetic
            □ Lorazepam (Ativan) – benzodiazepine
            □ Midazolam (Versed) – sedation and amnesiac
- Postoperative Care
    o Assessment priorities – Evaluate the client prior to administering pain medication.
        - Pulmonary
            □ Verify airway and check gag reflex.
            □ Check for bilateral breath sounds.
            □ Encourage coughing and deep breathing.
        - Neurological
            □ Evaluate the level of consciousness.
            □ Assess reflexes and movement.
        - Circulatory
            □ Compare vital signs to baseline.
            □ Assess tissue perfusion.
        - Gastrointestinal
            □ Assess for bowel sounds.
            □ Assess for abdominal distention.
        - Genitourinary
            □ Monitor I&O.
            □ Assess urinary output (color, clarity, and amount).
        - Equipment
            □ Verify IV fluid type, rate, and site.
            □ Check dressings for type and amount of drainage.
            □ Identify drainage tubes and amount and color of drainage.

□ If NG tube, determine type and amount of suction ordered.

 o Nursing Interventions
- Maintain NPO status until the client is alert and a gag reflex returns.
- Encourage the client to cough and deep breathe every hour.
- Assess vital signs according to policy.
- Monitor I&O.
- Place in semi-Fowler's position (based on the procedure) to provide for a safe airway.
- Provide pain control by using nonpharmacological interventions such as positioning, back rub, and relaxation techniques.
- Pharmacologic interventions
    □ PRN scheduling – Medication is given as the client requests and as it is prescribed.
    □ Fixed scheduling – Medication is given at specified times, around the clock, to control or prevent pain.
    □ PCA pump – The client self-administers pain medication through an infusion system.

SECTION 4

GASTROINTESTINAL, HEPATIC, AND PANCREATIC DISORDERS

Nursing Assessment

- Health History
    o Description of present illness or chief report
        - Onset, course, and duration of problem
        - Location and any alleviating factors
    o Contributing factors
        - Low fiber diet
        - Smoking or alcohol consumption
        - Inactivity or stress
        - Familial predisposition to gastrointestinal disorders

---

NOTES

- Assessment of Gastrointestinal System
  - Pain
    - Location, quality of pain or discomfort (stabbing or dull ache), and duration
    - Measures that alleviate pain
      - Positional changes
      - Over-the-counter medications
      - Use of home remedies
  - Examination of abdomen
    - Inspection – color, contour, distention, scars
    - Auscultation – bowel sounds
    - Percussion – tympany or dullness
    - Palpation – tenderness or masses
  - Elimination pattern
    - Constipation/laxative use
    - Diarrhea/rectal bleeding
  - Nutritional issues
    - Loss of appetite/anorexia
    - Difficulty swallowing
    - Nausea and vomiting
  - Other associated manifestations
    - Flatus/eructation (belching)
    - Heartburn
    - Dark urine/jaundice
    - Excessive weight loss or gain

Diagnostic Procedures

- Barium Swallow Series – Examination of upper gastrointestinal tract under fluoroscopy after ingesting barium sulfate (radiopaque) to detect anatomical or functional abnormalities of the esophagus, stomach, and/or small intestines.

  - Nursing Interventions
    - Preparation
      - NPO after midnight.
      - No smoking or chewing gum before the procedure.

- Postprocedure
  - Instruct the client to increase fluids to assist in passage of the barium.
  - A laxative may be ordered postprocedure to assist with passage of the barium. As the barium is eliminated, monitor stools for a chalky-white appearance.

- Barium Enema Study – Lower gastrointestinal study done by x-ray and fluoroscopic examination of the large intestine after the rectal insertion of barium (radiopaque).
  - Preparation
    - Clear liquid diet and laxatives the day before the procedure.
    - NPO after midnight.
    - Cleansing enema the morning of the test.
  - Postprocedure
    - The client must drink fluids to assist in the passage of the barium.
    - A laxative may be prescribed after the procedure. Monitor stools for a chalky-white appearance, as the barium is eliminated.
    - Notify the provider if there is no bowel movement in 48 hr.

- Endoscopic Studies – Visualization of the lower gastrointestinal tract using a flexible endoscope.
  - Colonoscopy – Endoscopic visualization of the lining of the large intestine, allowing biopsies and polypectomies.
  - Sigmoidoscopy/proctoscopy – Examination of the rectum and sigmoid colon, allowing biopsies and polypectomies.
  - Anoscopy – Rigid scope to examine the anal canal.
  - Preparation
    - Evacuation and cleansing of colon is necessary for visualization; specifics of cleansing regimen depend on the health care provider, but include
      - Clear liquid diet the day before.
      - Take osmotic laxative (Fleet Phospho-Soda) or polyethylene glycol and electrolyte solution (Golytely) the day before.

NOTES

- □ NPO after midnight.
  - ■ Administer Midazolam (Versed) in IV for conscious sedation.
  - o During examination
    - □ Monitor cardiac and respiratory functions.
    - □ Position the client on the left side with knees drawn up to chest (position may be changed to facilitate passage of scope).
  - o Postprocedure
    - ■ The client should remain on bed rest until fully alert.
    - ■ Monitor for manifestations of perforation such as pain or bleeding.
- Esophagogastroduodenoscopy – Visualization of the upper gastrointestinal tract (esophagus, gastric wall, sphincters, and duodenum) using a flexible scope. The scope allows for biopsies.

 o Nursing Interventions
  - ■ Preparation
    - □ NPO after midnight.
    - □ Administer Midazolam (Versed) in IV for conscious sedation.
  - ■ During examination
    - □ Monitor cardiac and respiratory functions.
    - □ Position the client on the left side (position may be changed to facilitate passage of scope).
  - ■ Postprocedure
    - □ The client should remain on bed rest until fully alert.
    - □ Monitor for manifestations of perforation such as pain or bleeding.
    - □ NPO until a gag reflex returns; observe for dysphasia.
- Analysis of Gastrointestinal Secretions – Laboratory analysis of stool or other fecal matter; to determine presence of urobilinogen, nitrates, bacteria, parasites, or blood.

 o Nursing Interventions
  - ■ Do not refrigerate the specimen.
  - ■ Promptly send the specimen to the laboratory.

- Gastric Analysis – Passage of an NG tube into the client's stomach to aspirate gastric contents (measures the amount of acid secreted, which is useful for diagnostic purposes).
  - o Pernicious anemia – deficiency of vitamin B_{12} to a lack of intrinsic factor in stomach acid
  - o Zollinger-Ellison syndrome – increased levels of gastrin, causing the stomach to produce excess hydrochloric acid

 o Nursing Interventions
  - ■ NPO after midnight.
  - ■ No antacids or H_2-receptor antagonists for 24 to 48 hr prior to the procedure.
  - ■ Instruct the client to avoid smoking and chewing gum or tobacco for 6 hr prior to the test.
- Evaluation of the Gallbladder and Liver – X-ray imaging procedure, known as cholecystogram, used to diagnose diseases of the liver and gallbladder.

 o Nursing Interventions
  - ■ Check for allergies to the x-ray contrast material.
  - ■ Instruct the client to consume a high-fat meal at noon, followed by a low-fat evening meal the day prior to the procedure.
  - ■ Twelve hours before the procedure, the client should take tablets containing the contrast medium.
  - ■ After taking the tablets, the client will be NPO until after the test.
- Percutaneous Transhepatic Cholangiogram (PTHC) – An x-ray of the bile ducts inside and outside of the liver; taken after the contrast medium is injected in the liver bile duct. PTHC can assist in identification of a blockage causing jaundice or pancreatitis.
  - o Procedure – A long, flexible needle is inserted through the right upper quadrant of the abdomen into the liver under fluoroscopy, where the bile duct is located.
  - o The contrast medium is injected, allowing for visualization of the ducts.

NOTES

- o Nursing Interventions
  - Assess for allergy to the contrast medium prior to the procedure.
  - Postprocedure
    - ☐ Monitor the client for complications that may include bleeding, infection (sepsis or peritonitis), or inflammation of the bile ducts.
- Abdominal X-ray (KUB or flat plate) – To identify suspected problems in the urinary system or a blockage in the intestine. The x-ray may also assist in diagnosing abdominal pain, distention, or unexplained nausea.
- Liver Biopsy – A needle is inserted into the right upper quadrant of the liver under fluoroscopy, to obtain a sample for a biopsy or microscopic examination.

- o Nursing Interventions
  - NPO after midnight.
  - Verify that the informed consent has been signed.
  - Review coagulation studies (PT, INR, platelet count).
  - Place the client in a supine or left lateral position.
- o Postprocedure
  - The client will be positioned on his right side for 1 to 2 hr.
  - Monitor for complications that may include bleeding, pneumothorax, shock, and infection.
- Paracentesis – The removal of abdominal fluid accumulated in the peritoneum.
  - o Contributing factors
    - New onset of ascites
    - History of ascites with sudden fever, painful abdominal distention, peritoneal irritation, dyspnea, hypotension, encephalopathy, or sepsis
    - Suspected malignancy
    - Peritoneal dialysis for clients with suspected peritonitis

- o Nursing Interventions
  - Verify that the informed consent has been signed.
  - Have the client void before the procedure.
  - Record the client's weight and abdominal girth before the procedure.
  - Client should be in a supine position, with his head elevated 30°.
  - Support the client while local anesthetic is administered into the abdominal wall, followed by the insertion of a paracentesis needle.
  - Up to 4 L of fluid can be gradually removed (may take 30 to 90 min)
  - If fluid is greater than 5 L, IV serum albumin may be given to prevent hypotension.
- o Postprocedure
  - Record the client's weight and abdominal girth and compare to preprocedure measurements.
  - Ensure that the client remains in the supine position for 2 to 4 hr.
  - Observe for complications such as hypovolemia shock or infection.
- Liver Function Tests – Blood tests to determine the quality and functional level of hepatic function.
  - o Alkaline phosphatase – A nonspecific indicator of liver or bone disease, hypoparathyroidism; also used to detect malignancy of the liver or bone.
  - o Prothrombin time – A test to evaluate blood clotting. The value is prolonged with liver damage.
  - o Blood ammonia – Assesses the liver's ability to break down protein byproducts (normal ammonia level is 35 to 65 mcg/dL).
  - o Cholesterol (acceptable norms)
    - Total < 200 mg/dL
    - LDL ("bad") < 140 mg/dL
    - HDL ("good") > 40 to 70 mg/dL
    - Triglycerides < 159 mg/dL

NOTES

- Bilirubin
  - Direct – measured directly in the blood
  - Indirect – derived from the total and direct bilirubin measurements
- Gastrointestinal Intubation – Insertion of a tube through the oral or nasal route for infusion or removal of fluids.
  - Types
    - Nasogastric tube – decompression of the stomach
    - Salem sump – for continuous or intermittent suction
    - Miller-Abbot – intestinal suction requiring that the client be repositioned every hour; movement into the intestines
    - Sengstaken-Blakemore – for treatment of esophageal varices; can cause potential trauma and complications for the client, such as rebleeding, pneumonia, and respiratory obstructions
- Nasogastric Tube Feeding/Suction

  - Nursing Interventions
    - Feeding
      - Assess placement of the tube before each feeding, and every 4 hr with continuous feeding.
      - Maintain a semi-Fowler's position while feeding is infusing.
      - Check for residual in the stomach and refeed the residual (unless the amount exceeds 100 mL).
      - Provide nose and mouth care.
    - Suction
      - Drains contents from the stomach.
      - After insertion, the nurse should expect to assess a decrease in volume and change in the color of the drainage over time.
- Gastrostomy/Jejunostomy Tubes
  - These tubes are inserted through the skin and occasionally sutured in place. The nurse should assess skin integrity and provide skin care frequently.
  - Tubes are primarily used for long-term feeding.

- Percutaneous Endoscopic Gastrostomy (PEG)
  - No need to check the placement.
  - Primarily used for long-term feeding.
  - PEG is preferred over the gastrostomy tube because of its ease of insertion and care.
- Total Parenteral Nutrition (TPN) – IV administration of a hyperosmotic solution made up of glucose, nitrogen, lipid, electrolytes, and other nutrients. Meant for clients whose nutritional requirements cannot be achieved by dietary intake alone. TPN must be administered through a central line.
  - Contributing factors
    - Gastrointestinal mobility disorders
    - Inability to achieve or maintain adequate nutrition for body requirements
    - Disorders that impair absorption

  - Nursing Interventions
    - Perform a chest x-ray for proper placement immediately after central line insertion.
    - Assess daily weight, baseline electrolytes, glucose, and albumin levels.
    - Verify provider order for type of solution and infusion rate.
    - Change all tubing and filter every 24 hr; dispose of any remaining TPN after 24 hr.
    - Maintain sterile technique during central line dressing changes.
    - Observe for complications, which include
      - Infection – change filters and tubing with every bottle
      - Hypoglycemia/hyperglycemia – Check the client's blood sugar every 4 hr (if behind in administration rate, do not attempt to speed up administration of TPN).
      - Air embolism – Never open a central line to air. The chance of an air embolism is decreased with multiple lumen setups and peripherally inserted central catheters. When central line caps are changed, have the client perform the Valsalva maneuver and place her in the Trendelenburg position.
      - Pneumothorax – Particularly at risk during insertion of the subclavian central line.

NOTES

- □ Fluid overload – Rate should be increased gradually, and the nurse should frequently assesses for fluid overload.
- □ Hyperglycemic, hyperosmolar nonketotic coma
- □ Monitor for electrolyte imbalances.
  - Continually evaluate the effectiveness of therapy.
  - Follow the protocol for discontinuing TPN.
  - Turn off TPN for 1 min before drawing all labs from central line.
- Gastroesophageal Reflux Disease – A condition in which the lower esophageal sphincter does not close properly and stomach contents backup into the esophagus.
  - o Contributing factors
    - Hiatal hernia
    - Obesity
    - Pregnancy
    - Smoking or alcohol use
  - o Manifestations
    - Persistent heartburn and dysphagia
    - Chest pain
    - Hoarseness in the morning, dry cough
    - Halitosis
  - o Nursing Interventions
    - Teach the client to avoid alcohol consumption and smoking.
    - Encourage the client to maintain his ideal body weight.
    - Avoid citrus fruits, chocolate, caffeine, fried foods, garlic, onions, tomato-based foods, and foods that are fatty or spicy.
    - Teach the client to eat frequent, small meals, and avoid lying down for 3 hr after a meal.
    - Inform the client that loose-fitting clothes can facilitate a feeling of comfort.
  - o Administer medications
    - Antacids

- H_2 blockers – cimetidine (Tagamet), famotidine (Pepcid), ranitidine (Zantac), nizatidine (Axid)
- Proton-pump inhibitors – omeprazole (Prilosec), lansoprazole (Prevacid), pantoprazole (Protonix), esomeprazole (Nexium) rabeprazole (Aciphex)
  - o Complications
    - Bleeding or esophageal ulcers
    - Barrett's esophagus
    - Aggravation of asthma, chronic cough, and pulmonary fibrosis
- Hiatal Hernia – A portion of the stomach herniates through the esophageal hiatus of the diaphragm.
  - o Nursing Interventions
    - Instruct the client to eat small, frequent meals while in an upright position during and after each meal.
    - Ensure that the head of the bed is elevated, particularly at night.
    - Avoid anticholinergic medications.
    - Avoid coughing.
    - Reduce intraabdominal pressure by avoiding lifting or wearing tight-waisted clothes.
    - Decrease the client's intake of spicy foods.
- Duodenal Ulcer – The most common type of ulcer, found close to the pylorus of the stomach and occurring between the ages of 25 to 50.
  - o Contributing factors
    - Helicobacter pylori bacteria
    - Smoking
  - o Manifestations
    - The client appears well nourished.
    - Pain occurs 2 to 3 hr after a meal, or early in the morning when the stomach is empty.
    - Sharp pain or gnawing sensation to the midepigastric area or the back
    - Hypersecretion of stomach acid.
    - Indigestion is relieved with food.
    - Presence of melena is noted.

NOTES

- Chronic Gastric Ulcer – An ulceration located in the lesser curvature of the stomach, most common in men over the age of 50.
  - Contributing factors
    - Excessive ingestion of salicylates
    - Smoking
  - Manifestations
    - The client is malnourished.
    - Pain occurs 30 to 60 min after a client ingests food.
    - Vomiting (hematemesis) occurs frequently and actually relieves pain.
    - There is normal secretion of stomach acid.
- Inflammatory Bowel Disease – A group of conditions of the large intestine (and in some cases the small intestine). Do not confuse with irritable bowel syndrome, which is less severe. Included in this group is Crohn's disease and ulcerative colitis.
- Crohn's Disease – Disease of unknown origin affecting the small bowel, particularly the ileum and right colon, frequently found in clients of Jewish origin.
  - Manifestations
    - Diarrhea that is constant and uncontrolled.
    - Abdominal pain that occurs with ingestion of food.
    - Colicky pain and weight loss occurs.
    - Bleeding is rare.
  - Treatment
    - Steroids and antifungals
    - Immune modulators – infliximab (Remicade)
    - Hyperalimentation
    - May need to remove diseased section of bowel
- Ulcerative Colitis – Disease of unknown origin that causes ulcerations in the lining of the lower colon and rectum, frequently found in clients of Jewish origin.
  - Manifestations
    - Frequent, severe rectal bleeding
    - Mild to severe pain after eating
    - Weight loss

- Treatment
  - Steroids and antiinflammatory meds
  - Immune modulators (Remicade)
  - Possible surgical interventions (Ileostomy)
- Stress Ulcers – May be caused by physical as well as psychological stress.
  - Curling's ulcer (secondary to burns)
    - Located in the duodenum
    - During steroid therapy
    - Usually occurs at least 1 to 2 weeks after stressor
    - Diagnosed due to presence of gastric bleeding, resulting in low hemoglobin and hematocrit
  - Nursing Interventions (major goal is to prevent complications, allowing ulcer to heal)
    - Physiological and emotional rest is essential to help lower stress.
    - Encourage the client to eliminate stimulates such as caffeine, alcohol, spicy food, and cigarette smoking.
    - The client's diet has no therapeutic effect; milk may actually increase discomfort.
    - Antacids – aluminum hydroxide (Amphojel); magnesium carbonate (Maalox)
    - Cimetidine (Tagamet, Zantac) – decreases acid production
    - Sucralfate (Carafate) – protects lining of the stomach
    - Omeprazole (Prilosec) – decreases gastric-acid production
    - For Helicobacter pylori – antibiotics and symptomatic relief (Pepto-Bismol)
- Gastric Resection
  - Types
    - Billroth I (gastroduodenostomy)
    - Billroth II (gastrojejunostomy)
    - Total gastrectomy – causes pernicious anemia
  - Nursing Interventions
    - Do not irrigate or remove the gastric tube, as this may cause bleeding at the surgical site.

NOTES

- Administer fluids and electrolyte replacements IV, as prescribed; monitor I&O.
- NPO until the suture line is totally healed.
- Assess drainage – initially is sanguineous, but should change to green in 2 to 3 days.
- Complications
  - Hemorrhage
  - Pulmonary complications
  - Dumping syndrome – Rapid entry of ingested food into the jejunum without proper mixing during the normal digestive process of the duodenum.
    - Early (5 to 30 min after eating) – vertigo, sweating, diarrhea, and nausea due to fluid shifts
    - Late (2 to 3 hr after meals) – hypoglycemia due to excessive insulin secretion
      - Interventions for dumping syndrome
        - The client should avoid salty, high-carbohydrate meals.
        - Instruct the client to eat small, frequent meals high in protein, high in fat, and low in carbohydrates.
        - The client should avoid consuming fluids with meals.
        - The client should lie down after meals for at least 30 to 60 min.
        - Antispasmodics are occasionally prescribed to delay gastric emptying.
  - Major complications – peritonitis
- Diverticulitis and Diverticulosis – An out-pouching of the inner lining of the colon, generally in the large intestine, which accumulates fecal material. When the out-pouching becomes inflamed, it is referred to as diverticulitis. An obstruction or rupture of the area can lead to peritonitis.

  - Nursing Interventions
    - Instruct the client about the importance of maintaining a low-residue diet for healing, and eventually increasing fiber intake for prevention.
    - The client should avoid any food with seeds.

- Prevent constipation by using bulk agents and increasing water intake.
- Irritable Bowel Syndrome (IBS) – A disorder in which the colon is sensitive to certain foods and stress. The specific etiology is unknown, but is thought to be autoimmune.
  - Manifestations
    - There is no specific diagnostic test for IBS, although testing (x-ray, colonoscopy, and stool sample) may be done to rule out other conditions. If the results are negative, IBS may be diagnosed on the basis of the manifestations.
    - Cramping abdominal pain is typically relieved by having a bowel movement.
    - Abdominal distention
    - Bowel pattern disturbance
      - Constipation, diarrhea
      - Constipation alternating with diarrhea
      - Manifestations may subside and return, or may progressively become worse.

  - Nursing Interventions
    - Instruct the client to eat small, frequent meals.
    - The client should avoid foods known to aggravate the condition, such as wheat, rye, barley, chocolate, and milk products.
    - Instruct the client to avoid alcohol and caffeine.
    - Instruct the client to consume adequate fluids and fiber.
    - Medications may include fiber supplements; antispasmodics; tegaserod maleate (Zelnorm) may be prescribed for 4 to 6 weeks.
- Hernia – Protrusion of the bowel through the muscle wall of the abdominal cavity.
  - Serious complications – strangulation and gangrene of the bowel
  - Types
    - Umbilical
    - Ventral
    - Inguinal

NOTES

---

o Nursing Interventions

- Abdominal binder for support of the herniated area
- Prevent constipation
- Open or laparoscopic surgery (with or without mesh)
- No heavy lifting greater than 10 lb for 4 to 6 weeks

• Intestinal Obstruction – A condition in which the normal peristaltic action of the colon is impaired by scar tissue, adhesions from prior surgery, malignant lesions, inflammation and edema of the gastrointestinal tract, decreased gastrointestinal motility, or incarcerated hernia.

  o Manifestations

  - Constipation or no bowel movements for more than 4 to 5 days
  - Pain
  - Abdominal distention
  - Vomiting (projectile from reverse peristalsis); fecal vomiting
  - Hypovolemia and shock

 o Nursing Interventions

  - Insert NG tube and connect to low wall suction.
  - Encourage early ambulation to promote peristalsis.

• Colostomy – A surgical procedure that brings the end of the intestine through the abdominal wall, creating an opening for the evacuation of fecal material.

  o Contributing factors

  - Cancer or tumors
  - Obstructive bowel disease
  - Severe diverticulitis or Crohn's disease
  - Trauma

  o Manifestations

  - Stoma should be pink or beefy-red in color.
  - May have blood-tinged mucoid discharge.
  - Should be above level of skin after surgery.

- Stool may be formed or liquid, based on the location of the stoma in the intestinal tract.

 o Nursing Interventions

- Instruct the client to avoid foods that cause excessive gas formation and odor.
- May temporarily require daily irrigation.
- Instruct the client in stoma care and irrigations as prescribed.
- Teach the client how to burp the flange to remove gas and prevent the bag from dislodging.
- Offer emotional support and encourage the client to verbalize feelings associated with an altered body image.

• Ileostomy – A surgical procedure that brings a portion of the small bowel (ileum) through the abdominal wall, creating an opening for the evacuation of fecal material

  o Contributing factors

  - Temporary for Crohn's disease
  - Temporary or permanent for ulcerative colitis

  o Manifestations

  - Stool is a dark green liquid.
  - Client has no control over evacuation.
  - Client must wear appliance at all times.
  - Client is at risk for dehydration and metabolic acidosis.

  o Preoperative care

  - Emotional support (anticipatory grieving)
  - Encourage the client to express concerns related to impending surgery (ileostomy/colostomy).

 o Nursing Interventions

  - Instruct the client to avoid foods that cause excessive gas formation.
  - Demonstrate how to change flange when there is constant leakage of stool.
  - Teach the client to carefully inspect skin for excoriation from liquid stool.
  - Offer emotional support and encourage the client to verbalize feelings associated with an altered body image.

NOTES

COMPARISON OF HEPATITIS A, B, C

	Hepatitis A (Infectious Hepatitis)	Hepatitis B (Serum Hepatitis)	Hepatitis C
Cause	• Virus transmitted by fecal/oral contact. • Often seen following natural disasters from contaminated water or shellfish.	• Virus is transmitted through infected blood or unprotected sex with infected persons. • It occurs in infants born to mothers who are infected. • It is responsible for 80% of primary hepatocellular cancer cases.	Virus transmitted via contaminated blood transfusions, IV drug use, health care worker exposure, or from unprotected sex.
Manifestations	Manifestations include fever, fatigue, malaise, nausea, vomiting, anorexia, right upper-quadrant pain with dark urine, jaundice, and hepatomegaly.	• Its manifestations are similiar to type A. • Chronic process may result in cirrhosis.	Develop chronic infection, cirrhosis, and cancer.
Nursing Interventions	Take enteric precautions, encourage bed rest with a low-fat diet, increase fluids, avoid acetaminophen and liver-toxic medications.	• Take precautions with blood and body fluids. • Monitor for antiviral therapy side effects, which include fatigue, flu-like manifestations, neutropenia, depression.	• Take precautions with blood and body fluids. • Encourage rest and nutritional diet . • Monitor liver function test. • Teach safe sex practices.
Prevention	• Follow hand hygiene and good sanitation. • If in contact with an infected client, administer immune globulin within 2 to 7 days. • Hepatitis A vaccine is available.	• Mandate screening of blood donors; one-time use of needles and syringes. • Administer hepatitis B immune globulin 2 to 7 days after exposure. • Give hepatitis B vaccine (series of three timed injections over 6 months).	• No sharing of needles among drug users. • Avoid accidental needle sticks (health care workers).

NOTES

- o Postoperative care
  - Psychological support
  - Maintain patency of NG tube.
  - A healthy stoma is red; a color change to blue or black should be reported to the provider immediately.
  - Drainage will be dark green and progress to yellow when the client resumes eating.
  - Teach self-care to client.
    - □ Instruct the client about the correct type and use of equipment.
    - □ Provide frequent skin care.
    - □ Diet should be decreased in fat and gas-forming foods.
    - □ Irrigation should be done at the same time each day to develop a regular elimination pattern.
- Hepatitis A, B, and C – An inflammation of the liver; manifestations, prognosis, and treatment depend on the cause.
  - o See Table on page 51 for comparison of Hepatitis, A, B, and C
  - o Hepatitis D (HDV) – A defective virus, which occurs only in clients with HBV infections. Typical clients include IV drug users and their sexual partners. Clients with the coinfection of HBV and HDV have a greater risk for liver failure and cirrhosis. Clients with HBV should be tested for HDV.
- Cirrhosis – A chronic, progressive liver disease in which normal cells are replaced by scar tissue. Causes include Laennec's cirrhosis (alcohol induced), post necrotic cirrhosis (hepatitis, exposure to chemicals), biliary cirrhosis (chronic, biliary obstruction), and cardiac cirrhosis (severe right-sided heart failure).
  - o Functions of the liver
    - Synthesis of clotting factors (fibrinogen, prothrombin, factors VII, IX, X)
    - Metabolism of hormones (aldosterone, antidiuretic hormone, estrogen, testosterone)
    - Synthesis of albumin (maintains normal colloid osmotic pressure)
    - Carbohydrate metabolism

- Protein metabolism
- Fat metabolism through bile production
- Filtration removes bacteria and toxins, antigens, drugs
- Storage – blood, fat, and water soluble vitamins (A, D, E, K, B vitamins), as well as minerals (copper and iron)
- o Manifestations
  - Early stage
    - □ Enlarged liver
    - □ Jaundice
    - □ Gastrointestinal disturbances
    - □ Abdominal discomfort
  - Late stage
    - □ Liver becomes smaller and nodular
    - □ Splenomegaly
    - □ Ascites, distended abdominal veins; increased pressure in the portal system
    - □ Bleeding tendencies; decreased vitamin K and prothrombin, anemia
    - □ Esophageal varices, internal hemorrhoids; increased pressure in the portal area
    - □ Dyspnea from ascites and anemia
    - □ Pruritus from dry skin
    - □ Clay-colored stools, no bile in stool
    - □ Tea-colored urine, bile in urine
  - End stage
    - □ Prodromal – slurred speech, vacant stare, restlessness, neuro deterioration
    - □ Impending – asterixis (flapping tremors), apraxia, lethargy, confusion
    - □ Stuporous – marked mental confusion, somnolence
    - □ Coma – unarousable, fetor hepaticas, seizures, high mortality rate
- o Nursing Interventions
  - Encourage the client to rest.
  - Avoid hepatotoxic medications such as acetaminophen and alcohol.

NOTES

- Maintain a high-calorie, low-protein (20 to 40 g/day), low-fat, low-sodium diet (maintain protein restriction during stages I and II of encephalopathy; no protein allowed during stages III and IV).

- Fat-soluble vitamin supplements and folic acid may need to be given IV.

- Restrict sodium and fluid intake as prescribed.

- Use Albumin IV to decrease third spacing.

- Weigh the client daily and measure abdominal girth.

- Assess skin integrity frequently.

- Monitor I&O.

- Assess for bleeding and hemorrhoids.

- Diuretics – spironolactone (Aldactone), Furosemide (Lasix)

- Neomycin – Reduces intestinal bacteria, thereby decreasing the breakdown of protein-reducing ammonia levels

- Lactulose (Chronulac) – Decreases ammonia levels.

- Provide supplemental vitamins (B_1 and B complex, A, C, and K; folic acid; and thiamine) as prescribed.

- Bleeding Esophageal Varices – Dilated veins in the lower esophagus secondary to portal hypertension. Life-threatening hemorrhage of varices occurs from rupture, secondary to coughing, trauma, or vomiting, and is a medical emergency.

  o Nursing Interventions

    - Maintain patent airway prior to the insertion of the Sengstaken-Blakemore tube.

    - When the tube is in place, maintain traction for stability and patency.

    - Provide oral suctioning if the client is unable to swallow saliva.

    - Keep scissors at the bedside to cut the tube if respiratory obstruction occurs.

    - Administer medications as prescribed to decrease portal hypertension.

    - Monitor the client's vital signs and I&O frequently.

    - May need to administer vitamin K and vasopressin (Pitressin) for vasoconstriction.

- Gall Bladder Disease – A disease process in which the gall bladder is unable to store or release bile for the digestion of fats. It can be caused by a blockage from gall stones or inflammation of the organ.

  o Contributing factors

    - Females (2:1), ages 20 to 40

    - Obesity

    - History of Crohn's disease or diabetes mellitus

    - Diet high in fat, or frequent fast food meals

  o Manifestations

    - Severe right upper quadrant or mid-epigastric pain that radiates through to the back

    - Nausea, vomiting, fever

    - Diaphoresis and chills

    - Intolerance of high-fat meals

    - Excessive belching or eructation

    - Positive Murphy's sign – Palpate the right lower subcostal area, then have the client inhale deeply. Pain occurring with inspiration is a positive indication of gall bladder disease.

  o Treatments

    - Laparoscopic cholecystectomy – Removal of the gall bladder with a laparoscope, using four ½ inch incisions to insert the instruments.

      □ Least invasive, fewer complications

      □ Client may complain of shoulder or ribcage pain from gas (carbon dioxide) instilled for visualization during the procedure

    - Open cholecystectomy – Gall bladder is removed through a standard abdominal incision.

      □ More invasive, but provides enhanced visualization for large quantities of stones.

      □ May need a drain if the gall bladder is infected.

      □ Resume the diet after bowel sounds return.

  o Nursing Interventions

    - Assess the client's level of pain and symptoms.

NOTES

- Monitor I&O.
- Instruct the client on a low-fat diet.
- Administer an antiemetic if needed.

- Pancreatitis – An inflammation that occurs when pancreatic enzymes, normally not active until reaching the stomach, begin to self-digest the pancreas.
  - Contributing factors
    - Alcohol or cirrhosis
    - Gall bladder stones or disease
  - Manifestations
    - Extreme upper abdominal pain
    - Nausea, vomiting, fever, anorexia
    - Distended abdomen, pale, bulky stools
    - Elevated amylase and lipase levels
  - Treatment (will depend on severity of the disease and whether it is acute or chronic)
    - May include NG tube placement
    - With long-term pancreatitis, the client may need a central line for infusion of total parenteral nutrition.
    - May be prescribed anticholinergics or fat-soluble vitamins
    - Replacement of pancreatic enzymes
    - Narcotics for pain control
   o Nursing Interventions
    - NPO to prevent vomiting or stimulation of pancreatic enzymes.
    - If ordered, place an NG tube.
    - Provide consistent pain control.
    - Teaching
      - The client should consume a low-fat diet and avoid alcohol.
      - If on TPN, teach the client how to manage the infusion from home.
      - Report changes in symptoms such as increased pain, fever, nausea, vomiting, and respiratory distress.

- Rheumatoid Arthritis – A chronic systemic disease of unknown origin marked by recurrent inflammation of the lining of all joints and organs; most likely autoimmune; most common in females, appearing around ages 20 to 50.
  - Manifestations
    - Periods of remission and exacerbation
    - Bilateral joint involvement
    - Tenderness, swelling, warmth, and redness
    - Development of subcutaneous nodules
    - Symptoms most severe upon rising
    - Positive C-reactive protein
    - Elevated sedimentation rate and antinuclear antibody
   o Nursing Interventions
    - Focus on relieving the symptoms.
    - Encourage the client to implement a gentle exercise routine.
    - Encourage frequent rest periods with extremities in an extended position.
    - Instruct the client about methods of weight control and maintenance. Refer him to a nutritionist if appropriate.
    - Manage the client's pain with NSAIDS or corticosteroids.
    - May benefit from methotrexate (Rheumatrex)
- Osteoarthritis – Degenerative process in which the cartilage of joints wears away from repeated use over a period of years; most common in females (20:1) and appears around middle age.
  - Manifestations
    - Pain and stiffness, particularly after short periods of inactivity
    - Crepitus or grinding noted with movement
    - Joint deformity/presence of Heberden's nodes or Bouchard's nodes

---

NOTES

---

o Nursing Interventions

- Teach the client range of motion or gentle exercises (isometric).
- Encourage the client to use ice or heat for comfort.
- Teach the client to maintain an ideal body weight.
- Manage the client's pain with NSAIDS or possible corticosteroids.
- The client may eventually need joint replacement.

- Fractures – A disruption of bone caused by a direct or indirect force.
  - o Types of Fractures
    - Closed (skin remains intact)
    - Comminuted (multiple small fragments of bone)
    - Compression (crushing of bone)
    - Greenstick (break does not extend completely through the bone)
    - Spiral (most commonly found in cases of abuse)
    - Pathological

 o Nursing Interventions
    - Immediate
      - □ Maintain the airway.
      - □ Monitor for shock.
      - □ Immobilize the fracture.
      - □ Reassess vascular status.
    - Ongoing care
      - □ Assess circulation, movement, and sensation, also known as the five Ps.
        - ▸ Pain
        - ▸ Pallor
        - ▸ Pulselessness
        - ▸ Paresthesia
        - ▸ Paralysis
  - o Manifestations
    - Monitor for fat embolism up to 2 weeks following fractures of long bones (humerus and femur)

- Restlessness or altered mental status
- Tachypnea and tachycardia
- Fever
- Petechiae

- Traction – The use of a pulling force maintained continuously to align bones and prevent muscle spasms.
  - o Types
    - Skin
      - □ Buck's traction (5 to 10 lb maximum)
      - □ Pelvic (up to 20 lb maximum)
    - Skeletal
      - □ Thomas splint with Pearson attachment
      - □ Crutchfield tongs, Cervical Halo

 o Nursing Interventions
    - Assess pulses and vascular status.
    - Maintain proper body alignment.
    - Verify that weights are hanging freely.
    - Monitor for pressure points or breakdown secondary to shearing forces.
    - Provide pin care every shift with skeletal traction.
    - Provide strengthening exercises for uninvolved extremities.
    - Consult physical therapy regarding crutch walking.

- Casts – Application of plaster or fiberglass to immobilize and maintain alignment of the bone until it is healed.

 o Nursing Interventions
    - Handle the cast with the palms wet, and assess the neurovascular integrity.
    - The cast should be allowed to air dry.
    - Elevate the cast on a pillow and apply ice to manage the pain.
    - Maintain skin integrity and petal edges of the cast to prevent skin breakdown.
    - Monitor for signs or symptoms of compartment syndrome.
      - □ Severe pain at rest with burning and tightness

NOTES

- ☐ Weak or absent pulses, skin cool to touch, edema, or delayed capillary return
- ☐ Paralysis is a late finding with increased risk of amputation.
- ☐ Absence of pulse for 6 hr or more requires amputation of the extremity.
- Hip Fractures – A disruption in the hip bone integrity from the neck of the femur to the trochanteric area.
  - o Treatment
    - ■ Skin traction for immobilization (preoperative) to decrease pain and muscle spasms
    - ■ Trochanter roll to prevent external rotation
    - ■ Open reduction and internal fixation
    - ■ Total hip replacement (insertion of artificial joint)
  - o Contributing Factors
    - ■ Arthritis or congenital hip dysplasia
    - ■ Severe hip fracture
    - ■ Failed reconstructive surgery
  - o Nursing Interventions
    - ■ Preoperative care
      - ☐ Maintain immobilization and assess the vascular status frequently.
      - ☐ Administer anticoagulation therapy as prescribed.
    - ■ Postoperative care
      - ☐ Maintain proper leg alignment.
        - ▸ Use abduction pillow while in bed.
        - ▸ Never flex operative hip more than 90°.
        - ▸ Limit flexion during transfers and while sitting, keeping the hips higher than the knees at all times.
        - ▸ Do not cross legs.
        - ▸ Use an elevated seat chair and a raised toilet seat.
      - ☐ Monitor for deep vein thrombosis formation.
        - ▸ Perform range of motion to affected extremity.
        - ▸ Apply elastic stockings.

- ▸ Administer anticoagulants as prescribed.
- ▸ Observe for dislocation of hip prosthesis, incisional infection, or hemorrhage.

- Osteoporosis – Demineralization of the bones; leading cause in crippling hip fractures in women.
  - o Contributing factors
    - ■ Prolonged immobility
    - ■ Low calcium diet
    - ■ Menopause, men 65 and older, and underweight females
    - ■ Smoking or steroid use
  - o Nursing interventions
    - ■ Teach the client the benefits of supplemental calcium with vitamin D, generally prescribed by a health care provider in the following amounts – 1,200 mg premenopause; 1,500 mg postmenopause.
    - ■ Teach the client fall precautions.
    - ■ Encourage the client to perform weight-bearing exercises.
    - ■ Bisphosphonate therapy
      - ☐ Alendronate (Fosamax); the client must remain upright for at least 30 min following dose.
      - ☐ Ibandronate (Boniva)

- Pelvic Fractures
  - o Nursing Interventions
    - ■ Assess the client for potential bladder injuries and observe for hematuria.
    - ■ Assess for bowel injuries and observe for signs of peritonitis.
    - ■ Monitor for signs of shock and internal bleeding.
    - ■ Maintain bed rest.
    - ■ Keep the client in a pelvic sling (may be removed intermittently).

- Amputation – The surgical removal of an extremity or part of an extremity.; most commonly related to advanced peripheral arterial disease; above- or below-the-knee amputation is the most common site.

NOTES

- o Contributing factors
  - ▪ Diabetes mellitus
  - ▪ Peripheral vascular disease
- o Nursing Interventions
  - ▪ Provide psychological support.
  - ▪ Perform standard preoperative teaching.
  - ▪ Teach the client to perform exercises to increase his upper body strength.
  - ▪ Elevate the surgical extremity for the first 24 hr, and then monitor for flexion deformity.
  - ▪ Apply ice for the first 24 hr.
  - ▪ Medicate for phantom pain.
  - ▪ Teach the client safe and effective transfer techniques.
- o Stump conditioning to prepare for prosthesis
  - ▪ Apply stump shrinker daily.
  - ▪ Toughen the stump by rubbing it briskly with a dry washcloth after the incision has healed.
  - ▪ Compression dressing
- • Gout – An inflammatory type of arthritis caused by deposits of urate crystals in and around the joints secondary to hereditary error in the metabolism of purine resulting in excessive uric acid production.
  - o Contributing factors
    - ▪ Alcoholism
    - ▪ Chemotherapy
    - ▪ Heredity
  - o Manifestations
    - ▪ Severe pain, often beginning in the great toe
    - ▪ Joints are red, warm, painful, and swollen
    - ▪ Accumulations of uric acid crystals in the joints (tophi) and connective tissue
    - ▪ Joint damage and deformity increase with each attack
    - ▪ Hyperuricemia – > 7 mg/dL
    - ▪ Sporadic and usually diet related

- • Treatment
  - o NSAIDS
    - ▪ Can cause bone marrow suppression and liver damage
    - ▪ Indomethacin (Indocin)
    - ▪ Probenecid (Benemid)
  - o Allopurinol (Zyloprim) for daily maintenance
  - o Colchicine during an acute attack only
    - ▪ Reduces uric acid
    - ▪ Stop if the client develops diarrhea
  - o Corticosteroid for the short-term to manage pain and inflammation
- o Nursing Interventions
  - ▪ Keep the client on bed rest during acute attacks.
  - ▪ Use a bed cradle to keep linens elevated above the affected joint.
  - ▪ Apply heat or cold as tolerated by the client.
  - ▪ Fluid intake should be 2,000 mL or more daily.
  - ▪ Limit the intake of high purine foods such as organ and red meats, wine, and alcohol.
  - ▪ Discuss weight loss strategies with the client.
- • Total-knee Replacement – Implantation of metal or acrylic prosthesis designed to provide functional, joint stability to clients that are experiencing severe pain and functional disabilities related to joint destruction.
- o Nursing Interventions
  - ▪ Assess the client for swelling, manifestations of infection, neurovascular status, and pain.
  - ▪ Assess drains for quality and quantity drainage.
  - ▪ Premedicate prior to using a passive motion device.
  - ▪ Apply ice consistently to control or reduce edema.
  - ▪ Review weight-bearing status orders.

NOTES

SECTION 6

ENDOCRINE SYSTEM FUNCTIONS AND DISORDERS

- Pituitary Gland – The anterior lobe of the pituitary gland promotes growth of body tissue, is responsible for the secretory activity of the adrenal cortex, and controls the activity of thyroid hormone secretion. The anterior lobe is the major producer of thyrotropic hormone (TSH), adrenocorticotropic hormone (ACTH), luteinizing hormone (LH), follicle-stimulating hormone (FSH), and gonadotropic hormones.
  - o Disorders of anterior pituitary
    - Acromegaly – Hypersecretion of growth hormone (GH) that occurs in adulthood; commonly associated with benign pituitary tumors.
  - o Manifestations
    - Enlargement of skeletal extremities
    - Protrusion of the jaw and orbital ridges
    - Visual problems, blindness
    - Hyperglycemia, insulin resistance
    - Hypercalcemia
  - o Treatment
    - Irradiation of pituitary
    - Bromocriptine (Parlodel) with surgery or radiation
  - o Nursing Interventions
    - Provide emotional support.
    - Provide symptomatic care.
- Gigantism – Hypersecretion of GH that occurs in childhood.
  - o Manifestations
    - Proportional overgrowth in all body tissue
    - Overgrowth of long bones – height during childhood may reach 8 or 9 ft
  - o Treatment (same as acromegaly)
  - o Nursing Interventions (same as acromegaly)

- Dwarfism – Hyposecretion of GH during fetal development or childhood that results in an adult height of < 4 ft 10 inches.
  - o Manifestations
    - Head and extremities are disproportionate to torso.
    - Progressive bowed legs and lordosis
    - Delayed adolescence
  - o Treatment
    - Limb-lengthening surgery
    - Human growth hormone injections
    - Measures are adapted to meet activities of daily living.
  - o Nursing Interventions (same as acromegaly)
- Disorder of Posterior Pituitary – The posterior pituitary, controlled mainly by the hypothalamus, directly affects the function of the other endocrine glands; known as the master gland.
  - o Diabetes insipidus – Hyposecretion of antidiuretic hormone due to insufficient production of vasopressin, head injury, or tumors; considered idiopathic or genetic.
    - Manifestations
      - □ Polyuria and polydipsia
      - □ Hypernatremia
      - □ Weight loss
      - □ Dehydration or dry skin
    - Medication treatment
      - □ Vasopressin (desmopressin/DDAVP)
      - □ Lypressin (Diapid) nasal spray
    - Nursing Interventions
      - □ Weigh the client daily.
      - □ Monitor urine-specific gravity.
      - □ Assess the client's blood pressure and heart rate.
      - □ Maintain fluid and electrolyte balance.
      - □ Avoid foods with diuretic action.
- Syndrome of Inappropriate Secretion of Antidiuretic Hormone (SIADH) – The inappropriate, continued release of antidiuretic hormone resulting in water intoxication; caused by neoplastic tumors, respiratory disorders, and drugs.

NOTES

- Manifestations
  - Mental confusion and irritability
  - Lethargy and seizures
  - Dilutional hyponatremia
  - Weight gain
  - Anorexia, nausea, and vomiting
  - Weakness
- Treatment
  - Correct hyponatremia with fluid restriction and hypertonic solutions.
  - Give demeclocycline (Declomycin) to inhibit the vasopressin receptors.
  - Treat the underlying cause with surgery, chemotherapy, and/or radiation.
- Nursing Interventions
  - Assess the client's neurologic status frequently.
  - Monitor I&O.
  - Weigh the client daily.
- Adrenal Gland
  - Disorders of adrenal cortex
  - Addison's disease – The hyposecretion of adrenal cortex hormones from insufficiency of cortisol, aldosterone, and androgens; can be induced by abrupt steroid medications.
  - Manifestations
    - Fatigue, muscle pain and weakness, and joint pain
    - Anorexia and weight loss
    - Hyperpigmentation (known as the perpetual tan)
    - Hypotension and syncope
    - Hypoglycemia, hyponatremia, hyperkalemia
    - Craving salty foods
    - Irritability and depression
    - Diminished libido
  - Treatment (replacement of steroids)
    - Medication – hydrocortisone (Cortef) to replace the insufficiency of cortisol
    - Fluid and electrolyte balance

  - High-protein and high-carbohydrate diet
- Nursing Interventions
  - Monitor for Addisonian crisis (sudden extreme weakness; severe abdominal, back, and leg pain; hyperpyrexia; coma; death) secondary to stress caused by infection, trauma, surgery, pregnancy, or stress.
  - Monitor for side effects of hormone replacement, which are the same symptoms as hypersecretion of this gland.
  - Provide emotional support to the client and provide instruction on life-long disease management (medications, prompt treatment of infection, illness, and stress management).
  - Monitor fluid and electrolyte balance.
- Cushing's Syndrome – The hypersecretion of the glucocorticoids from an overdose of steroid medications; may also result from adenoma of pituitary gland stimulating increased production of the adrenocorticotropic hormone.
  - Manifestations
    - Upper body obesity, moon face, buffalo hump, and neck fat
    - Skin fragility with purple striae
    - Osteoporosis
    - Hyperglycemia, hypernatremia, hypokalemia
    - Hirsutism
    - Amenorrhea
    - Elevated triglycerides and hypertension
    - Sexual dysfunction
    - Immunosuppression
    - Peptic ulcer
  - Treatment
    - Adrenalectomy – unilateral or bilateral
    - Chemotherapy – bromocriptine (Parlodel), mitotane (Lysodren), or aminoglutethimide (Cytadren)
    - High-protein, low-carbohydrate, low-sodium diet with potassium supplement
    - For pituitary adenoma, the client may need a transsphenoidal adenomectomy

---

NOTES

- o Nursing Interventions
    - Monitor the client for infection.
    - Protect the client from accidents and falls due to osteoporosis.
    - Educate the client concerning lifelong self-administration of hormone suppression therapy.
    - Provide steroid replacement for anti-inflammatory and antiautoimmune properties.
        - □ Indications
            - ▸ Crisis (shock, bronchial obstruction)
            - ▸ Long-term therapy (postadrenalectomy, arthritis, leukemia)
        - □ Side effects due to prolonged use
        - □ Dosage schedule
            - ▸ Large dosages should be given at 0800 ($^2/_3$), smaller doses at night ($^1/_3$), to simulate the normal excretion by the body.
            - ▸ Steroids should be taken at the same time every day.
            - ▸ Withdraw steroids in tapered dosages, or the client may develop symptoms of Addison's disease.
            - ▸ Give steroids with antacids to minimize gastrointestinal upset and ulceration.
- Aldosteronism (Conn's syndrome) – The hypersecretion of aldosterone from the adrenal cortex (usually due to a tumor).
    - o Manifestations
        - Hypokalemia and hypernatremia
        - Hypertension from hypernatremia
        - Muscle weakness and cardiac problems related to hypokalemia
    - o Treatment
        - Surgical removal of tumor/adrenal gland
        - Potassium replacement
        - Antihypertensive medications – spironolactone (Aldactone)

- o Nursing Interventions
    - Provide the client a quiet environment.
    - Monitor the client's blood pressure and cardiac activity.
    - Monitor the client's potassium level.
- Disorders of Adrenal Medulla
    - o Pheochromocytoma – A benign tumor of the adrenal medulla that causes hypersecretion of epinephrine and norepinephrine.
    - o Manifestations (sudden onset) – Seen in young women and men.
        - Hypertensive crisis
        - Tachycardia
            - □ Diaphoresis
            - □ Apprehension
            - □ Palpitations secondary to tachycardia
            - □ Nausea, vomiting
            - □ Orthostatic hypotension
            - □ Headache
        - Pallor
        - Flight or fight symptoms
        - Hyperglycemia
        - Headache
    - o Treatment
        - Immediate surgical removal of tumor.
        - Alpha and beta-blocker medication to diminish the effect of norepinephrine prior to the surgery.

- o Nursing Interventions
    - Provide a high-calorie, nutritious diet and avoid caffeine.
    - Encourage frequent rest periods.
    - Preoperative – It is essential to control hypertension to prevent stroke secondary to hypertensive crisis.

___

NOTES

___

- Thyroid Gland
  - ○ Myxedema – A malfunction of the thyroid gland in which there is a slow, but progressive decrease in secretion of thyrocalcitonin, hyposecretion of thyroxine (T_4) and triiodothyronine (T_3); more commonly seen in women, peaking between the ages of 50 to 60.
  - ○ Manifestations
    - ▪ Fatigue and weakness
    - ▪ Increased sensitivity to cold
    - ▪ Constipation
    - ▪ Dry skin, brittle hair and nails
    - ▪ Weight gain
    - ▪ Deepened, hoarse voice
    - ▪ Joint pain and stiffness
    - ▪ Hyperlipidemia and anemia
    - ▪ Depression
    - ▪ Heavy menstrual cycle
    - ▪ Facial edema/goiter
    - ▪ Puffy appearance (nonpitting)
  - ○ Treatment
    - ▪ Synthetic thyroid – replacement hormone levothyroxine (Synthroid)
      - □ Administer the medication on an empty stomach.
      - □ Monitor the client for toxicity – palpitations, insomnia, increased appetite, and tremors.
  - ○ Nursing Interventions
    - ▪ Provide the client a warm environment.
    - ▪ Provide a low-calorie, low-cholesterol, and low-fat diet.
    - ▪ Increase roughage and fluids.
    - ▪ Avoid sedatives.
    - ▪ Plan rest periods for the client.
    - ▪ Weigh the client daily.
    - ▪ Observe for manifestations of overdose of thyroid preparations (these will be the same as the manifestations of hyperthyroidism).

- Hyperthyroidism (Graves' Disease) – The hypersecretion of thyroxine from the immune system; attacks the thyroid gland and is more common in women older than 20.
  - ○ Manifestations
    - ▪ Anxiety and irritability
    - ▪ Insomnia and fatigue
    - ▪ Tachycardia
    - ▪ Tremors
    - ▪ Diaphoresis
    - ▪ Intolerance of heat
    - ▪ Weight loss (despite food intake)
    - ▪ Exophthalmos and photosensitivity
    - ▪ Diarrhea
    - ▪ Light or absent menstrual cycle
  - ○ Treatment
    - ▪ Beta-blocker medications are needed to manage tachycardia, anxiety, and tremors.
      - □ Nadolol (Corgard), propranolol (Inderal), atenolol (Tenormin), metoprolol (Lopressor)
      - □ Propylthiouracil (Propyl-Thyracil or PTU) – blocks thyroid hormone production
      - □ Methimazole (Tapazole) – short-term use to block production of thyroxine; usually used no more than 8 weeks
    - ▪ Monitor CBC frequently for occurrence of agranulocytosis.
      - □ Iodides decrease vascularity and inhibit the release of thyroid hormones.
        - ▸ Lugol's solution (use is decreasing)
        - ▸ Saturated solution of potassium iodide (SSKI); used prior to thyroidectomy
      - □ A radioactive iodine treatment shrinks the thyroid gland prior to surgery.
        - ▸ Saturated solution of potassium iodide (SSKI)
      - □ Thyroidectomy requires a lifelong intake of levothyroxine (Synthroid) and calcium.
  - ○ Nursing Interventions
    - ▪ Encourage the client to get adequate rest in a cool, quiet environment.

NOTES

- Provide a high-caloric (4,000 to 5,000 cal/day), high-protein, and high-carbohydrate diet without stimulants or extra fluids.
- Weigh the client daily.
- Provide her emotional support.
- Provide eye protection for the client by giving ophthalmic medicine, taping her eyes at night, and decreasing sodium and water.
- Elevate the head of the client's bed.
- Be alert for complications.
  - □ Corneal abrasion
  - □ Heart disease
  - □ Thyroid storm (after thyroid surgery)
- Thyroidectomy – The removal of part or all of the thyroid gland.
  - o Preoperative goals
    - Decrease thyroid function toward normal range using a saturated solution of potassium iodide (SSKI).
  - o Nursing Interventions (postoperative care)
    - Place the client in the semi-Fowler's position.
    - Monitor the client's dressing, especially the back of the neck.
    - Observe for respiratory distress. Keep a tracheostomy tray, oxygen, and suction apparatus at the client's bedside.
    - Monitor for signs of hemorrhage.
    - Note any hoarseness, which is indicative of laryngeal nerve injury; limit talking.
    - Observe for signs of tetany (Chvostek's and Trousseau's sign); may indicate damage or accidental removal of parathyroid glands.
    - Keep a calcium gluconate IV at the client's bedside.
    - Observe for thyroid storm (life-threatening); caused by an increased release of the thyroid hormone.
      - □ Fever
      - □ Tachycardia
      - □ Delirium and irritability
    - Gradually increase the range of motion to the neck and support the client when he sits up.

- Parathyroid Gland
  - o Hypoparathyroidism – The hyposecretion of PTH, resulting in hypocalcemia and hyperphosphatemia.
  - o Manifestations
    - Paresthesia
    - Muscle cramps and tetany
    - Chvostek's sign – Tapping the side of the cheek causes muscle spasms and twitching around the mouth, throat, and cheeks
    - Trousseau's sign – Pressure from the blood pressure cuff induces muscle spasms in the distal extremity.
    - Alopecia
    - Dry skin, brittle hair and nails
    - Painful menstruation
    - Poor development of tooth enamel
    - Lethargic
    - Thin hair and brittle nails
    - Mental retardation
    - Circumoral paraesthesia with numbness and tingling of the fingers
  - o Treatment
    - Acute – IV calcium gluconate
    - Chronic
      - □ Oral calcium salts
      - □ Vitamin D and aluminum hydroxide gel (Amphojel)
      - □ High-calcium, low-phosphorous diet
  - o Nursing Interventions
    - Place the client in a quiet room with no stimulus.
    - Assess the client for signs of neuromuscular irritability.
- Hyperparathyroidism (caused by tumor or renal disease) – A hypersecretion of PTH with loss of calcium from the bones and into the serum, resulting in hypercalcemia and hypophosphoremia.

NOTES

- o Manifestations
  - Kidney stones and hyperuricemia
  - Osteoporosis
  - Hypercalcemia and hypophosphoremia
  - Abdominal pain, nausea, and vomiting
  - Muscle weakness and fatigue
  - Polyuria and polydipsia
  - Hypertension
- o Treatment
  - Subtotal surgical resection of the parathyroid gland
  - Hydration and diuretics - furosemide (Lasix) promotes excretion of excess calcium
  - Plicamycin (Mithracin) or gallium nitrate (Ganite)
- o Nursing Interventions
  - Force fluids.
  - Provide the client a low-calcium, low-vitamin D diet.
  - Prevent constipation and fecal impaction.
  - Strain all of the client's urine.
  - Instruct the client about safety measures to prevent breaks.
  - Calcitonin binds phosphate in renal failure.
- Pancreas – A gland that produces insulin designed to decrease blood glucose by stimulating active transport of glucose into muscle and adipose tissue, stimulating protein synthesis, and promoting the conversion of glucose to glycogen for storage; also produces glucagon, which converts glycogen back to glucose when needed.
  - o Diabetes mellitus – A chronic disorder of carbohydrate metabolism, characterized by an imbalance between insulin supply and demand; either a subnormal amount of insulin is produced or the body requires abnormally high amounts.
    - Type 1 – insulin-dependent diabetes mellitus; usually juvenile onset
    - Type 2 – Noninsulin-dependent diabetes mellitus; usually adult onset
    - Of the 21 million Americans with diabetes mellitus, approximately 90% have type 2.
    - Diabetes mellitus is caused by the dual defects of insulin resistance and beta-cell secretory dysfunction.
  - o Glycemic control
    - Maintaining tight glycemic control substantially reduces the risk for the onset or progression of the complications of diabetes mellitus.
    - Glucose control is monitored on a day-to-day basis by capillary blood glucose levels.
      - Normal preprandial (fasting) blood glucose is 70 to 99 mg/dL
      - Normal postprandial blood glucose is 70 to 140 mg/dL
    - Glucose control is monitored on a long-term basis by the HbA1c (glycosylated hemoglobin).
      - Normal (nondiabetic) HbA1c level is less than 6%.
      - The goal of the American Diabetes Association is an HbA1c level of less than 7%.
  - o Manifestations: "3 Polys"
    - Polyuria
    - Polydipsia
    - Polyphagia
  - o Nursing Interventions
    - Balance the client's diet with insulin and exercise.
    - Administer insulin therapy.
      - Insulin is necessary to open the door for glucose to enter the cell and be used for energy.
      - When mixing insulins
        - ‣ Draw up the Regular insulin first, then the NPH insulin (clear, then cloudy).
        - ‣ Do not mix long-acting insulins (glargine, detemir) with any other insulin or solution. Separate syringes and sites must be used when giving a long-acting and rapid-acting insulin.

NOTES

INSULIN PREPARATIONS

Insulin Preparation	Onset of Action	Peak	Duration of Action	Type
Lispro/aspart/glulisine (NovoLog, Humalog)	5 to 15 min	1 to 2 hr	4 to 5 hr	Rapid acting
Human Regular (Humulin R, Novolin R)	30 to 60 min	2 to 4 hr	8 to 10 hr	Short acting
NPH (Humulin L, Lente, Novolin NPH)	1 to 2 hr	4 to 8 hr	10 to 20 hr	Intermediate acting
Glargine/detemir/ insulin zinc suspension, extended (ultralente) (Lantus, Humulin U)	1 to 4 hr	Relatively flat	Up to 24 hr	Long acting

NOTES

- □ Insulin pump – An external device that provides a basal dose of Regular insulin with a bolus dose before meals; does not read blood glucose.
  - ▸ Needles are inserted into subcutaneous abdominal tissue (change site every 24 to 48 hr).
  - ▸ Complications
    - ▹ Secondary to continuous administration of insulin
- ■ Sulfonylurea medications stimulate the pancreas to produce insulin.
  - □ Glipizide (Glucotrol)
  - □ Chlorpropamide (Diabinese)
  - □ Glyburide (DiaBeta)
  - □ Metformin (Glucophage)
  - □ Glimepiride (Amaryl)
- ■ Maintain diet therapy.
  - □ Provide the client with adequate nutrients for proper cell growth and function.
  - □ Maintain a balance between the amount of glucose in the body and the amount of insulin present to use that glucose.
  - □ The provider may advise the client to follow the food exchange from the American Diabetes Association's diet.
- ■ Monitor for complications.
  - □ Hypoglycemia occurs when the blood glucose level falls below 60 mg/dL.
    - ▸ Causes – decreased dietary intake, excess insulin, and increased exercise
- o Manifestations
  - ■ Tachycardia
  - ■ Diaphoresis
  - ■ Weakness, fatigue
  - ■ Irritability, anxiety
  - ■ Confusion
- o Nursing Interventions
  - ■ Give the client 10 to 15 g of a fast-acting simple carbohydrates (hard candy, 4 tsp of sugar, one Tbsp of honey, ½ cup fruit juice).

- ■ Follow with a snack or carbohydrates such as cheese, a slice of bread, or graham crackers with peanut butter.
- ■ For severe hypoglycemia (blood glucose of less than 20 mg/dL), the client may not be able to swallow. If he is unconscious or seizing, administer 1 mg of glucagon IM or subcutaneous.
- Diabetic Ketoacidosis – Complication of diabetes mellitus due to deficient insulin production; exacerbated hyperglycemia causes production of ketones resulting from fat used for energy; the most common is type 1 diabetes mellitus.
  - o Contributing factors
    - ■ Illness, fever, or infection
    - ■ Surgery
    - ■ Fever
    - ■ Substance abuse
    - ■ Noncompliance with insulin therapy
  - o Manifestations
    - ■ Exacerbated polyuria, polydipsia, polyphagia
    - ■ Anorexia, nausea, and vomiting
    - ■ Metabolic acidosis with ketonuria
    - ■ Kussmaul's respirations
    - ■ Fruity, scented breath
    - ■ Level of consciousness changes
  - o Nursing Interventions
    - ■ Provide vascular support.
    - ■ Administer fluid and electrolyte replacements as prescribed by the provider.
    - ■ Administer Regular insulin IV therapy.
- Lipodystrophy – Indurated areas of subcutaneous tissue secondary to injecting cold insulin or not rotating sites.
  - o Hyperglycemic hyperosmolar nonketotic coma
    - ■ Extremely high glucose levels cause dehydration
    - ■ No ketosis; elevated BUN
    - ■ Treatment
      - □ Replace fluids as prescribed.

NOTES

- □ Administer insulin and electrolytes as prescribed.
- ○ Nursing Interventions
  - Teach the client proper foot care.
    - □ Cleanse feet daily in warm, soapy water; rinse and dry carefully; don't break blisters; trim nails to follow natural curve of the toe; always wear breathable shoes such as leather; no crossing of the legs; no cream between toes; inspect each foot daily.
  - Perform injection techniques and site rotation.
  - Instruct the client about the importance of weight management.
  - Encourage the client not to smoke.
  - Teach stress-reduction techniques.
- ○ Long-term complications
  - Diabetic neuropathy – Causes pain in the legs, decreased sensation; causes impotence in men.
  - Renal – Affects microcirculation of the kidneys, results in renal failure.
  - Cardiovascular – Clients with diabetes mellitus are 4 times more likely to have a MI; also increases the occurrence of hypertension and decreased peripheral circulation.
  - Eyes – The number one cause of blindness and occurrence of cataracts.
  - Infections – Increased glucose in body fluids makes for an ideal medium for growth of micro-organisms, urinary tract infections, and cellulitis.

- ○ Nursing Interventions
  - Assess all systems for complication.
  - Assist the client in developing lifestyle changes that support the maintenance of dietary insulin and blood glucose control. Referral to a diabetic educator is appropriate.

- Anemia – A deficiency of RBCs characterized by a decreased RBC count and a below normal Hgb and Hct; the result is a decrease in oxygen to the cells directly related to the degree of anemia present.
  - ○ Causes
    - Acute or chronic blood loss (gastrointestinal ulcers)
    - Greater than normal destruction of RBCs (spleen diseases)
    - Abnormal bone marrow function (chemotherapy)
    - Decreased erythropoietin (renal failure)
    - Inadequate maturation of RBCs (cancer)
  - ○ Manifestations
    - Fatigue, dizziness, and weakness
    - Pallor – first seen in conjunctival area (Caucasian) and oral area (dark-skinned population)
    - Cardiac, if there is decreased oxygen to heart
    - Decreased activity tolerance
    - Decreased Hgb, Hct, RBC levels
    - Shortness of breath and dyspnea
  - ○ Nursing Interventions
    - Encourage activity as tolerated by the client with frequent rest periods.
    - Monitor skin integrity and implement measures to prevent breakdown.
    - Provide oxygen therapy to the client as needed.
    - Administer blood products as prescribed.
- Blood Transfusions
  - ○ Equipment
    - Y-type tubing with filter
    - 0.9% sodium chloride
    - Blood

NOTES

- o Nursing Interventions
  - Check the client's ID, name, and blood type. Make sure the information is verified by two nurses.
  - Prior to administration, assess baseline vital signs, including temperature.
  - For the first 15 min, stay with the client and infuse slowly, monitoring for any reaction.
  - Infuse within 4 hr and discard any remaining blood.
  - Monitor the client for transfusion reaction.
    - □ Allergic (pruritus, respiratory distress, urticaria), flushing; if there is a minor reaction, the nurse may give diphenhydramine (Benadryl) if prescribed, and continue to infuse.
    - □ Hemolytic – ABO-incompatibility (flank pain, chest pain, fever, chills, tachycardia, tachypnea)
  - Treat transfusion reaction.
    - □ Stop blood immediately and take the client's vital signs.
    - □ Maintain IV access with NS.
    - □ Notify the health care provider.
    - □ Follow facility policy (send urine sample, CBC, send bag and tubing to laboratory for analysis).
- Types of Anemias
  - o Hypoproliferation anemia – Bone marrow is unable to produce an adequate numbers of cells
    - Anemia secondary to renal disease (lack of erythropoietin); treat by administering synthetic erythropoietin (Procrit, Epogen)
    - Iron deficiency anemia
      - □ Due to chronic blood loss (bleeding ulcer); treat the ulcer.
      - □ Due to nutritional deficiency; administer iron preparations.
      - □ Common in infants, young adult women, and older adults.

- o Aplastic anemia – Lack of precursor cells in the bone marrow with a decrease in all blood cell components (WBC – leukopenia; platelet – thrombocytopenia; RBC – anemia) due to medications, virus, toxins, and irradiation.
  - Treatment
    - □ Administer steroid therapy, bone marrow transplantation, antibiotics, and splenectomy.
  - Manifestations
    - □ Hypoxia, fatigue, and pallor (related to anemia)
    - □ Increased susceptibility to infection (related to leukopenia)
    - □ Hemorrhage, ecchymosis/leukopenia (related to thrombocytopenia)
  - Nursing Interventions
    - □ Implement protective barrier precautions.
    - □ Provide the client protective isolation.
    - □ Monitor for manifestations of infection.
    - □ Provide emotional and psychological support to the client.
- o Megaloblastic anemia (deficiency of B_{12} and folic acid)
- o Pernicious anemia – A vitamin B_{12} deficiency due to a lack of the intrinsic factor in gastric juice or diet.
  - Causes
    - □ Atrophy of the gastric mucosa/hypochlorhydria
    - □ Total gastrectomy
    - □ Malabsorption (secondary to Crohn's disease, pancreatitis)
    - □ Malnutrition
  - Manifestations (low Hgb and Hct)
    - □ Numbness and tingling of extremities
    - □ Paresthesia/hypoxemia
    - □ Gait disturbances
    - □ Behavioral problems

NOTES

- Nursing Interventions
  - Administer cobalamin (Vitamin B$_{12}$) 1,000 mcg IM daily for 2 weeks, then weekly until Hct level is therapeutic, and then monthly for life.
  - Cobalamin (Nascobal) is available intranasally. Instruct about the need for lifelong, self-injection if nasal administration is not available.
  - Promote rest for the client and encourage a balanced dietary intake.
  - Limit the client's consumption of alcohol.
- Hemolytic anemia – due to excessive RBC destruction
  - Contributing factors
    - Trauma
    - Lead poisoning
    - Tuberculosis
    - Infections
    - Transfusion reactions
    - Toxic agents

  - Nursing Interventions
    - Administer steroids as prescribed.
    - Treat the underlying disease.
- Congenital anemias
  - Sickle cell anemia – A genetic defect found in clients of African-American or Mediterranean origin, in which the Hgb molecule assumes a sickle shape and oxygen in venous blood is low; the sickle cells become lodged in the blood vessels, especially the brain and the kidneys.
    - Manifestations
      - Severe pain and swelling
      - Fever
      - Jaundice
      - Susceptibility to infection
      - Hypoxic damage to organs
    - Risk factors that precipitate crisis by enhancing sickling in the cells
      - Stress
      - Dehydration

- Hypoxia
- High altitudes
  - Nursing Interventions (symptomatic)
    - Maintain adequate hydration.
    - Provide oxygen therapy to the client.
    - Administer hydromorphone (Dilaudid) to manage the client's pain.
    - Encourage the client to rest.
    - Teach the client to identify triggers, get immunizations in a timely manner, and refer for genetic counseling.

Administering Iron Preparations

- Oral
  - Dilute liquid preparations with juice or water and administer with a plastic straw to avoid staining the client's teeth.
  - Orange juice fortified with vitamin D helps to facilitate absorption.
  - Avoid antacids, coffee, tea, dairy products, or whole grain breads concurrently and for 1 hr after administration due to decreased absorption.
  - Monitor the client for constipation and gastrointestinal upset.
- Intramuscular
  - Use a large bore needle (19 to 20 gauge, 3-inch needle).
  - Use 1 needle to draw up iron; change the needle before administering to prevent staining.
  - Use Z-track (to the buttocks only, never the deltoid).
  - Do not massage.

SECTION 8

CARDIOVASCULAR SYSTEM DISORDERS

Cardiovascular System in Failure

- Deficits Present in at Least One Area
  - Efficiently pumps blood to all parts of the body, indicating healthy working cardiac muscles and system.

NOTES

- o Adequate circulating blood volume to meet the body's needs.
- o Peripheral vascular resistance must be sufficient to maintain adequate blood pressure.
- o Normal heart rate is 60 to 100/min.

Diagnostic Procedures

- Laboratory Tests
  - o Blood electrolytes
  - o Sedimentation rate (less than 20 mm/hr); increased with MI
  - o Blood coagulation tests
    - PT (16 to 40 seconds); most significant if the client is on heparin therapy
    - PT (11 to 14 seconds); most significant if the client is on warfarin sodium (Coumadin) therapy
    - Clotting time (10 min)
    - INR
      - □ Normal INR is 1.
      - □ Universal test is not affected by variations in laboratory norms.
      - □ If the client requires anticoagulation, the desired value is increased to approximately 2 to 3.
  - o BUN (7 to 20 mg/dL); reflects renal function and perfusion; levels increase with MI
  - o Total serum cholesterol desirable; less than 200 mg/dL; risk for cardiac or stroke event with levels greater than 200
    - Low-density lipids; desirable less than 140 mg/dL
    - High-density lipids; desirable greater than 40 mg/dL for men, 50 mg/dL for women
    - Triglycerides desirable less than 150 mg/dL
  - o Enzymes (indicates death of myocardial muscles; heart attack)
    - Creatine phosphokinase MB Isoenzyme (CPK-MB) is an enzyme that increases within 5 hr after MI and peaks at 24 hr.

- Troponin is a protein that is considered the gold standard in diagnosing MI. A series of 3 tests completed over 12 hr can remain elevated for 1 to 2 weeks following an event.
- Central Venous Pressure (normal = 5 to 10 cm water)
  - o Provides an indication of pressure in the right atrium
  - o Trends are more important than values
- ECG – A record depicting the electrical activity of the heart
  - o Interpretation
    - P wave – atrial depolarization
    - QRS complex – ventricular depolarization
    - T wave – ventricular repolarization
    - PR interval – 0.12 to 0.2 seconds
    - QRS – 0.08 to 0.1 seconds
  - o Atrial dysrhythmias (impacts ventricular function and heartbeat)
    - Atrial fibrillation
      - □ Irregular, rapid rate referred to as irregularly irregular
      - □ Often asymptomatic with increased risk for a stroke event
      - □ Managed with cardioversion, beta-blocker medication, and warfarin (Coumadin)
    - Atrial tachycardia
      - □ Heart rate exceeds 100/min
      - □ Occurs with hypoglycemia, hypokalemia, digoxin toxicity, anxiety, and stimulants
      - □ Treated with medications or by removing the cause
    - Atrial bradycardia
      - □ Rate below 60/min
      - □ Normal in athletes
      - □ Significance related to how it affects cardiac output
      - □ Treated by administering anticholinergic medication (Atropine)
    - Atrioventricular (AV) heart block – Cardiac electrical conduction transmission is blocked from sinoatrial node to the AV node causing bradycardia, syncope, and palpitations.

NOTES

- First degree
  - ▸ Delayed transmission of impulse through the AV node
  - ▸ Prolonged PR interval (greater than 0.2)
  - ▸ No treatment necessary
- Second degree
  - ▸ Not all impulses pass through the AV node
  - ▸ May process to more lethal heart block
  - ▸ Pacemaker may be necessary
- Third degree
  - ▸ No impulses pass through AV node
  - ▸ Atria and ventricles beat independently of each other
  - ▸ Ventricular pacemaker takes over; the ventricles are slow and an unreliable source to generate cardiac heart rate
  - ▸ Indication for a permanent pacemaker

○ Ventricular dysrhythmias
- Premature ventricular contraction
  - Ventricle contracts prematurely, causing palpitations
  - Side effects – slowing of the heart rate, decreased blood pressure, and tissue perfusion
  - Could lead to cardiac arrest or ventricular tachycardia
  - Treat with antiarrhythmic medications
    - ▸ Procainamide hydrochloride (Pronestyl)
    - ▸ Lidocaine (Xylocaine)
- Ventricular tachycardia
  - Pulse rate above 150/min
  - Decreases cardiac output
  - Treatment – cardioversion
- Ventricular fibrillation
  - Most serious dysrhythmia
  - Synonymous with cardiac arrest; treat with CPR and defibrillation

- Arteriography/Angiography – Injection of contrast medium into the vascular system to outline an area of the body; when done to the vessels around the heart, it is usually done with cardiac catheterization.
  - ○ Purpose
    - To obtain information regarding coronary anatomy and structural abnormalities of the coronary artery.
  - ○ An angiography will assess circulation, movement, and sensation bilaterally. It may require the use of Doppler on the affected extremity.
- Cardiac Catheterization – A diagnostic procedure where a catheter is introduced into the right or left side of the heart through either the femoral or brachial artery.
  - ○ Purpose
    - Measure oxygen concentration, saturation, tension, and pressure in various chambers of the client's heart.
    - Detect coronary shunts.
    - Obtain blood samples.
    - Determine cardiac output and pulmonary blood flow.
    - Determine the client's need for cardiac bypass surgery.
  - ○ Nursing Interventions
    - Prior to catheterization
      - Know approach for shave prep – right (venous) side, or left (arterial) side.
      - NPO for 6 hr prior to the procedure.
      - Mark distal (baseline) pulses.
      - Explain to the client that the procedure may leave a metallic taste, and he may feel flushed when the dye is injected.
      - Verify that the client does not have any history of allergy to dye or shellfish.
      - Verify that procedural consent has been obtained.
    - After catheterization
      - Monitor the client's blood pressure and apical pulse every 15 min for 2 to 4 hr.

NOTES

- Perform a neurovascular assessment on the client every 15 min, for the first 2 hr; then every 30 min until the client is able to sit up.
- Monitor puncture sites for bleeding.
- Apply pressure for a minimum of 15 min to prevent bleeding or hematoma formation.
- Assess the client for chest pain.
- Keep the extremity extended for 4 to 6 hr.
- Maintain bed rest; no hip flexion and no sitting up in bed.
- Increase fluid intake to enhance flushing of dye.

Disorders

- Angina – A manifestation of myocardial ischemia caused by arterial stenosis or blockage, uncontrolled blood pressure, or cardiomyopathy.

  - Nursing Interventions
    - Assess the client's pain.
      - Location – jaw and/or arm, as well as chest
      - Character
      - Duration – relieved with rest and/or nitroglycerine (Nitro-Bid)
      - Precipitating factors (once identified, eliminate or minimize to avoid attacks)
    - Educate the client regarding lifestyle changes to prevent further episodes of angina.
      - Avoid excessive activity in cold weather.
      - Avoid overeating.
      - Stop smoking.
      - Avoid constipation.
      - Rest after meals.
      - Exercise.
      - Decrease stress.
    - Teach the client about the disease process (peripheral vasodilation decreases myocardial oxygen demand; coronary artery vasodilation increases the supply of oxygen to the myocardium).
      - Provide teaching on the correct use of nitroglycerin.

- As needed at onset of chest pain or tightness or in preparation of exertional activity
- Take nitroglycerin as prescribed, at onset of attack, and every 5 min up to three doses. If pain is not relieved, call 911.
- Store nitroglycerin in a dark, dry spot and replace every 6 months.
- Side effects of taking nitroglycerin include headache and hypotension.
- Types of nitroglycerin – tablets, ointment, patch, or spray
  - If the client is given nitroglycerin for prevention, he must be nitroglycerine free daily for 12 hr to prevent developing a tolerance.
  - If the client uses a nitro patch, instruct him to apply it in the morning and remove it at bedtime.
  - Instruct the client to take nitroglycerine (Nitrostat) while sitting down and stopping all activity.
  - Erectile dysfunction therapy is contraindicated with the use of nitrates.

- MI – The process by which myocardial tissue is destroyed due to reduced coronary blood flow and lack of oxygen; actual necrosis of the heart muscle (myocardium) occurs.
  - Contributing factors
    - Atherosclerotic heart disease
    - Coronary artery embolism
  - Manifestations
    - Severe chest pain
      - Unrelieved with nitroglycerin or rest
      - Crushing quality, radiates to jawline, left arm, neck, and/or back
      - Diabetics and women often report no pain
    - Diaphoresis, nausea, vomiting, anxiety, fear
    - Vital sign changes – tachycardia, hypotension, dyspnea, dysrhythmias
    - Laboratory results – elevated troponin and CK-MB enzymes, elevated LDH
    - ECG changes – ST elevation, T-wave inversion

NOTES

- o Nursing Interventions – Aimed at resting the myocardium and preserving the heart muscle.
    - Early
        - ☐ Administer oxygen
        - ☐ Medications
            - ► Antidysrhythmics – lidocaine (Xylocaine), amiodarone HCL (Cordarone)
            - ► Analgesics – morphine sulfate
            - ► Anticoagulants – heparin IV
            - ► Thrombolytics within 6 hr of a cardiac event – tissue plasminogen activator (TPA), streptokinase (Streptase), alteplase recombinant (Activase)
            - ► Vasodilators – nitroglycerine
            - ► Beta-blockers – metoprolol (Lopressor)
            - ► Calcium channel blockers – verapamil HCL (Calan), nifedipine (Procardia)
        - ☐ Frequently monitor vital signs, O_2 saturation, and ECG.
        - ☐ Provide emotional support to the client.
    - Later
        - ☐ Administer stool softeners to prevent straining with bowel movements and/or Valsalva maneuver.
        - ☐ Provide the client a soft, low-fat, low-cholesterol, low-sodium diet.
        - ☐ Use a bedside commode, which causes less energy than using a bedpan.
        - ☐ Promote self-care, but instruct the client to stop at the onset of pain.
        - ☐ Plan for cardiac rehabilitation.
            - ► Initiate an exercise program, but stop if fatigue or chest pain occurs.
            - ► Teach and encourage the use of stress-management techniques.
            - ► Teach the client to modify any risk factors.
                - ▷ Obesity
                - ▷ Stress
                - ▷ Diet
                - ▷ Hypertension
                - ▷ Smoking
                - ▷ Lack of exercise
            - ► Recognize the risk factors that cannot be modified.
                - ▷ Heredity
                - ▷ Race
                - ▷ Age
                - ▷ Sex
                - ▷ Type-A personality
            - ► Bleeding precautions with anticoagulant therapy.
            - ► Initiate long-term medication therapy.
                - ▷ Anticoagulants – heparin, aspirin, warfarin (Coumadin), enoxaparin (Lovenox)
                - ▷ Antihypertensives – metoprolol (Lopressor), hydrochlorothiazide (Hydrodiuril), and calcium channel blockers diltiazem (Cardizem)
                - ▷ Vasodilators – nitroglycerin
                - ▷ Antilipidemics – simvastatin (Zocor), atorvastatin (Lipitor)

- • Heart Failure – The inability of the heart to meet tissue requirements for oxygen (not pumping effectively); the body tries to compensate by increasing the rate (tachycardia), increasing the size of the muscle, and increasing the length of the heart fibers.
    - o Left-ventricular failure – An inadequate ejection of blood into the systemic circulation, usually associated with MI and hypertension.
        - Manifestations (primarily respiratory symptoms)
            - ☐ Dyspnea and paroxysmal nocturnal dyspnea
            - ☐ Moist cough
            - ☐ Crackles, wheezing
            - ☐ Orthopnea
        - Pulmonary edema results, causing excessive fluid in pulmonary interstitial spaces evidenced by
            - ☐ Moist crackles and frothy sputum
            - ☐ Severe anxiety

NOTES

- □ Marked dyspnea and cyanosis
- ■ Nursing Interventions
  - □ Administer morphine sulfate to decrease respiratory rate and increase effective breathing. This will cause a pooling of blood in the peripheral vessels, which will decrease cardiac return and therefore decrease the work of the heart.
  - □ Administer furosemide (Lasix) as prescribed.
  - □ Deliver high-flow oxygen therapy.
  - □ Monitor respiratory status and the need for possible intubation.
  - □ Maintain bed rest in the semi-Fowler's position.
  - □ Administer digitalis (Digoxin) to increase the efficiency of the myocardium as a pump.
- ○ Right-ventricular failure – Congestion due to blood not adequately pumped from systemic system to the lungs; also related to COPD/Cor pulmonale.
  - ■ Manifestations
    - □ Dependent peripheral edema
    - □ Distended neck veins
    - □ Weight gain (greater than 2 lb in 1 day)
    - □ Enlarged liver
    - □ Elevated central venous pressure, wedge pressures
    - □ Hypotension and tachycardia

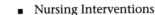

  - ■ Nursing Interventions
    - □ Provide the client psychological support for the relief of anxiety and stress.
    - □ Administer oxygen as prescribed.
    - □ Decrease her fluid intake to decrease cardiac preload.
    - □ Improve myocardial contraction with digitalis and dobutamine hydrochloride (Dobutrex).
  - ■ Digitalis Therapy – Decreases the heart rate, improves ventricular filling, stroke volume, coronary artery perfusion, and improves strength of contraction.

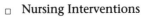

- □ Monitor for signs of toxicity and monitor digitalis level in serum (0.8 to 2 ng/mL is normal).
- □ Nursing Interventions
  - ▶ Monitor the client's potassium levels (decreased levels enhance digitalis toxicity).
  - ▶ Monitor her apical heart rate (verify greater than 60/min before each dose).
  - ▶ Monitor the client for digitalis toxicity.
    - ▷ Normal digitalis level in serum is 0.8 to 2 ng/mL
    - ▷ Manifestations of digoxin toxicity
      - ◆ Early – nausea, vomiting, anorexia, bradycardia, depression
      - ◆ Late – frequent premature ventricular complex, green-yellow halos in visual field, hyperkalemia, photophobia, diplopia
  - ▶ Teach the client to assess her pulse, report signs of toxicity, keep laboratory appointments, avoid St. John's wort and licorice because of risk of toxicity, encourage intake of foods low in sodium and high in potassium.
- ● Valvular Disorders – Results in narrowing of valve that prevents or impedes blood flow (stenosis) or impaired closure that allows backward leakage of blood (regurgitation); affects mitral, aortic, or tricuspid (history of endocarditis and rheumatic fever is frequently the cause).
  - ○ Manifestations
    - ■ Right-sided heart failure (mitral stenosis, mitral regurgitation, tricuspid stenosis)
    - ■ Left-sided heart failure (aortic stenosis, insufficiency)
    - ■ Murmurs
    - ■ Decreased cardiac output
  - ○ Nursing Interventions
    - ■ Encourage the client to implement a low-sodium, low-cholesterol diet.
    - ■ Adhere to digoxin and diuretic therapy.

NOTES

- Use prophylactic antibiotic therapy to prevent endocarditis.
  - o Surgical management
    - Heart valve replacement (click can be heard on auscultation)
    - Mitral commissurotomy (valvulotomy)

      - □ Nursing Interventions
        - ▸ Allow activities as tolerated.
        - ▸ Implement a low-sodium, low-cholesterol diet.
        - ▸ The client must take anticoagulation medication for life.
        - ▸ Instruct the client in lifelong need for antibiotics prior to any invasive procedures and dental work.
- Aortic Aneurysm – Local distention of an artery wall, usually thoracic or abdominal (4 times more common).
  - o Monitored until above 5, when the rate of rupture increases and surgery is required.
  - o Contributing factors
    - Infections
    - Congenital
    - Atherosclerosis or hypertension
  - o Manifestations (frequently asymptomatic)
    - Thoracic – pain, dyspnea, hoarseness, cough, dysphagia
    - Abdominal – abdominal pain, persistent or intermittent low back or flank pain; may be asymptomatic; pulsating abdominal mass; shock
  - o Treatment usually requires surgery
    - Preoperative – careful monitoring for possible rupture; prepare the client for abdominal surgery
    - Postoperative – careful monitoring of peripheral circulation below the level of the aneurysms
    - Postoperative complications
      - □ MI or emboli
      - □ Renal failure
      - □ Spinal cord ischemia

- Hypertension – Persistent blood pressure above 140/systolic and 90/diastolic; is often called the silent killer.
  - Primary hypertension
    - □ Most common type (90%)
    - □ Hereditary disease; cause unknown
    - □ More common among African Americans
    - □ Late manifestations – headaches, fatigue, dyspnea, edema, nocturia, blackouts
    - □ Usually no signs or symptoms until end-organ involvement occurs
  - Secondary hypertension
    - □ Due to identifiable cause
    - □ Pheochromocytoma
    - □ Renal pathology

  - Nursing Interventions
    - □ Teach the client weight control methods.
    - □ Encourage the client to stop smoking.
    - □ Avoid stimulants by decreasing alcohol and caffeine intake. A moderate amount is less than 1 oz of alcohol or 24 oz of beer a day.
    - □ Promote a program of regular physical exercise.
    - □ Promote a lifestyle with reduced stress.
    - □ The client should maintain a sodium-restricted diet.
    - □ Teach the client risk factors.
  - o Antihypertensive medications
    - Potassium-depleting diuretics
      - □ Loop diuretic-furosemide (Lasix), bumetanide (Bumex)
      - □ Thiazide-hydrochlorothiazide (HCTZ), chlorothiazide (Diuril)

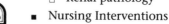

      - □ Nursing Interventions
        - ▸ Administer potassium supplements to the client as prescribed.
        - ▸ Teach dietary sources of potassium.
        - ▸ Possible interaction between low potassium and digitalis (Digoxin) preparations.

NOTES

- Potassium-sparing diuretics
  - Spironolactone (Aldactone)
  - Triamterene (Dyrenium)
  - Monitor for increased potassium level
- Beta-blockers
  - Propranolol HCl (Inderal)
  - Atenolol (Tenormin)
  - Metoprolol (Lopressor)
  - Nursing Interventions
    - Watch for major side effects of bradycardia.
    - Monitor the client's pulse daily.
    - Monitor for manifestations of heart failure.
    - Noncardioselective beta-blockers may be contraindicated in asthmatics.
    - Watch for reflex tachycardia due to decreased cardiac output and hypotension.
- Central-acting alpha-blockers (sympatholytics)
  - Clonidine HCL (Catapres)
    - Constipation
    - Sexual dysfunction
    - Dry mouth
    - Depression
  - Guanfacine HCL (Tenex)
    - Rebound hypertension
    - Drowsiness
    - Bradycardia
  - Methyldopa (Aldomet)
    - Aplastic anemia
    - Thrombocytopenia
- Angiotensin-converting enzyme (ACE inhibitors)
  - Captopril (Capoten)
  - Enalapril (Vasotec)
  - Lisinopril (Zestril)

- Major side effects
  - Cough
  - Headache
  - Angioedema of face and limbs
- Calcium-channel blockers
  - Nifedipine (Procardia)
    - Headache/dizziness
    - Bradycardia
    - Peripheral edema
  - Verapamil (Calan), diltiazem (Cardizem)
    - Flushing
    - Arrhythmias
    - Constipation
- Thrombophlebitis – Clot within the vein with inflammation of the wall.
  - Contributing factors
    - Stasis
    - Hypercoagulability
    - Damage to intima of blood vessels/trauma
    - Pregnancy or estrogen (oral contraceptives)
    - Malignancy or obesity
  - Manifestations
    - Edema of affected limb
    - Local swelling, bumpy, knotty
    - Red, tender, local induration
  - Nursing Interventions
    - Maintain bed rest.
    - Elevate the affected extremity and apply moist, warm compresses.
    - Administer anticoagulant therapy.
    - Initiate antiembolism stockings/support hose.
    - Administer pain medication.
    - Increase fluids.
    - Encourage deep breathing to enhance oxygenation.
    - Assist the client with range of motion.
    - Avoid eating excessive amounts of green, leafy vegetables while on warfarin (Coumadin).

NOTES

- Varicose Veins
  - Precipitating factors
    - Prolonged standing
    - Pregnancy
    - Obesity
    - Heredity
  - Manifestations
    - Enlarged, tortuous veins in lower extremities
    - Pain
    - Edema (after upright)

  - Nursing Interventions
    - Avoid prolonged sitting or standing.
    - Instruct the client to wear supportive antiembolism stockings, especially during air flights and pregnancy.
    - Avoid crossing legs, engage in daily exercise, and maintain an ideal body weight.
    - Elevate the client's lower extremities to reduce edema and promote venous return.
    - Promote her circulation with thigh-high antiembolism stockings, ambulation, and elevation.
  - Ulcers
    - Arterial – looks punched-out; no edema present
    - Venous – usually around the ankle; reddened and bluish; edema often present
- Arterial Disorders of the Peripheral Vascular System
  - Intermittent claudication – Pain or cramping in the lower extremities due to atherosclerosis of the lower extremity arteries (popliteal); the muscles do not receive adequate blood supply.
  - Manifestations
    - Pain with walking
    - Calf muscle atrophy
    - Skin appears shiny with hair loss and thickened toenails
    - Poor neurovascular integrity
    - Necrotic ulcers
    - Tingling and numbness of the toes
    - Cool extremities with poor pulses

- Surgical treatment
  - Femoral popliteal bypass surgery
  - Angioplasty or stenting

- Nursing Interventions
  - Encourage the client to stop smoking.
  - Provide instruction about maintaining a low-fat diet.
  - Administer pentoxifylline (Trental) and cilostazol (Pletal).
  - The client should avoid crossing his legs.
- Arteriosclerosis obliterans usually affect the aorta or the arteries of the lower extremities.
  - Contributing factors
    - Diabetes mellitus
    - Hypertension
    - Cerebrovascular disease and coronary artery disease
    - Renal failure
    - Smoking
  - Surgical management
    - Vascular grafts
    - Patch grafts
    - Endarterectomy
  - Nursing Interventions
    - Assess the client's extremities frequently for pulses, color, and temperature.
    - Observe the client for signs of paralysis of the lower extremities after a thoracic aorta procedure.
    - Assess perfusion, central venous pressure, and monitor I&O.
    - Teach the client to avoid dependent positions, elevate extremities, and use support hose/antiembolism stockings.
    - Administer heparin.
- Buerger's disease (thromboangiitis obliterans) – Recurring inflammation of the arteries and veins of the lower and upper extremities, resulting in thrombus with occlusion (cause unknown).

NOTES

THE COMPREHENSIVE NCLEX®-RN REVIEW

- Manifestation
  - Occurs in men ages 20 to 40
  - Most common manifestations – pain in legs relieved by inactivity, numbness and tingling of toes and fingers in cold weather/intermittent claudication
  - Cessation of smoking is important; avoid cold or constrictive clothing
  - Ulcerations and gangrene with amputation are common
- Raynaud's syndrome – Vasospastic or obstructive condition of the arteries that occur from exposure to the cold or stress and primarily affect the hands.
  - Manifestations
    - Arteriolar vasoconstriction results in coldness, pallor, and pain
    - Occasional ulceration of the fingertips
    - Color changes from white to blue to red (can be bilateral or symmetrical)
  - Nursing Interventions
    - Teach the client to avoid the cold and keep extremities warm. He should wear warm, but nonconstrictive gloves.
    - Encourage the client to stop smoking and limit his caffeine intake.
    - Administer nifedipine (Procardia).

Cardiac Surgery

- Pacemaker – An electronic device that provides repetitive electrical stimuli to the heart muscle, in order to control the heart rate.
  - Types
    - Permanent pacemakers
      - Ventricular demand – Fires at a preset rate when the client's heart rate drops below a predetermined/preprogrammed rate.
      - Ventricular fixed – Fires constantly at a preset/preprogrammed rate, regardless of the client's own heart rate.
      - Dual chamber – Stimulates both the atria and the ventricles.
      - Atrial demand – Fires as needed when the atria do not originate a rhythm.
      - Variable rate – Senses oxygen demands and increases the firing rate to meet the client's needs.
    - Temporary pacemakers
      - Transcutaneous (skin) – external, for use in emergency pacing situations
      - Transvenous
  - Nursing Interventions
    - Postoperative care
      - Monitor ECG for dysrhythmias and check the client's pulse rate.
      - Assess the wound for hematoma or infection.
      - Administer analgesics as necessary.
      - Maintain an electrically safe environment. Instruct the client to avoid large generators, magnets, and magnetic resonance imaging machines.
      - Observe the client for hiccoughs, which indicates that the pacemaker is malpositioned and is pacing the diaphragm.
      - Use the aseptic technique at the insertion site when caring for the wound.
      - To prevent accidental dislodging of the electrode, the client should not to raise his arms over his head until the site is healed.
      - Observe for pacemaker malfunction (failure to capture, sense, or pace).
    - Teach the client to:
      - Carry identification information at all times.
      - Change the batteries at intervals (3 to 15 years for lithium batteries).
      - Transmit data via telephone from the pacemaker to the health care provider.
      - Wear loose-fitting clothes.
      - Avoid contact sports.

NOTES

□ Lower the limit rate. All permanent pacemakers are set at a definitive lowest rate, when the pacemaker will fire and stimulate the heart if the pulse rate drops below the predetermined/preprogrammed rate. The nurse must know this rate to assess and teach the client. If the pulse ever drops below this rate, it must be reported.

- Percutaneous Transthoracic Cardiac Angioplasty – A variety of procedures used to treat plaque in the arteries of the heart; most commonly, a balloon is passed into the diseased vessel and inflated, compressing the plaque and dilating the narrowed artery so that blood can flow more easily.

  o Procedure is performed through a left cardiac catheterization.

  o A stent may be placed into the vessel to maintain patency.

   o Nursing Interventions

    ■ Follow this procedure the same as postangioplasty care.

    ■ Monitor for vasospasm, dysrhythmia, or rupture of the coronary vessel leading to a MI.

- Coronary Artery Bypass Graft – To replace damaged coronary arteries and re-establish perfusion in areas of myocardium.

  o Most procedures require an open chest/heart approach with a bypass machine; however, the latest techniques may not use bypass resulting in a shorter recovery period for some clients.

    ■ Preoperative/general care

      □ Provide psychological support as needed

    ■ Postoperative care

      □ Bilateral chest tubes

      □ General postoperative care including pain management and care of wound

      □ Client often has an endotracheal tube for a day postoperative; prepare the client and provide sterile technique when caring for the tube and suctioning

      □ Assess all systems affected by decreased cardiac output (vital signs, urine output, circulation in legs, chest pain).

□ Assess for complications such as MI, pleural effusion, dysrhythmia, and stroke.

Shock

- Lack of oxygen and nutrients at the cellular level due to impaired tissue perfusion for cellular metabolism

- Types

  o Cardiogenic – failure of the heart to pump adequately

  o Hypovolemic – decreased blood volume

  o Distributive (vasogenic)

    ■ Neurogenic – increased size of vascular bed due to loss of vascular tone

    ■ Anaphylactic – hypersensitivity reaction

    ■ Septic – systemic vasodilation due to infection

- Manifestations (related to decreased tissue perfusion)

  o Tachycardia with hypotension

  o Tachypnea

  o Oliguria

  o Cold, moist skin

  o Color ashen – pallor

  o Metabolic acidosis

  o Decreased level of consciousness

  o Septic shock – initially warm, flushed skin, fever

- Nursing Interventions

  o Position the client in a modified Trendelenburg.

  o Secure a large bore IV line (16 or 18 g).

  o Administer oxygen.

    ■ Record the client's vital signs every 5 min.

    ■ Promote rest and decrease movement.

    ■ Monitor the client's urine output.

NOTES

- Emergency Medications
  - Atropine – increases heart rate
  - Dopamine (Intropin) – vasoconstrictor; increases blood pressure, tissue, and renal perfusion
  - Epinephrine HCl (Adrenalin) – increases the body's reaction to stress
  - Isoproterenol (Isuprel) – increases heart rate and cardiac output
  - Dobutamine (Dobutrex) – inotropic; increases the force of myocardial contraction in cardiogenic shock and increases blood pressure
  - Norepinephrine levarterenol (Levophed) – vasoconstrictor; increases tissue perfusion
  - Sodium bicarbonate – decreases acidosis

Cardiopulmonary Resuscitation (CPR)

- Indications
  - Absence of palpable carotid pulse
  - Absence of breath sounds
- Purpose
  - Establish effective circulation and respiration
  - Prevent irreversible cerebral anoxic damage
- Procedure
  - Determine that the client is unresponsive and make sure the scene is safe.
  - Activate the emergency response system and get an automated external defibrillator.
  - Open the client's airway by tilting the head and lifting the chin, unless there is a suspected neck or spine injury; in that case, the airway is opened with a jaw thrust. Check to see if the client is breathing.
  - Give the client 2 breaths and then check the carotid pulse.
  - Follow the American Heart Association 2006 recommendations:
    - Ratio – 30 compressions to 2 ventilations for 1 or 2 rescuers
    - Compression rate – 100/min for all age groups

- Complications
  - Fractured ribs
  - Punctured lungs
  - Lacerated liver
  - Abdominal distension
- Stop CPR When
  - A health care provider pronounces the client dead.
  - The rescuer is exhausted.
  - Help arrives.
  - The client's heartbeat returns.
- Automated External Defibrillator – A computerized defibrillator that analyzes cardiac rhythm once pads are placed on the client's chest.
  - A mechanical voice tells the rescuer if/when to deliver shock to the client.
  - AED is frequently found in public locations, since it is easy for nontrained individuals to use.
  - Do not use an AED on children who are 1 month to 12 months.
- Obstructed Airway
  - Conscious
    - Establish that the client is choking.
    - Perform the Heimlich maneuver until it is successful or the client becomes unconscious.
  - Unconscious
    - If a conscious choking adult becomes unresponsive, look for the foreign object in the pharynx and perform a finger sweep.
    - Begin CPR. Every time you open the airway to give breaths look for the object.
    - Continue CPR.

NOTES

SECTION 9

GENITOURINARY SYSTEM DISORDERS

Assessment of the Kidney

- Functions of the Kidney
  - Regulates acid-base balance
  - Excretes metabolic wastes (creatinine, urea)
  - Regulates blood pressure – renin (stimulated by decreased blood pressure or blood volume) stimulates the production of angiotensin I, which is converted to angiotensin II in the lungs; angiotensin II is a strong vasoconstrictor and stimulates aldosterone secretion; vasoconstriction and sodium reabsorption results in increased blood volume and increased blood pressure
  - Secretes erythropoietin
  - Converts vitamin D to its active form for absorption of calcium
  - Excretes water-soluble medications and medication metabolites
- Contributing Factors
  - History of genitourinary disorder
  - Family history of renal disease
  - Incontinence or prostatic problems
  - Incontinence in women; benign prostate hypertrophy
- Manifestations
  - Flank pain radiating to upper thigh, testis, or labium
  - Changes in voiding – hematuria, proteinuria, dysuria, frequency, urgency, burning, nocturia, incontinence, polyuria, oliguria, anuria
  - Thirst, fatigue, generalized edema

Diagnostic Tests

- Urinalysis
  - Specific gravity – range tested 1.010 to 1.030
  - Color – yellow or amber
  - Negative glucose, protein, RBCs, and WBCs
  - pH – 5 to 8
  - First voided morning sample preferred; 15 mL
  - Sent to laboratory immediately or refrigerate
  - If clean catch, get urine for culture prior to starting antibiotics
    - Cleanse labia, glans penis
    - Obtain midstream sample
- Renal Function Tests (several tests over a period of time are necessary)
  - BUN – 7 to 20 mg/dL
  - Creatinine – 0.5 to 1 mg/dL
  - 24 hr creatinine clearance – 75 to 120 mL/min
    - Have the client void and discard the first specimen.
    - Draw serum creatinine before the start of collection.
    - Collect all urine from the client for the next 24 hr (refrigerate or keep container on ice).
    - At the completion of the 24 hr, the test is stopped following the client's last void.
  - Uric acid (serum) – 3.5 to 7.8 mg/dL
  - Prostate-specific antigen – greater than 10 increases the risk of prostate cancer
- Radiologic Test
  - Kidneys, ureters, bladder (x-ray) – shows the size, shape, and position of kidneys, ureters, and bladder; no preparation is necessary (verify that the client is not pregnant)
  - IV pyelography (IV bolus) – to help in visualization of the urinary tract

NOTES

- Nursing Interventions
  - □ Verify that informed consent has been signed.
  - □ Verify the client's last creatinine level.
  - □ The client should remain NPO for 8 hr; fluids may be permitted.
  - □ Administer laxatives as prescribed.
  - □ Give him an enema or suppository on the morning of the test (as necessary).
  - □ Check for allergies to iodine or shellfish.
  - □ Inform the client of potential sensations during the exam – He may experience flushing, warmth, nausea, a metallic or salty taste, or incontinence.
  - □ Emergency equipment should be readily available during the test.
  - □ Encourage fluids to help flush out the dye.
  - ○ Renal angiography – Visualization of renal arterial supply; contrast material injected through a catheter.

- Nursing Interventions (preprocedure)
  - □ Femoral or brachial artery approach.
  - □ Locate and mark peripheral pulses.
  - □ Have the client void before the procedure.
  - □ Explain that the procedure may create the feeling of warmth along the vessel and it takes ½ to 2 hr.

- Nursing interventions (postprocedure)
  - □ Maintain bed rest for 6 to 8 hr.
  - □ Monitor the client's vital signs until stable.
  - □ Observe him for swelling and hematoma.
  - □ Palpate peripheral pulses/vascular checks.
  - □ Monitor the client's I&O including urinary status.
- Cystoscopy – An invasive procedure in which a scope is passed to view the interior of the bladder, urethra, or the position of urethral orifices.
  - ○ Purpose – To remove calculi from the urethra, bladder, and ureter; to treat lesions of the bladder, urethra, and prostate.

- ○ Nursing Interventions (preoperative)
  - ■ Maintain NPO if the client is given general anesthesia, and liquids if given local anesthesia.
  - ■ Administer preoperative cathartics/enemas as ordered.
  - ■ Teach the client deep breathing exercises to relieve bladder spasms.
  - ■ Monitor for postural hypotension.
  - ■ Inform the client that pink-tinged or tea-colored urine is common following the procedure, but bright, red urine or clots should be reported.
  - ■ Provide nonpharmacological pain management techniques following the procedure.
    - □ Leg cramps due to lithotomy position
    - □ Back pain or abdominal pain
    - □ Warm sitz baths comforting
  - ■ Push fluids/analgesics.
  - ■ Monitor the client's I&O.
- Renal Biopsy

  - ○ Nursing Interventions (preprocedure)
    - ■ Obtain bleeding, clotting, and prothrombin times.
    - ■ Obtain results of prebiopsy x-rays of kidney, IV bolus.
    - ■ Maintain NPO status for 6 to 8 hr.
    - ■ Position the client with a pillow under her abdomen and her shoulders on the bed.
  - ○ Nursing Interventions (postprocedure)
    - ■ Maintain the client in the supine position. The client should remain in bed for 24 hr.
    - ■ Monitor her vital signs every 5 to 15 min for 4 hr.
    - ■ Maintain pressure to the puncture site for 20 min.
    - ■ Observe the client for any pain, nausea, vomiting, and blood pressure changes.
    - ■ Encourage fluid intake.
    - ■ Assess Hct and Hgb 8 hr after procedure.

NOTES

- Monitor the client's urine output.
- Make sure the client avoids strenuous activity, sports, and heavy lifting for at least 2 weeks.
- Indwelling Urinary Catheterization
  - Purpose – A sterile procedure to empty the contents of the bladder, obtain a sterile specimen, determine residual urine, initiate irrigation of the bladder, or bypass an obstruction.
  - Nursing Interventions
    - Maintain a closed system.
    - Measure the client's output every shift.
    - Keep a drainage bag below the level of the client's bladder.
    - Have him increase his daily fluid intake.
    - Prevent dependent loops in the catheter tubing.
    - Discontinue as soon as possible due to increased risk for urinary tract infection.

Specific Disorders and Nursing Interventions

- Cystitis – Inflammation of the urinary bladder
  - Contributing factors
    - Wiping back to front after toileting, secondary to ascending infection from *Escherichia coli*
    - Prolonged baths with excessive soap (common in females).
    - Benign prostatic hypertrophy (males)
  - Manifestations
    - Frequency and urgency, and only voiding small amounts of urine each time
    - Dysuria with hematuria
    - Suprapubic tenderness; pain in the bladder region or flank pain
    - Fever, malaise, chills
    - Cloudy, foul-smelling urine
  - Nursing Interventions
    - Obtain the client's urine for culture and sensitivity before initiating antibiotic therapy.

- Administer antimicrobial medications – Sulfonamides are the medications of choice unless the client is allergic (sulfamethoxazole-trimethoprim [Bactrim] and nitrofurantoin microcrystal [Macrodantin]).
- Maintain acidic urine pH.
- Force fluids (greater than 3,000 mL/day).
- Give urinary analgesics (phenazopyridine [Pyridium]). Inform the client that the medication will temporarily turn urine orange.
- Apply heat to the perineum for comfort.
- Instruct the client to
  - Follow appropriate perineal care (wiping front to back).
  - Wear cotton underwear.
  - Avoid bubble baths (it can be irritating to urethra).
  - Maintain an increased fluid intake.
  - Void after sexual intercourse.
  - Drink cranberry juice daily.

- Glomerulonephritis – An acute renal disease involving the renal glomeruli of both kidneys; thought to be an antigen-antibody reaction that damages the glomeruli of the kidney (usually in children), the prognosis is good if treatment is implemented.
  - Contributing factors
    - Beta-hemolytic streptococcal
    - Can follow tonsillitis or pharyngitis
  - Manifestations
    - Hematuria (cola or tea-colored urine), with proteinuria
    - Edema (especially facial and periorbital; ascites)
    - Oliguria or anuria
    - Hypertension with headache
    - Increased BUN; elevated BUN is azotemia
    - Flank or abdominal pain
    - Anemia

NOTES

- o Nursing Interventions
    - Maintain bed rest to protect the kidney.
    - Administer penicillin for streptococcal infection (substitute other antibiotics for clients allergic to penicillin).
    - Administer corticosteroids for inflammatory disease.
    - Treat manifestations symptomatically (antihypertensives for increased blood pressure).
    - Reduce protein and sodium in the client's diet, but increase calories.
    - Restrict fluids.
- Nephrosis – A clinical disorder associated with protein-wasting; secondary to diffuse glomerular damage.
    - o Contributing factors
        - May be autoimmune; the glomerular membrane more permeable
    - o Manifestations
        - Insidious onset of pitting edema (generalized edema is anasarca)
        - Proteinuria
        - Anemia
        - Hypoalbuminemia
        - Anorexia malaise and nausea
        - Oliguria
        - Ascites
    - o Nursing Interventions
        - Maintain bed rest (during severe edema only) to preserve renal function.
        - Make sure the client maintains a low-sodium, low-potassium, moderate-protein, high-calorie diet.
        - Protect the client from infection.
        - Monitor I&O.
        - Weigh the client and measure abdominal girth daily.
    - o Medication therapy
        - Loop diuretics – furosemide (Lasix)
        - Steroids – prednisone (Deltasone)

- Immunosuppressive agents – cyclophosphamide (Cytoxan)
- Urolithiasis (Urinary calculi) – Stones in the urinary system
    - o Contributing factors
        - Obstruction and urinary stasis
        - Uric acid stones (excessive purine intake)
        - Dehydration and immobilization
        - More common in men ages 20 to 40 and tends to reoccur
    - o Manifestations (based on location and size of the stone)
        - Pain – severe renal colic (ureter); dull, aching (kidney); radiates to the groin
        - Nausea, vomiting, diarrhea, or constipation
        - Hematuria
        - Manifestations of a urinary tract infection
    - o Nursing Interventions
        - Goals – to eradicate the stone and prevent nephron destruction.
        - Force fluids – at least 3,000 mL/day (IV or by mouth).
        - Strain all urine.
        - Provide the client pain control.
        - Maintain proper urine pH (depends on type of stone).
        - Avoid foods high in oxalates if it is a calcium oxalate stone (spinach, black tea, rhubarb, chocolate).
        - Administer allopurinol (Zyloprim) for uric acid stones.
        - Use the lithotripsy method to crush the stone through sound waves.
- Acute Renal Failure – An abrupt reversible cessation of renal function; may be the result of trauma, allergic reactions, kidney stones, or shock.
    - o Contributing factors
        - Prerenal – disrupted blood flow to the kidneys; hypovolemic shock, dehydration, heart failure, burn injury, and anaphylaxis

---

NOTES

- Renal – renal tissue damage; trauma, hypokalemia, acute glomerulonephritis, hemolytic uremic syndrome (infection caused by *Escherichia coli*; common in children), substance abuse
- Postrenal – the renal filtration of urine compromised; kidney stones, prostate hypertrophy, tumors, and strictures

o Manifestations (3 phases)

- Oliguric (8 to 15 days) – sudden onset, less than 400 mL in 24 hr, edema, elevated BUN, creatinine and potassium; decreased specific gravity; acidosis; heart failure; dysrhythmias
- Diuretic – urine output increases followed by diuresis of up to 4,000 to 5,000 mL/day, indicating recovery of damaged nephrons; hypotension and fluid and electrolyte imbalances are a concern
- Recovery – may take up to 1 year until urine function returns to normal (baseline); older adults are at increased risk for residual impairment

o Nursing Interventions

- Eliminate or prevent cause.
- Correct metabolic acidosis, hyperkalemia, Hyperphosphatemia, and hypocalcemia.
  - □ Kayexalate (an ion exchange resin given orally or by enema)
  - □ IV glucose and insulin (causes potassium to enter cells)
  - □ Calcium IV or sodium bicarbonate to stabilize cell membrane
- Implement diet.
  - □ For oliguric phase – low-protein, high-carbohydrate diet and restrict potassium intake
  - □ For diuresis phase – low-protein, high-calorie diet and restrict fluids as indicated
- Administer phosphate binders to lower phosphorus while replacing calcium (Phos-Lo, Calcium acetate).
- Bed rest in the oliguric phase.
- Monitor daily weights.
- Monitor I&O.

- Implement dialysis (as ordered) until renal function returns.
- Assess for pericarditis; friction rubs.

- Chronic Renal Failure – Progressive failure of the kidneys to function that results in death unless hemodialysis or transplant is performed; is irreversible.

o Contributing factors

- Diabetes mellitus (leading cause)
- Uncontrolled hypertension (second cause)
- Chronic glomerulonephritis
- Pyelonephritis
- Congenital kidney disease

o Stages of renal failure

- Diminished renal reserve (creatinine 1.6 to 2)
- Renal insufficiency (creatinine 2.1 to 5)
- Renal failure (creatinine > 8)
- Uremia – end stage (creatinine > 12)

o Manifestations (progressively worsen)

- Fatigue secondary to anemia
- Headache and hypertension
- Nausea, vomiting, diarrhea
- Irritability
- Convulsions, coma
- Edema
- Hypocalcemia, hyperkalemia
- Pruritus, uremic frost
- Pallid, gray-yellow complexion
- Metabolic acidosis; elevated BUN and creatinine; decreased glomerular filtration rate

o Nursing Interventions

- Maintain bed rest.
- Implement a renal diet for the client – low-protein, low-potassium, high-carbohydrate, vitamins and calcium supplements, low-sodium, and low-phosphate.
- Monitor the client for and treat hypertension as prescribed.

NOTES

- Strict I&O; fluid replacement – 500 to 600 mL more than previous 24-hr urine output.
- Monitor the client's electrolytes, especially potassium.
- Administer phosphate binders.
- Do not administer antacids with magnesium or enemas with phosphorous
- Maintain dialysis.
- Administer diuretics in early stages.
- Provide meticulous skin care.
- Provide emotional support to the client and the client's family.
- Assess for bleeding tendencies.
- Administer epoetin alfa/erythropoietin (Epogen, Procrit) for anemia to stimulate RBC formation and transfuse as necessary.

- Dialysis
  - Goals
    - Remove end products of metabolism (urea and creatinine) from the client's blood.
    - Maintain a safe concentration of the serum electrolytes.
    - Correct acidosis and restore blood buffer system.
    - Remove excess fluid from the client's blood.
  - Hemodialysis – The process of cleansing the blood of accumulated waste products; used for end stage renal failure or clients who are acutely ill and require short-term treatment.

    - Nursing Interventions
      - Weigh the client before and after the procedure.
      - Monitor the client's blood pressure continuously during the procedure.
      - Provide care to the access site, to prevent clotting and infection.
      - Assess for presence of thrill and bruit.
      - Provide adequate nutrition as prescribed.
      - Post a sign above the client's bed that warns of no blood pressure readings or blood work on the side of the fistula.
      - Maintain fluid restrictions.

- Withhold regular morning medications prior to dialysis.
  - Peritoneal Dialysis – Artificially induced kidney function during failure using the peritoneum as a dialyzing membrane; usually short term; a peritoneal catheter is inserted by the provider.

    - Nursing Interventions
      - Assist the client to void prior to the procedure.
      - Weigh the client daily.
      - Monitor the client's vital signs and baseline electrolytes.
      - Maintain asepsis.
      - Keep an accurate record of the client's fluid balance.
      - Procedure
        - Warm dialysate (1 to 2 L of 1.5, 2.5, or 4.25% glucose solution)
        - Allow to flow in by gravity
        - 5 to 10 min inflow time; close clamp immediately
        - 30 min of equilibration (dwell time)
        - 10 to 30 min of drainage (should be clear and pale yellow)
        - Continue treatment for 2 full days.
        - Monitor for complications (peritonitis, bleeding, respiratory difficulty, abdominal pain, bowel or bladder perforation).
  - Continuous Ambulatory Peritoneal Dialysis (CAPD) – A dialyzing method involving almost continuous peritoneal contact with dialysis solution for clients with end-stage renal disease.
    - Procedure (differs from acute peritoneal dialysis)
      - Permanent indwelling catheter inserted into peritoneum
      - Fluid infused by gravity (1.5 to 3 L)
      - Dwell time – 4 to 10 hr
      - Dialysate drains by gravity – 20 to 40 min
      - Four to 5 exchanges daily, 7 days/week (some clients may elect to do at night with automatic cycling machines; 10 to 14 hr, 3 times/week)

NOTES

- Nursing Interventions
  - Monitor the client for complications.
  - Watch the client for peritonitis (rebound tenderness, fever, cloudy outflow).
  - Check for bladder perforation (yellow outflow).
  - Hypotension
  - Monitor for bowel perforation (brown outflow).
- Advantages to CAPD
  - More independence
  - Free dietary intake and better nutrition
  - Satisfactory control of uremia
  - Least expensive dialysis
  - Decreased likelihood of future transplant rejection
  - More closely approximates normal renal function

- Urinary Tract Surgery
  - Kidney transplantation
    - For individuals with irreversible end-stage renal disease
    - Requires a well-matched donor
      - Living donors (most desirable)
      - Cadaver donors
    - Preoperative management
      - Interventions are prescribed to correct the client's metabolic status.
      - Administer immunosuppressive therapy.
      - Perform hemodialysis within 24 hr.
      - Provide the client emotional support.

    - Nursing Interventions (postoperative management)
      - Maintain homeostasis.
      - Administer immunosuppressive medications to the client such as azathioprine (Imuran), cyclosporine (Sandimmune), or steroids.
      - Monitor the client for rejection. This could include oliguria, edema, fever, tenderness over graft site, fluid and electrolyte imbalance, hypertension, elevated BUN, creatinine, and elevated WBCs.
      - Monitor the client for infection and maintain protective isolation.
      - Provide emotional support and monitor for depression.

- Urinary Diversion – Removal of the bladder and transplant of ureters into a pouch under the abdominal skin; can be continent or incontinent; care of a stoma plus general interventions.

  - Nursing Interventions
    - Monitor the client's vital signs (hemorrhage and shock are frequent complications).
    - Provide the client with pain control.
    - Observe for manifestations of paralytic ileus, which are very common.
    - Provide adequate fluid replacement.
    - Weigh the client daily.
    - Maintain function and patency of the drainage tubes.
      - Indwelling urinary catheter (dependent position, tape tubing to the thigh)
      - Nephrostomy tube
        - Never clamp.
        - Irrigate only with prescription for 10 mL of 0.9% sodium chloride.
        - Assess for leakage of urine.
      - Ureteral catheters
        - Each catheter drains ½ of the urinary system.
        - Bloody drainage expected after surgery, but should clear within 24 to 48 hr.
        - Never irrigate the surgical implant.
        - Aseptic technique required.

- Benign Prostatic Hyperplasia – Enlargement of the prostate that may accompany the aging process in males; exact cause is unknown.

NOTES

- o Manifestations
  - Difficulty starting stream/dribbling
  - Decrease in force of the urinary stream
  - Frequent urinary tract infections
  - Nocturia
  - Hematuria
- o Diagnosis and treatment
  - Digital rectal exam or cystoscopy
  - Prostate-specific antigen for diagnosis
- o Treatments
  - Urinary antibiotics
  - Alpha-blocker medications to promote urinary flow – terazosin (Hytrin), tamsulosin (Flomax), alfuzosin (Uroxatral), and doxazosin (Cardura)
  - Enzyme inhibitors to decrease the size of the prostate gland – dutasteride (Avodart) and finasteride (Proscar)
  - Transurethral resection of prostate (TURP)

    - □ Nursing Interventions (Preoperative)
      - ‣ Insert indwelling urinary catheter.
      - ‣ Administer antibiotics as prescribed.
    - □ Nursing Interventions (Postoperative)
      - ‣ Monitor the client for shock and hemorrhage.
      - ‣ Teach the client to avoid heavy lifting, prolonged sitting, constipation, or straining (which could cause a rebleed).
      - ‣ Monitor for continuous bladder irrigation (expect bloody drainage; monitor I&O carefully).
      - ‣ Encourage fluid intake (at least 3,000 mL/day).
      - ‣ Assess for TURP syndrome – a cluster of manifestations resulting from absorption of irrigating fluids through prostate tissue (hyponatremia, confusion, bradycardia, hypo/hypertension, nausea, vomiting, and visual changes).
      - ‣ Medicate for pain control – the client may need medication and narcotics to decrease bladder spasm.

- ‣ Keep the catheter taped tightly to the client's leg (for hemostasis at the surgical site by catheter balloon).
- ‣ Teach the client Kegel exercises (there may be temporary or permanent loss of sexual function or urinary control).

- Prostate Cancer – A slow-growing cancer of the prostate gland.
  - o Contributing factors
    - Men age 50 and older
    - African American
    - Family history
    - Elevated testosterone levels
    - High-fat diet
  - o Manifestations
    - Asymptomatic in early stages
    - Hematuria
    - Prostate-specific antigen greater than 10
    - Rectal exam – hard, pea-sized nodule
  - o Treatment
    - Radical prostatectomy
    - External radiation therapy
    - Internal radioactive seeds
    - Hormone therapy
- Incontinence
  - o Types
    - Urge – The client cannot hold urine when stimulus to void occurs.
    - Functional – Cannot physically get to the bathroom or is not aware of the stimulus to void.
    - Stress – Pressure such as coughing, straining, lifting, bearing down, or laughing causes incontinence; very common in middle-age women.
  - o Nursing Interventions
    - Use adult incontinency devices.
    - Decrease the client's fluid intake after 1800.
    - Maintain a regular toilet schedule.
    - Perform the Credé maneuver as needed.

NOTES

- Monitor the client for signs of cystitis.
- Teach the client Kegel exercises to strengthen the sphincter.
- Assure that the physical environment enhances the ability to get to the bathroom.
  - ○ Urine retention
    - Caused by a physical obstruction of the urethra from acute or chronic causes (edema, tumor, inflammation or inability of the bladder to work; postanesthesia, stroke).

    - Nursing Interventions
      - □ Stimulate relaxation of the urethral sphincter by providing the client privacy, placing the client's hands in warm water (or just turning on the water), and encouraging guided imagery.
      - □ Administer bethanechol chloride (Urecholine).
      - □ Position the client upright.
      - □ Ensure adequate fluid intake.
  - ○ Medications
    - Urge incontinence
      - □ Anticholinergics – tolterodine (Detrol) and Oxybutynin (Ditropan)
    - Stress incontinence
      - □ Tricyclic antidepressant – imipramine (Tofranil)

SECTION 10

NEUROSENSORY DISORDERS

Neurological Assessment

- History of Present Illness
- Mental Status
  - ○ Level of consciousness (alert, lethargic, obtunded, stupor, coma)
  - ○ Orientation (person, place, time)
  - ○ Affect
  - ○ Mood
  - ○ Speech (clarity, consistency, word-finding ability)
  - ○ Cognition (judgment and abstraction ability)

- Cranial Nerves (I through XII)
  - ○ CN I Olfactory – sensory smell
  - ○ CN II Optic – sensory vision
  - ○ CN III Oculomotor – motor eye
  - ○ CN IV Trochlear – motor eye
  - ○ CN V Trigeminal – sensory face, motor chewing
  - ○ CN VI Abducens – motor eye
  - ○ CN VII Facial – motor facial movements, sensory taste
  - ○ CN VIII Acoustic – sensory hearing, balance
  - ○ CN IX Glossopharyngeal – sensory posterior taste
  - ○ CN X Vagus – sensory throat, motor swallow, and speak
  - ○ CN XI Spinal accessory – motor shoulders
  - ○ CN XII Hypoglossal – motor tongue
- Motor Function
  - ○ Muscles
    - Size
    - Symmetry
    - Tone
    - Strength
  - ○ Coordination
  - ○ Movement
    - Voluntary control/involuntary movements
    - Tremors
    - Twitches
    - Balance and gait
  - ○ Posturing
    - Decorticate – An abnormal posturing indicated by rigidity, flexion of the arms to the chest, clenched fists, and extended legs; indicative of damage to the corticospinal tract (the pathway between the brain and the spinal cord).
    - Decerebrate – An abnormal body posturing indicated by rigid extension of the arms and legs, downward pointing of the toes, and backward arching of the head; indicative of deterioration of structures of the nervous system, particularly the upper brain stem.

NOTES

- Reflexes
  - To absent
  - 1+ diminished
  - 2+ normal
  - 3+ brisk
  - 4+ hyperactive
- Client's Response to Stimulus – Glasgow coma scale
- Scale – normal is 8 to 15; 7 or less indicates a coma
  - Best eye-opening response
    - Spontaneously = 4
    - To speech = 3
    - To pain = 2
    - No response = 1
  - Best motor response
    - Obeys verbal command = 6
    - Localizes pain = 5
    - Flexion – withdrawal to pain = 4
    - Flexion – abnormal (decorticate) = 3
    - Extension – abnormal (decerebrate) = 2
    - No response to pain on any limb = 1
  - Best verbal response
    - Oriented x 3 = 5
    - Conversation (confused) = 4
    - Speech – inappropriate = 3
    - Sounds – incomprehensible = 2
    - No response = 1
- Pupil Check
  - Pupils compared for size equality, movement, and response to light
  - Normal finding – pupils equal and reactive to light
- Vital Signs
  - Blood pressure or pulse changes may indicate increased intracranial pressure

Diagnostic Procedures

- Lumbar Puncture – Procedure to measure pressures within the cerebrospinal fluid and to collect a sample of fluid for testing; fluid is used to diagnose neurological disorders, infections, brain or spinal cord damage.

  - Nursing Interventions
    - Verify that informed consent has been signed.
    - Have the client empty his bladder and bowel.
    - Position the client on his side with his knees pulled toward his chest and his chin tucked downward.
    - Insert the spinal needle between the third and fourth lumbar vertebrae.
    - Measure the spinal fluid pressure and collect fluid.
    - Postprocedure
      - Encourage fluid intake.
      - Check puncture site for redness, swelling, and clear drainage.
      - Assess movement of the client's extremities.
- Computed tomography (CT scan)
  - Head CT – A computerized tomography image (with or without dye) is used to evaluate cranial-facial trauma, subarachnoid or intracranial hemorrhage, and headaches; also used to diagnose a stroke or determine abnormal development of the head and neck.

  - Nursing Interventions (preprocedure; if dye is used)
    - Verify that informed consent has been signed.
    - Check for any allergies to iodine, contrast dyes, or shellfish.
    - Instruct the client to lie still and flat.

  - Nursing Interventions (postprocedure; if dye is used)
    - Increase fluids to clear dye from the client's system.
    - Assess dye injection site and monitor the client's distal pulses.

NOTES

- Cerebral Arteriogram – Injection of dye into the carotid arteries, via the femoral artery, to allow visualization of the cerebral arteries and assess for brain lesions.

  - Nursing Interventions (preprocedure)
    - Verify that informed consent has been signed.
    - Check for any allergies to iodine, contrast dyes, or shellfish.
    - Keep client NPO 4 to 6 hr before the procedure.
    - Mark distal peripheral pulses.
    - Instruct the client that her face may feel warm during the procedure.

  - Nursing Interventions (postprocedure)
    - Monitor the client for an altered level of consciousness and sensory or motor deficits.
    - Check for hematoma at the insertion site. Keep the client's leg straight for 2 hr with a sand bag at the insertion site and maintain bed rest for 12 hr.
    - Use an ice cap to decrease the client's swelling.
    - Check the client's peripheral pulses, color, and temperature of extremities.

- Myelogram – An injection of contrast medium or air into subarachnoid space to detect abnormalities of the vertebrae and/or spinal cord.

  - Nursing Interventions (preprocedure)
    - Verify that informed consent has been signed.
    - Check for any allergies to iodine, contrast dyes, or shellfish.
    - Maintain NPO for 4 hr before the procedure.

  - Nursing Interventions (postprocedure)
    - Keep the client horizontal for 12 to 24 hr after the procedure.
    - Monitor his vital signs and output.
    - Encourage fluid intake.
    - Monitor the client for fever, stiff neck, and back pain.

- Electroencephalogram (EEG) – Detects problems in the electrical activity of the brain; electrodes are placed over multiple areas of the scalp to detect and record patterns of electrical activity, and they also check for abnormalities such as seizure disorders, confusion, evaluation of head injuries, tumors, infections, degenerative diseases, metabolic disturbances, or to confirm brain death.

  - Nursing Interventions (preprocedure)
    - Verify that informed consent has been signed.
    - Verify which medications should be administered before the EEG.
    - Instruct the client to avoid caffeine 8 hr before the test.
    - Advise the client to wash her hair the night before the test, because it must be free of oils, sprays, and conditioners.
    - Verify if the test is to be done awake, asleep, or sleep-deprived.

- Electromyography (EMG) – A test to assess the health of the muscles and the nerves controlling the muscles; a needle electrode is inserted into the muscle where electrical activity is detected.

- Magnetic resonance imaging (MRI) – A noninvasive procedure that uses magnets and radio waves to construct clear, detailed pictures of the brain and nerve tissues without obstruction.

  - Nursing Interventions
    - Verify that informed consent has been signed.
    - Assess the client for claustrophobia.
    - Remove all metal objects such as body piercings, jewelry, credit cards, and watch.
    - No special test, diet, or medications are required.

- Increased Intracranial Pressure – Increase in normal brain pressure due to an increase in the cerebrospinal fluid pressure; can be caused by lesions or swelling within the brain; causes compression of the brain structures and restricts blood flow through the brain.

NOTES

- o Contributing factors
  - Head injury with subdural or epidural hematoma
  - Cerebrovascular accident or cerebral edema
  - Brain tumor
  - Hydrocephalus
  - Ruptured aneurysm and subarachnoid hemorrhage
  - Meningitis, encephalitis
- o Manifestations – vary depending on cause and location; will affect the client's level of consciousness
  - Lethargic, drowsy, stupor; motor and sensory changes
  - Headache, irritability, restlessness
  - Nausea and vomiting, often projectile
  - Pupil changes – dilated, unequal, nonreactive
  - Diplopia
  - Changes in vital signs
    - □ Widening pulse pressure; bradycardia with increased systolic blood pressure is Cushing's syndrome
    - □ Irregular or decreasing respirations (Cheyne-Stokes respirations)
    - □ Elevated temperature
- o Nursing Interventions
  - Monitor the client's vital signs and neurological function.
  - Keep head of bed the elevated 30° to 45°.
  - Keep the client's head in a neutral position to enhance drainage.
  - Avoid coughing, sneezing, straining, and suctioning.
  - Maintain maximum respiratory exchange (hyperventilation causes CO_2 to decrease, leading to vasoconstriction. This causes a decrease in the intracranial pressure).
  - Administer oxygen to increase the supply to the client's brain.
  - Monitor fluid I&O and restrict fluids to prevent increased cerebral edema.
  - Administer medications as prescribed.

- □ Avoid opiates and sedatives (contraindicated).
- □ Barbiturates (pentobarbital [Nembutal]) may be prescribed for uncontrolled, increased intracranial pressure to place the client into a therapeutic coma with ventilatory support and close monitoring of cardiac status.
- □ Acetaminophen (Tylenol) for fever.
- □ Administer osmotic diuretics (mannitol [Osmitrol]) and steroids (dexamethasone [Decadron]) to decrease cerebral swelling.
- □ Give antihypertensive or anticonvulsant medications if necessary.
  - Use hypothermia as ordered to decrease intracranial pressure.
  - Decrease environmental stimuli.
  - Intensive care is required when monitoring intracranial pressure (ventriculostomy).
- Hyperthermia – Body temperature above 40.5° C (105° F)
  - o Contributing factors
    - Infections
    - Cerebral edema
    - Environmental heat
- Manifestations
  - o Nausea, vomiting, shivering
  - o Hypoxia
  - o Nursing Interventions
    - Assess neuro status every hour.
    - Use a cooling blanket as ordered, or place ice packs to axilla, groin, and back of the neck.
    - Monitor the client for tachycardia and dysrhythmias.
    - Monitor for manifestations of dehydration by checking I&O and weighing the client daily.
    - Initiate seizure precautions.
    - Prevent shivering.
      - □ Decreases risk of increased intracranial pressure and oxygen consumption
      - □ Chlorpromazine hydrochloride (Thorazine)

NOTES

- □ Meperidine hydrochloride (Demerol)
- Seizure Disorders – Sudden, excessive discharge of electrical activity within the brain.
    - o Contributing factors
        - Genetics
        - Trauma
        - Brain tumors
        - Toxicity or infection
    - o Classifications
        - Generalized seizures (4 types)
            - □ Tonic-clonic (formerly grand-mal)
            - □ Absence (formerly petit-mal)
            - □ Myoclonic
            - □ Atonic or akinetic (drop-attacks)
        - Partial seizures (2 types)
            - □ Complex (loss of consciousness)
            - □ Simple (no loss of consciousness)
    - o Nursing Interventions
        - Maintain patent airway (turn to side after tonic phase).
        - Protect the client from injury.
        - Do not restrain the client.
        - Do not put anything her mouth.
        - Turn her head to the side to prevent aspiration.
        - Document the length of seizure (most important).
        - Watch for prodromal signs such as irritability, mood change, and insomnia preceding the aura (a sensory warning that the seizure is about to occur).
        - Document how long the client is unconsciousness and the length of any incontinence.
        - Precipitating factors (if any).
        - Monitor the client for respiratory difficulty.
        - Note the client's behavior during the postictal phase (period of lethargy and limpness following seizure).

- Teach the client to
    - □ Take medications consistently and never to stop abruptly.
    - □ Get adequate rest and exercise.
    - □ Avoid alcohol.
- Administer anticonvulsants
    - □ Phenytoin (Dilantin) – gum hypertrophy (must visit the dentist routinely), ataxia, and diplopia; monitor medication levels.
    - □ Carbamazepine (Tegretol) – nystagmus, ataxia, blood dyscrasias; monitor CBC, liver function tests, and medication levels.
    - □ Valproic acid (Depakene) and divalproex sodium (Depakote) – nausea, bleeding problems, and liver damage; monitor liver function tests and medication levels.
    - □ Phenobarbital (Luminal) – side effect includes drowsiness; monitor liver function test and medication levels.
- Institute seizure precautions for clients that are prone to multiple seizures and/or are in poor control
    - □ Bed rest should include padded side rails.
    - □ Ensure that immediate access is available for oxygen administration and suction.
- Status Epilepticus – A life-threatening condition characterized by prolonged or clustered seizures that develop into continuous seizures for 30 min or more; may be caused by a sudden withdrawal of anticonvulsant medications; can lead to brain damage or death
    - o Nursing Interventions
        - Initiate seizure precautions.
        - Administer benzodiazepine and anticonvulsant therapy.
            - □ Lorazepam (Ativan) is the medication of choice at a loading dose of 4 mg IV every 2 min, up to a maximum of 8 mg.
            - □ Diazepam (Valium) may also be used in status epilepticus beginning with a loading dose of 5 to 10 mg IV every 10 min up to a maximum of 30 mg.
            - □ Phenytoin (Dilantin) 500 to 1,000 mg IV slowly administering no more than 50 mg/min.

NOTES

- ▸ Do not mix with glucose; administered in 0.9% sodium chloride only.
  - ▸ Monitor for bradycardia and heart block.
- Transient Ischemic Attacks (TIA) – Temporary episode of neurological dysfunction lasting minutes or seconds secondary to decreased blood flow to the brain; may be a warning sign of an impending stroke, especially in the first 4 weeks after TIA.
- Contributing factors
  - Atherosclerosis
  - Microemboli from atherosclerotic plaque
  - Cerebral artery spasm
  - ○ Manifestations
    - Sudden change in visual function
    - Sudden loss of sensory or motor functions
  - ○ Diagnostic testing
    - Carotid Doppler studies
    - CT scan and/or MRI
    - Arteriography
  - ○ Treatment
    - Antiplatelet medications
      - ▫ Clopidogrel (Plavix)
      - ▫ Dipyridamole (Aggrenox)
      - ▫ Ticlopidine (Ticlid)
    - Anticoagulant medications
      - ▫ Warfarin (Coumadin)
    - Angioplasty
      - ▫ Carotid endarterectomy (removal of plaque from one or both carotid arteries)
  - ○ Nursing Interventions
    - Encourage the client to stop smoking and limit alcohol intake.
    - Maintain a diet low in cholesterol and sodium.
    - Stress the importance of maintaining ideal body weight with regular exercise.

- Cerebrovascular Accident (CVA) – Commonly referred to as a stroke, CVA is the sudden loss of brain function resulting from a disruption of blood supply to the involved part of the brain; causes temporary or permanent neurological deficits.
  - ○ Risk factors
    - Hypertension and obesity
    - Smoking or cocaine use
    - Hypercholesterolemia
    - Diabetes mellitus or peripheral vascular disease
    - Aneurysm or cranial hemorrhage
  - ○ Manifestations – The severity of the neurological deficit is determined by location and the extent of tissue ischemia; symptoms manifest on the side opposite of damage to the brain, due to a cross-over effect.
    - Loss of motor balance or function, coordination
    - Slurred speech, aphasia, and dysphagia
    - Hemiparesis, hemiplegia
    - Visual disturbance
    - Cranial nerve disturbance
  - ○ Nursing Interventions
    - Maintain an adequate airway.
    - Monitor the client's neurological function and vital signs routinely. Establish level of function and Glasgow coma scale.
    - Maintain fluid and electrolyte balance.
    - Monitor for aspiration due to risk of dysphagia; feed the client slowly, place food in the back of his mouth and to the unaffected side.
    - Provide psychological support to the client and his family.
    - Establish means of communication with a client who is experiencing aphasia (expressive, receptive, global). Encourage slow deliberate speech.
    - Participate in acute and rehabilitation phases.
      - ▫ Range of motion – to prevent flexion contractures; keep extremities in a position of extension or neutrality.

NOTES

- □ Hemiparesis, hemiplegia – will cause safety issues in the client; consult occupational or physical therapy.
- □ Hemianopsia – place articles within client's visual range.
- □ Help the client to achieve bowel and bladder control.
- Spinal Cord Injury – Partial or complete disruption of nerve tracts and neurons; resulting in paralysis, sensory loss, altered activity, and autonomic nervous system dysfunction.
  - o Risk factors
    - Men ages 16 to 25
    - High-risk activities
      - □ Driving while intoxicated
      - □ Not wearing a seat belt
      - □ No protective sports gear
      - □ Firearm use
      - □ Diving accidents
  - o Types
    - Contusion
    - Laceration
    - Compression of the cord
    - Complete transection
  - o Level of injury (determines manifestations)
    - Cervical – causes quadriplegia
      - □ Respiratory dysfunction (the client may be ventilator dependent)
      - □ Paralysis of all 4 extremities
      - □ Loss of bladder and bowel control
      - □ Injury above C3 is usually fatal
    - Thoracic injury – causes paraplegia
      - □ Loss of bladder and bowel control
      - □ Paralysis of lower extremities and major control of body trunk
      - □ Potential complication of autonomic dysreflexia – injury above T6

- Lumbar
  - □ Paralysis of lower extremities (remain flaccid)
  - □ Loss of bladder and bowel control
- o Nursing Interventions
  - Immobilize the client as ordered
    - □ Spinal board
    - □ Halo traction
    - □ Gardner-Wells traction or Crutchfield tongs
  - Provide care for spinal shock/neurogenic shock (flaccid paralysis below level of injury resulting in spastic reflexes).
  - Maintain respiratory function.
  - Monitor for autonomic hyperreflexia or dysreflexia – A life-threatening syndrome with sudden, severe hypertension triggered by noxious stimuli below damage of cord. May be caused by impaction, bladder distension, pressure points or ulcers, or pain.
  - o Manifestations
    - Hypertension (250 to 300/100) with bradycardia
    - Headache, flushing, nausea
    - Blurred vision and restlessness
- o Nursing Interventions
  - Place the client in the high-Fowler's position, to help decrease blood pressure.
  - Determine stimuli and correct.
  - Teach the client bowel and bladder management.
  - Administer dexamethasone (Decadron) to reduce edema.
  - Consult with occupational or physical therapy regarding rehabilitation issues; self care deficits.
- Head Injury – Any trauma that leads to injury of the scalp, skull, or brain, ranging from concussion to skull fracture; classified as either closed or penetrating.
  - o Closed-head injury – Head sustains blunt force trauma caused by striking against an object.
    - Concussion

NOTES

- Contusion
- Fracture
  - ☐ Basilar skull fracture
    - ▸ Manifestations
      - ▹ Bleeding from the nose and ears
      - ▹ Otorrhea, rhinorrhea – cerebrospinal fluid from the ears or nose; must differentiate between cerebrospinal fluid and mucus by assessing the glucose content of the drainage
    - ▸ Raccoon eyes (periorbital edema and ecchymosis)
    - ▸ Battle's sign (postauricular ecchymosis) noted on mastoid bone
- Hematomas
  - ☐ Epidural hematoma – Bleeding into the space between the skull and the dura.
    - ▸ Commonly involves the middle meningeal artery
    - ▸ Typical presentation – the client sustains the injury, followed by a brief loss of consciousness; this is followed by a lucid interval, then rapid deterioration
    - ▸ Emergency management – burr holes to relieve increasing intracranial pressure
  - ☐ Subdural hematoma – bleeding below the dura
    - ▸ Usually venous
    - ▸ May be acute, subacute, or chronic
    - ▸ Management – craniotomy
  - ○ Penetrating head injury – An object penetrates the skull and enters the brain.

  - ○ Nursing Interventions
    - Assess the client frequently for signs of increased intracranial pressure.
    - Same interventions as head trauma

- Laminectomy – A surgical procedure to remove a portion of vertebrae for the treatment of severe pain and disability resulting from compression of spinal nerves by a ruptured disk or bony compression; also an option to relieve persistent pain or to treat progressive neurological problems due to nerve compression.

  - ○ Nursing Interventions
    - Monitor the client for circulatory impairment.
    - Assess the client for loss of sensation in lower extremities.
    - Monitor the dressing for spinal fluid leakage, bleeding, or signs of infection.
    - Log roll the client.
    - Address the client's sexual concerns.
- Multiple Sclerosis (MS) – Chronic, progressive disease of the CNS, characterized by patches of demyelination in the brain and spinal cord (exact cause unknown, probable autoimmune basis).
  - ○ Manifestations
    - Occurs in young adults 20 to 40 years of age
    - Nystagmus, blurred vision, diplopia
    - Slurred hesitant speech and fatigue
    - Spastic weakness of extremities, paresthesia, and difficulty with balance
    - Emotionally labile, depression
    - Intention tremors
    - Spastic bladder
    - MRI shows sclerotic patches through the brain and spinal cord
  - ○ Management
    - There is no cure or specific treatment, only symptomatic relief. MS is characterized by long periods of remissions and exacerbations.
    - During exacerbation, administer corticosteroids as prescribed.
    - Stress management techniques may be helpful to prevent exacerbations.
    - Immunosuppressants – azathioprine (Imuran) or beta-interferon (Betaseron)

NOTES

- Muscle spasticity and tremors – baclofen (Lioresal), gabapentin (Neurontin), clonazepam (Klonopin)
- Urinary problems and constipation – oxybutynin (Ditropan), tolterodine (Detrol), propantheline (Pro-Banthine), psyllium (Metamucil)
- Depression – amitriptyline (Elavil), imipramine (Tofranil), sertraline (Zoloft), fluoxetine (Prozac)
- Sexual difficulties – sildenafil (Viagra)
- Fatigue – amantadine (Symmetrel), modafinil (Provigil)

  o Nursing Interventions
- Encourage the client to live an active and normal life.
- Teach the client self-catheterization techniques.
- Promote daily exercise with fall precautions.
- Instruct the client to avoid stressors that exacerbate the condition (infections).
- Teach the client self-injection technique for beta interferon (Betaseron).

- Parkinson's Disease – Chronic, progressive neurologic disorder affecting the brain centers that are responsible for control and regulation of movement; extrapyramidal tract; loss of pigmented cells of substantia nigra and depletion of dopamine.
  o Manifestations
- Bradykinesia with rigidity
- Resting tremor
- Expressionless, fixed gaze; mask-like and depression
- Drooling and slurred speech
- Constipation
- Retropulsion, propulsion
  o Stages
- Unilateral flexion of upper extremity
- Shuffling gait with progressive weakness and difficulty ambulating
- Progressive, permanent disability

  o Management
- Medication Therapy
  □ Antiparkinsonian agent – levodopa (Dopar); levodopa (Sinemet), side effects include hypotension and gastrointestinal upset; administer on an empty stomach ½ to 1 hr before meals
  □ Antiparkinsonian agent – carbidopa (Lodosyn); side effects include hypokinesia, hyperkinesia, and psychiatric manifestations
  □ Dopamine agonist – bromocriptine mesylate (Parlodel)
  □ Anticholinergic – benztropine (Cogentin); trihexyphenidyl (Artane); side effects include dry mouth, mydriasis, constipation, and confusion
  □ Antiviral, antiparkinsonian – amantadine HCl (Symmetrel); side effects include tremor, rigidity, and bradykinesia

  o Nursing Interventions
- Teach the client fall precautions.
- Encourage the client to wear clothing that fosters independence (no snaps, buttons, or zippers).
- Encourage a high-fiber diet.

- Amyotrophic Lateral Sclerosis (ALS) – Rapidly progressive, invariably fatal neurological disease that attacks nerve cells (neurons) that control voluntary muscles; also known as Lou Gehrig's disease.
- Progression
- Most commonly affects men 40 to 60 years of age.
- Presents with muscle weakness in extremities and slurred speech, and progresses to inability to swallow, chew, communicate, breathe, and perceive sensory or tactile stimulation.
- Greatest risk of respiratory failure or pneumonia is within 3 to 5 years of onset.
- Eventually the client loses the ability to breathe without ventilatory support and dies from respiratory failure or pneumonia.

NOTES

- ALS does not affect the client's sensory or cognitive abilities; all senses remain intact.
  - Manifestations
    - Twitching, cramping, and stiffness of muscles
    - Muscle weakness affecting an arm or leg
    - Slurred or nasal speech with difficulty forming words (dysarthria)
    - Difficulty chewing and swallowing (dysphagia)
    - Overactive gag reflex
    - Fatigue
    - Difficulty with manual dexterity
  - Management
    - Etiology unknown; no known cure, treatment is symptomatic
   Nursing Interventions
    - Speech therapy to assist with communication and swallowing needs.
    - Occupational therapy to assist with adaptive devices to foster independence.
    - Physical therapy to maintain muscle strength and tone.
    - Support respiratory needs with mechanical respirator devices.
    - Medication to provide relief from excessive salivation, pain, muscle cramps, constipation, and depression.
    - Provide supportive services to the client and family with anticipatory grieving.
- Myasthenia Gravis – Disorder of unknown origin affecting the neuromuscular transmission of the voluntary muscle of the body; loss of acetylcholine receptors on the postsynaptic membrane of the neuromuscular junction (probable autoimmune basis).
  - Manifestations
    - Extreme muscular weakness – increased with fatigue and relieved by rest
    - Progressive deterioration, particularly the respiratory system, and muscle wasting
    - Early manifestations – diplopia, ptosis, dysphagia

  - Medical treatment
    - Medication management
      - Anticholinesterase medications that increase the amount of acetylcholine in the neuromuscular function
      - Pyridostigmine (Mestinon); Neostigmine (Prostigmin)
      - Atropine is antidote for medications
      - Steroids – prednisone (Deltasone)
    - Thymectomy (excision of the thymus)
    - Crisis
      - Cholinergic – usually from overmedication; causes severe tremors
      - Myasthenic – spontaneous or from infection; drooling and severe ptosis; can actually cause respiratory arrest
      - Differentiate between the two with the Tensilon test – edrophonium (Tensilon) injected response expected in 30 seconds; if no response, it becomes a cholinergic crisis
   Nursing Interventions
    - Maintain patent airway.
    - Plan activities for the client early in the day to avoid fatigue.
    - Teach the client manifestations of crisis.
    - Give the client his medications on time.
- Guillain-Barré Syndrome – An acquired acute inflammatory disease of peripheral nerves resulting in demyelination characterized by ascending, reversible paralysis; severity determines verbal or motor manifestations.
  - Manifestations
    - Disease is preceded by an infection (respiratory or gastrointestinal).
    - Initial manifestations – tingling of the legs that may progress to upper extremities, trunk and facial muscles; ascending paralysis is a classic disease presentation.
    - Progresses to paralysis and possible respiratory failure.
    - Recovery takes anywhere from several months to one year in descending form (the last lost is the first recovered)

NOTES

■ Immunotherapy prescribed – plasma exchange or IV immune globulin

o Nursing Interventions

■ Maintain the client's airway; monitor respiratory status, oximetry.

■ Monitor her blood pressure and heart rate.

■ Provide nutrition, especially if the client has difficulty chewing and swallowing. May need parenteral feedings.

■ Manage bowel and bladder problems.

■ Collaborate with physical therapy to maintain the client's muscle strength, flexibility, and contractures.

■ Prevent complications of immobility – pneumonia, deep vein thrombosis, urinary tract infection atelectasis , and skin breakdown.

Sensory Assessment

- Evaluation of Visual Acuity

  o Assessment of the client's ability to see objects at specified distances

  o Manifestation

    ■ Myopia (nearsightedness) – Distant objects appear blurred.

    ■ Hyperopia (farsightedness) – Close objects appear blurred.

    ■ Presbyopia (farsightedness associated with aging) – A progressive condition in which the lens of the eye loses its ability to focus.

    ■ Macular degeneration (loss of visual acuity associated with aging) – A progressive disorder of the retina causing decreased vision and potentially the loss of central vision.

- Treatment of Visual Acuity Problems

  o Abnormal refractory findings are typically treated with corrective lens.

  o Lasik surgery – A surgical procedure that permanently changes the shape of the cornea and (in most cases) restores 20/20 vision.

- Auditory Assessment

  o Audiology exam (audiogram) tests the client's ability to hear sounds at varying intensity and decibels.

  o Presbycusis (hearing deficit associated with aging) – A progressive disorder characterized by a loss of the ability to hear sounds at high frequencies; may lead to deafness.

  o Client may need hearing aides to amplify desirable environmental sounds.

- Ménière's Disease – Disorder of the inner ear in which an increase in fluid causes change in sensory perception.

  o Manifestations

    ■ Vertigo

    ■ Tinnitus

    ■ Hearing loss

    ■ Pressure in the ear

  o Nursing Interventions

    ■ Medication

      □ Meclizine (Antivert) to manage vertigo

      □ Hydrochlorothiazide (HCTZ) to reduce inner ear fluid volume and pressure

      □ Dexamethasone (prednisone) to reduce inflammation

    ■ Encourage the client to implement a low sodium diet.

    ■ Instruct the client to eat six small meals/day.

    ■ Encourage him to avoid caffeine.

    ■ Manage his anxiety and stress.

    ■ Initiate and teach the client fall precautions.

    ■ Maintain a quiet environment for the client.

    ■ Assist him with identifying triggers such as bright lights, loud music, caffeine, stress, and nicotine.

- Detached Retina – Occurs when the sensory retina separates from the pigment epithelium of the retina; vitreous humor fluid flows between the layers when a tear occurs in the retina; can be related to age and trauma.

NOTES

- o Manifestations
    - Sudden visual disturbances
    - Flashes of light
    - Blurred vision with floaters
    - Curtain or shadow over visual field
- Nursing Interventions (preoperative)
    - Immediate bed rest with head of the bed elevated.
    - Tell the client to avoid coughing, sneezing, and straining.
    - Surgical intervention – scleral buckling, photocoagulation, cryosurgery
- Nursing Interventions (postoperative)
    - Maintain bed rest with both of the client's eyes bandaged for 24 hr.
    - Avoid jarring or bumping head.
    - Teach regular self administration of eye drops on schedule.
- Cataract – Slow, progressive clouding of the lens by development of thickening material.
    - o Manifestations
        - Diplopia, blurred vision, and photophobia
        - Frequent change in eyeglasses prescription
        - Halos around lights and colors appear pale
    - o Surgical treatment – removal of the lens under local anesthesia, with intraocular lens implant
    - o Nursing Interventions (preoperative – dilate the eye)
        - Mydriatics
        - Cycloplegics
    - o Nursing Interventions (postoperative)
        - Keep the client's operative eye covered.
        - Elevate head of bed 30° to 45° and do not turn the client onto operative side.
        - Instruct the client to avoid bending at the waist, lifting, sneezing, coughing, and to not touch the eye area.
        - Prevent vomiting or straining.
        - Report severe pain immediately, as it may indicate the development of glaucoma.

- Glaucoma – Increased intraocular pressure due to the inability of aqueous humor to drain; if uncorrected, glaucoma may lead to atrophy of the optic nerve and blindness
    - o Manifestations
        - Acute (closed angle)
            - Results from an obstruction to the outflow of aqueous humor
            - Severe pain in and around the client's eye
            - Lights appear to have a rainbow of colors around them.
            - Cloudy and blurred vision with dilated pupils
            - Nausea and vomiting
            - Within hours, the client may develop gastrointestinal, sinus, neuro, and dental manifestations.
    - o Chronic (open angle)
        - Insidious onset with slowly decreasing peripheral vision
        - Tired feeling in the client's eye
        - Halos around lights
        - Progressive loss of visual field
    - o Nursing Interventions
        - Administer medications consistently on time.
        - Medication causes pupils to contract and the iris to pull away from the corneas.
        - Aqueous humor may drain through lymph spaces (meshwork) into Schlemm's canal.
        - Types (avoid anticholinergic medications)
            - Pilocarpine hydrochloride (Pilocar) lasts 6 to 8 hr; medication of choice for glaucoma
            - Acetazolamide (Diamox) decreases production of aqueous humor; a side effect includes gastric distress
            - Mannitol (Osmitrol), IV; reduces intraocular pressure by increasing blood osmolality; indications – treatment of acute attacks and preoperatively
            - Isosorbide (Isordil), oral; cautions – safer than IV medication for cardiac clients; may cause diuresis, which is troublesome in men with prostatitis

---

NOTES

- o Surgical care
  - Procedures
    - □ Iridencleisis
    - □ Thermosclerectomy
  - Teach the client that glaucoma is controllable, but not curable.
  - Avoid emotional upsets, extreme exertion, lifting, and colds.
  - Encourage moderate exercise, regular bowel habits, daily use of medicines, medical checkups, and the importance of wearing a Medic-Alert bracelet; monitor fluid intake.

SECTION 11

ONCOLOGY NURSING

Neoplastic Diseases

- Healthy cells transformed into malignant cells upon exposure to certain etiological agents – viruses, chemical, and physical agents
- Failure of Immune Response
  - o Contributing factors
    - Rapid cell division
    - Malignant cells metastasize and extend directly into adjacent tissue, moving through lymph system, entering body circulation, and diffusing into body cavity
  - o Tumors
    - Classified according to type of tissue from which they evolve
    - Carcinomas begin in epithelial tissue (skin, gastrointestinal tract lining, lung, breast, uterus).
    - Sarcomas begin in nonepithelial tissue (bone, muscle, fat, lymph system).
    - Cell type affects appearance, rate of growth, and degree of malignancy (epithelial basal cells are basal cell carcinoma; bone cells are osteogenic carcinoma; gland epithelium are adenocarcinoma).

- Manifestations Suggesting Malignant Disease (American Cancer Society 7 Warning Signs)
  - o C – Change in bowel or bladder habits
  - o A – A sore that does not heal
  - o U – Unusual bleeding or discharge
  - o T – Thickening or lumps in breast or elsewhere
  - o I – Indigestion or difficulty swallowing
  - o O – Obvious change in wart or mole
  - o N – Nagging cough or hoarseness
- Cancer Therapy – Administered to cure the client or minimize functional and structural impairment results from the disease.
  - o If a cure is not possible, goals involve:
    - Preventing further metastasis as long as possible.
    - Providing symptomatic relief of manifestations.
    - Maintaining quality of life.
  - o Chemotherapy
    - Medications interfere with cell division; combination of medications usually given
    - Classification (all cause bone marrow depression)
      - □ Alkylating agents – uracil mustard (Nitrogen mustard), cyclophosphamide (Cytoxan)
      - □ Antimetabolite – fluorouracil (5-FU), methotrexate (MTX) (Folex)
      - □ Antibiotics – doxorubicin hydrochloride (Adriamycin), bleomycin (Blenoxane), dactinomycin (Actinomycin D)
      - □ Plant alkaloids – vincristine (Oncovin), vinblastine (Velban)
      - □ Hormones – estrogen, progesterone, tamoxifen citrate (Tamofen)
      - □ Biological modifiers (Procrit, Neupogen)
      - □ Common side effects and interventions to counteract
      - □ Bone marrow depression – expected side effect of all chemo drugs

NOTES

- ▸ Leukopenia (WBC less than 1,000 mm³) – Measures to enhance the immune system include a balanced diet, rest, handwashing, filgrastim (Neupogen) medication to increase WBC production, protective isolation during hospitalization; routine laboratory work.

- ▸ Anemia (Hgb less than 10) – Oxygen therapy, iron-rich foods, blood transfusions, erythropoietin (Epogen), epoetin alfa (Procrit) to increase RBCs; routine laboratory work.

- ▸ Thrombocytopenia (platelets less than 50,000) – Platelet transfusion, oprelvekin (Neumega) to increase platelets, bleeding precautions, and avoiding use of aspirin or alcohol.

- ☐ Alopecia – Hair loss 2 weeks after start of treatment. Apply ice to the client's scalp during chemotherapy to slow hair loss. Use gentle shampoo, hats, scarves, and sunscreen. The American Cancer Society provides wigs and supportive services.

- ☐ Anorexia, nausea and vomiting – Administer antiemetic prior to therapy. The client should drink cool beverages and eat small, favorite meals high in potassium with high-calorie supplements. Avoid unpleasant odors. Take loperamide (Imodium A-D) to manage diarrhea. Soft, bland, high-protein foods at room temperature for stomatitis, and use a straw for fluids. Rinse mouth with a topical anesthetic, may need topical steroids and zinc supplements.

- ☐ Elevated uric acid, crystal, and urate stone formation – allopurinol (Zyloprim) therapy; increase fluid intake

- ☐ Specific medications have specific toxic effects

- ☐ Doxorubicin hydrochloride (Adriamycin) – irreversible cardiomyopathy

- ☐ Cisplatinum (Platinol) – renal toxicity

- ☐ Vincristine sulfate (Oncovin) – peripheral neuropathy

- ■ Provide emotional support to the client and his family.

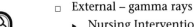

- ○ Radiation – Use of radiation externally or internally to cure disease or provide palliative relief from pain.
  - ■ Types
    - ☐ External – gamma rays
      - ▸ Nursing Interventions
        - ▷ Give antiemetic before treatment – ondansetron (Zofran).
        - ▷ Premedicate with pain medication.
        - ▷ Provide psychological support.
        - ▷ Provide skin care – dermatitis 3 to 6 weeks after start of treatment; teach the client to wash with water; avoid lotions, powders, and sunlight.
        - ▷ Wet reaction – skin's response to radiation; skin becomes dry or develops blisters which may break, causing pain and the potential for infection. If dry reaction, keep clean and lubricated. If wet reaction, clean and cover to prevent infection.
    - ☐ Internal – cesium needles
      - ▸ Nursing Interventions
        - ▷ Maintain time, distance, and shielding, because the client is radioactive.
        - ▷ Follow institutional guidelines for radiation protection.
        - ▷ Limit visitors; private room; position area of body being irradiated toward the outside of the building.
        - ▷ Prone to inflammation at site of radiation (intrauterine may lead to proctitis and cystitis; oral insertion may lead to stomatitis).
          - ◆ Observe for signs of complications.
          - ◆ Rest the area; indwelling urinary catheter.
          - ◆ Increase fluids, low residue, soft.

NOTES

- ◆ Administer medications to decrease inflammation; steroids, urinary antiseptics, and aesthetics.
  - ▷ If the radiation source is dislodged, do not touch it with bare hands.
    - ◆ Use lead forceps to pick up and place in lead container.
    - ◆ Follow institution guidelines for radiation containment.

SECTION 12

IMMUNOLOGIC DISORDERS

- AIDS – Infectious disease characterized by severe deficits and destruction of cellular immune function; manifested clinically by opportunistic infection and/or unusual neoplasms
  - o Etiology – HIV
  - o Risk factors
    - Unprotected intercourse with an infected or high-risk partner/multiple partners
    - IV drug abusers sharing needles
    - Blood transfusions (hemophiliacs, surgical clients; blood supply testing for HIV began in 1985)
    - Infants of mothers who are infected
  - o Manifestations
    - Flu-like symptoms
    - Swollen lymph glands
    - Weight loss with wasting syndrome
    - Chronic diarrhea and fever
    - Night sweats
    - CD4 lymphocyte count less than 200 (800 to 1,200 is normal)
    - Dementia complex
    - Bacterial infections
      - □ Pneumonia
      - □ Tuberculosis
      - □ Salmonellosis – severe diarrhea, abdominal pain, and fever

- Viral infections
  - □ Cytomegalovirus – can cause blindness
  - □ Herpes simplex virus – genital and systemic
  - □ Human papillomavirus (HPV)
- Fungal infections
  - □ Candidiasis – tongue, esophagus, vagina
  - □ Cryptococcal meningitis
- Pneumocystis carinii pneumonia
- Toxoplasmosis
- Kaposi's sarcoma
- Non Hodgkin's lymphoma

 o Nursing Interventions

- Provide the client respiratory support.
- Monitor fluid and electrolyte balance.
- Prevent the spread of infection by using standard precautions and blood and body fluid precautions.
- Observe for signs and symptoms of Kaposi's sarcoma.
- Provide high-nutrition, low-residue meals.
- Teach the client about abstinence, safer sex practices, monogamy, good hand hygiene, and use of condoms.
- Medication therapy – World Health Organization; highly active antiretroviral therapy guidelines (HAART) (research findings are constantly being updated).
  - □ Efavirenz (Sustiva), azidothymidine (AZT), and lamivudine (Epivir)
    - ▸ Common adverse effects – neutropenia, gastrointestinal distress, anemia, insomnia
    - ▸ Zidovudine (AZT) recommended for protecting the unborn fetus of women who are HIV positive
  - □ Interferon (Roferon)
  - □ Pneumocystis pneumonia prophylaxis – Pentamidine (Pentam 300)
  - □ Antifungals – metronidazole (Flagyl) and amphotericin B (Fungizone)
  - □ Antituberculosis medications as needed

NOTES

- □ Acyclovir (Zovirax) herpes treatment
- □ Protease inhibitors – saquinavir (Fortovase), ritonavir (Norvir)
- □ Antivirals – zalcitabine, dideoxycytidine (Hivid)

- ○ Point to Remember – The disease has a long incubation period, sometimes up to 10 years until late in the infection

- Systemic Lupus Erythematosus (SLE) – Chronic inflammatory disease of unknown origin that involves the vascular and connective tissue of multiple organs; may be autoimmune.
  - ○ Manifestations
    - ▪ Insidious onset
    - ▪ Characterized by remissions and exacerbations
    - ▪ Erythematous "butterfly rash" on both cheeks and across the bridge of the nose; rash deepens on exposure to sunlight (most common manifestation)
    - ▪ Polyarthralgia; also Raynaud's phenomenon
    - ▪ Normochromic, normocytic anemia
    - ▪ Fever, malaise, weight loss
    - ▪ Positive for antinuclear antibodies

  - ○ Nursing Interventions
    - ▪ Supportive (depends on organs involved)
    - ▪ Encourage uninterrupted sleep and daytime naps.
    - ▪ Instruct the client to use sunscreen and wear protective clothing.
    - ▪ Encourage the client to get 30 min of exercise/day.
    - ▪ Avoid smoking.
    - ▪ Identify triggers (stress, oral contraceptives, sunlight, foods, and pregnancy).
    - ▪ Select a barrier contraceptive method (no intrauterine contraceptive device).
  - Points to Remember
    - ○ Lupus nephritis occurs early in the disease
    - ○ Treatment for nephritis
      - ▪ NSAIDS and Salicylates

- ▪ Antimalarial hydroxychloroquine (Plaquenil); monitor for visual changes and muscle weakness.
- ▪ Corticosteroids
- ▪ Dialysis

SECTION 13
BURNS

Assessment

- Rule of Nines for Body Surface Area (BSA)
  - ○ Adults – Rule of nines
    - ▪ Head and neck – 9%
    - ▪ Anterior trunk – 18%
    - ▪ Posterior trunk – 18%
    - ▪ Arms (9%) – 18%
    - ▪ Legs (18%) – 36%
    - ▪ Perineum – 1%
  - ○ Infants and young children
    - ▪ Head and neck – 21%
    - ▪ Arms and hands – 10%
    - ▪ Chest and stomach – 13%
    - ▪ Back – 13%
    - ▪ Buttocks – 5%
    - ▪ Legs and feet – 13.5%
    - ▪ Groin – 1%
- Depth of Burn
  - ○ Superficial (formerly called first degree)
  - ○ Superficial partial thickness (formerly called second degree)
  - ○ Deep partial thickness (formerly called third degree)
  - ○ Full-thickness
- Type of Burn
  - ○ Thermal
  - ○ Chemical
  - ○ Electrical
  - ○ Radiation

NOTES

Treatment

- Acute Phase
  - Assess for possible inhalation injury (soot around the nostrils or mouth).
  - Establish and maintain airway.
  - Verify the time of injury and percentage of BSA burned.
  - Initiate large bore IV for rapid fluid replacement.
  - Insert urinary catheter.
  - Insert NG tube as prescribed.
  - Administer tetanus toxoid.
  - Monitor for shock.
  - Nursing Interventions
    - Maintain airway.
    - Fluid replacement therapy.
      - Goal is to maintain vital organ perfusion
      - Shock phase – 24 to 48 hr (monitor vital signs)
        - Fluid shifts from plasma to interstitial space (third spacing)
        - Hct rises while potassium leaves cells, increasing K+ serum levels
      - Metabolic acidosis
        - Fluid and protein loss
        - Monitor urine output (goal of 50 mL/hr)
      - Parkland formula
        - Give 4 mL/kg/% burn.
        - Give half of total fluids in first 8 hr.
        - Give second half over remaining 16 hr.
        - Deduct any fluid given prehospital from the amount to be infused in the first 8 hr.
      - Diuretic phase
        - Capillary permeability stabilizes and fluid shifts from interstitial spaces to plasma.
        - Observe for pulmonary edema.
        - Assess vital signs and central venous pressure.
        - Monitor output.
        - Check laboratory values (particularly low potassium; high sodium).
  - Nursing Interventions
    - Control the client's pain.
      - Medication depends on severity (morphine sulfate, PCA pump, fentanyl and NSAIDS)
      - Give IV due to poor absorption
    - Assess the client's nutritional needs.
      - NPO until bowel sounds return (usually has NG tube)
      - High caloric needs (most common) 6,000 to 8,000 calories/day; use enteral or total parenteral nutrition
      - Diet should be high in protein, carbohydrates, fats, and vitamins for healing.
      - Prevent stress ulcers (Curling's Ulcer) – antacids, H2-receptor antagonists
    - Monitor for and prevent complications.
      - Infection
        - Asepsis – reverse isolation
        - Wound care (debridement, hydrotherapy)
        - Antimicrobial therapy – oral, IV, or topical
      - Contractures and deformities
        - Range of motion as tolerated by the client initiated first postburn day
        - Place in position of function (pressure garments, Jobes, and splints)
      - Provide emotional support to the client and family.
        - Support is essential for long-term adjustment
        - Alteration in body image
        - The nurse is aware that clients with burns often experience complex psychosocial, emotional, and spiritual challenges.

NOTES

Methods of Treating Burns

- Open-Exposure Method
  - Allows for drainage of burn exudate
  - Eschar forms hardened crust (may constrict circulation, requiring escharotomy)
  - Use of topical therapy; asepsis crucial
  - Skin easily visualized and assessed
  - Range of motion easier
  - Disadvantages
    - Increases pain and heat loss
    - Difficult to manage burns of hands and feet
- Closed Method
  - Gauze dressing wrapped distal to proximal
  - Decreased fluid and heat loss
  - Limited mobility may result in contractures
  - Wound assessment only during dressing changes
- Topical Antimicrobial
  - Silver sulfadiazine (Silvadene)
    - Broad-spectrum coverage including yeast
    - Can be removed with water
  - Mafenide acetate (Sulfamylon)
    - Broad-spectrum coverage
    - Penetrates tissue wall
    - Must be open to air; no dressings
    - Breakdown of medication may cause metabolic acidosis
    - Painful
  - Bacitracin
- Biologic Dressings and Tissue Grafts
  - Homograft or allograft (human tissue donors)
  - Xenograft or heterograft (animal sources)
  - Amniotic membrane
  - Biosynthetic (Biobrane) or synthetic (transparent film)
- Skin Care Following Discharge
  - Control the client's swelling and reduce scarring.
    - Wear pressure garment 23.5 hr/day.

- Engage in regular exercise per physical therapy.
- Elevate affected areas as much as possible.
  - Keep skin moisturized.
  - Control itching with cool baths and loose, cotton fabric.
  - Avoid sun exposure.
  - Change in appearance of skin as scars fade from red to near natural coloration.
  - Encourage the client to take in extra calories and protein.

SECTION 14

NUTRITION: THERAPEUTIC DIETS

Adult Nutritional Requirements

- Protein – 0.8 to 1 g/kg daily
- Fat – < 30% of total kcal
- Carbohydrates – 45 to 65% of daily caloric intake
- Calcium – 1,000 mg/daily
  - Postmenopausal – 1,500 mg/day
- Potassium – 2,300 mg/day
- Iron
  - Men (19 and older) 8 mg/day
  - Women (19 to 50) 18 mg/day
  - Women (> 51) 8 mg/day
- Daily fluid requirement in mL = Body weight in lb x 15
- Fiber – 30 to 38 g/day

Nutrient Modification

- Low-Protein Diet
  - Indicated for renal impairment, hepatic coma, and advanced cirrhosis
  - Controls end products of protein metabolism by limiting protein intake.
  - Encourage high-carbohydrate foods.
  - Limit foods high in protein such as eggs, meat, milk, and milk products.

NOTES

- High-Protein Diet
  - Used for tissue building, burns, correction of malabsorption syndromes, mild to moderate liver disease, undernutrition, and pregnancy.
  - Corrects protein loss and/or maintains and rebuilds tissues.
  - Encourage high-protein foods such as fish, fowl, organ and meat sources, and dairy products.
  - May include protein supplements.
- Abnormalities in Amino-Acid Metabolism
  - Use for phenylketonuria, galactosemia, and lactose intolerance.
  - Reduce or eliminate the offending enzyme.
  - Avoid milk and milk products for all three diets.
  - Use milk substitutes.
- Low-Cholesterol Diet
  - Indicated for cardiovascular diseases, diabetes mellitus, and high-serum cholesterol levels
  - Controls cholesterol levels by limiting cholesterol intake
  - Limit foods high in low-density lipoproteins, saturated fats, and trans-fatty acids such as animal products (egg yolks, organ meats, bacon, fatty meats, and butter).
  - Encourage low-cholesterol foods, foods containing high-density lipoproteins, and unsaturated fats (including omega-3 fatty acids such as fatty fish, shellfish, walnuts, flaxseed oil, raw or cooked vegetables, fruits, lean meats, and skinless fowl).
- Modified-Fat Diet
  - Indicated for malabsorption syndromes, cystic fibrosis, gallbladder disease, obstructive jaundice and liver disease, and obesity
  - Fat content in the diet is lowered
    - To stop contractions of the diseased organs
    - When there is inadequate absorption of fat
    - To decrease fat storage in the body
  - To reduce fat intake, avoid gravies, fatty meat and fish, cream, fried foods, rich pastries, whole milk products, cream soups, salad and cooking oils, nuts, and chocolate; allow 2 to 3 eggs/week, lean meat, and butter and margarine.

- For a fat-free diet, restrict all fatty meats and fat; allow vegetables, fruits, lean meats, fowl, fish, bread, and cereal.
- High-Polyunsaturated Fat Diet
  - Indicated for cardiovascular diseases
  - Reduce saturated fats and transfatty acids by avoiding foods from animal sources, whole-milk products, egg yolks, organ meats, bacon, fatty meats, tropical oils, and partially hydrogenated vegetable oils.
  - Increase polyunsaturated fats by including vegetable sources, corn/soybean/safflower oils, foods high in omega-3 fatty acids such as fatty fish and walnuts.
- Carbohydrate Modification (diabetic diet or American Diabetes Association diet)
  - Principles of diabetic diet management
    - Attain or maintain ideal body weight.
    - Ensure normal growth.
    - Maintain plasma glucose levels as close to normal as possible.
    - Provide 30 calories/kg of ideal body weight.
    - Provide 25% of calories at each meal and 25% for snacks.
    - Provide 20% of calories as protein, 55 to 60% as carbohydrates, and 20 to 30% as fats.
    - Include unsaturated fats, high fiber, and complex carbohydrates.
  - Develop meal plans designed for individual needs using exchange lists.
    - Milk exchanges
    - Vegetable exchanges
    - Fruit exchanges
    - Bread exchanges
    - Fat exchanges

NOTES

Mineral Alterations

- Potassium-Modified Diets
  - Increase potassium intake for diabetic acidosis, thiazide diuretics, 48 hr after burns, vomiting, or fevers.
  - Reduce potassium intake for kidney failure.
  - Foods high in potassium include fruits and fruit juices (orange, grapefruit, banana, apple), avocados, prunes, dried apricots, dried beans, soy beans, lima beans, kidney beans, squash, baked potatoes, milk, and broiled meats.
  - Foods low in potassium include breads, cereals, sugar, fats, and cranberry and grape juice.
- Sodium-Restricted Diets
  - Sodium is restricted in hypertension, heart failure, MI, hepatitis, adrenal cortical diseases, kidney disease, lithium carbonate therapy, cystic fibrosis, and conditions such as cirrhosis of the liver and preeclampsia, which cause persistent edema.
    - Mild restriction is 2 to 3 g of sodium
    - Moderate restriction is 1,000 mg of sodium
    - Strict restriction is 500 mg of sodium
    - Severe restriction is 250 mg of sodium
  - Limit foods high in sodium, such as potato chips and other salted snack foods; canned soups and vegetables; baked goods that contain baking powder or soda; cereals; seafood; beef; processed meats such as bologna, ham, and bacon; dairy products, especially cheese; pickles; olives; and condiments such as soy sauce, steak sauce, Worcestershire sauce; and salad dressings.
  - Encourage low-sodium foods such as fresh fruits and vegetables, chicken, salt substitutes, and low-sodium products.
- Iron Alterations
  - Increased iron intake is indicated for correction or prevention of iron deficiency anemia, which is most likely to occur in infants, toddlers, adolescents, and pregnant women.
  - Food sources high in iron include fish, meats (particularly organ meats), green leafy vegetables, enriched breads, cereals and macaroni products, whole grain products, dried fruits such as raisins and apricots, and egg yolks.
  - Vitamin C enhances absorption of iron from the gastrointestinal tract.
  - Administration of iron supplements.
    - Oral administration with a straw.
    - Maximum absorption occurs when administered between meals.
    - Fewer gastrointestinal side effects occur when administered with meals
    - Injectable iron administered deep IM with Z track
  - Calcium alterations
    - Increased calcium intake is indicated for growing children and adolescents, pregnant and lactating women, and postmenopausal women (prevents osteoporosis).
    - Decreased calcium intake is indicated in the presence of kidney stones composed of calcium.
    - Food sources high in calcium include milk and milk products like yogurt and cheese; dark green vegetables, such as collard greens, kale, broccoli; dried beans and peas; and shellfish and canned salmon.
    - Some antacids contain calcium.
    - Vitamin D enhances absorption of calcium from the gastrointestinal tract.

Consistency Modifications

- Clear-Liquid Diet
  - Indicated for resting the gastrointestinal tract, maintaining fluid balance; immediately postoperative; for diarrhea, nausea, and vomiting
  - Includes water, tea, broth, gelatin, apple juice
  - Not nutritionally adequate
- Full-Liquid Diet
  - When clear liquids are tolerated well, progress to full liquids
  - Include clear liquids plus milk and milk products, such as custard, pudding, creamed soups, ice cream, sherbet, and fruit juices

---

NOTES

- Soft Diet
  - Include full liquids plus pureed vegetables, eggs that are not fried, tender meats, potatoes, and cooked fruit
- Bland Diet
  - Used to promote healing of gastric mucosa by eliminating chemically and mechanically irritating food sources.
  - Indicated for gastric and duodenal ulcers and postoperative stomach surgery.
  - Given in small, frequent feedings to assist in diluting or neutralizing stomach acid; protein foods are good at neutralizing; fat has some ability to inhibit the secretion of acid and delays stomach emptying.
  - Foods usually introduced in stages with gradual addition of foods
  - Foods allowed include milk, butter, eggs that are not fried, custard, vanilla ice cream, cottage cheese, cooked, refined, or strained cereal, enriched white bread, gelatin, homemade creamed/pureed soups, and baked or broiled potatoes.

SECTION 15

LABORATORY VALUES

Serum Electrolytes

- Sodium (Na+) = 135 to 145 mEq/L
- Potassium (K+) = 3.5 to 5 mEq/L
- Calcium (Ca++) = 8.5 to 10 mg/dL
- Magnesium (Mg++) = 1.8 to 3 mg/dL
- Phosphorus (PO4) = 2.5 to 4.5 mg/dL
- Creatinine (Cr) = 0.5 to 1 mg/dL
- BUN = 10 to 20 mg/dL
- Glucose (fasting) = 70 to 110 mg/dL

ABGs

- pH = 7.35 to 7.45
- $PaCO_2$ = 35 to 45 mm Hg
- PaO_2 = > 80 mm Hg
- HCO_3 (bicarbonate) = 22 to 26 mEq/L

- SaO_2 = 90 to 100%

CBC

- RBCs males 4.6 to 6.2 mm³
- RBCs females 4.2 to 5.4 mm³
- WBCs 4,800 to 10,800 mm³
- Hgb males 13 to 18 g/dL; Females 12 to 16 g/dL
- Hct males 45 to 52%; Females 37 to 48%

Other Hematologic Values:

- Glycosylated hemoglobin (HbA1c) 5% (up to 7% in clients who have diabetes mellitus)
- Erythrocyte sedimentation rate < 20 mm/hr

Coagulation Times

- Bleeding time = 4 to 7 min
- Therapeutic INR = 2.0 to 3.0
- Platelets = 150,000 to 450,000 cu/mm
- PT = 11 to 14 seconds
- Activated partial thromboplastin time = < 40 seconds

Liver Function Tests

- Albumin = 3.8 to 5 g/dL
- Ammonia = 35 to 65 mcg/dL
- Total bilirubin = 0.0 to 1.5 mg/dL
- Total protein = 6 to 8 gm/dL

Urinalysis

- Specific gravity = 1.010 to 1.030
- pH = 4.5 to 7.5
- Glucose = negative
- RBCs = negative
- WBCs = negative
- Albumin = negative

Therapeutic Medication Monitoring

- Digoxin level = 0.8 to 2 ng/mL
- Lithium level = 0.8 to 1.2 mEq/L

NOTES

- (Note: "Need to know values" are those listed in the 2007 Detailed Test Plan for the NCLEX-RN examination under the heading of "Physiological Adaptation: Reduction of Risk Potential, Laboratory Values")

- "Need to Know" laboratory values have been taken from the United States National Library of Medicine at the National Institutes for Health. Different institutions or laboratories may use slightly different normal laboratory values and ranges. NCLEX exam questions addressing laboratory values will include easily identifiable high and low laboratory values.

NOTES

UNIT FOUR

MENTAL HEALTH NURSING

SECTION 1

OVERVIEW

- Mental Health Nursing – A personal state of being in which a person has a positive self-perception, the ability to cope adaptively with stressors, and is able to consistently develop toward autonomy and self-actualization.
  - Client outcomes
    - Dealing with emotional responses to stress and crisis
    - Satisfying basic needs
    - Learning more effective behavior
    - Achieving positive coping skills
- Theoretical Models of Treatment
  - Psychoanalytical Model (Sigmund Freud) – Focuses on uncovering childhood trauma and repressed feelings that cause conflicts later in life.
    - Mind structure
      - Id – contains primitive drives
      - Ego – mediates demands of primitive id and superego
      - Superego – values that guide behavior
      - Conscious – ability to recall events without difficulty
      - Unconscious – memories that do not enter awareness
    - Nursing Interventions
      - Establish guidelines for understanding human behaviors.
      - Determine adaptive and maladaptive traits.
      - Individualize client teaching based on psychosexual development.
- Psychosocial Developmental Model (Erik Erikson) – A process in which emotional and developmental growth is achieved through the accomplishment of designated tasks in each of the eight life cycles.
  - Failure in any stage decreases the likelihood of achieving success in future stages.
  - Wellness is viewed as a continuum.

 o Nursing Interventions
  - Identify the client's current stage of psychosocial development.
  - Assist the client to complete the current stage.
  - Set goals to advance to the next stage.
- Basic Human Needs Model (Maslow) – A hierarchy of needs; a belief that needs are fulfilled in a progressive order.
  - Levels
    - Physiologic
      - Oxygen
      - Food
      - Sleep
      - Sexual expression
    - Safety
      - Physical safety
      - Avoiding harm
      - Sense of protection
    - Love and belonging
      - Group identity
      - Mutual caring
    - Self-esteem
      - Self-confidence
      - Self-acceptance
    - Self-actualization
      - Self-fulfillment
      - Environmental mastery

NOTES

ERIKSON'S STAGES OF DEVELOPMENT

Stage	Task	Behavior	Definition
Newborn/Infant (Birth to 1 year)	Trust vs. mistrust	Hopefulness, trusting vs. withdrawn, alienated	Newborns/infants learn to trust one consistent parent (not necessarily the mother).
Toddler (1 to 3 years)	Autonomy vs. shame, doubt	Self-control vs. compliance and compulsiveness, uncertainity	Toddlers learn independence and self-control; learn how to affect the environment with direct manipulation.
Preschooler (3 to 6 years)	Initiative vs. guilt	Realistic goals – explores, tests reality vs. strict limits on self-worry	Preschoolers engage in personal exploration and set goals that influence the environment; they evaluate their own behavior.
School-age child (6 to 12 years)	Industry vs. inferiority	Explores, persistent, competes vs. incompetent, low self-esteem	School-age children develop a sense of self and competency; they learn to create and interact.
Adolescent (12 to 20 years)	Indentity vs. role diffusion	Sense of self vs. confusion, indecision	Adolescents integrate life experiences that allow them to seek a sense of self (try new roles to see what fits); peer pressure creates tumultuous rebellions. Adolescents also examine their own sexual identity.
Young adult (20 to 35 years)	Intimacy vs. isolation	Commitment in love/work/play vs. superficial, impersonal	Young adults develop intimate or committed relationships, between work and family life; seek balance in life.
Middle adult (35 to 65 years)	Generativity vs. stagnation	Productivity, caring about others vs. self-centered and indulgent	Middle adults establish and guide the next generation by giving back to society in terms of volunteering and being productive through reminiscing.
Older adult (Over 65 years)	Integrity vs. despair	Sense of accomplishment vs. hopelessness, depression	Older adults undergo a review of life (necessary); they learn to accept one's life as purposeful, worthwile, and/or successful; want to provide a legacy.

NOTES

Copyright© 2009 Assessment Technologies Institute®, LLC

- ■ Nursing Interventions
  - ☐ Prioritize client care based on Maslow's hierarchy of needs.
  - ☐ Assist the client to advance through the stages of learning to fulfill his own needs.
  - ☐ Assist the client to develop new behaviors that reduce stress and prevent recurrences of mental dysfunction.
- Behaviorist Model – Maladaptive behavior is learned; therefore, positive changes can be accomplished using learning theory.

- ○ Nursing Interventions
  - ■ Positive reinforcement – Use rewards to increase or reinforce positive behaviors (adding food, attention, or phone privileges).
  - ■ Negative reinforcement – Extinguish an undesirable behavior by removing aversive consequences.
  - ■ Positive punishment – Decrease behavior by adding aversive consequences (time outs).
  - ■ Negative punishment – Decrease behavior by withdrawing privileges (no phone calls).

- ○ Main uses
  - ■ Children or clients who are regressed
  - ■ Personality disorders
  - ■ Phobias or eating disorders
  - ■ Clients who are mentally delayed
- Community Mental Health Model – Treatment provided on all levels in the community setting, with the nurse as the case manager and resource guide.
  - ○ Treatment concepts
    - ■ Primary prevention – Promotion of health and teaching risk factors.
    - ■ Secondary prevention – Early diagnosis and treatment (crisis intervention).
    - ■ Tertiary prevention – Rehab and follow up to avoid permanent disability.
  - ○ Nursing Interventions
    - ■ Provide holistic care.
    - ■ Initiate therapeutic nurse/client relationship.
    - ■ Identify the client's strength and align them with appropriate resources.
- Nurse/Client Relationship – An interpersonal and collaborative process characterized by a sequence of events leading to a mutually identified goal.
  - ○ Phases
    - ■ Preinteraction phase
      - ☐ Assess the client's feelings.
      - ☐ The nurse should assess her feelings.
      - ☐ Gather data from a secondary source.
    - ■ Orientation phase
      - ☐ Introduce responsibilities.
      - ☐ Establish trust, honesty, and empathy with the client.
    - ■ Assess the client's
      - ☐ Ability to perform ADLs.
      - ☐ Physical and emotional status.
      - ☐ Memory (long and short term).
      - ☐ Intellectual capacity.
      - ☐ Family and spiritual history.
      - ☐ Drug or alcohol history.

NOTES

- Formulate contract
  - Establish the time of meetings.
  - Ensure confidentiality.
  - State goals in behavioral terms.
- Working phase
  - Establish collaborative goals.
  - Explore thoughts, feelings, and actions.
  - Problem solve.
- Termination phase
  - Begin this phase on admission or first contact with the client.
  - Evaluate behavioral goals.
  - Transfer care to other support systems.
  - Assist the client to express separation of feelings or anger.
  - Do not continue relationship with the client past this phase.
- Crisis Intervention – An event characterized by overwhelming feelings of helplessness in which coping mechanisms fail, and the nurse should focus on safety, support, and the strengths of the client (crises are self-limiting – 4 to 8 weeks).
  - Type of crisis
    - Situational – unanticipated (death, divorce, termination from job)
    - Transitional – maturational, anticipated (birth, marriage)
    - Cultural/social (war)
  - Manifestations
    - Physiologic ("fight and flight")
    - Psychologic (panic, helplessness, fear)
    - Behavioral (talkative or withdrawn)
  - Nursing Interventions
    - Maintain a calm, controlled atmosphere.
    - Focus on the client's positive coping skills.
    - Keep the client focused on the immediate problem.
    - Set specific goals for resolution.
    - Use simple concrete statements to promote effective communication.

- Assist the client to develop more adaptive coping behaviors.
- Group Therapy – A collection of 7 to 10 individuals interacting together who a share a purpose and goals.
  - Group functions include problem-solving, developing a feeling of cohesiveness, and maintaining standards of behavior
  - Nursing Interventions
    - Assume a leadership role.
    - Direct the group toward common goals.
    - Set limits to prevent scapegoating.
    - Clarify issues to support group members.
      - Alcoholics anonymous, Al-Anon
      - Ostomy groups, cancer groups
- Family Therapy – Type of psychotherapy that focuses on the family unit in treatment.
  - Nursing Interventions
    - Help to reestablish communication between family members.
    - Assist in redefining roles and goals.
    - Identify scapegoating of the member who has manifestations of the illness.
    - Teach problem-solving techniques.
- Milieu Therapy – Management of the client's environment by replicating a positive living experience to facilitate recovery.
  - Nursing Interventions
    - Assist the client to develop shared responsibilities and cooperation.
    - Provide guidance to help the client learn to cope more effectively.
    - Help manage the client's daily activities.
  - Adjunctive Therapies – Alternative therapies that are used to increase social skills, encourage expression of feelings, relieve tension, and raise self-esteem.
  - Nursing Interventions
    - Allow free expression through art (clay, painting, drawing).
    - Encourage release of tension (dance, volleyball, recreation).
    - Point to Remember: A nurse should work collaboratively with an interdisciplinary team to promote and maintain mental health for all clients.

NOTES

MENTAL HEALTH/ILLNESS CONTINUUM		
Adaptive		Maladaptive
Healthy (Latent Phase)	Neurosis	Psychosis
Adaptive coping (confrontation)	←——————→	Maladaptive coping; withdrawal or aggressiveness
Reality oriented (x3)	←——————→	Psychotic: denies reality, creates new environment
Interacts with real environment	←——————→	Hallucination/delusion
Socially acceptable behavior; insight	←——————→	Bizarre behavior (gesturing posturing), little insight

---

NOTES

- Mental Health – A positive attitude toward self, positive personal growth, and the ability to cope adaptively with stress.
- Mental Illness Continuum – Characterized by maladaptive behavior in which the individual cannot manage stress or relate in socially acceptable ways.
- Unconscious Defense Mechanisms
  - Denial – The avoidance of an unpleasant reality by ignoring or refusing recognition ("I can quit drinking any time I want.").
  - Rationalization – Offering a socially acceptable explanation for unacceptable impulses ("I failed the exam because it was a bad test.").
  - Displacement – Transferring feelings to a neutral object (had a bad day at work, so go home and yell at family).
  - Projection – Blaming one's own thoughts or actions on another person ("You made me angry; you made me hit you.").
  - Compensation – Putting more effort toward achievements in areas of real or imagined deficiency (a student who fails a class later becomes the valedictorian).
  - Reaction formation – Displaying behaviors or attitudes directly opposite of unacceptable conscious or unconscious thoughts (being friendly with an individual you dislike).
  - Identification – Subconsciously adopting the characteristics of an individual who is admired (Elvis impersonator).
  - Sublimation – Directing unacceptable behaviors into a socially acceptable area (individual with violent thoughts writes a murder mystery novel).
  - Regression – Going back to an earlier developmental level (becoming dependant on another for all decisions).
  - Undoing – Compulsive, unconscious act meant to reverse previous unacceptable impulses (mother spanks child, then begins to bake cookies).
  - Introjection – Incorporating the emotions of another (a nurse becomes depressed while caring for a client who is depressed).
  - Isolation – A splitting-off response in which the psych blocks unpleasant feelings (an individual is inappropriately calm when told of the death of a loved one).
  - Splitting – A viewpoint of absolutes in which individuals are all bad or all good.
  - Repression – Involuntary forgetting of painful memories, feelings, or actions (denying occurrence of child abuse).
  - Conscious defense mechanism
    - Suppression – Deliberately forgetting or delaying painful acts or thoughts (an individual repeatedly cancels dentist appointments).
- Communication Tools – Method of using conversation to enhance a client's verbalization of feelings in a nonjudgmental environment.
  - Listen – Use nonverbal cues, eye contact, and face the client with proactive body language.
  - Offer self – "I will stay with you."
  - Focus – Only concentrate on the present.
  - Broad openings – "How are things today?"
  - Clarify – "What does that mean to you?"
  - Reflect – Verbalize ideas back to the client, or feelings conveyed such as, "You say you feel tense when you fight?"
  - Show empathy – State a feeling implied by the client.
  - Summarize – "Today we have discussed…"
  - Silence – Convey interest through the use of body language.
  - Share perceptions – "You seem angry."
  - Restate main idea – "You are sad?"
  - Validate – "I hear you saying that…"
- Communication Blocks – Statements or questions that can be answered with "yes" or "no," or verbal interactions that prevent the client from freely verbalizing his own feelings or thoughts.
  - False reassurance – "Don't worry."
  - Present own opinion – "I think you did the right thing."
  - Advise – "You should…"
  - Judge – "That was good."

NOTES

- o Belittle – "Everyone feels like that."
- o Defend – "All of our doctors are great."
- o Approve – Classify an action as good or bad.
- o Focus on the nurse – "I feel that way, too."
- o Change the subject or ignore the client.

- o Nursing Interventions
  - ▪ Avoid communication blocks.
  - ▪ Use open-ended statements or questions.
  - ▪ Avoid asking "why" questions.
  - ▪ Limit client questions to one idea at a time.
  - ▪ Mention nonverbal cues observed – "I notice your hands are shaking."
  - ▪ Do not invade the client's space (3 to 6 ft).
  - ▪ Use touch cautiously, because it can often be misinterpreted as a threat.

SECTION 2

ANXIETY

- • A stress-based sense of apprehension in response to a perceived physiological or psychological threat, resulting in feelings of fear and helplessness.
  - o Manifestations
    - ▪ Psychological
      - □ Sense of fear and helplessness
      - □ Poor self-confidence and insecurity
      - □ Anger or guilt
    - ▪ Physiological
      - □ Fight or flight mechanisms
      - □ Elevated vital signs
      - □ Palpitations, diaphoresis
      - □ Dry mouth, sweaty palms
      - □ Hyperventilation, diarrhea
      - □ Fidgeting, giggling, talkative

  - o Point to Remember – The initial nursing priority is to reduce the client's anxiety to levels that are tolerable, since progress cannot be made until the anxiety is manageable.

- o Maladaptive responses to anxiety
  - ▪ Panic attacks – Sudden onset of intense apprehension, fear, or terror that is out of proportion to occurring external events (may last from minutes to hours).
  - ▪ Manifestations
    - □ Dyspnea and faintness
    - □ Chest pain with palpitations
    - □ Hyperventilation and choking
    - □ Fear of dying or going crazy

  - ▪ Nursing Interventions
    - □ Stay with the client to provide support.
    - □ Provide calm reassurance to the client.
    - □ Remove anxiety-producing stimuli.
    - □ Distract the client by encouraging deep breathing into a paper bag.
- o Generalized anxiety disorder – Excessive worry regarding numerous issues out of proportion to actual events (finances, job responsibilities, health).
  - ▪ Manifestations
    - □ Restlessness and irritability
    - □ Poor concentration and insomnia

  - ▪ Nursing Interventions
    - □ Encourage the client to discuss concerns.
    - □ Assist the client to identify the source of the anxiety.
    - □ Help the client to identify personal strengths.
    - □ Teach the client how to develop positive coping skills.
- o Phobic disorders – Irrational fear of a specific object, activity, or situation that leads to avoidance (fear of flying).
  - ▪ Types
    - □ Agoraphobia – Fear of being places outside of the home.
    - □ Arachnophobia – Fear of spiders.
    - □ Social phobia (most common) – Also referred to as social anxiety disorder, which is an irrational fear of embarrassment or ridicule in any social setting or event.

NOTES

LEVELS OF ANXIETY				
Level	Physiologic Response	Cognitive State	Behavioral Changes	Nursing Interventions
Mild (+)	Slight discomfort, restlessness, tension relief, fidgeting, tapping	Perceptual field can be heightened; learning can occur	Restlessness (inability to work toward goal)	• Listen to the client. • Promote insight and problem solving. • Discuss alternatives with the client.
Moderate (++)	Increased pulse, respirations, shakiness, voice tremors, difficulty concentrating, pacing	Perceptual field narrows; client is selective in attention	• Focuses on immediate events • Benefits from the guidance of others	• Remain calm and rational in discussion. • Encourage the client to engage in relaxation exercises.
Severe (+++)	Elevated blood pressure, tachycardia, somatic reports, hyperventilation, confusion	Perceptual field greatly reduced; attention scattered and unable to focus	• Feelings of increasing threat; purposeless activity • Feeling of impending doom	• Listen to the client. • Encourage the client to express his feelings. • Establish concrete activity with the client. • Reduce the client's stimuli with simple tasks.
Panic (++++)	• Immobility or severe hyperactivity, cool, clammy skin, pallor, dilated pupils, chest pain and palpitations • Prolonged anxiety can lead to exhaustion	• Perceptual field diminished • Hallucinations or delusions may occur • Effective decision making is impossible	• Mute or psychomotor agitation • May strike out physically or withdraw • Loss of control	• Isolate the client from stimuli. • Stay with the client. • Remain very calm. • Protect the client's safety. • Do not touch the client.

NOTES

- Nursing Interventions
  - Use gradual desensitization experiences.
  - Employ behavior-modification techniques.
  - Teach relaxation techniques and biofeedback.
  - Avoid decision-making or competitions.
- Obsessive-compulsive disorder – Obsession is a persistent recurring fixed idea or thought that cannot be voluntarily removed from consciousness, and compulsion is an irresistible impulse to perform an action, regardless of its logic (may occur together or separately).
  - Manifestations
    - Feelings of inferiority, low self-esteem
    - Irrational coping to handle guilt
    - Compulsive need to repeat act to decrease severe anxiety

  - Nursing Interventions
    - Do not interrupt the client's compulsive act.
    - Schedule time for the client to complete his ritual (client may perform ritual slowly).
    - Decrease the time and frequency of the client's rituals.
    - Distract and substitute self-esteem building activities.
    - Provide safety, structure, and activities.
    - Demonstrate acceptance of the client's feelings.
    - Give antianxiety medications, if prescribed.
- Posttraumatic stress disorder – A severe anxiety disorder that occurs following exposure to a major traumatic event, which results in repeated flashbacks, nightmares, or emotionally crippling fear responses.
  - Manifestations
    - Persistent flashbacks of the events
    - Hypervigilance or startle responses
    - Feelings of detachment or emptiness
    - Irritability, insomnia, nightmares

- Nursing Interventions
  - Teach stress reduction techniques to the client.
  - Identify community support systems for the client.
  - Encourage the client to attend a support group.
- Somatoform disorders – A group of disorders characterized by reports of physical symptoms, with no organic pathology (a soldier paralyzed during a war, but has no physical injury).
- Conversion disorders (hysteria) – Alteration in physical function that is an expression of an unconscious physical need.
  - Manifestations
    - Sensory – blindness, deafness, and/or loss of sensation in extremities
    - Motor – mutism, ataxia, paralysis
    - Visceral– migraines, dyspnea
    - La belle indifference – lack of concern about manifestations
    - Primary purpose is to suppress anxiety and gain sympathy

  - Nursing Interventions
    - Redirect the client away from manifestations.
    - Encourage the client to express his feelings.
    - Teach the client relaxation and stress-reduction techniques.
    - Schedule daily activities for the client to decrease the time focused on symptoms.
  - Hypochondriasis – Exaggerated preoccupation with physical health; no organic pathology.
  - Manifestation
    - Varies with the individual and changes frequently
    - Client ponders manifestations
    - Constantly seeks medical care from multiple health care providers

  - Nursing Interventions
    - Set limits on pondering.

NOTES

- □ Do not feed into the client's manifestations.
- □ Help the client express his feelings.
- o Psychophysiological/psychosomatic disorders – True pathology originating with stress-related factors; physical manifestations must be treated or can progress to death.
  - ■ Manifestation
    - □ Migraines
    - □ Ulcerative colitis or peptic ulcers
    - □ Eczema
    - □ Cancer
    - □ Rheumatoid arthritis
    - □ Other autoimmune disorders
  - ■ Nursing Interventions
    - □ Care for the client's physical disorder using Maslow's hierarchy of needs.
    - □ Educate the client about body/mind connection.
    - □ Teach the client relaxation techniques.
    - □ Encourage the client to express his feelings.
    - □ Encourage the client to care for himself (regulation activities, relaxation, exercise, positive lifestyle changes).
- o Dissociative disorders (hysterical neuroses) – A condition in which there is a disruption in the awareness, memory, or perception of one's identity (common in cases of child abuse); may lead to multiple personalities.
  - ■ Manifestations
    - □ Dissociative identity disorder (multiple personalities)
    - □ Dissociative fugue or amnesia
    - □ Depersonalized disorder
  - ■ Nursing interventions
    - □ Assess the client to rule out organic pathology.
    - □ Encourage the client to express his feelings.
    - □ Use expressive therapy to deal with maladaptive anxiety.

 o Point to Remember – Antianxiety medications are not a cure, but rather a temporary means to reduce anxiety. Antianxiety medications can be highly lethal in overdose; therefore, clients who are suicidal should be monitored closely. Older adult clients are easily sedated and therefore are at risk for falls.

SECTION 3
SCHIZOPHRENIA

- • A mental disorder characterized by regression, thought disturbances, and bizarre dress that may be accompanied by delusions, hallucinations, and/or abnormal motor behaviors.
  - o Manifestations
    - ■ Delusions – fixed false beliefs of grandeur
    - ■ Hallucinations – visual or auditory
    - ■ Perceptions without environmental stimuli
    - ■ Illusions – misinterpretation of actual stimuli, such as believing an extension cord is a snake
    - ■ Ideas of reference – only personalizing environmental stimuli to self
    - ■ Neologisms – self-coined words
    - ■ Circumstantiality – cannot come to a point
    - ■ Blocking – sudden interruption of speech due to distraction of thoughts
    - ■ Echolalia – the repetition of words or phrases heard from another individual
    - ■ Echopraxia – imitation of movement or gestures of another individual
    - ■ Pressured speech – speaking rapidly
  - o Types
    - ■ Disorganized – incoherent, severe thought disturbance with inappropriate behaviors
    - ■ Catatonic – psychomotor
    - ■ Stupor – decreased responses
    - ■ Excitement – increased activity
    - ■ Waxy flexibility – bizarre posturing
    - ■ Negativism – doing the opposite of what is asked
    - ■ Mutism – refusal to speak

NOTES

ANTIANXIETY AGENTS AND ADVERSE REACTIONS

Chemical Class	Generic Name	Trade Name	Medication Alerts
Benzodiazepine compounds	• chlordiazepoxide • diazepam • oxazepam • lorazepam • alprazolam • clonazepam	• Librium • Valium • Serax • Ativan • Xanax • Klonopin	• Benzodiazepines ○ Warn the client about the effects of sedation. ○ Have the client avoid activities that require alertness. ○ Monitor the client for signs of medication dependance. A sudden withdrawal may cause seizures; therefore, wean the client off of the medication over a 2-week time frame.
Sedating antihistamines	hydroxyzine	Vistaril, Atarax	Antihistamines tend to cause drying and sedation, but are nonaddictive.
Beta-blockers	propranolol	Inderal	None
Selective serotonin reuptake inhibitors	paroxetine	Paxil	It is shown to be effective with social anxiety disorder; allow 2 to 3 weeks to note effects.
Anxiolytics	buspirone	BuSpar	BuSpar is nonsedating and nonaddicting. Allow 2 to 3 weeks to note effects, and avoid using concurrently with alcohol or in clients who have a history of hepatic disease.

Anticholinergic Side Effects of Antianxiety Agents	Nursing Interventions
Dry mouth	Provide candies, fluids.
Blurred vision	Inform the client that this will disappear within a week.
Urinary retention	Monitor the client's I&O. Monitor for distention by runnning water.
Drowsiness or sedation	Instruct the client not to drive. Avoid giving with other CNS depressants.
Ataxia	Use siderails and remain with the client when he is out of bed.
Tremors	Observe for the severity of tremors.
Hypotension	Check the client's blood pressure often and institute safety measures.
Tolerance	Observe the client for proper usage and effects and then withdraw gradually.

Medication Interactions

- CNS depressants – action potentiated; therefore, avoid alcohol and concurrent use of MAOIs.
- Tolerance does develop; therefore, discontinue slowly to minimize symptoms and rebound symptoms of insomnia or anxiety.
- Older adults are more vulnerable to adverse reactions; safety risk.
- Possible paradoxical reactions can occur in children and older adults.
- Stopping usage suddenly may cause seizures or death.

- Paranoid – behaviors escalate rapidly that can be destructive to self and others
- Hallucinating – persecutory
- Delusion – grandeur
- Emotions – anger, suspicion, excess religiosity of a punitive nature

- o Nursing Interventions
  - Provide for physical needs
  - Promote client safety
  - Establish nurse/client relationship
  - Re-orient to reality and include family
  - Provide structure to the day
  - Keep instructions simple and concrete
  - Deal with hallucinations:
    - □ Distract client but do not confront.
    - □ Seek to establish feelings.
    - □ Point out that others do not share the same perceptions, but do not deny that client sees it.
    - □ Avoid leaving client alone (clients hallucinate more while alone).
    - □ Engage client in group activities.
- Paranoid Personality Disorder – Insidious development of a permanent delusional system in which others are viewed as hostile, threatening and malevolent.
  - o Manifestations
    - Delusions of grandeur and persecution
    - Loneliness and general distrust of others
    - Mistrust and resistance to all treatment
    - Hostile, suspicious, and argumentative
    - Failed Erikson's first stage (trust vs mistrust)
    - Fear of being poisoned:
      - □ Serve food in covered containers.
      - □ Do not hide medications in food.
      - □ Medication should be packaged and opened in presence of client.
    - Respect client's personal space and avoid touching as client may strike out in fear

- Avoid any verbal and nonverbal communication that could be interpreted as threatening
- Difficulty concentrating and easily distracted
- Poor attention span, failure to complete a task
- Impulsive actions without thought of possible consequences

- o Nursing Interventions
  - Encourage effective communication
  - Assist to learn adaptive coping behaviors
  - Assess for client safety and intervene as needed initiate educative techniques between parent and child, using play therapy, family therapy, and cognitive-behavioral therapy.
- o Medication therapy
  - Methylphenidate hydrochloride (Ritalin)
  - Amphetamine sulfate (Adderall)
  - Dextroamphetamine sulfate (Dexedrine)
  - Atomoxetine (Strattera)
- Antipsychotic Medications
  - o Block dopamine receptors to decrease:
    - Combativeness and negativism
    - Hallucinations and delusions
    - Disorganization and suspiciousness
  - o Improve self-care deficits
  - o Medications cannot improve
    - Apathy or lack of interest
    - Insight or judgment
    - Lack of interest

SECTION 4

PERVASIVE DEVELOPMENTAL DISORDERS

- Autism – A severe developmental disorder of varying degrees that affects language, reasoning, and social interactions.
  - o Manifestations
    - Lack of interest in human contact
    - No social play or interaction
    - Compulsive need for consistent routines

NOTES

- Autoerotic behaviors (rocking)
- Self-mutilation (head-banging)
- Abnormal speech patterns

 o Nursing interventions
- Assess the client's physical and psychologic status.
- Determine the ability of the client's family to understand and cope.
- Facilitate communication between the client and her family.
- Assist the client to reach her optimal level of function.

- Asperger's Disorder – A milder form of autism that displays mild cognitive and/or language delay, and is generally identified late in childhood.
  - o Manifestations
    - Peculiar, repetitive speech patterns
    - Intense and focused areas of interest
    - Higher functioning than true autism
    - Difficulty with peer relationships

 o Nursing interventions
- Encourage one-on-one interactions with the client.
- Use positive reinforcement to encourage desired behaviors.
- Encourage the client to communicate with his family.

- Attention Deficit Hyperactivity Disorder – A chronic biobehavioral disorder that is usually diagnosed in children and characterized by a lack of attention, impulsiveness, and excessive hyperactivity.
  - o Manifestations
    - Difficulty concentrating and easily distracted
    - Poor attention span, failure to complete a task
    - Impulsive actions without thought of possible consequences

 o Nursing Interventions
- Encourage effective communication in the client.
- Assist the client to learn adaptive coping behaviors.

- Assess the client's safety and intervene as needed.
- Initiate educative techniques between the parent(s) and child by using play therapy, family therapy, and/or cognitive-behavioral therapy.

o Medication therapy
- Methylphenidate hydrochloride (Ritalin)
- Amphetamine sulfate (Adderall)
- Dextroamphetamine sulfate (Dexedrine)
- Atomoxetine (Strattera)

SECTION 5
MOOD DISORDERS

- Grief – A profound mental anguish or sense of sorrow, sadness, and mourning as the result of a social, physical, or emotional loss; adaptive grief may last up to 2 years.
  - o Contributing factors
    - Death in the family
    - Separation or divorce
    - Physical illness or disability
    - Failure at work

 o Point to Remember – Unresolved grief produces psychotic and neurotic manifestations such as chronic depression, acting-out behaviors, and psychosomatic disorders.

- Moderate Mood Disorders
  - o Types
    - Dysthymia – chronically depressed mood
    - Cyclothymic – cycles of depression and hypomania (not as severe as mania)
  - o Manifestations
    - Social withdrawal with pessimism
    - Insomnia or hypersomnia
    - Feelings of worthlessness, irritability
    - Low energy, indifference

NOTES

- o Nursing Interventions (based on the severity of the disorder)
  - Refer the client to a support group.
  - Encourage the client to actively seek professional assistance.
- Major Depression – Maladaptive response that interferes with a client's ability or desire to perform usual ADLs.
  - o Manifestations
    - Weight gain or loss
    - Insomnia or overwhelming fatigue
    - Loss of pleasure in usual activities
    - Feelings of helplessness/hopelessness
    - Inability to make decisions or concentrate
    - Social withdrawal or suicidal ideation
    - Poor self-care, pain, and indigestion

  - o Nursing Interventions
    - Promote the physical well-being and/or needs of the client.
    - Communicate with the client to build trust.
    - Initiate suicide precautions with the client.
    - Encourage the client to focus on his strengths.
    - Schedule nonintellectual activity time for the client.
- Suicide – Self-inflicted death stemming from depression, a sense of hopelessness, and/or a loss of desire to live.
  - o Contributing factors
    - Hallucinations or delusions
    - Substance abuse
    - Organic mental disorders
    - Adolescence/older adults
    - Chronic or painful illnesses
  - o Danger signs
    - Giving away personal possessions
    - Completing a will/finalizing business
    - Sudden changes in behavior
    - Previous suicide attempts
    - States, "Everything is figured out."

- o Nursing Interventions
  - Initiate suicide precautions.
  - Never leave the client unattended.
  - Take all of the client's gestures seriously.
  - Remove potentially harmful objects.
  - Understand that it is impossible to "sterilize" the client's environment.
  - Establish a safety contract with the client.
  - Encourage the client to verbalize her feelings.
  - Nurture and maintain positive goals with the client.
- Electroconvulsive Therapy – A medical procedure in which a small amount of electricity is quickly passed through the brain, inducing a grand mal seizure; used for clients who are severely depressed or have not responded to other therapeutic modalities.
  - o Contributing factors
    - Used after other methods have failed
    - Requires consent of the client
    - Electric current is passed through the client's temporal lobe and hypothalamus for 0.1 seconds
    - The nurse may observe a slight grimace or plantar flexion in the client
    - The client may undergo 6 to 10 treatments; three per week

  - o Nursing Interventions
    - The day prior to the procedure, instruct the client to be NPO after midnight.
    - Check and assess the client's preoperative vital signs.
    - Verify that the client has signed the informed consent.
    - Remove the client's jewelry/prosthetics.
    - Have the client empty her bladder.
    - Instruct the client and her family that short-term memory loss is temporary for up to 2 months.
    - Administer preoperative medications to the client as prescribed.

NOTES

ANTIDEPRESSANT AGENTS

Chemical Class	Generic Name	Trade Name	Teaching Points
Tricyclic antidepressants (more adverse reactions)	• imipramine • desipramine • amitriptyline	• Tofranil • Norpramin • Elavil	May cause cardiovascular effects such as arrhythmias, conduction disturbances, and T wave abnormalities
Selective serotonin reuptake inhibitors (SSRIs)	• fluoxetine • sertraline • paroxetine • escitalopram • citalopram	• Prozac • Zoloft • Paxil • Lexapro • Celexa	SSRIs have fewer adverse effects and can be used safely in older adults, but are potentially lethal in cases of accidental or purposeful overdose
Serotonin norepinephrine reuptake inhibitor (SNRI)	• duloxetine • venlafaxine HCL	• Cymbalta • Effexor	Also used in treating diabetic neuropathy
Miscellaneous antidepressants	• trazodone • bupropion HCL	• Desyrel • Wellbutrin/Zyban	• Effective in the treatment of depression • Wellbutrin must be tapered off slowly to prevent seizures. • Wellbutrin must not be given at the same time as Zyban. (Both are different trade names for bupropion.)

Adverse Reactions of Antidepressants		Nursing Interventions	Teaching Points

• Anticholinergic effects (can be treated - usually clear in 1 week)
  o Dry mouth
  o Constipation
  o Urinary retention
  o Blurred vision
  o Aggravated glaucoma
		• Increasing fluids, good oral hygiene
		• Bulk, diet, exercise, stool softeners
		• Monitoring I&O
		• Corrective lenses or large print
		• Ophthalmologist consult
			All antidepressant medications can cause dry mouth, constipation, blurred vision, drowsiness, and hypotension; these are treatable side effects.

• Cardiovascular effects
  o Postural hypotension
  o Direct effects on the heart: tachycardia, arrhythmia, conduction defects
  o Fluid retention secondary to irregular rhythm and ineffective pumping action: can lead to heart failure
		• Take blood pressure regularly, sitting and standing to monitor cardiovascular effects
		• Use smaller divided doses in clients with known heart disease; avoid in those with recent MI.
		• Weigh the client daily; check for fluid retention
			• The provider should do an ECG prior to prescribing antidepressants to check for undiagnosed heart disease.
			• Teach clients to take own pulse at home; have blood pressure checked frequently, and report weight gain of more than 2 lb in 24 hr to the provider.

o Photosensitivity
  o Insomnia
  o Tremors and seizures
  o Excessive perspiration
  o Erection/orgasm difficulty (may cause noncompliance)
		• Protect skin with clothing, carefully check for sunburn
		• Single morning dose
		• Monitor client for new onset tremors or seizures
		• Observe, report, provide comfort measures.
		• Switch to a lower dose or to a less anticholinergic preparation.
			• Encourage the client to wear sunscreen at all times, even during overcast days.
			• Advise the client to avoid caffeinated beverages.
			• Advise the client to shower frequently, and wear light cotton clothing.

Medication Interactions	Adverse Reactions	Teaching Points
MAOIs	14-day waiting period before changing from MAOI to antidepressant or vice versa	Do not use tricyclic or SSRIs concurrently with MAOIs
Antihypertensives and heart medications	Causes hypotension or hypertension	Report chest pain or palpitations to the provider immediately.
Antacids	Inhibits absorption	Do not use antacids without consulting the provider.
CNS depressants/alcohol	Potentiated effects	

ANTIDEPRESSANT AGENTS: MAOIS

Chemical Class	Generic Name	Trade Name
MAOIs	• isocarboxazid • phenelzine • tranylcypromine	• Marplan • Nardil • Parnate

Adverse Reactions	Nursing Interventions	Teaching Points
Hypertensive crisis: elevated blood pressure, palpitations, diaphoresis, chest pain, and headache that can lead to intracranial hemorrhage and death	Monitor client's blood pressure and assess for report of headache.	Teach client to avoid foods with high tyramine content such as aged cheeses, femented foods, chocolate, liver, bean pods, yeast, sausage and bologna, beer, Chianti and vermouth wines; limit amounts of ETOH, sour cream, yogurt, raisins, soy sauce; teach client to avoid OTC and prescription medications such as antidepressants, sedatives, cough and cold preparations, which interact to produce hypertensive crisis
Anticholinergic disturbances: dry mouth, constipation	Increase fluids, bulk in diet, and exercise.	
CNS effects: drowsiness, fatigue, headache, restlessness	Some can be expected to last for a short period; increase activity, short afternoon naps	
Insomnia	Give single morning dose; relax several hours before bedtime.	

Medication Interactions	Adverse Reactions	Medication Alerts
Tricyclic antidepressants Dibenzoxazepines	Hypertensive crisis	Must wait 2 weeks before changing to a different antidepressant medication
CNS depressants	Decrease liver function	
Amphetamines	Potentiate action	

ANTIMANIA AGENTS AND MOOD STABILIZERS

Chemical Class	Generic Name	Trade Name	Teaching Points
• Lithium ○ Blood level: 0.8 to 1.5 mEq/L, therapeutic; above 1.5 mEq/L, toxic; 2.0 mEq/L, lethal	• lithium	• Eskalith • Lithonate	• A client who is to start lithium should be ruled out for thyroid, cardiac, and renal problems first; lithium should be discontinued prior to surgery, ECT, and pregnancy; it is essential to monitor lithium levels routinely to maintain a therapeutic range. • Half-life is 24 hr
• Anticonvulsants	• valproic acid • gabapentin • carbamazepine	• Depakote • Neurontin • Tegretol	• Depakote should not be used in clients with liver or hepatic disease; must monitor LFTs, CBCs. • Do not stop anticonvulsant medication suddenly, may have seizures. • Anticonvulsants are used in the maintenance treatment of bipoloar disorder to act as a mood stabilizer.

ANTIPSYCHOTIC AGENTS

Chemical Class	Trade Name	Teaching Points
Phenothiazine	• Thorazine	• Photosensitivity • Orthostatic hypotension
Phenothiazine	• Mellaril	
Phenothiazine	• Prolixin • Trilafon • Stelazine	At greater risk for extrapyramidal effects (EPS)
Butyrophenone	• Haldol	
Dibenzoxazepine	• Clozaril • Seroquel	• Can cause agranulocytosis • Weekly CBCs required
Thienobenzodiazepine	• Zyprexa	• Mirrored after Clozaril • Does not require weekly CBCs • Can cause significant weight gain.
Benzisoxazole	• Risperdal • Geodon	• Less risk of EPS • Can be used safely in older-adult clients

Adverse Reactions in Antipsychotic Medications	Nursing Interventions	Medication Alert
Sedation	Most comon in low potency antipsychotics; entire dose can be given at bedtime	Sedation is common in Thorazine and Mellaril.
Extrapyramidal effects (EPS): parkinsonian symptoms (e.g., fine hand tremors, pill rolling, drooling)	Report to the primary care provider; mediations may be changed; or antiparkinsonian medication given to control manifestations	EPS is usually associated with high potency (Stelazine, Haldol)

ANTIPSYCHOTIC AGENTS

Dystonia: muscle spasm of the face and neck; eyes rolling back in head	Reports to provider; usually an antiparkinsonian medication is given or the antipsychotic medication is changed.	Dystonia is most common in males taking Haldol, Prolixin, Stelazine.
Akathisia: restlessness, inability to sit still	Call provider; may treat with antiparkinsonian medications, may need to change antipsychotic medication	Akathisia is associated with the use of antipsychotics, lithium, benzodiazipines, and L-dopa medications.
Tardive dyskinesia: lip smacking, involuntary tongue protrusion, jerking of the head and neck, extension and flexion of the fingers, back and forth movement of the spine	Careful observation in clients on long-term use; discontinue medication at first sign to prevent permanent disability; abnormal involuntary movement scale (AIMS) is used to assess clients for permanent disability	Frequently assess the client for adverse movement reaction. Also, teach the client/family to notify the nurse of any new and/or unusual movements.
• Anticholinergic • Dry mouth • Constipation • Urinary retention • Blurred vision • Nasal congestion • Orthostatic hypotension • Caution client to stand up slowly	• Provide candies, fluids. • Provide laxatives; modify diet • Monitor I&O. • Client teaching: effects transient and disappear in a week. • Increase humidity • Monitor blood pressure using orthostatic measurements.	Thorazine, Mellaril, Risperdal, and Zyprexa have potential to cause orthostatic hypotension, especially in older adults
Photosensitivity	Sunscreen; cover up with clothing	Thorazine: exposure to sun causes dark purplish pigmentation of skin.
Agranulocytosis	Observe for signs of infection or nosebleeds report immediately to the provider if present; discontinue medication; monitor weekly CBCs.	Most often seen with Clozaril
Retinopathy	Sunglasses	Thorazine and Mellaril may cause retinopathy
Neuroleptic malignant syndrome (NMS) (Can be fatal)	Discontinue medication and report immediately if manifestations occur (altered consciousness, unstable blood pressure and pulse, fever, muscle rigidity, diaphoresis	Teach the client to report any flu-like symptoms or fever immediately; an extreme emergency situation.
• Decreased libido • Appetite increase, weight gain	• Decrease dose or change medication. • Exercise/diet regimen	• Neuroendocrine effects are most often seen with Mellaril; these symptoms are related to decreased hypothalamic function. • Most common adverse effect of Zyprexa is weight gain; Seroquel is an alternative medication to use if the client has extreme weight gain.
Drug Interactions: MAOIs, Anticonvulsants		

ANTIPSYCHOTIC AGENTS

Medication Interactions	Adverse Reactions	Teaching Points
• Diuretics • Antipsychotics • Sodium bicarbonate • ECT/surgery • Pregnancy	• Increase risk or lithium toxicity, do not use with Haldol • Promote excretion, lowering serum level • May cause neurotoxicity • Crosses placental barrier	• Do not take while pregnant; must be discontinued prior to any surgical procedure. • Monitor levels carefully in hot weather if prone to excessive sweating due to loss of sodium.

SLEEP AGENTS

Chemical Class	Generic Name	Trade Name	Teaching Points
Benzodiazepine	• flurazepam • temazepam • lorazepam	• Dalmane • Restoril • Ativan	• For short-term use to treat insomnia • Teach client not to increase dose or stop medication suddenly. • Monitor for paradoxical hyperactivity, especially in older adults and children
Newer sleep agents	• zolpidem • eszopiclone	• Ambien • Lunesta	• For short-term treatment of insomnia.

NOTES

SUBSTANCE ABUSE			
Drug	Manifestations of Intoxication	Withdrawal Manifestations	Nursing Interventions
Hallucinogens – LSD, marijuana, "gateway drugs"	Flushing of skin, dilated pupils, transient increase in pulse rate and blood pressure, hallucinations, psychosis, paranoia	None	• Treat with diazepam (Valium) to decrease anxiety. • Stay with the client to provide verbal reassurance and emotional support; flashbacks may occur for several months.
Stimulants – amphetamines, cocaine (see below)	Restlessness, irritability, anxiety, tachycardia, cardiac arrhythmia, paranoia, psychosis with clear sensorium, elation, psychotic behavior, weight loss with prolonged use	• High doses are associated with a rapid withdrawal • Persecutory delusions • Aggressiveness and hostility • Anxiety • Psychomotor agitation • Suicidal ideations	• The client may need antianxiety medications to manage aggression and hostility. • Monitor the client for safety issues, particularly suicide attempts; psychiatric hospitalization for severe withdrawal symptoms.
Cocaine/crack	• Same as for amphetamines • Overdose: syncope, chest pain, seizures, death may result from cardiac and respiratory failure; • High-dose use: visual and tactile hallucinations and "cocaine bugs"	• Sleepiness, depression, malaise and fatigue, poor concentration, irritability, "cocaine craving," psychosis • Use of cocaine during pregnancy may cause a stroke in the fetus	• Hospitalize clients who are high-dose "crack" or freebase users or poly addicted. • Monitor the client for hallucinations during withdrawal. • Monitor the client for respiratory depression, which can be treated as outpatient, but this is less successful.
Opiates – heroin, morphine, Dilaudid, Demerol, codeine, methadone	Mitosis, euphoria, drowsiness, dysphoria, apathy, psychomotor retardation, slurred speech, impaired attention or memory, impaired social judgement; chronic use can lead to manourishment, criminal behavior, STDs, HIV/AIDS with IV drug use	Withdrawal begins 8 to 12 hr after and lasts for 3 to 5 days; severity varies with the extent of abuse; lacrimation, rhinorrhea, sweating, piloerection, diarrhea, yawning, mild hypertension, tachycardia, fever, insomnia, dilated pupils, restlessness, abdominal cramps, anxiety	The client can quit "cold turkey" or medically manage his addiction with antianxiety agents, methadone or clonidine (Catapres).
Sedative-hypnotics – barbiturates, benzodiazepines, lorazepam (Ativan), chlordiazepoxide (Librium), diazepam (Valium), alprazolam (Xanax)	Mental impairment, confusion, and lack of motor coordination, depression; frequently used with alcohol	Weakness, insomnia, nausea, postural hypotension develops within the first 48 hr; seizures may occur at any time; delirium may develop between days 3 and 7	• Manifestations can be a medical emergency, and hospitalization is required. • Monitor the client for sudden seizure activity. Anticonvulsants may be used to prevent precipitous withdrawal.

- Understand that general anesthesia will be used.
- Succinylcholine chloride (Anectine) is given to relax the client's muscles.
- Atropine sulfate dries the client's secretions and blocks vagal reflexes.

  o Postprocedure interventions
  - Maintain a patent airway.
  - Monitor the client's vital signs every 15 min until they are stable.
  - Observe the client for decreased respirations, which are an adverse effect of succinylcholine chloride.
  - Frequently reorient the client with himself, place, and time.
  - Assist the client to ambulate as soon as possible.
  - Provide the client with symptomatic relief for residual nausea or vomiting.

SECTION 6

PERSONALITY DISORDERS

- Antisocial/sociopath – Unstable personality traits reflecting maladaptive chronic inflexibility with impaired social and emotional functioning.
  o Contributing factors
  - Genetic abnormalities
  - Can be learned responses
  - Deficient ego/superego development
  - Inappropriate or nonexistent parent and child relationship
  o Manifestations
  - Lack of remorse or guilt
  - Inability or refusal to accept responsibility
  - Failure at school/work/relationships
  - Superficial, but manipulative charm/wit
  - Reckless disregard for rights of others
  - Delinquency and violation of rules
  - Does not seek treatment and behavior does not change with punishment

- Borderline Personality – A behavioral disorder characterized by instability of moods and an altered sense of self.
  o Contributing factors
  - Mostly seen in women
  - Can be learned responses
  - Poor parental relationships
  o Manifestations
  - Impulsive, unpredictable, and self-destructive behaviors (sex/gambling)
  - Intense, unstable relationships
  - Manipulative, splitting behaviors
  - Intolerance of being alone, easily bored
  - Identity disturbance, poor self-image
  - Self-mutilation, suicidal gestures
  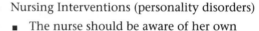 o Nursing Interventions (personality disorders)
  - The nurse should be aware of her own feelings.
  - Confront the client regarding his behaviors.
  - Set clear rules and boundaries with the client.
  - Reinforce consequences with the client for rule violations.
  - Protect other clients from the client's physical and verbal abuse.
  - Establish a contract for behavioral changes.
  - Use group therapy to identify the client's manipulative behaviors and encourage accountability.

SECTION 7

SUBSTANCE ABUSE

- Substance-Related Disorders – A client's use of psychotropic drugs, including alcohol, to the extent of significant interference where his physical, social, and/or emotional well-being is characterized by a preoccupation with obtaining and/or using a particular substance(s).
  o Contributing factors
  - Genetic predisposition
  - Peer pressure and availability
  - Low self-esteem or socioeconomic status

NOTES

- Inappropriate coping skills
- Family, work, and/or relationship problems
- Isolation and withdrawal
  - ○ Psychological/behavioral effects
    - Reduces anxiety and promotes a false sense of well-being
    - Decreases inhibitions and the ability to reason
  - ○ Addiction – Physical dependence that occurs with long-term use of a substance.
  - ○ Dependence – A psychologic need for a substance.
  - ○ Nursing Intervention – Based on type of substance, length of addiction, and presence of multiple drugs or comorbidities.
- Alcohol Abuse and Dependence – Alcohol is a CNS depressant that affects all systems of the body, eventually creating a compulsive physical and psychological need for alcohol.
  - ○ Manifestations of long-term use
    - CNS system – progresses from mild dysphoria to impaired motor activities, psychosis, stupor, seizures, and Wernicke-Korsakoff syndrome
    - Neuro system – memory loss, ataxia, and confusion secondary to thiamine and niacin deficiencies
    - Cardiac system – arrhythmias, myopathy, and hypertension
    - Gastrointestinal system – gastritis, cirrhosis, pancreatitis, ulcers, and esophageal varices
    - Respiratory system – COPD (secondary to the use of cigarettes while drinking), pneumonia, and cancer
    - Genitourinary system – fetal alcohol syndrome (in pregnant women) and decreased libido
    - Skin – spider angiomas and fractures
    - Emotional effects
    - Impulsive or abusive behavior
    - Poor judgment and loss of memory
    - Family dysfunction/job loss
    - Depression and low self-esteem

- Isolation/suicide
- Alcohol Withdrawal Syndrome – Painful physical manifestations that develop within 6 to 8 hr of the abstinence of alcohol.
  - ○ Manifestations – reflects stimulation of the autonomic nervous system
    - Shakiness and tremors
    - Anxiety and mood swings/insomnia
    - Confusion and elevated vital signs
  - ○ Nursing Interventions (based on the degree of intoxication and addiction)
    - Initiate fluid replacement (generally IV).
    - Administer antianxiety medications (benzodiazepines, such as chlordiazepoxide [Librium], diazepam [Valium], or oxazepam [Seraz]).
    - Replace depleted vitamins (thiamine/niacin).
    - Decrease stimuli and reorient the client frequently.
    - Administer antidiarrheal medication.
    - Avoid restraining the client.
    - Implement a high-protein, low-fat, low-salt, high-carbohydrate diet.
- Delirium Tremens – Acute state of advanced withdrawal that occurs 2 to 48 hr after a client's last drink and can be fatal if not treated within 72 hr.
  - ○ Manifestations – All manifestations of withdrawal plus the following
    - Disorientation and confusion
    - Visual and auditory hallucinations
    - Seizures and death
  - ○ Nursing Interventions
    - Provide a quiet, dimly lit room.
    - Provide rest and nutrition.
    - Observe the client for physical complications.
    - Monitor the client for depression and suicide.
    - Provide firm limits/monitor the client's visitors.

NOTES

- o Discharge teaching
  - Encourage the client to participate in a rehabilitation program such as Alcoholics Anonymous.
  - Disulfiram (Antabuse) is given to deter the use of alcohol, which is a type of aversion therapy to sensitize the client to alcohol.
  - If the client ingests alcohol while taking disulfiram, a physical reaction occurs, which includes symptoms of shock, chest pain, dyspnea, confusion, with circulatory collapse, and death.
  - Medication cannot be initiated until 2 weeks after the client's last drink. If the client stops medication, no alcohol can be consumed for at least 2 weeks.
  - Warn the client about "hidden alcohol": mouthwash, after-shave lotions, cough syrup and salad dressings.

SECTION 8

ORGANIC MENTAL DISORDERS

- Delirium – An acute brain disorder resulting in psychological or behavioral behaviors secondary to an identifiable and reversible cause.
  - o Etiology
    - Medical
      - □ Fever/infection
      - □ Acid/base or electrolyte imbalances
    - Surgical
      - □ Anesthesia/blood loss
    - Pharmacological
      - □ Medication interactions
      - □ Overdose of medication
    - Neurological
      - □ Cerebrovascular accident/intracranial pressure
      - □ Brain tumor
  - o Manifestations (based on cause)
    - Sleep disturbances and restlessness
    - Short attention span, easily distracted
    - Disorganized speech patterns/illusions

- Dementia – A chronic, progressive deterioration of the cognitive processes, personality and motor skills, as well as a loss of behavioral control.
  - o General manifestations
    - Insidious onset, often attributed to aging
    - Deterioration of personality and judgment
    - Language disorders (confabulation)
    - Loss of thought process and memory
  - o Types
    - Wernicke-Korsakoff syndrome (dementia related to alcoholism)
    - Long- and short-term memory loss
    - Confabulation and confusion
    - Polyneuritis/ataxia
    - Flat affect/learning impaired
    - Alzheimer's disease – Primary degenerative dementia, cause unknown.
      - □ Onset – generally affects those who are 45 years old or older
      - □ Progressive; usually 5 to 15 years
      - □ Disorientation/agitation
      - □ Forgetting words and meanings
      - □ Delusions/hallucinations/paranoia
      - □ Physical deterioration
  - o Nursing interventions (follow Maslow's criteria)
    - Manage the client's physical symptoms first.
    - Give the client finger foods and small meals.
    - Provide opportunities for the client to exercise and rest (range of motion, walks).
    - Allow the client frequent rest periods.
    - Monitor the client's I&O and limit bed time fluids. The client may need stool softeners.
    - Encourage ADLs.
    - Allow the client to be independent.
    - Promote client safety.
    - Optimize the client's cognitive abilities.
    - Maintain consistency and simple routines.
    - Frequently reorient the client and use visual cues.
    - Provide socialization opportunities.

NOTES

- Use alternative therapies (music, pets, children).

- o Point to Remember – A nurse's responsibility is to focus on the basic principles of care for the client who is cognitively impaired while facilitating the highest level of safe and independent function.

SECTION 9

EATING DISORDERS

- Anorexia Nervosa – An eating disorder characterized by an extreme fear of obesity and altered perception of one's own body weight.
  - o Contributing factors
    - Adolescent struggles with independence
    - Poor self-image, loss of control/introvert
    - Family issues (conflict, chaos, denial)
    - Type-A personality/manipulative
  - o Manifestations
    - Usually manifests between ages 13 to 22
    - Preoccupied with food/weight
    - More than 20% under normal body weight
    - Muscle atrophy, emaciated, no fatty tissue
    - Dryness of hair/presence of lanugo
    - Hypotension/amenorrhea
    - Electrolyte imbalances – death due to cardiac arrhythmias

  - o Nursing interventions
    - Monitor the client for the need to be hospitalized.
    - Provide appropriate nutrition for the client.
    - Monitor the client for 30 to 60 min after meals.
    - Do not allow the client to exercise after meals.
    - Initiate a behavior-modification plan.
    - Give positive reinforcement for weight gain.

- Bulimia – An uncontrollable compulsion to consume large amounts of food in a short period of time (binging), followed by a compensatory need to rid the body of the calories consumed, usually accomplished by inducing vomiting (purging).
  - o Contributing factors
    - Family genetics/family problems
    - Excessive parental and peer pressure
    - Distorted body image/feelings of ineffectiveness/extrovert
  - o Manifestation
    - Onset between ages 15 to 26
    - Normal or slightly overweight
    - Admits eating behavior is abnormal
    - Dental cares/gingival infections
    - Hides/hoards high-calorie foods
    - Binges, then purges – induces vomiting
    - Uses laxatives, diuretics, drugs
    - May have calluses on back of hands

  - o Nursing Interventions
    - Encourage the client to recognize and verbalize feelings.
    - Promote acceptance of self-responsibility.
    - Set limits to provide consistency.
    - Initiate family therapy.
    - Refer the client to self-help groups.

  - o Point to Remember – Clients who have eating disorders are extremely resistant to change and progress may be slow. However, eating disorders are life-threatening, so a nurse must focus on reinforcing the seriousness to a client.

SECTION 10

DEVELOPMENTAL DISABILITIES

- Mental Retardation – Deficits in adaptive abilities and intellectual functioning with noted alterations in developmental growth and self-care deficiencies.

NOTES

- o Etiology
  - Genetic (chromosomal)
    - Down syndrome (trisomy 21) – Congenital mental retardation with motor involvement.
    - Klinefelter's syndrome (XXY) – Gonadal defect with subnormal intelligence and social adaptation.
  - Errors of metabolism
    - Phenylketonuria (PKU) – Accumulation of phenylalanine, which is toxic to the brain; retardation may be limited through strict dietary avoidance of phenylalanine.
    - Tay-Sachs Disease – Inherited disorder generally in families of Jewish descent, in which lipid metabolism causes mental retardation, blindness and muscle weakness.
  - Acquired
    - Prenatal – viruses/toxins
    - Perinatal – anoxia/injury/disease (rubella)
    - Postnatal – infections/poisons/abuse
- o Levels of mental retardation (based on standard IQ ranges; normal is 80 to 110)
  - Mild – IQ range of 50 to 70
    - May be self-sufficient as an adult
    - Can learn vocational skills
    - Mental age of approximately 8 to 10 years
  - Moderate – IQ range of 35 to 49
    - Can perform simple ADLs
    - Poor awareness of social interactions
    - May perform skills, but needs close supervision
    - Mental age of 5 to 6 years
  - Severe – IQ range of 20 to 34
    - Needs constant supervision/care
    - Poor motor and speech skills
    - Mental age of a toddler
  - Profound – IQ below 20
    - No self-care ability
    - Mental age of an infant

- o Nursing Interventions
  - Assess the client's physical needs/abilities.
  - Determine the client's developmental level based on Erikson's stages.
  - Assist the parents with the grieving process and encourage participation in support groups.
  - Refer the client to available community resources.

- o Point to Remember – A client who has a developmental disability may still have a full range of emotions and is subject to all mental illnesses.

SECTION 11

FAMILY VIOLENCE

- Family Violence – Purposeful infliction of physical, verbal, or emotional harm occurring within families of all socioeconomic levels, across all races, and cultural lines.
  - o Contributing factors
    - History of previous family violence
    - Caregiver is experiencing family stress
    - Victim is physically or cognitively impaired
    - Victim is isolated
  - o Types of abuse
    - Physical – unsolicited use of force that results in injury, pain, or impairment
    - Emotional – inflicting mental anguish through threats, humiliation or intimidation
    - Sexual – nonconsensual or illegal sexual contact
    - Neglect – failure to provide essential food, clothing, shelter, or medical, including abandonment
    - Social isolation – from other family members or outside support systems
    - Economic – (particularly among older adults) includes theft, embezzlement, or misuse of life savings
  - o Characteristics of perpetrator
    - Poor coping skills/low self-esteem

NOTES

- Has anxiety/abuses substances
- Victim of previous childhood abuse
- Impulsive/immature/poor anger management
- Characteristics of victim
  - Feelings of helplessness/hopelessness/suicide
  - Submissive/fearful of being harmed
  - Emotionally dependent on abuser
  - Codependency issues
- Manifestations
  - Frequent emergency room visits in which explanation of injuries does not fit the pathology of the injury
  - Unexplained fractures (especially spiral), burns, bruises/difficulty walking
  - Poor hygiene/hunger/dehydration
  - Venereal disease or STDs, especially in children
  - Anxiety/fear/hesitant to speak openly
  - Depression/runaway behaviors/anger
  - Suicidal ideation or attempts
- Nursing Interventions
  - Identify signs of abuse in all clients, particularly those who are < 18 or > 65.
  - Be aware that most adult victims will deny being abused due to the fear of reprisal or shame.
  - Build trust/be nonjudgmental toward the client.
  - Ask specific details of the client and look for inconsistencies.
  - Offer assistance in seeking a safe shelter.
  - Report all suspected cases of child and/or older adult abuse to the appropriate group (the nurse does not have to prove that abuse occurred). The burden of proof belongs to the legal system.
  - Assist the client to identify support systems and crisis intervention resources.
  - Encourage the client to keep clothes, money, and important papers in a safe location.

SECTION 12
SEXUAL ASSAULT (RAPE)

- Rape – A violent crime involving nonconsensual forced sexual contact.
  - False concepts regarding rape
    - The victim is promiscuous.
    - The victim provoked the event through a mode of dress or actions.
    - Only women are raped.
    - Victims cannot be raped against their will.
    - Only young adults are raped.
  - Manifestations
    - Experiences Rape Trauma syndrome
    - Fear and disorganized thinking
    - Physical and emotional stress
    - May have nightmares and flashbacks
    - Will eventually face family or relationship dysfunctions
- Nursing Interventions
  - The client will initially need a safe/secure environment.
  - Stay with the client to offer emotional support/empathy.
  - Encourage the client to verbalize feelings.
  - Do not begin the exam until the client is ready.
  - Allow for choices to help the client regain her sense of control.
  - Take a detailed history and perform an assessment.
  - Collect evidence in the presence of law enforcement and according to the facility policy to preserve the chain of evidence.
  - Arrange for a follow up to check for STDs/AIDS.
  - Refer the client to counseling for posttraumatic stress disorder.

NOTES

SECTION 13

LEGAL ASPECTS OF MENTAL HEALTH NURSING

- Types of Admissions
  - Voluntary
    - Admits self
    - Consents to all treatment
    - Can refuse treatment, including medications, unless a danger to self or others
    - Can demand and receive discharge
  - Involuntary
    - Client deemed by lawful authority to be a danger to self or others.
    - At the end of a specified time, the client must have a hearing or be released.
  - Informed consent required for
    - Electroconvulsive therapy
    - Medications
    - Seclusion
    - Restraints
  - Client rights
    - Right to receive or refuse treatment
    - Access to stationery and postage
    - Receipt of unopened mail
    - Visits by health care provider/attorney or clergy
    - Daily interaction with visitors or phone access
    - Have and/or spend money
    - Storage space for personal items
    - Own property/vote/marry
    - Make wills and contracts
    - Access educational resources
    - Sue, or be sued, including challenging one's hospitalization
  - Point to Remember – A nurse's priority is to promote and provide care to a client in the least restrictive environment possible.

NOTES

MENTAL HEALTH TERMS

Terms	Definitions
Affect	Mood or feeling tone
Akathisia	Regular restless movements or pacing
Anhedonia	Inability to experience pleasure
Apraxia	Loss of purposeful motor movements
Associative Looseness	Disturbance of thinking in which ideas shift from one subject to another in unrelated themes
Binge	Ingestion of large quantities of food in a short period of time
Blackouts	A person that drinks heavily and appears to function normally, but later is unable to recall prior events
Catatonia	State of psychological immobilization that can revert to episodes of extreme agitation
Clanging	Meaningless rhyming of words
Comorbidity	The prescence of one or more disorders (or diseases) in addition to a primary disease or disorder; often used to identify when a client has manifestations of both physical illness and a psychiatric illness
Compulsion	Repetitive purposeless ritualistic behavior performed in accordance with specific rules or routine manner in an attempt to reduce anxiety
Concrete Thinking	Thinking characterized by immediate experiences rather than abstract thought
Confabulation	A compensatory mechanism for memory loss; filling in the memory gaps with imaginary stories the tell believes to be true
Countertransference	Experience where the therapist transfers his or her feelings for significant others onto the client
Crisis	A conflict that cannot readily be resolved by using usual coping mechanisms
Defense Mechanisms	Mental strategies used to help cope with areas of conflict
Delusion	A fixed false belief held to be true even with evidence to the contrary
Denial	Unconscious attempt to escape unpleasant realities by denying their existence
Desensitization	Gradual systematic exposure of the client to feared situations under controlled conditions
Dissociation	Disturbance in the integrated organization of memory, identity, perception, or consciousness
Echolalia	Repetition by one person of what is said by another
Echopraxia	A meaningless imitation of movement
Enabling	Helping a chemically dependent person avoid experiencing the consequence of his or her drinking or drug use
Extrapyramidal Reaction	A reversible side effect of some psychotropic drugs characterized by muscle rigidity, drooling, restlessness, shuffling gait, and blurred vision
Flight of Ideas	Rapid flow of speech in which the person jumps from one idea to another before the first idea had been concluded
Grandiosity	Exaggerated belief or claim about one's importance or identity
Grief	An emotional response to a recognized loss
Hallucination	False sensory perception without external stimuli that can involve any of the senses
Hypomania	An elevated mood with symptoms less severe than those of mania
Ideas of Reference	False impressions that outside events have special meaning for oneself
Illusions	Misinterpretation of a real, external sensory experience
Insight	Understanding and awareness of the reasons and meanings behind one's motives and behaviors
Judgment	The ability to make logical or rational decisions
Labile	Having rapidly shifting emotions

MENTAL HEALTH TERMS	
Terms	Definitions
Limit Setting	Clear statement of rules with consistent reinforcement
Mania	Unstable elevated mood
Manipulation	Behavior that is self-directed to get needs met at the expense of others
Milieu Therapy	Management of the client's environment to promote a positive living experience and facilitate recovery
Narcissism	Self-involvement with lack of empathy for others
Neologism	Coined word with special meaning to the user
Neuroleptic Malignant Syndrome	A rare and sometimes fatal reaction to high-potency antipsychotic medications. Symptoms include muscle rigidity, fever, and elevated WBC
Obsession	Repetitive, uncontrollable thought
Paranoid	Irritable suspicions of distrust that are defended without basis in reality
Phobia	A persistent, irrational fear of a specific object, activity or situation, as the result of severe unrelieved anxiety.
Premorbid	Occuring before development of a disease
Psychosis	State in which there is impairment in a person's ability to recognize reality, communicate and relate to others appropriately
Purging	Purposeful vomiting or elimination of a substance that has been ingested
Reframing	A technique that involved changing one's viewpoint of a situation and replacing it with another viewpoint that alters the entire meaning
Secondary Gains	Benefits from being ill, such as attention
Self-esteem	The degrees of feeling worthwhile or valued
Self-image	One's thoughts about one's own self
Somatization	The expression of a psychological stress through physical symptoms
Splitting	The tendency to label individuals into "all good" or "all bad" categories
Tardive Dyskinesia	Irreversible, involuntary tonic muscular spasms of the tongue, fingers, toes, neck, and pelvis that results from long-term use of antipsychotic medications
Transference	Unconscious phenomenon in which feelings, attitudes, and wishes toward significant others in one's early life are linking to and projected onto others, usually a therapist in one's current life
Waxy Flexibility	The extremities remain in a fixed position for a long period of time
Word Salad	Spoken words and phrases having no apparent meaning or logic

NOTES

UNIT FIVE

MATERNAL NEWBORN NURSING

SECTION 1

FEMALE REPRODUCTIVE NURSING

Pregnancy

- Female Reproductive Organs
  - Ovaries
  - Fallopian tubes
  - Uterus
  - Cervix
  - Vagina
- Fertilization and Fetal Development
  - Conception (fertilization) – union of sperm and ovum
    - Conditions necessary for fertilization
      - Mature egg and sperm
      - Timing of deposit of sperm
        - Lifetime of ovum is 24 hr
        - Lifetime of sperm in female genital tract is 72 hr
        - Menstruation begins approximately 14 days after ovulation if conception has not occurred.
      - Climate of the female genital tract
        - Vaginal and cervical secretions are less acidic during ovulation (sperm cannot survive in a highly acidic environment)
        - Cervical secretions are thinner during ovulation (sperm can penetrate more easily)
    - Process of fertilization (7 to 10 days)
      - Ovulation occurs
      - Ovum travels to fallopian tube
      - Sperm travels to fallopian tube
      - One sperm penetrates the ovum
      - Zygote forms (fertilized egg)
      - Zygote migrates to uterus
      - Zygote implants in uterine wall

- Progesterone and estrogen are secreted by the corpus luteum to maintain the lining of the uterus and prevent menstruation until the placenta starts producing these hormones (note – progesterone is a thermogenic hormone that raises body temperature, an objective sign that ovulation has occurred).
- Placental development
  - Chorionic villi develop that secrete human chorionic gonadotropin (HCG), which stimulates production of estrogen and progesterone from the corpus luteum (production of HCG begins on the day of implantation and can be detected by day 6).
  - Chorionic villi burrow into the endometrium, forming the placenta.
  - The placenta secretes HCG, human placental lactogen (HPL), and (by week 3) estrogen and progesterone.
- Fetal membranes develop and surround the embryo and fetus
  - Amnion – inner membrane
  - Chorion – outer membrane
  - Umbilical cord
    - Two arteries carrying deoxygenated blood to the placenta
    - One vein carrying oxygenated blood to the fetus
    - No pain receptors
    - Encased in Wharton's jelly (thick substance that surrounds the umbilical cord that acts as a buffer, preventing pressure on the vein and arteries in the umbilical cord)
    - Covered by chorionic membrane
- Amniotic fluid
  - Production origins
    - Maternal serum during early pregnancy
    - Replaced every 3 hr
    - 800 to 1,200 mL at end of pregnancy

NOTES

ADAPTATIONS TO PREGNANCY

Adaptations to Pregnancy	Trimester	Nursing Interventions
• Gastrointestinal/digestive ○ Nausea/vomiting ○ Constipation, flatulence, and heartburn ○ Bleeding gums ○ Gallstones ○ Heartburn	• 1 • 2, 3 • 2, 3 • 2, 3 • 2, 3	• Instruct the client to eat small frequent meals such as crackers or dry toast before getting up in the morning. Have the client consume dry meals and drink liquids between meals. • Encourage the client to exercise, increase fluid and fiber in her diet, and take stool softeners as recommended by the provider. • Advise the client to use a soft toothbrush for dental care. • Tell the client to avoid foods high in fat. • Instruct the client to eat small frequent meals, avoid spicy and fatty foods, avoid sodium bicarbonates as antacid, and only take antacids that are recommended by the provider.
• Urinary ○ Kidney and renal function increased ○ Renal blood flow and glomerular filtration rate increased by 50% ○ Pressure of uterus on bladder causes urinary frequency and urgency ○ Decrease in bladder tone due to pressure in the pelvic area can cause urinary stasis and infection	• 1, 3 • 2, 3	• Instruct the client to void when she first feels the urge. Have her wear a pad to prevent leaking. • Encourage the client to perform Kegel exercises. • Instruct the client to limit fluid intake minimally only before bedtime. • Instruct the client to report pain or a burning sensation to the provider.
• Breasts ○ Increase in size and nodularity, striae ○ Tenderness and tingling ○ Hypertrophy of Montgomery tubercles ○ Darkening seen around the nipples ○ Colostrum secreted at the end of the third month	• 1 • 1 • 2 • 2 • 2, 3	• Instruct the client to wear a supportive bra. • Encourage the client to wear pads to absorb discharge, and wash breasts with warm water and keep dry. • Advise the client that breast tenderness may interfere with sexual expression.
• Vagina ○ Epithelium undergoes hypertrophy and hyperplasia ○ Increased vascularity, deepening of color to dark red or purple (Chadwick's sign) ○ Increased pH – optimal for growth of Candida albicans (thrush) ○ Increase in discharge; leukorrhea is common	• 1, 2, 3 • 1	• Instruct client about normal changes associated with pregnancy. • Instruct the client to report itching and burning to the provider. • Instruct the client to bathe daily and avoid douching and nylon undergarments.

ADAPTATIONS TO PREGNANCY

Adaptations to Pregnancy	Trimester	Nursing Interventions
• Respiratory system ○ Maternal oxygen requirement increases in response to increased metabolic rate, tissue mass, and fetal needs ○ Diaphragm is pushed upward; ribcage flares out; breathing changes from abdominal to chest ○ Increase in oxygen consumption by 15% ○ Stuffiness, epitaxis, and changes in the voice occur as a result of increased estrogen levels ○ Dyspnea – shortness of breath is common with exertion due to pressure on the diaphragm	• 1 • 3 • 3	• Encourage the client to use relaxation techniques that focus on deep breathing. • Advise the client that cool moist air may help to alleviate symptoms of stuffiness. Instruct her to avoid over-the-counter decongestants and sprays. • Instruct her maintain an upright posture and sleep with head propped up.
• Skin ○ Areola darkens ○ Abdominal striae, linea nigra ○ Diaphoresis – secondary to increased sebaceous and sweat gland activity ○ Chloasma – mask of pregnancy ○ Vascular spider nervi; chest, neck, arms, and legs	• 2, 3	• Instruct the client that skin changes are not preventable and usually disappear slowly after delivery. • Remind the client to keep her skin clean and dry.
• Metabolism/nutrition ○ Basal metabolic rate increase, but varies considerably in women; returns to nonpregnant level approximately 5 to 6 days after delivery ○ The client may experience heat intolerance ○ Due to the increase in maternal blood volume and fetal growth, dietary iron needs to increase. ○ A pattern of weight gain is important and recommendation is determined by prepregnancy weight (normal – 11 to 16 kg [25 to 35 lb])	• 2, 3 • 2, 3	• Encourage the client to increase rest and sleep, especially in the first trimester. • Instruct the client to increase her caloric intake by 300 kcal/day. • Instruct the client to increase protein intake by 26 g/day. • Instruct the client to increase iron intake to 30 mg/day. • Instruct the client to increase folate (Folic Acid) to 600 mcg/day. • Instruct the client to increase fluid intake to 2 L/day.

ADAPTATIONS TO PREGNANCY

Adaptations to Pregnancy	Trimester	Nursing Interventions
• Cardiovascular		
○ Cardiac output increases by 30% to 50% by 32 weeks of gestation	• 3	
○ Blood volume increases by 50% by the end of the second trimester.	• 2	
○ Plasma volume increases greater than RBC and Hgb, resulting in pseudo anemia		
○ Pulse rate increases by 10 to 15/min; may experience sinus arrhythmia, premature atrial contractions, and premature ventricular systole	• 2	
○ Blood pressure drops slightly in the second trimester due to peripheral dilatation effects of progesterone and returns to normal by the third trimester	• 2, 3	• Provide close supervision to the client who has preexisting heart disease. In a healthy client with no underlying heart disease, no therapy is needed.
○ Peripheral vasodilation allows for normal blood pressure despite increased blood volume	• 1, 3	• Instruct the client to elevate her legs when possible to enhance venous return. Instruct her to avoid standing for long periods of time and constrictive clothing.
○ Varicose veins may develop		
○ Increased tendency to clot due to increase in clotting factors (VII, VIII, IX, and X)		
• Uterus		• Encourage the client to perform Kegel exercises.
○ Growth is influenced by estrogen		• Encourage the client to void frequently.
○ 500 to 1,000-fold increase in capacity		• Elevate legs and avoid standing for long periods of time to relieve increasing pressure;
○ Enlargement from increased vascularity and dilation of blood vessels		• Increase in weight from 2 ounces to approximately 2 pounds by the end of gestation
○ Increase in weight from 2 oz to approximately 2 lb by the end of gestation	• 2, 3	
○ After third month, uterine enlargement is primarily a result of the growing fetus		
○ Uterine anteflexion after 6 weeks of gestation causes the fundus to press on the bladder		
○ Cervical secretions form the mucus plug		
• Endocrine		
○ Increase in size and activity of thyroid		
○ Increase in size and activity of anterior lobe of pituitary		
○ Increase in size and activity of adrenal cortex	• 2, 3	• Review hormones and their effects on pregnancy with the client. Profound changes are essential for pregnancy maintenance.

□ Functions

▸ Maintains constant body temperature of the fetus

▸ Protects from trauma and heat loss

▸ Prevents umbilical cord compression

▸ Facilitates musculoskeletal development by allowing for movement of the fetus

▸ Facilitates symmetric growth and development

▸ A source of oral fluid for the fetus

■ Placental transfer of material to and from the fetus

□ Diffusion across membrane (gases, water, electrolytes)

□ Active transport via enzyme activity (glucose, amino acids, calcium, iron)

□ Pinocytosis – small particles engulfed and carried across the cell (fats)

□ Leakage – small defects in the chorionic villi that cause slight mixing of material and fetal blood cells

□ Nutrients and wastes are exchanged in the placenta, but the blood does not intermingle

- Intrauterine Development

  ○ Preembryonic – conception to day 14

  ○ Embryonic – day 15 to 8 weeks of gestation

  ○ Fetal – 9 to 40 weeks of gestation

  ■ Full term – between 37 and 42 weeks of gestation, or more than 2,500 grams

  ■ Preterm – 20 to 37 weeks of gestation, or between 500 and 2,500 grams

  ■ Postterm – more than 42 weeks of gestation

- Terminology

  ○ Gravida – Number of times a woman has been pregnant, including present pregnancy.

  ■ Variations – primigravida, multigravida

  ○ Para – Number of pregnancies delivered after the age of viability, whether born alive or dead.

  ■ Variations – nullipara, primipara, multipara

○ Five-digit system

■ G – Gravida is the number of pregnancies

■ T – Term births is the number of deliveries after 37 weeks of gestation

■ P – Preterm is the number of preterm deliveries, or deliveries between 20 and 37 weeks of gestation

■ A – Abortions are the number of medical abortions before 20 weeks of gestation or viability

■ L – Number of living children (For GTPA count multiples as one number. For L count the number of living children.)

Signs of Pregnancy

- Presumptive Signs (subjective symptoms or objective signs experienced by the woman that may indicate a pregnancy)

  ○ Amenorrhea – missed periods

  ○ Nausea and vomiting – morning sickness, probably due to HCG; usually lasts about 3 months

  ○ Fatigue – first trimester

  ○ Urinary frequency – caused by an enlarging uterus pressing on bladder

  ○ Breast changes – tenderness and tingling, nipples pronounced, full feeling, increased size, areola darker

  ○ Quickening – mother's perception of fetal movement around 16 to 20 weeks of gestation; fluttering sensation

  ○ Increased pigmentation, linea nigra, and striae gravidarum

- Probable Signs (primarily uterine changes observed by an examiner leading to suspicion of pregnancy)

  ○ Chadwick's sign – a bluish coloration of the mucous membranes of the cervix, vagina, and vulva

  ○ Goodell's sign – softening of cervix; occurs beginning of the third month

  ○ Hegar's sign – softening of the isthmus of the uterus, between the body of the uterus and cervix; occurs around 6 weeks of gestation

---

NOTES

- o Enlargement of abdomen – uterus is just above the symphysis at 8 to 10 weeks of gestation; it's at the umbilicus at 20 to 22 weeks of gestation
- o Braxton-Hicks contractions – painless contractions that occur at irregular periods throughout pregnancy; most commonly felt after 28 weeks of gestation
- o Uterine souffle – soft blowing sound; blood flow to placenta same rate as maternal pulse
- o Pregnancy test positive – HCG in serum and urine
- o Ballottement – can push fetus and feel it rebound
- Positive Signs (can only be explained by a pregnancy)
  - o Fetal heartbeat – by Doppler at 8 to 10 weeks of gestation
  - o Fetal movements – felt by examiner
  - o Fetal outline – on ultrasound

Assessment of Date of Delivery

- Nägele's rule – first day of last menstrual period minus 3 months plus 7 days; in most cases, add 1 year
- Other parameters – fundal height, quickening, sonograms

Physical Adaptations and Discomforts of Pregnancy

- See Adaptations to Pregnancy table on pages 143 to 145.

Teratogenic Effects on Fetal Development

- Teratogen – Nongenetic factor that produces malformations of the fetus; greatest effect on those cells undergoing rapid growth; thus, time is important.
  - o Types
    - Chemical agents (insecticides)
    - Radiation
    - Drugs/medications – alcohol, tetracycline (Sumycin), chemotherapeutic agents, phenytoin (Dilantin), narcotics, nicotine, megavitamins, warfarin (Coumadin), lead, lithium, carbamazepine (Tegretol), and mercury

- Bacteria and viruses
  - □ Syphilis
    - ▸ Spirochete does not cross the placenta until after 18 weeks of gestation. Treat it as soon as possible. Can also be treated later, since penicillin does not cross the placenta.
    - ▸ It can cause late abortions, stillbirths, and congenitally infected infants.
  - □ Gonorrhea – causes injury to the eyes at birth (ophthalmia neonatorum)
  - □ TORCH syndrome – severe effects on the fetus
    - ▸ Toxoplasmosis – protozoan contracted by ingesting raw meat or feces of an infected animal (cats); pregnant women should not change cat litter boxes
    - ▸ Rubella – first trimester most serious; causes congenital heart problems, cataracts, hearing loss; clients cannot receive the rubella vaccine during pregnancy as it is a live virus; if they receive the immunization in the postpartum period, they must understand that they should not become pregnant for at least 3 months
    - ▸ Cytomegalovirus – member of the herpes family; causes congenital and acquired infection; principal organs affected: liver, brain, and blood; most common mode of transmission is respiratory droplet; employees in day care centers, developmentally delayed, and health care settings are especially at high risk
    - ▸ Herpes simplex virus, Type 2 (HSV-2)
      - ▹ It is transmitted to the neonate vaginally in intrauterine cavity or during delivery. Do not deliver the neonate vaginally if active lesions are present.
      - ▹ It affects blood, brain, liver, lungs, CNS, eyes, and skin.

NOTES

▷ Perinatal mortality – 96%; 50% of survivors have neurological or visual abnormalities

☐ Chlamydia – causes conjunctivitis and pneumonia in the newborn

☐ AIDS

▸ Transmitted via breast milk

▸ 25.5% chance of transmission in utero or during delivery

▸ Treatment of mother with zidovudine (AZT) while pregnant can reduce chance of transmission to fetus to approximately 8.3%

Emotional and Psychological Adaptations to Pregnancy

- Stressors
  - Circumstances of pregnancy
  - Meaning of pregnancy to the mother
  - Responsibilities associated with parenthood
  - Available socioeconomic resources
- Development Tasks of Pregnancy
  - First trimester – Accept the biological fact of being pregnant. It is common to feel ambivalent early in the pregnancy.
  - Second trimester – Accept the growing fetus as a newborn that will need to be nurtured.
  - Third trimester – Prepare for the birth and parenting of the newborn.
- Emotional Responses
  - Self-concept related to body image
  - Mood swings related to biophysical and social changes
  - Ambivalence related to fear and anxiety
  - Sexual concerns related to biophysical changes

Prenatal Care

- Initial Assessment
  - Complete history (includes reproductive and obstetrical history)
  - Baseline laboratory data – CBC, blood type and Rh-antibody, urinalysis, STD, streptococcus ß-hemolytic, Group B, alpha-fetoprotein, rubella titer, tuberculosis skin test, test offer of HIV
  - Vital signs, weight, and urine test for protein and glucose
  - Physical exam – fundal height, FHR, fetal activity
  - Recent illness or infection – recent environmental exposures
  - Current medications
  - Internal exam
    - Adequate pelvic outlet, signs of pregnancy (First visit)
    - Cervical changes, especially in last few weeks (ripe cervix)
    - Vaginal smear for *Neisseria gonorrhea*, Chlamydia, streptococcus ß-hemolytic, Group B, human papillomavirus (HPV) cultures, and pap test
  - Family history including genetic disorders
  - Psychosocial assessment
- Health Teaching
  - Nutrition
    - Maternal weight gain recommendation varies according to the appropriateness of the prepregnancy weight
    - Caloric intake should increase by approximately 300 to 400 kcal/day
    - Protein requirements should increase by 25 g throughout pregnancy
    - Iron intake should increase to 30 mg/day
    - Folate intake should increase to 600 mcg/day to prevent neural tube defects
  - Expected discomforts
    - Danger signs (A nurse should be able to differentiate potential complications from the normal discomforts or physical adaptations of pregnancy.)
      - ☐ Ruptured membranes prior to 37 weeks of gestation
      - ☐ Vaginal bleeding
      - ☐ Abdominal pain
      - ☐ Severe headaches

NOTES

- □ Elevated temperature
- □ Dysuria
- □ Blurred vision
- □ Edema of face or hands; epigastric pain
- □ Symptoms of hyper/hypoglycemia
- ○ Childbirth education and alternative birthing methods
  - ■ Childbirth class instruction
    - □ Fetal growth and development
    - □ Breathing exercises
    - □ Positioning for relaxation and comfort
- ○ Follow-up prenatal visits
  - ■ Every 4 weeks until 28 weeks of gestation
  - ■ Every 2 weeks until 28 to 36 weeks of gestation
  - ■ Every week until 36 weeks of gestation to delivery
- Diagnostic Procedures
  - ○ Ultrasound – Consists of high-frequency sound waves that are used to visualize internal organs and tissues of the developing fetus and maternal structures. Allows for early diagnosis of complications, permitting early intervention.
    - ■ Locates placenta
    - ■ Diagnoses multiple pregnancy
    - ■ Identifies congenital anomalies
    - ■ Determines gestational age
  - ○ Nursing Intervention
    - ■ Assure that the client has a full bladder.

Fetal Assessment

- Fetal Monitoring
  - ○ Purpose
    - ■ Determine FHR (normal rate is 110 to 160/min).
    - ■ Recognize periodic changes in FHR.
    - ■ Determine frequency and duration of contractions.

 Point to Remember

- ○ Reassuring FHR patterns consist of a heart rate of 110 to 160/min with beat-to-beat variability of 15/min, lasting at least 15 seconds, with a return to baseline in less than 2 min with no decelerations.
- ○ Types
  - ■ Auscultation with fetoscope; palpation
  - ■ External electronic monitoring
  - ■ Internal electronic monitoring
    - □ Provides actual intrauterine pressures
    - □ Provides beat-to-beat variability of the FHR, which is an indication of the sympathetic and parasympathetic nervous system status
  - ■ Indications for continuous fetal monitoring
    - □ Multiple gestations, placenta previa, abruption placenta, oxytocin (Pitocin) infusion, fetal bradycardia, maternal pregnancy-induced hypertension, postdates, meconium staining, abnormal findings on a stress test, and/or abnormal contractions.
- ○ Periodic changes
  - ■ Early decelerations – associated with head compression
  - ■ Variable decelerations – associated with cord compression
  - ■ Late decelerations – associated with uteroplacental insufficiency
  - ■ Accelerations – usually a sign of fetal well-being
- ○ Nonreassuring FHR patterns associated with fetal hypoxia
  - ■ Fetal bradycardia
  - ■ Fetal tachycardia
  - ■ Absence of FHR variability
  - ■ Late decelerations
  - ■ Variable decelerations

NOTES

- Kick Counts or Daily Fetal Movement Count – Maternal tracking and counting of fetal movement as a reliable screening of fetal well-being during the third trimester of both low- and high-risk pregnancies.
  - Types of fetal movement counted include kicks, turns, twists, swishes, rolls, and jabs
- Parameters
  - A healthy fetus should have 10 kicks in less than 2 hr
  - Most fetuses will take less than 30 min to achieve 10 kicks

 Nursing Interventions
  - Tell the client to assess kick count daily, or as recommended by the primary care provider.
  - Tell the client to select the time of day when the fetus is most active; after a meal, after an activity, or in the evening.
  - Tell the client to assess the kick count at the same time every day, or as recommended by the primary care provider.
  - Have the client perform assessment in a lying or otherwise comfortable position. Encourage the client to relax.
  - Have the client write down the time of first and tenth kick.
  - If the fetus is sleeping, tell client to awaken it with a glass of juice.

 Point to Remember
  - Fetal movements may be temporarily decreased if the client is taking a depressant medication, drinks alcohol, and/or smokes. Obesity also decreases the perception of fetal movements and the ability of the mother to monitor fetal activity.

- Nonstress Test (NST)
  - Purpose
    - It assesses fetal well-being.
    - Look for an increase in FHR (accelerations) with fetal activity (reactive NST).
  - A nonreactive, NST is not reassuring.
- Contraction Stress Test
  - Types

- Oxytocin challenge test
- Nipple stimulation test
  - Purpose
    - It looks for three contractions in 10 min.
    - No late decelerations will determine fetal well-being.
  - A negative CST is reassuring.
- Biophysical Profile
  - Purpose
    - It determines fetal well-being after a questionable NST.
    - It determines the amount of amniotic fluid.

 Nursing Interventions
    - Provide client education.
    - Provide emotional support.
- Amniocentesis (performed after 16 weeks of gestation)
  - Purpose
    - It determines fetal anomalies, sex, and fetal maturity.
    - It determines lecithin-sphingomyelin (L/S) ratio, bilirubin levels, and creatine levels.

 Nursing Interventions
    - Provide client education.
    - Assess for premature labor and hemorrhaging.
    - Provide RhoGAM for client who is Rh-negative.
- Chorionic Villi Sampling
  - Purpose
    - It determines fetal anomalies and genetic defects.
    - It is an early test that is given at 8 to 10 weeks of gestation.

 Nursing Interventions
    - Provide client education.
    - Provide RhoGAM for client who is Rh-negative.

Components of Labor

- Power (uterine contractions)

NOTES

STAGES OF LABOR

Stages	Characteristics	Nursing Interventions
• First Stage – (stage of dilatation) begins true labor; ends with complete cervical dilatation; composed of three phases ○ Latent phase ○ Active phase ○ Transitional phase	• Duration ○ Primigravida 3.3 to 19.7 hr ○ Multigravida 0.1 to 14.3 hr ○ 0 to 4 cm dilatation; mild to moderate contractions every 5 to 30 min, lasting 10 to 30 seconds; backache, cramping, bloody show; mother talkative, cheerful, anxious ○ 5 to 7 cm dilatation; strong contractions every 3 to 5 min, lasting 30 to 45 seconds ○ 8 to 10 cm dilatation; strong contractions of 2 to 3 min, lasting 45 to 90 seconds; legs may cramp; nausea/vomiting, perspiration on forehead and upper lip: dark, profuse bloody show; mother may have amnesia between contractions, is irritable, anxious, and self-oriented	• Perform an admission assessment that includes a medical and obstetrical history, vital signs, FHR, signs of labor, weight, and vaginal exam (if no active vaginal bleeding). • Provide the client with diversional activities, time contractions, assess maternal-fetal status, instruct the client in the pelvic rock method, promote hydration, have the client use breathing patterns, and evaluate the client's labor progress. • Assess the maternal-fetal status, give the client backrubs, and provide her with comfort measures. The client may feel apprehensive, so provide encouragement and analgesia or anesthesia if she requests and it is appropriate. Instruct the client to maintain hydration and elimination and to keep her perineum clean. Have the client rest between contractions and evaluate her labor progress. • Assess the maternal-fetal status and provide reassurance and comfort measures. Encourage the client to use the pant/blow method when she feels the urge to push. Be supportive and help the client maintain control with breathing, and evaluate her labor progress.
• Second Stage – (stage of delivery) begins with complete dilatation of the cervix and ends with delivery; composed of three phases ○ Latent phase ○ Descent phase ○ Transition phase	• Duration ○ Primigravida 0.3 to 1.9 hr ○ Multigravida 0.9 to 0.69 hr; contractions 2 to 3 min, lasting 50 to 90 seconds; client has urge to push and is exhausted	Assess the maternal-fetal status. Coach pushing, encourage short breath holds, promote comfort, record time of delivery, an episiotomy/lacerations, medications, or anesthetics, and evaluate the client's labor progress.
• Third Stage – (placental stage) begins with delivery of the neonate; ends with delivery of placenta	Mild contractions continue until placenta expelled, normally within 30 min; client may have to push to help placenta	Assess the maternal status and blood loss. Note the time that the placenta was delivered. Administer an oxytocic after placenta separation, if prescribed. Promote maternal/newborn bonding, and be aware of cultural variations regarding care of the placenta.
• Fourth Stage – first 1 to 2 hr after delivery; client usually remains in birthing unit until stable	• Cramping uterine discomfort; rubra vaginal discharge with small clots; intense tremors and shivering common; discomfort if episiotomy done; client feels happy, relieved, and excited • Initiating breastfeeding aids in contraction of the uterus and prevents hemorrhage	Assess maternal vital signs, fundus, lochia, and the perineum. Usual protocol is every 15 min for the first hour, every 30 min for 2 hr, and every 60 min for 1 hr. Provide comfort measures for the client (blanket for warmth) and assist with initial breastfeeding.

MEDICATIONS USED IN LABOR AND DELIVERY

Name: Generic (Trade)	Use
• Oxytocin (Pitocin)	• Induces labor, stimulates labor, or contracts the uterus after delivery
• Methylergonovine maleate (Methergine)	• Contracts the uterus after delivery
• Nifedipine (Procardia)	• Calcium-channel blocker that suppresses contractions; can cause hypotension
• Terbutaline sulfate (Brethine)	• Treats premature labor
• Indomethacin (Indocin)	• Suppresses labor by blocking production of prostaglandins
• Hydralazine hydrochloride (Apressoline)	• CNS depressant; relaxes smooth muscles, lowers blood pressure
• Magnesium sulfate	• Controls convulsions when used with PIH; treats premature labor
• Calcium gluconate (generic only)	• Antidote for magnesium sulfate toxicity
• Naloxone HCl (Narcan)	• Treats respiratory depression
• Betamethasone (Celestone)	• Stimulates fetal lung maturation
• Prostaglandin E_2 gel (Cervidil)	• Softens and thins the cervix

NOTES

- o Frequency – from the beginning of one contraction to the beginning of the next contraction
- o Duration – from the beginning of one contraction to the end of that same contraction
- o Intensity – strength of contraction, measured with fingertips lightly on the fundus (mild, moderate, and strong); accurate measurement can only be made with an internal monitor
- o Regularity – establish a pattern that increases in frequency and duration
- o Effacement – thinning of cervix, 0 to 100%
- o Dilatation – opening of cervix, 0 to 10 cm
- Passenger (fetus)
  - o Lie – relationship of the cephalocaudal axis of the fetus to the cephalocaudal axis of the mother
    - Transverse lie
    - Longitudinal lie
  - o Presentation – body part of the passenger that enters the pelvic passageway first is called the "presenting part"
    - Cephalic
      - □ Vertex – occiput (most common)
      - □ Brow – sinciput
      - □ Face – mentum
    - Breech
      - □ Complete – sacrum
      - □ Frank
      - □ Footling
    - Shoulder
  - o Position – relationship of the landmark on the presenting fetal part to the front, sides, and back of the maternal pelvis
    - Maternal pelvis includes left or right posterior, anterior, and transverse aspects
    - Fetal landmarks – occiput (O), mentum (M), sacrum (S), and scapula (Sc)
    - Most common is left occiput anterior (LOA)
  - o Attitude or habitus – the relationship of the fetal parts to one another; usually referred to as fetal position

- o Station – the relationship between the presenting part and the ischial spines; O-station is engagement
- o Cardinal movements of descent
  - Descent
  - Flexion
  - Internal rotation
  - Extension
  - External rotation or restitution
- Passageway (maternal pelvis)
  - o False pelvis helps support pregnant uterus
  - o True pelvis forms bony canal; inlet, pelvic cavity, and outlet
  - o Types
    - Gynecoid – normal female (50%), which is best for delivery
    - Android – normal male (20%), which is not favorable
    - Platypelloid – flat female pelvis (5%), which is not favorable
    - Anthropoid – apelike (25%), which is not favorable
  - o Cephalopelvic disproportion

SECTION 2

LABOR AND DELIVERY

Nursing Care During the Stages of Labor

- Assessment During Admission to Birthing Facility
  - o Review of antepartum care and birth plan
  - o A 20 to 30 min baseline monitoring of FHR and maternal contractions
  - o Vital signs
  - o Status of amniotic membranes
  - o Vaginal bleeding

 Point to Remember

  - o In the presence of vaginal bleeding, a vaginal exam should be avoided until placenta previa or abruptio placenta is ruled out. Vaginal exams should be done by the primary care provider.

NOTES

Signs of Impending Labor

- Lightening
- Braxton-Hicks contractions
- Weight loss (1 to 3 lb)
- Cervical changes
- Increase in back discomfort
- Bloody show
- Rupture of membranes
- Sudden burst of energy

 Nursing Interventions
  - Monitor FHR.
  - Check for prolapsed cord.
  - Test vaginal secretions for alkalinity with Nitrazine paper.
  - Watch for signs of infection/meconium.

Pain Management and Pharmacological Interventions

- Analgesia in Labor – It is important to perform nursing assessments of the mother, fetus, and labor status prior to administering analgesia. If given too early, analgesia can slow down labor. If given too close to delivery, analgesia can result in respiratory depression of the neonate. Ideally, active labor (at least 4 cm) should be established before analgesics are administered.

 Point to Remember
  - Nonpharmacologic management
    - The laboring mother's perception of the birth process as good or bad is often associated with how successfully her pain management goals were met. The nurse should look for cues to identify if the client's nonpharmacologic pain management practices are meeting her pain management goals.
  - Methods
    - Hypnosis, patterned breathing, controlled relaxation techniques, biofeedback, massage and touch, walking, rocking, changing positions, heat and cold, and water therapy

Complications During Labor and Delivery

- Preterm Labor – Uterine contractions and cervical changes that occur between 20 and 37 weeks of gestation.
  - Etiology
    - Previous preterm labor or birth
    - Multifetal pregnancy
    - Hydramnios
    - Bleeding or acute or recurrent infection
    - Placental problems
    - Gestational hypertension
    - Diabetes mellitus
    - Lack of prenatal care
    - Age < 17 or > 35

 Nursing Interventions
    - Provide modified bed rest with bathroom privileges.
    - Encourage rest in the left-lateral position to increase blood flow to the uterus.
    - Assess for vaginal drainage or discharge, noting color, consistency, and odor.
    - Monitor the client's vital signs including temperature.
    - Monitor FHR.
    - Maintain adequate hydration in the client.
    - Administer tocolytic medications as prescribed.
    - Prepare the client for delivery if near term.

- Fetal Distress
  - Etiology
    - Uteroplacental insufficiency
      - Acute uteroplacental insufficiency
        - Excessive uterine activity associated with induction and use of oxytocin (Pitocin)
        - Maternal hypotension – epidural, venacaval compression, supine position, internal hemorrhage
        - Placental separation – abruptio, previa

NOTES

- □ Chronic uteroplacental insufficiency
  - ▸ Pregnancy-induced hypertension
  - ▸ Diabetes mellitus
  - ▸ Postmaturity
- ○ Nursing Interventions
  - ■ Stop oxytocin induction.
  - ■ Administer 8 to 10 L of oxygen/face mask.
  - ■ Turn the client onto her left side.
  - ■ Increase the client's IV fluids.
  - ■ Notify the provider.
- Premature Rupture of Membrane (PROM)
  - ○ Etiology
    - ■ Infection
    - ■ Trauma
  - ○ Nursing Interventions
    - ■ Assess FHR.
    - ■ Assess the client for infection.
    - ■ Assess her for a prolapsed cord.
    - ■ Give the client ampicillin 4 g IV load then 2 g every 4 hr.
- Umbilical Cord Compression
  - ○ Etiology
    - ■ Prolapsed cord – Pressure on the umbilical cord during pregnancy, labor, or delivery that reduces blood flow from the placenta to the fetus.
      - □ Causes – abnormal presentation, inadequate pelvis, presenting part at high station, multiple gestation, prematurity, premature rupture of membranes, and/or polyhydramnios
      - □ Complications – fetal asphyxia
      - □ Nursing Interventions
        - ▸ Place the client in the Trendelenburg or knee-chest position.
        - ▸ Perform a sterile vaginal exam to support the presenting part and relieve pressure on the cord.
        - ▸ Administer 8 to 10 L of oxygen to the client via a face mask.
        - ▸ Prepare the client for delivery.

- ■ Nuchal cord (cord around neck)
- Emergency Childbirth
  - ○ Have the mother pant, unless the fetus is in breech presentation.
  - ○ Support the perineum.
  - ○ Rupture the membranes if they have not yet ruptured.
  - ○ Feel for the cord around the neonate's neck, and gently slip it over his head.
  - ○ Clear out mucus and keep the neonate dry and warm.
  - ○ Do not cut the cord.
  - ○ Deliver the placenta. Expect a gush of blood and a lengthening of the cord. Save the placenta.
  - ○ Massage the client's uterus to shrink it. Place the neonate on the client's breast.
- Amniotic Fluid Emboli – Occurs when amniotic fluid, fetal cells, hair, or other debris enter the maternal circulation, triggering a complex series of events leading to life-threatening maternal symptoms.
  - ○ Etiology
    - ■ Fluid enters the maternal circulation as a result of an opening in the amniotic sac or maternal uterine veins accompanied by intrauterine pressure
  - ○ Manifestations
    - ■ Respiratory distress
    - ■ Circulatory collapse
    - ■ Hemorrhage
    - ■ Seizure activity
  - ○ Nursing Interventions
    - ■ Administer 10 L of oxygen to the client via a face mask.
    - ■ Prepare the client for intubation.
    - ■ Initiate and/or assist with CPR.
    - ■ Administer IV fluids.
    - ■ Administer blood or blood products.
    - ■ Prepare for an emergency birth.
    - ■ Provide emotional support.
      - □ Happens at delivery

NOTES

       □ Emergency situation and often fatal

- Dystocia – prolonged, difficult labor
  - Etiology
    - Dysfunction of uterine contractions
    - Abnormal position
    - Cephalopelvic disproportion
    - Maternal exhaustion
  - Manifestations
    - Short stature, overweight status
    - Age > 40 years
    - Multifetal pregnancy
    - Inappropriate timing of analgesia
  - Nursing Interventions
    - Assess fetus and status of the client's labor.
    - Assist with the application of a fetal scalp electrode.
    - Encourage the client to void and ambulate regularly.
    - Assist the client in positioning and coaching during contractions.
    - Prepare the client for a possible forceps, vacuum-assisted, or cesarean birth.

Operative Obstetrics

- Episiotomy – An incision that is made into the perineum to enlarge the vaginal outlet during delivery.
  - Indications
    - To spare muscles from overstretching/ lacerations; to avoid difficulty holding urine later in life
  - Nursing Interventions
    - Assess the client for healing, infection, laceration of the anal sphincter (4th-degree tear), and hemorrhage.
    - Encourage the client to perform Kegel exercises to improve and restore perineal muscle tone.

- Forceps – Obstetric instrument used to aid in delivery of the fetal head.
  - Indications
    - Poor progress
    - Fetal distress
    - Persistent occiput posterior position
    - Abnormal presentation
  - Nursing Interventions
    - Assess the neonate for intracranial hemorrhage, facial bruising, and facial palsy.
    - Assist with the delivery as needed.
    - Check FHR before traction is applied.
  - Complications
    - Lacerations to cervix or vagina
    - Bladder or urethral injury
    - Urine retention
    - Hematoma formation in the pelvic soft tissues
- Vacuum Extraction – Attachment of a vacuum cup to the fetal head to assist in birth of the head.
  - Indications
    - Similar to those of outlet forceps
    - Preferred method when compared to forceps assistance
  - Nursing Interventions
    - Continue to encourage the client to push during contractions.
    - Assess the neonate for trauma at the application site and cerebral irritation (poor suck, listlessness).
    - Assess the neonate for cerebral trauma.
    - Inform the parents that caput will begin to disappear in a few hours.
- Cesarean Birth – Birth of fetus through a transabdominal incision of the uterus.
  - Types
    - Low transverse – decrease chance of uterine rupture with future pregnancies; less bleeding after delivery
    - Classical – good for emergency delivery; provides more room

---

NOTES

- o Indications
  - Fetal distress
  - Cephalopelvic disproportion
  - Placenta previa, abruptio
  - Uterine dysfunction
  - Prolapsed cord
  - Diabetes mellitus
  - Toxemia
  - Malpresentation such as breech or shoulder
- o Nursing Interventions
  - Perform postoperative assessment.
  - Perform postpartum assessment.
  - Assess effects of anesthesia.
  - Maintain patent airway.
  - Assess for and treat pain.
  - Monitor vital signs.
  - Assess incisional dressing, fundus, and lochia.
  - Assess I&O.
  - Have the client turn, cough, and take deep breaths.
  - Facilitate maternal/newborn bonding and attachment.
  - Initiate breastfeeding when the mother is able.
- Induction of Labor – The process of initiating labor.
  - o Indications
    - Maternal disease – cardiac, pregnancy-induced hypertension, diabetes mellitus
    - Placental malfunctions (partial previa)
    - Fetal conditions (anomaly, death)
    - Postmaturity
  - o Chemical methods used to soften cervix
    - Cervidil – placed in cervix then removed after 12 hr; start oxytocin 1 hr after removal
    - Prostaglandin E (Cervidil) – used before induction to soften and thin the cervix
  - o Methods used to initiate induction
    - IV oxytocin (Pitocin)
    - Rupture of membranes; amniotomy

- o Nursing Interventions
  - Perform a vaginal exam for effacement, dilation, and station.
  - Monitor the client's vital signs every 4 hr.
  - Monitor the client's contraction pattern.
  - Assess the client's I&O.
  - Assess the client's level of maternal discomfort and provide pain management.
  - Observe the client's emotional responses and provide support.

SECTION 3

POSTPARTAL ADAPTATIONS AND NURSING ASSESSMENT

Postpartum Assessment

- Puerperium – The period of time during which the body adjusts and returns to a prepregnancy state; usually lasts 6 weeks, but can last up to 1 year
  - o Breasts
  - o Uterus
  - o Bladder
  - o Bowel
  - o Lochia (rubra, serosa, alba)
  - o Episiotomy
  - o Deep vein thrombosis
  - o Emotion
  - o Uterus (involution)
    - Fundus is 2 cm below the umbilicus immediately after delivery; 1 fingerbreadth above umbilicus 12 hr after delivery; by 24 hr after delivery, it descends 1 to 2 cm every 24 hr
    - Fundus involutes faster if the client breastfeeds her infant
  - o Nursing Interventions
    - Assess the client for hemorrhage and increased lochia.
    - Assess the client for pain and medicate as needed.

NOTES

- Administer oxytocin (Pitocin) to the client as prescribed.
- Encourage the client to breastfeed her infant.
- Provide client education.
- Lochia – Vaginal discharge following delivery.
  - Color
    - Rubra (1 to 4 days)
    - Serosa (4 to 9 days)
    - Alba (10 days to 6 weeks)
  - Odor – if foul smelling, may indicate infection
  - Amount – moderate at first, but will increase with activity
  - Menstruation – resumes in about 6 to 8 weeks in mothers who are not breastfeeding; can vary with mothers who breastfeed
- Breasts
  - Engorgement

  - Nursing Interventions
    - Nonbreastfeeding
      - Avoid stimulation.
      - Provide ice.
      - Have client wear a supportive bra.
      - Give pain medication.
    - Breastfeeding
      - Encourage frequent hot showers.
      - Encourage frequent feedings.
      - Give massage.
- Perineum
  - Episiotomy or laceration
    - Edema
    - Pain

  - Nursing Interventions
    - Encourage warm sitz baths.
    - Provide pain management.
    - Encourage performance of Kegel exercises.
- Gastrointestinal
  - Sluggish bowels secondary to decreased muscle tone
  - Hemorrhoids

  - Nursing Interventions
    - Administer stool softeners.
    - Instruct the client to increase her dietary fiber and fluids.
    - Suggest that the client use sitz baths and/or witch hazel pads for comfort.
- Urinary Tract
  - Postpartal diuresis within 12 hr after birth
  - Lessened sensation of bladder fullness
  - Urinary retention
  - Decreased urge to void; bladder distension can cause subinvolution of the uterus

  - Nursing Interventions
    - Monitor the client's I&O.
    - Gently palpate the client's bladder.
    - Encourage the client to void frequently.
- Temperature
  - In the first 24 hr, there can be an increase up to 38° C (100.4° F) in the client's temperature due to dehydration. The client's metabolic rate may increase.
  - The client's WBC is normally elevated. Ten to 12 days following delivery, WBC count can increase to 20,000 to 25,000/mm³.
- Postpartal Chill
  - Neurologic or vasomotor response to impending delivery
  - Normal immediately following delivery

  - Nursing Interventions
    - Maintain client comfort.
    - Provide the client with a warm blanket.
    - Monitor the client's vital signs.
- Cardiac
  - Heart rate and blood pressure return to prepregnant state within 10 days
  - Tachycardia may occur in first 10 days of postpartum secondary to decreasing blood volume

  - Nursing Interventions
    - Assess the client's vital signs every 4 hr.

NOTES

- Monitor Hct, Hgb, and CBC laboratory values.

Psychological Adaptation

- Self-Concept
  - Body image
  - Fatigue
  - Discomfort
- Maternal Role – Reva Rubin's Stages
  - Taking-in phase – lasts 2 to 3 days after birth; the mother is preoccupied with herself and her own needs
  - Taking-hold phase – begins 2 to 3 days after birth; the mother takes responsibility for her newborn and is open to learning
  - Letting-go phase – begins at 4 to 5 weeks after birth; mother totally surrenders to her newborn and her role as a mother
- Postpartum Depression
  - Mood swings, depression
  - Usually peaks on 5th day; if it lasts longer than 10 days, the primary care provider should be notified
  - Risk factors
    - Young age, low socioeconomic status, history of depression, anxiety, and low partner support
  - Nursing Interventions
    - Provide the client teaching prior to discharge.
    - Assess her emotional status and mood on first postpartal visit.
    - Instruct the client to notify the provider if symptoms persist.
    - Provide the client with a referral to available community help resources.

Complications During the Postpartum Period

- Hemorrhage – Blood loss of more than 500 mL for a normal spontaneous vaginal delivery, or blood loss of more than 1,000 mL for a cesarean birth.
  - Etiology
    - Early – atony
    - Late – retained placenta

- Lacerations, hematomas
- Ruptured uterus
- Placental abruption or previa
- Uterine subinvolution

 Nursing Interventions
- Atony
  - First, massage the fundus.
  - Assess the bladder.
  - Administer oxytocic medications.
    - Prostaglandin F2a, Hemabate (Carboprost Tromethamine) may be prescribed if other measures do not stop the bleeding. Avoid giving these medications to clients who have asthma, pelvic inflammatory disease, and/or cardiac, pulmonary, renal or hepatic conditions
  - Surgery may be necessary for a retained placenta, lacerations, and/or hematomas.
- Thromboembolic Disease – Results from the formation of a blood clot inside a blood vessel caused by inflammation or partial obstruction of the vessel.
  - Etiology
    - Increased clotting factors postpartum
    - Venous stasis
    - History of heart disease, endometritis, and leg varicosities
  - Nursing Interventions
    - Assess the client's lower extremities for edema, tenderness, varices, and warmth.
    - Check for Homan's sign.
    - Maintain the client on bed rest and elevate her affected extremity.
    - Never massage the extremity and monitor the client for pulmonary embolus.
    - Administer anticoagulant medication to the client as prescribed.

NOTES

- Infection – Reproductive organs becomes infected, which may occur within 28 days of miscarriage, abortion, or childbirth (temperature greater than 38° C [100.4° F]).

  o Nursing Interventions

    ■ Assess the client for fever, chills, pelvic discomfort or pain, vaginal discharge, and an elevated WBC count.

    ■ Monitor the client's vital signs and temperature every 4 hr.

    ■ Use isolation precautions as needed to protect the newborn.

    ■ Monitor culture results.

    ■ Administer prescribed antibiotics.

    ■ Encourage the client to increase her fluid intake.

    ■ Encourage the client to eat a nutritious diet that is high in calories and protein.

    ■ Provide discharge teaching.

SECTION 4

REPRODUCTIVE RISKS AND COMPLICATIONS

- Medical Problems
  - o Cardiac disease
    - ■ Etiology
      - □ Pregnancy expands plasma volume, which increases cardiac output and causes an increased work load on the heart
      - □ Can result in heart failure or death
    - ■ Prognosis
      - □ Occurs in 1% of all women who are pregnant
      - □ Danger of maternal death
        - ▸ When blood volume peaks at the end of the second trimester (30 to 50% increase in volume)
        - ▸ During labor – there is an increase of up to 20% from the "milking" effect of contractions

        - ▸ During delivery – due to a sudden increase in the volume at birth when the uterus contracts fully
    - ■ Manifestations
      - □ Cough, dyspnea, and fatigue
      - □ Palpitations and tachycardia
      - □ Peripheral edema
      - □ Pulmonary edema
      - □ Angina
      - □ Respiratory infection
    - ■ Nursing Interventions
      - □ Prenatal care
        - ▸ Prevent infection.
        - ▸ Instruct the client to consume a diet that is high in protein and will restrict weight gain. Tell the client not to limit her salt intake unless this is ordered.
        - ▸ Monitor the client for anemia.
        - ▸ Provide anticoagulant therapy. Use heparin, and not warfarin sodium (Coumadin).
        - ▸ Instruct the client to decrease her activity, encourage rest, and reduce stress.
      - □ Labor and delivery
        - ▸ Tell the client to avoid frequent position changes.
        - ▸ Give the client an epidural to decrease pain.
        - ▸ Avoid a cesarean birth. Deliver the neonate vaginally with aid of forceps.
        - ▸ Have ECG, FHR monitor, and oxygen ready.
        - ▸ Monitor the IV carefully.
        - ▸ Use oxytocin (Pitocin) with caution.
      - □ Postpartum
        - ▸ Observe the client for the first 48 hr after delivery (heart failure).
        - ▸ Watch for hemorrhage if oxytocin is not used.
        - ▸ Monitor the client's I&O (cardiac failure).

NOTES

- ▸ Avoid placing stockings on the client's legs.
- ▸ Assess the client for infection. Give prophylactic antibiotics to (prevent endocarditis).
- ▸ Plan for the client's discharge. The client will need assistance and instruction if she chooses to breastfeed her newborn.
- ○ Diabetes mellitus
  - ▪ Etiology
    - □ Maternal insulin – does not cross the placenta; by 12 weeks of gestation, the fetus produces insulin, but this does not lower blood glucose level (maternal control)
    - □ First trimester – the fetus draws large amounts of glucose for growth, so the maternal requirement decreases; the client may not need any insulin
    - □ Second trimester – human placental lactogen and other hormones secreted by the placenta after 18 weeks of gestation have anti-insulin effect; the need for insulin will increase

  - ▪ Nursing Interventions
    - □ Prenatal care
      - ▸ Provide the client teaching related to her diet, insulin administration, exercise, and blood glucose monitoring.
      - ▸ Assess maternal HbA1c. Blood glucose control is imperative for a good outcome.
      - ▸ Monitor the client's ability to control her glucose levels. Failure to do so may cause congenital anomalies and stillbirths.
    - □ Labor and delivery
      - ▸ Assess the fetus for maturity and well-being by an amniocentesis, stress and nonstress testing, and estriol levels.
      - ▸ A cesarean birth after 37 weeks of gestation may be necessary if the placenta deteriorates.

- □ Postpartum
  - ▸ The client will need insulin, because it drops rapidly after delivery of the placenta.
  - ▸ Assess the neonate for hypoglycemia.
  - ▸ Assess the client for infection.
- ▪ Complications
  - □ Pregnancy-induced hypertension
  - □ Polyhydramnios
  - □ Hypo/hyperglycemia
  - □ Fetal death
  - □ Macrosomia (dystocia)
  - □ Spontaneous abortion
- ○ Gestational diabetes (second to third trimester)
  - ▪ May be controlled by diet alone
  - ▪ 10 to 15% of clients require insulin
  - ▪ Normal after delivery; there is an increased risk of the client being diagnosed with diabetes mellitus later in life
- • Hyperemesis Gravidarum – Persistent nausea and vomiting that continues beyond the first trimester of pregnancy.
  - ○ Etiology – may be hormonal or psychological

  - ○ Nursing Interventions
    - ▪ Assess the client for nausea and vomiting.
    - ▪ Assess the client for weight loss.
    - ▪ Observe the client for signs of dehydration and nutritional deficits.
    - ▪ Monitor the client's I&O.
    - ▪ Administer IV fluids.
    - ▪ Introduce foods slowly.
    - ▪ Decrease the client's stress. Obtain a consult for psychiatric care if necessary.
    - ▪ Assess the client for metabolic alkalosis.
- • Polyhydramnios – Excessive amniotic fluid.
  - ○ Etiology
    - ▪ Maternal diseases (toxemia, diabetes mellitus)
    - ▪ Fetal malformation (esophagus not complete)
    - ▪ Erythroblastosis
    - ▪ Multiple pregnancies

NOTES

- o Treatment
  - Relieve pressure by amniocentesis
  - Delivery
- Abortion – Expulsion of the fetus, usually before 20 weeks of gestation (spontaneous or induced).
  - o Etiology
    - Abnormal fetus
    - Infection
    - Anomaly of reproductive tract
    - Injury
    - Unwanted pregnancy
  - o Terminology
    - Spontaneous – miscarriage
      - □ Therapeutic – termination of a pregnancy by medical intervention
      - □ Criminal – abortion done outside medical facilities; against the law
  - o Nursing Interventions
    - Save all pads and any tissues passed.
    - Assess the client for shock, infection, disseminated intravascular coagulation, and thrombophlebitis.
    - Administer RhoGAM if the client is Rh-negative.
    - Provide emotional support. Do not give false encouragement (grieving necessary).
- Ectopic Pregnancy – Occurs outside the uterus; usually in the fallopian tube; can be on the ovary, in the abdomen, or interligaments.
  - o Etiology
    - Malformation of tubes
    - Pelvic inflammatory disease
    - Tumors
    - Adhesions secondary to surgery or endometriosis
  - o Manifestations
    - Sharp abdominal pain (rupture of tube)
    - Shock
    - Mild manifestations initially (little or no bleeding)

- o Diagnosis and treatment
  - Culdocentesis (blood does not clot)
  - Removal of tube; may need blood transfusion
- o Nursing Interventions
  - Observe the client for shock.
  - Provide usual postoperative care.
  - Provide emotional support, especially if the client fears that it will happen again (only one tube remains).
- Hydatidiform Mole/Molar Pregnancy – abnormal degeneration of the products of conception
  - o Etiology (actual cause is unknown)
    - Abnormal ova
    - Protein deficiency
  - o Manifestations
    - Bleeding – spotting too profuse; client passes tan-colored, grape-like clusters (anemia secondary to blood loss)
    - Severe nausea and vomiting
    - Increased levels of human chorionic gonadotropin (HCG) continues to increase
    - Signs of pregnancy induced hypertension before 24 weeks of gestation
    - Uterus enlarges at a rapid rate
  - o Nursing Interventions
    - Check laboratory values for increased HCG.
    - Assist with an ultrasound.
    - Prepare the client for vacuum aspiration.
    - Monitor the client for postprocedure hemorrhage.
    - Instruct the client regarding birth control measures to prevent pregnancy for 1 year.
    - Monitor the client closely for possible cancer. Discourage her from becoming pregnant until cancer is ruled out (at least 1 year).
    - Monitor the client for signs of hypertension and hemorrhage.
    - Reinforce follow-up care with the client to screen for choriocarcinoma.
    - Provide the client with emotional support.

NOTES

- Incompetent Cervix – premature dilation of the cervix, which typically occurs in the fourth or fifth month of pregnancy
  - ○ Etiology
    - ▪ Associated with cervical trauma secondary to previous surgery or birth
  - ○ Manifestations
    - ▪ Vaginal bleeding
    - ▪ Fetal membranes visible through the cervix
  - ○ Nursing Interventions
    - ▪ Encourage the client to rest, increase hydration, and give her tocolytic agents, as prescribed.
    - ▪ Prepare the client for cerclage to close cervix.
    - ▪ Following the procedure, monitor the client for contractions, bleeding, rupture of membranes, and infection.
- Pregnancy-Induced Hypertension (PIH) – Hypertensive disorder of pregnancy that occurs after 20 weeks of gestation or early postpartum.
  - ○ Etiology
    - ▪ Increased sensitivity to angiotensin II causes cyclic vasospasms, which leads to vasoconstriction; this is responsible for most or all symptoms of PIH
  - ○ Terminology
    - ▪ Preeclampsia – may be mild or severe depending on the degree of manifestations; IV hydralazine (Apresoline) is the medication of choice for preeclampsia
    - ▪ Eclampsia – convulsions occur
  - ○ Manifestations
    - ▪ Edema – may be mild to severe swelling of the hands, face; pitting of legs (or sacrum)
    - ▪ Proteinuria – from 1 gm/24 hr to 5 gm or more/24 hr
    - ▪ Hypertension – from 140/90 mm Hg (or an increase of 30/15 mm Hg above base) to 160/110 mm Hg or increase in systolic of 50 above base
    - ▪ Decrease in urinary output (must have at least 30 mL/hr)
    - ▪ Weight gain from edema
    - ▪ Headaches, visual disturbances, vasospasm
    - ▪ Hemoconcentration
    - ▪ Epigastric pain
    - ▪ Hyperreflexia
  - ○ Occurrence
    - ▪ Primigravida with age extremes (< 16, > 40)
    - ▪ Any chronic medical condition that affects the vascular system (diabetes mellitus, chronic hypertension, kidney disease, cardiac disease)
    - ▪ Family history
    - ▪ Multiple pregnancies (twins, triplets)
    - ▪ Dietary deficiencies, especially protein
  - ○ Nursing Interventions (depends on degree of illness; status can change very quickly)
    - ▪ Assess the client's vital signs, weight, edema, and protein in urine.
    - ▪ Encourage the client to eat a diet that is high in protein. She should maintain adequate fluid intake and not restrict her salt intake unless ordered.
    - ▪ Instruct the client to maintain bed rest in a relaxed environment. She should lie on her left side.
    - ▪ Monitor the client's I&O.
    - ▪ Institute seizure precautions (have suction and oxygen ready).
    - ▪ Be prepared to stabilize the client and deliver the neonate.
      - ▫ Check the client's reflexes and then give magnesium sulfate ($MgSO_4$). Have calcium gluconate at the bedside (must be given slowly).
        - ▸ Magnesium sulfate may be continued for 14 to 48 hr. Monitor the client for signs of magnesium toxicity, which include flushing, sweating, hypotension, depressed deep tendon reflexes, and CNS depression.
      - ▫ Assess the client for precipitous delivery and abruptio placenta.
- Disseminated intravascular coagulopathy – A dangerous disorder of clotting that leads to hemorrhage.

NOTES

- HELLP syndrome – A laboratory diagnosis for severe preeclampsia that is characterized by hemolysis, elevated liver enzymes, and low platelets.
- Abruptio Placenta – Premature separation of the placenta from the uterus.
  - Etiology
    - Trauma
    - Pregnancy-induced hypertension
    - Multiparity
    - Cocaine use
  - Manifestations
    - Bleeding – either internal or external
    - Board-like abdomen, severe pain, tenderness, lack of contractions
    - Bradycardia or no FHR (uteroplacental insufficiency)
  - Treatment
    - Usually immediate cesarean birth
    - Treat client for blood loss
  - Nursing Interventions
    - Observe the client for shock.
    - Monitor vital signs and FHR.
    - Assess the client for diffuse intravascular coagulation, infection, and anemia.
- Placenta Previa – Placenta attaches low in the uterus, either near or covering the cervical os.
  - Etiology
    - Older clients
    - Multiparity
  - Types
    - Total – completely covers cervix
    - Partial – partial covering of cervical os
    - Low lying – near to cervical os
  - Manifestations – painless, bright red bleeding after the seventh month (bleeding may be intermittent)

- Nursing Interventions (depends on type, severity, and gestational age)
  - The client may require blood, bed rest, or an immediate cesarean birth.
  - Observe the client for hemorrhage, count pads, monitor vital signs and FHR, and be prepared for an emergency cesarean birth.
  - Provide the client with emotional support.
  - Avoid performing vaginal exams

Nursing Care of the Newborn

- Initial Care
  - Maintain a patent airway by using suctioning and proper positioning.
  - Maintain the newborn's temperature by drying and placing him on his mother or under a radiant heat source.
  - Perform an Apgar score at 1 and 5 min after birth.
    - Five areas scored – heart rate, respiratory effort, muscle tone, reflex irritability, and color
      - 7 to 10 – good
      - 3 to 6 – moderately depressed
      - 0 to 2 – severely depressed
  - Administer eye prophylaxis, which is either erythromycin or tetracycline. This protects the newborn's eyes against infections caused by chlamydia and gonorrhea.
  - Place identification on the newborn.
  - Administer vitamin K (Aquamephyton) 0.5 to 1 mg, as prescribed, in the newborn's vastus lateralis.
  - Clamp the newborn's cord for at least 24 hr after birth.
- Vital Signs
  - The newborn's temperature should range from 36° to 37° C (97° to 99° F). If it becomes too high, dehydration, sepsis, brain damage, and overheating may occur. If it becomes too low, infection, brain stem injury, and cold may occur.

NOTES

- o The newborn's heart rate should range from 120 to 150/min, depending on state. A murmur is common at first from the transient patent ductus arteriosus.
  - o Respirations
    - The newborn's respirations should be 30 to 50/min.
    - The newborn will exhibit respiratory distress by nasal flaring, intercostal or xiphoid retractions, expiratory grunting, and/or tachypnea.
  - o The newborn's blood pressure should be 80/40 mm Hg at birth, and 100/50 mm Hg by day 10.
- Head
  - o Measure head circumference.
  - o Assess fontanels.
    - Posterior – triangular-shaped, closes at 8 to 12 weeks
    - Anterior – diamond-shaped, closes at 18 months
    - Bulging – increased intracranial pressure; depressed means dehydration
  - o Observe for molding.
    - Caput succedaneum (edema of soft scalp tissue)
    - Cephalohematoma (hematoma between periosteum and skull bone)
- Eyes
  - o Blue-gray color
  - o Strabismus is common ("cross-eye")
  - o Small hemorrhage (clears in a few weeks)
  - o Cataracts
- Ears
  - o Low-set ears are associated with anomalies.
  - o Newborns hear acutely as mucus is absorbed.
- Nose
  - o Patency – newborns are obligatory nose breathers; can smell
  - o Symmetry

- Mouth
  - o Sucking reflex
  - o Epstein pearls (small white epithelial cysts along the newborn's midline of hard palate)
  - o Thrush (white patches that adhere to the newborn's tongue, palate, and buccal mucosa)
  - o Palate intact
- Breasts
  - o Engorgement
  - o Amount of breast tissue
- Abdomen
  - o Measure abdominal circumference.
  - o Palpate for masses.
  - o Inspect umbilical cord.
    - Three vessels (one vein, two arteries) "AVA"
    - Will fall off after 10 days; assess for infection
- Skin
  - o Normal variations
    - Acrocyanosis – immature circulation (cyanosis of hands and feet)
    - Milia – tiny white papules on the newborn's face, distended sebaceous glands
    - Toxic erythema – pink papular rash on the newborn's trunk
    - Vernix – white, cheese-like substance
    - Mongolian spots – birth marks (irregular areas of pigmentation)
    - Lanugo – fine, downy hair on the newborn's forehead, shoulders, and back
  - o Color
    - Assess birthmarks, Mongolian spots, cafe-au-lait, port wine stains, stork bites
- Skeletal
  - o Clavicles
  - o Hips – check for congenital hip dysplasia; feel for Ortolani click
- Genitals
  - o Female
    - Swollen
    - Pseudo menstruation

NOTES

- Vaginal tag
  - Male
    - Swollen
    - Hypospadias – opening on underside of penis
    - Phimosis – stenosis that prevents foreskin from being retracted back, which may lead to problems with urination; treatment is circumcision
- Elimination
  - The newborn should void in the first 24 hr; pink stains from urates
  - The newborn should pass meconium during the first 24 hr; patent rectum

Assessment for Gestational Age

- Physical Assessment (first 24 hr) – for full-term newborn
  - Resting posture
  - Vernix distribution (very little)
  - Skin
  - Nails
  - Lanugo (very sparse)
  - Sole creases (present at full term)
  - Skull firmness
  - Breast tissue
  - Ear formation and cartilage (firm; springs back)
  - Genitalia
  - Recoil
- Neurological Exam (after 24 hr)
  - Major reflexes
    - Sucking – response to nipple
    - Rooting – touch the newborn's cheek and he will turn his head to that side
    - Grasping – touch the newborn's palm and his fingers should curl
    - Moro – startle reflex
    - Tonic neck – turn the newborn's head to one side while he is in the supine position: he should extend the arm and leg on that side, but flex on the opposite side

- Care of Newborn
  - Weigh the newborn daily. The newborn will initially lose 10% of his birthweight. Newborns should regain birthweight back in 2 weeks.
  - Record the newborn's daily intake and number of wet and dry diapers.
  - Maintain the newborn's body temperature.
  - Discuss circumcision options with the newborn's parents.
    - Obtain a signed permit.
    - After the procedures, assess the newborn for hemorrhage and/or infection.
    - Circumcision is required or discouraged by some cultures, religions, or ethnic groups.
  - Perform tests.
    - Phenylketonuria – Lack of enzyme to convert phenylalanine to tyrosine; Guthrie test: 24 hr after first feeding, and performed again in 4 to 6 weeks.
    - Dextrostix – Assess the newborn's blood glucose level.
    - Cultures – To check for possible infection.
  - Educate the parents about general care such as feeding, bathing, dressing, cord and circumcision care.
  - Promote parent/newborn attachment.
  - Assess the need for parental support after discharge.

SECTION 5

HIGH-RISK NEWBORN

- Premature Newborn – Gestational age of less than 37 weeks, regardless of weight.
  - Etiology
    - Gestational hypertension
    - Multiple pregnancies
    - Lack of prenatal care
    - Substance abuse
    - Previous history of preterm delivery
    - Premature rupture of membranes
    - Placenta previa

NOTES

- o Physical adaptation
    - ▪ Respiratory
        - □ The newborn may lack surfactants.
        - □ The newborn may be at risk for respiratory distress syndrome.
            - ‣ Retractions
            - ‣ Nasal flaring
            - ‣ Expiratory grunt
            - ‣ Tachypnea
            - ‣ Newborn needs mechanical ventilation, oxygen, continuous positive airway pressure
- o Nutrition (fluid and electrolyte)
    - ▪ The newborn may lack a gag and sucking reflex if younger than 34 weeks.
    - ▪ The newborn should be fed by gavage or hyperalimentation.
- o Circulatory
    - ▪ Patent ductus arteriosus is common in a newborn that is premature.
    - ▪ Persistent fetal circulation is common in a newborn that is premature.
- o Complications
    - ▪ Hypothermia
    - ▪ Hypocalcemia
    - ▪ Hypoglycemia
    - ▪ Hyperbilirubinemia
    - ▪ Birth trauma
    - ▪ Sepsis
    - ▪ Intracranial hemorrhage
    - ▪ Necrotizing enterocolitis
    - ▪ Apnea
- o Nursing Interventions
    - ▪ Monitor the newborn's respiratory status and effort.
    - ▪ Monitor the newborn's vital signs.
    - ▪ Maintain the newborn's temperature.
    - ▪ Assess the newborn's hydration and nutrition status.
    - ▪ Monitor the newborn's weight daily.
    - ▪ Monitor the newborn's elimination status.
    - ▪ Promote attachment and bonding between the parents and the newborn.
- Small for Gestational Age (SGA) – Any newborn who falls below the 10th percentile on the growth chart at birth.
    - o Etiology
        - ▪ Placental insufficiency
        - ▪ Pregnancy-induced hypertension
        - ▪ Multiple pregnancies
        - ▪ Poor nutrition
        - ▪ Smoking, drugs, and/or alcohol
        - ▪ Adolescent pregnancy
    - o Complications
        - ▪ Perinatal asphyxia
        - ▪ Meconium aspiration syndrome
        - ▪ Hypoglycemia
        - ▪ Hypothermia
        - ▪ Infections
    - o Nursing Interventions
        - ▪ Support the newborn's respirations.
        - ▪ Provide neutral thermal environment for the newborn (isolette or radiant heat warmer).
        - ▪ Initiate early and frequent feedings.
        - ▪ Observe the newborn for complications.
        - ▪ Prevent infection in the newborn.
        - ▪ Support the parents and promote parent/newborn bonding.
- Large for Gestational Age (LGA) – A newborn whose weight is at or above the 90th percentile (may still be premature).
    - o Etiology
        - ▪ Diabetes mellitus
        - ▪ Genetic predisposition
        - ▪ Congenital defects
    - o Complications
        - ▪ Birth trauma (fractured clavicle)
        - ▪ Hypoglycemia
        - ▪ Polycythemia

NOTES

- If mother has diabetes mellitus, she is at same risk and requires same care as newborn that is premature
  - o Nursing Interventions
    - Assess the newborn for trauma.
    - Assess the newborn for congenital abnormalities.
    - Assess the newborn for hypoglycemia, especially if his mother has diabetes mellitus.
- Postmature Infant – Gestational age of more than 42 weeks.
  - o Physical findings
    - Dry, parchment-like skin
    - Longer, harder nails
    - Profuse scalp hair
    - Absent vernix
    - Hypoglycemia
  - o Complications
    - Progressive aging of placenta
    - Difficult delivery
    - High perinatal mortality
- Jaundice (Hyperbilirubinemia)
  - o Causes
    - Physiological
      - □ Not observed in the newborn during the first 24 hr; usually appears by the third day
      - □ Due to an immature liver
    - Bruising
    - ABO-incompatibility (Mother is O, newborn is A, B, or AB)
    - Rh-incompatibility (erythroblastosis fetalis)
      - □ A mother who is Rh-negative and has a newborn who is Rh-positive
      - □ Kernicterus (bilirubin encephalopathy) can lead to brain damage, anemia, and/or hepatosplenomegaly

- □ Treatment
  - ▸ Phototherapy, sunlight, and/or exchange transfusion is administered to the newborn.
  - ▸ RhoGAM administered at 28 weeks of gestation and within 72 hr of delivery.
    - ▹ RhoGAM may also be given to all mothers who are Rh-negative who abort after 8 weeks of gestation.
  - Breastfeeding
- Substance Abuse and the Newborn
  - o Drug dependent
    - Manifestations of withdrawal
      - □ Early manifestation is irritability
      - □ Sneezing and nasal stuffiness
      - □ High-pitched, weak cry
      - □ Tremors
      - □ Perspiration
      - □ Feeding problems (weak suck reflex)
      - □ Transient tachypnea
    - Nursing Interventions
      - □ Prevent overstimulation in the newborn to prevent possible seizures.
      - □ Swaddle and hold the newborn firmly.
      - □ Administer medications to the newborn as prescribed.
      - □ Provide small, frequent feedings to the newborn (may need to gavage).
  - o Fetal alcohol syndrome
    - Etiology
      - □ Linked to client's consumption of alcoholic beverages during pregnancy
    - Manifestations
      - □ Feeding problems (weak suck reflex)
      - □ Distinctive facial features (microcephaly, small eyes, thin upper lip)
      - □ CNS dysfunction (including mental retardation and seizures)
      - □ Physical defects (limb anomalies, hyperactivity, cardiocirculatory defects, deafness)
      - □ Withdrawal manifestations

NOTES

- Nursing Interventions
  - Protect the newborn from injury.
  - Administer medications to the newborn.
  - Monitor the newborn's fluid therapy.
  - Decrease the newborn's stimuli.
  - Provide support to the parents who may have to care for a newborn that is difficult.
  - Provide social service referral to the parents.

SECTION 6

NURSING CARE OF THE GYNECOLOGIC CLIENT

Vaginal Infections

- Candidiasis (thrush) – A fungal infection of any of the Candida species of which *Candida albicans* is the most common. Encompasses infections that range from superficial, such as oral thrush and vaginitis, to systemic and potentially life-threatening diseases.
  - Etiology
    - Use of oral contraceptives, frequent use of antibiotics, and frequent douching; diabetes mellitus and immunosuppression
  - Manifestations
    - A cheese-like discharge, itching, and discomfort; discomfort on urination and during intercourse
  - Nursing Interventions
    - Administer miconazole (Monistat) or fluconazole (Diflucan).
    - Discuss the importance of cleanliness and perineal care with the client.
    - Ensure that both partners are treated.

- Trichomoniasis – An infection caused by the single-celled protozoan parasite, *Trichomonas vaginalis*. The vagina is the most common site of infection in women, and the urethra is the most common site of infection in men.
  - Etiology
    - The parasite is transmitted sexually through penis-to-vagina intercourse or vulva-to-vulva contact with an infected partner. Women can acquire the disease from infected men or women, but men usually contract it only from infected women.
  - Manifestations
    - Yellow, green, or gray discharge; discomfort with urination and intercourse; irritation and itching

  - Nursing Interventions
    - Administer metronidazole (Flagyl) unless the client is in her first trimester of pregnancy.
    - Treat both sexual partners and instruct them to abstain from sexual intercourse during treatment.
- Condyloma – Genital warts, also known as venereal warts.
  - Etiology
    - Condyloma is one of the most common types of STDs. Genital warts affect the moist tissues of the genital area. The virus that causes genital warts is the Human papillomavirus, which has also been associated with cervical cancer.
  - Manifestations
    - Small, flesh-colored or gray swellings in the genital area; warts can clump together and take on a cauliflower shape; itching or discomfort in the genital area; bleeding may occur with intercourse

  - Nursing Interventions
    - Provide education related to risk factors, such as having unprotected sex with multiple partners, having had another STD, and/or becoming sexually active at a young age.
    - Administer medications such as imiquimod (Aldara) and podophyllin (Condylox).

NOTES

SEXUALLY TRANSMITTED DISEASES				
STD	Symptoms in Women	Symptoms in Men	Complications	Treatments
• Chlamydia ○ Symptoms may appear 7 to 28 days after infection	• Vaginal discharge • Vaginal bleeding • Painful/frequent urination • Abdominal pain • Fever/nausea	• White, watery penile discharge • Painful/frequent urination • Swollen/tender testicles	• Can pass to sexual partners and to neonate during childbirth • Damage to reproductive organs • Can lead to infertility in women and sterility in men	Caused by bacteria and can usually be cured with medication
• Genital herpes ○ Symptoms may appear anytime after infection	• Some have no symptoms • Blisters on mouth or genital region • Blisters last 7 to 21 days • Blisters can reoccur	• Some have no symptoms • Blisters on mouth or genital region • Blisters last 7 to 21 days • Blisters can reoccur	• There is no cure for herpes • Treatment is available • Can pass to sexual partners and to neonate during childbirth	• Caused by a virus • Antiviral medications are available to suppress herpes outbreaks
• Gonorrhea ○ Symptoms may appear 2 to 21 days after infection	• Yellow/gray vaginal discharge • Painful urination/bowel movement • Vaginal bleeding • Stomach cramps	• Yellow/green penile discharge • Painful urination/bowel movement • Frequent urination • Swollen/tender testicles	• Transmitted to sexual partner and to the neonate in uterus/during childbirth • Damage to reproductive organs • Can lead to infertility in women and sterility in men • Can cause heart problems, arthritis, and/or blindness	• Caused by bacteria and can usually be cured with medication • A health care professional can provide antibiotics to treat gonorrhea
• HIV ○ Symptoms can appear months to several years after infection	• Can be infected for several years without symptoms • Weight loss/fatigue • Recurring vaginal yeast infections • Diarrhea/flu-like symptoms • Oral thrush	• Can be infected for several years without symptoms • Weight loss/fatigue • Diarrhea/flu-like symptoms • Oral thrush	• There is no cure for HIV, but treatment is available • Can be passed by sex, sharing needles, to the fetus in uterus/during childbirth, or during breastfeeding • Can cause several illnesses and can lead to death	• HIV is a virus and there is no cure • Medication is available to slow down the progression of HIV

SEXUALLY TRANSMITTED DISEASES

STD	Symptoms in Women	Symptoms in Men	Complications	Treatments
• Human papilloma virus (HPV) ○ There are more than 100 strains of HPV; some may cause genital warts and others have been linked to cancer (cervical, anal) ○ Symptom appearance time varies	• Genital warts ○ Warts can reoccur • Itching/burning around the genitalia • Abnormal pap smear	• Genital warts ○ Warts can reoccur • Itching/burning around the genitalia	• There is no cure for HPV, but treatment is available • Can pass to sexual partners and neonate during childbirth • Warts can spread • Certain strains of HPV may lead to cancer	• HPV is a virus and there is no cure • Depending on the strain of HPV different treatment options are available
• Pelvic inflammatory disease (PID) ○ Several different bacteria can cause PID, and many cases have been related to Chlamydia and gonorrhea. When pushed from the vagina and cervix higher into the female reproductive tract, bacteria can cause PID.	• Lower abdominal pain • Vaginal discharge ○ May have unpleasant odor • Painful intercourse/ urination • Vaginal bleeding	PID does not occur in males	• Can cause ectopic pregnancy (pregnancy in the fallopian tubes) • Can cause damage to the reproductive organs • May require surgery to treat • Can lead to infertility • May cause chronic pain in abdominal area	• Depending on the severity of PID, the following may be used for treatment ○ Antibiotics ○ Hospitalization/ bed rest ○ Outpatient intensive treatment
• Syphilis ○ There are three stages of syphilis. Stage 1 symptoms can appear 1 week to 3 months after infection.	• Stage 1 ○ Sore(s) on genitalia or mouth ○ The sore(s) can last 2 to 6 weeks • Stage 2 ○ Rash on body ○ Flu-like symptoms Tertiary (last) Stage ○ Neurological/ cardiovascular complications	• Stage 1 ○ Sore(s) on genitalia or mouth ○ The sore(s) can last 2 to 6 weeks • Stage 2 ○ Rash on body ○ Flu-like symptoms • Tertiary (last) Stage ○ Neurological/ cardiovascular complications	• Can pass to sexual partners and to the neonate during pregnancy • May cause miscarriage in women • May cause heart disease, blindness, and/or brain damage • Can lead to death	• Syphilis is caused by bacteria and may be cured • A health care professional may provide penicillin for syphilis • Other antibiotics may be available for individuals allergic to penicillin
• Trichomoniasis (Trich) ○ Symptoms can appear 3 days to 2 weeks after infection	• Often no symptoms • Vaginal itching or burning • Yellow/green/gray vaginal discharge	• Often no symptoms • White, watery penile discharge • Painful/frequent urination	• Can pass to sexual partners • Continuation of unpleasant symptoms • Can lead to prostate infection in men	• Trich is caused by a parasite and may be cured • A health care professional may provide medication for Trich

- Provide teaching and support when surgery or cryotherapy is used as a treatment option.

Cancer

- Cervical Cancer – Forms in the tissue of the cervix.
  - Etiology
    - Human papillomavirus is responsible for most cervical cancer, and half of cervical cancer cases occur between the ages 35 and 55. A history of STDs, becoming sexually active at a young age, immunosuppression, and cigarette smoking are contributing factors.
  - Risk factors
    - Many partners with initial sex before age 18
    - History of STDs
    - Immunosuppression
    - Cigarette smoking
  - Manifestations
    - Abnormal bleeding
    - Pelvic pain or pain during intercourse
  - Screening
    - Annual Pap smear
    - HPV, DNA test
  - Treatment
    - Conization, laser surgery, loop electrocautery excision procedure, cryosurgery, hysterectomy, radiation, and/or chemotherapy
  - Prevention
    - Delay initial intercourse.
    - Avoid smoking.
    - Have fewer sexual partners.
    - Gardasil (Human Papillomavirus Quadrivalent) is a vaccine for ages 12 to 26 that is given as three injections over a 6-month period.
- Endometrial Cancer – Originates in the cells of the endometrium and is often detected at an early stage as it produces early vaginal bleeding between menstrual cycles or after menopause.

- Etiology
  - Obesity increases the risk three-fold for women who are 21 to 50 lb overweight; nulliparity; late menopause
- Screening
  - There is no specific diagnostic test. At the time of menopause, all women should be informed about the risks and symptoms of endometrial cancer, and to report any unusual bleeding to the provider.
- Manifestations
  - Postmenopausal bleeding
  - Abnormal bleeding
- Treatment
  - Radium
  - X-ray therapy
  - Hysterectomy
- Nursing Interventions
  - Assess the client for grieving.
  - Provide preoperative teaching.
  - Provide postoperative care.
  - Assess the client's psychosexual needs.
- Ovarian Cancer – Cancerous growth originating from different parts of the ovary.
  - Etiology
    - Contributing factors are unknown, but there is a high incidence with family history. Ovarian cancer is the fifth leading cause of cancer death after lung, breast, colorectal, and pancreatic. Mortality rates are greater in Caucasian women.
  - Risk factors
    - Age 50 and older
    - One or more relatives has a history (mother, daughter, sister)
  - Screening
    - CA 125 blood test – more than 35 u/mL is considered abnormal
    - Intravaginal ultrasound
    - Pelvic exam

NOTES

- o Manifestations
  - Early symptoms are not obvious. Later symptoms may include pressure or pain in the abdomen, pelvis, back or legs, a swollen or bloated abdomen, nausea and indigestion, constipation or diarrhea, fatigue, shortness of breath, frequent urination, and/or vaginal bleeding.
  - o Treatment
    - Chemotherapy, radiation, surgery
- Breast Cancer – abnormal growth of breast tissue
  - o Etiology
    - Initial menses before age 12, initial menopause after age 51
    - First pregnancy after age 35
    - Did not breastfeed
    - Never been pregnant
    - Family history of breast cancer
    - Overweight and sedentary lifestyle
    - Long-term use of hormone replacement therapy
    - Use of oral contraceptives
    - Alcohol use greater than one drink per day
  - o Screening
    - Mammogram – Women 40 and older should get a mammogram every 1 to 2 years.
    - Clinical breast exam – Women should receive this exam annually.
    - Breast self-exam – Women should perform this monthly, 1 week after menses.
  - o Manifestations
    - Lump in breast or armpit
    - Thickening, dimpling, redness, pain, or asymmetry in breasts
    - Pulling, discharge, or pain in nipple area
  - o Treatment
    - Surgery, chemotherapy, radiation, or hormone therapy

Uterine Disorders

- Myomas (uterine fibroids) – Benign fibroid tumors of the uterine muscle.
  - o Etiology
    - African Americans older than age 30 who have never been pregnant
  - o Manifestations
    - Pelvic pain or pressure
    - Hypermenorrhea
  - o Treatment
    - Medication, surgery
- Endometriosis – Endometrial tissue located outside of the uterus.
  - o Etiology
    - May involve retrograde menstruation, hereditary factors, and impaired immune function
  - o Manifestations
    - Severe dysmenorrhea
    - Lower abdominal pain, pain during intercourse, back and rectal pain
    - Abnormal bleeding
  - o Treatment
    - Oral contraceptives (hormone therapy), surgery, or pregnancy

Tubal Disorder

- Pelvic Inflammatory Disease – An infection of the female reproductive organs, which usually occurs when sexually transmitted bacteria spreads from the vagina to the upper genital tract.
  - o Etiology
    - Infections
    - Venereal disease
  - o Complications
    - Ectopic pregnancy
    - Infertility
    - Chronic pelvic pain.
  - o Manifestations
    - Vaginal discharge that is foul smelling, purulent
    - Pain in abdomen, and/or the lower back
    - Elevated temperature, nausea, and/or vomiting

NOTES

- o Treatment
  - Antibiotics
  - Treating all sexual partners
  - Avoiding sexual intercourse until treatment is completed
- o Nursing Interventions
  - Administer antibiotic therapy.
  - Educate the client.
- Menopause – complete cessation of menstruation for 1 year.
  - o Manifestations
    - Hot flashes
    - Palpitations
    - Diaphoresis
    - Osteoporosis
  - o Nursing Interventions
    - Assess the client's psychosocial response.
    - Discuss the merits of estrogen therapy, including prevention of osteoporosis and heart disease.
    - Use alternative therapies (diet, exercise, and/ or calcium supplements).
- Infertility – decreased capacity to conceive.
  - o Etiology
    - Abnormal genitalia
    - Absence of ovulation
    - Blocked fallopian tubes
    - Altered vaginal pH
    - Sperm deficiency or decreased motility
    - Infection
  - o Diagnosis
    - Examination of male reproductive organs
    - Examination of female reproductive organs
  - o Management
    - Medication
      - □ Clomiphene citrate (Clomid) or menotropins (Pergonal); is associated with multiple births

- □ Hormone replacement
- Artificial insemination
- In vitro fertilization
- Surrogate parenting
- o Nursing Interventions
  - Provide emotional support to the client.
  - Provide client education.

Contraception

- Nursing Assessment
  - o Determine the client's knowledge about and previous experience with family planning.
  - o Determine the client's need for genetic counseling.
  - o Identify infertility problems.
  - o Assess risks associated with the client's chosen contraceptive method.
- Types
  - o Natural (rhythm) method
    - Use of calendar, basal body temperature, and cervical mucus methods
  - o Nursing Intervention
    - □ Teach the method to the client.
  - o Oral contraceptives
    - Side effects are similar to pregnancy, which include initial discomforts, hypertension, clotting problems, and fluid retention
    - Contraindications
      - □ Older than age 35
      - □ Hypertensive
      - □ The client smokes
      - □ Client has a history of clotting disorder
    - Nursing Interventions
      - □ Teach the method to the client.
      - □ Assess the client for complications (increased blood pressure).
  - o Injectable contraceptive
    - Medroxyprogesterone acetate (Depo-Provera) administered every 3 months via an IM injection

NOTES

- Side effects include irregular, unpredictable menses
  - o Ortho Evra patch is a skin patch that is worn on the lower abdomen, buttocks, or upper body that releases progestin and estrogen
    - Less effective in women weighing more than 200 lb
    - Worn for 3 weeks and removed for 1 week during menses
  - o NuvaRing
    - A flexible 2-inch ring that is inserted into the vagina to release progestin and estrogen
    - Can cause vaginal discharge, vaginitis, and irritation
    - Worn for 3 weeks and removed for 1 week during menses
    - If the ring falls out for more than 3 hr, use back-up method until the ring has been in place for 7 consecutive days
  - o Intrauterine device
    - High risk of pelvic inflammatory disease, ectopic pregnancy, and perforation of the uterus; periods may be heavy (anemia)

    - Nursing Interventions
      - □ Instruct the client about the importance of follow up.
      - □ Instruct the client to receive regular pap tests.
      - □ Teach the client how to frequently feel for strings.
  - o Mechanical barriers
    - Diaphragm

      - □ Nursing Interventions
        - ▸ Teach the client how to insert the diaphragm.
        - ▸ Teach the client how to use spermicidal jelly with the diaphragm.
        - ▸ Teach the client to leave the diaphragm in for 6 to 8 hr after intercourse.
        - ▸ Teach the client to have the diaphragm refitted if she gains or loses weight or after childbirth.

- Condom

    - □ Nursing Interventions – female condom (vaginal sheath)
      - ▸ Teach the client how to use it with spermicide.
      - ▸ Tell the client that it protects against STDs, including HIV.
    - □ Nursing Interventions – male condom
      - ▸ Teach the client to leave a space at the end.
      - ▸ Teach the client how to prevent slipping or tearing during removal.
      - ▸ Tell the client that it protects against STDs, including HIV.
  - Cervical cap – can be left in place for up to 12 hr
  - o Chemical barriers (spermicides)

    - Nursing Interventions
      - □ Teach the client about possible allergic reactions.
      - □ Teach the client how to clean the equipment.
      - □ Advise the client not to douche for 6 to 8 hr after intercourse.
  - o Sterilization
    - Tubal ligation

      - □ Nursing Interventions
        - ▸ Discuss the permanency of this procedure with the client.
        - ▸ Discuss methods of obstructing the tubes.
    - Vasectomy
      - □ Nursing Interventions
        - ▸ Discuss the permanency of this procedure with the client.
        - ▸ Warn the client of the need for a negative sperm count three times before attempting to engage in unprotected intercourse.
  - o Methods that are not completely reliable
    - Withdrawal/coitus interruptus
    - Douching

NOTES

UNIT SIX

NURSING CARE OF CHILDREN

SECTION 1

GROWTH AND DEVELOPMENT

Newborn/Infant

AGE	VITAL SIGNS
Newborn – birth to 28 days	• Temperature: 97.7° to 99.5° auxiliary • Apical heart rate – 120 to 160/min • Respirations – 30 to 60 breaths/min • Blood pressure – 73/55 mm Hg
One year old – 1 month to 1 year	• Temperature – 97° to 99.0° auxiliary • Apical heart rate 90 to 130/min • Respirations – 20 to 40 breaths/min • Blood pressure – 90/56 mm Hg

- Physical characteristics
  - Height – increases by 50% in first year
  - Weight – birth weight doubles by 6 months; birth weight triples by 1 year
  - Head – 70% of adult size at birth; 80% of adult size by end of first year
    - Posterior fontanel – closes by 2 months of age
    - Anterior fontanel – closes between 12 to 18 months of age
      - Bulging – classic sign of increased intracranial pressure
      - Sunken – classic sign of dehydration
  - Dentition
    - Drools at 4 months
    - Six primary teeth by 1 year (age of child in months minus 6 equals number of teeth)

- Nursing Interventions
  - Avoid phenytoin (Dilantin), because it causes gingivitis and gingival hyperplasia. Also, avoid medications that may stain the infant's teeth (tetracycline, iron).
  - Teach the parents to watch for increased drooling, finger sucking, and biting on objects, which are all indicators of teething.
  - Inform the parents that cool or cold items such as teething rings are soothing.
  - Use acetaminophen (Tylenol) for continued irritability.
  - Educate the parents that once dentition occurs they should avoid giving the infant a nighttime bottle that contains juice or formula, because it increases the incidence of dental caries (bottle mouth caries).
  - Reflexes
    - Rooting (disappears by 3 to 4 months)
    - Tonic neck (disappears by 3 to 4 months)
    - Palmar grasp (disappears by 3 to 4 months)
    - Moro (disappears by 3 to 4 months)
    - Sucking (continues through infancy)
    - Stepping (disappears by 3 to 4 months)
  - Vital signs
    - Pulse ranges from 100 to 140/min, and may even be as high as 160/min depending upon activity
    - Respirations range from 30 to 40/min
    - Immature thermoregulatory mechanisms
    - Crying will increase all vital signs
- Nutrition
  - Infant feeding
    - Allow the infant to set his own schedule.
    - Breast or bottle feeding depends on the mother's preference.

NOTES

- Give vitamin supplements as prescribed; usually starting around 3 to 4 months (vitamin D and iron); fluoride supplements are prescribed for infants who are breastfed.
- Adequate infant growth requires between 100 to 110 calories/kg/day.

o Introduction of solid foods

- Physiologic readiness
  - □ Tongue extrusion reflex (fades by about 4 months)
  - □ Digestive enzymes
  - □ Motor skills – sits with support; head and neck control
  - □ Shows interest in solid food
- Nutritional guidelines
  - □ Introduce solid foods around 4 to 6 months.
  - □ Introduce foods one at a time, every 4 to 7 days, and watch for any allergies.
  - □ Introduce food in a sequence at 1-month intervals.
    - ▸ Rice cereal (a good source of iron; no wheat)
    - ▸ Vegetables and then fruits (yellow first, and then green)
    - ▸ Meats (begin with chicken, then turkey)
    - ▸ Egg yolks (avoid egg whites)
  - □ Begin table foods around 8 months to 1 year.
    - ▸ Avoid giving the infant nuts, foods with seeds, raisins, popcorn, or grapes, because of the risk for aspiration.
    - ▸ Give finger foods to the infant to help enhance the thumb-finger apposition.
  - □ When switching from formula to cow's milk, avoid skim milk. The infant needs whole milk, because it has more fat.
  - □ As the amount of solids increases, reduce the quantity of milk to no more than 30 oz/day.
  - □ Never mix food or medication with formula.

- □ Do not use sweeteners like honey or corn syrup, to avoid the risk of botulism.

o Weaning

- The infant should begin to wean around 4 to 6 months when he starts to sip from a cup. Parents can use a training cup with a sipper tube and/or handles.
- Introduce the cup gradually.
- Remove the bottle or breastfeeding one at a time. Remove the nighttime feeding last.
- By 12 to 14 months, the infant should be able to drink from a cup.

o Nutritional concerns

- Colic
  - □ Seen in infants younger than 3 months
  - □ Paroxysmal abdominal pain is associated with crying and accumulation of gas
  - □ Associated with overfeeding, air swallowing, and maternal insecurity
  - □ Nursing Interventions
    - ▸ Feed the infant slowly and burp him frequently.
    - ▸ Avoid feeding the infant excessively.
    - ▸ Increase bonding between the mother and the infant.
    - ▸ Teach the mother various feeding and holding techniques.
- Iron-deficiency anemia
  - □ A result of poor diet or low-iron stores in the infant
  - □ Seldom seen in the first 6 months, due to iron stores inherited from the mother
  - □ Most frequently seen in infants between 6 months and 1 year who ingest large quantities of milk
  - □ RBCs appear microcytic and hypochromic
  - □ Use an iron-fortified formula and/or cereal to prevent
  - □ Ferrous sulfate (Feosol) is the medication of choice

NOTES

- □ Nursing Interventions
  - ► Administer the medication between meals.
  - ► Administer with citrus juice for greater iron absorption.
  - ► Teach the parents that liquid preparations may stain the infant's teeth.
  - ► Inform the parents that iron may cause tarry stools.
- Activity/rest
  - o Normal infants sleep 14 to 16 hr/day
  - o Nocturnal pattern of sleep develops by 3 to 4 months
- Motor skills
  - o 2 months
    - Smiles socially
    - Demonstrates differentiated cry
    - Turns head from side to side
  - o 3 months
    - Follows object 180° horizontal and vertical (20/100 visual acuity at birth)
    - Discovers hands
    - Reaches for object
    - Lifts head off bed and bears weight on forearms
  - o 4 months
    - Recognizes familiar objects and moves extremities in response
    - Sits with support
    - Reaches for object
    - Laughs out loud
    - Begins to recognize parent
    - Rolls back to side
    - Exhibits almost no head lag
  - o 5 to 6 months
    - Rolls over completely
    - Bangs with object held in hand
    - Vocalizes displeasure when object is taken away
    - Rakes object
    - Exhibits no head lag
  - o 6 to 8 months
    - Holds own bottle (6 months)
    - Transfers toy (7 months)
    - Begins pincer grasp (8 months)
    - Shows a fear of strangers (stranger anxiety)
    - Sits alone (8 months)
  - o 9 to 12 months
    - Pulls self to feet (9 months)
    - Stands alone
    - Walks with help
    - Uses spoon, with spilling
    - Cruises (9 months); crawls well (10 months)
    - Claps hands on request
    - Imitates behavior
    - Smiles at image in the mirror
- Language development
  - o Vocalizes (distinct from crying) by 3 to 4 months
  - o Recognizes 'no' by 9 months; own name by 10 months
  - o Two to three words in addition to 'mama,' 'dada' by 12 months
- Developmental stages
  - o Psychosocial development (Erikson)
    - Trust vs. mistrust
    - Quality of parent/child relationship
  - o Cognitive development (Piaget)
    - Sensorimotor phase
      - □ Reflexive
      - □ Imitates and recognizes new experiences
    - Object permanence
      - □ Understands that self and object are separate (10 months)
      - □ Searches for lost object (12 months)

NOTES

□ Separation anxiety
(8 to 12 months)

- Play

  o Solitary

  o Characteristics

    ▪ 1 to 3 months – verbal, visual, tactile stimuli

      □ Toys should be brightly colored, washable, of various sizes, shapes, and textures

      □ Enhanced eye-hand coordination

        ▸ Mobiles, cradle gyms

        ▸ Busy box, toys with faces

      □ Stimulate auditory senses (rattles, music box)

    ▪ 4 to 6 months – initiates and recognizes new experiences

      □ Mobility increasing

      □ Hand coordination increasing

      □ Starts having a memory

      □ Types of toys

        ▸ Mirrors to see image

        ▸ Chewable, large toys

        ▸ Brightly colored rattles, beads

        ▸ Squeeze toys, teething rings

        ▸ Cradle gym should be removed to avoid accidents

    ▪ 6 to 12 months

      □ Increased self-awareness

      □ Repeats pleasurable activities

      □ Object permanence

      □ Imitates behavior at 10 months (peek-a-boo)

      □ Increased desire to explore

      □ Types of toys

        ▸ Large boxes, kitchen utensils

        ▸ Water play with supervision

        ▸ Texture play (sand, dirt)

        ▸ Pouring, filling, dumping

        ▸ Playing with food (the start of self-feeding)

  o Safety measures

    ▪ Toys should be large with short strings.

    ▪ Toys should be constructed out of nontoxic materials.

    ▪ Always supervise the infant.

    ▪ Inspect toys for rough edges or parts that can be pulled off and swallowed.

  o Health maintenance

    ▪ Safety

      □ Avoid overstimulation and rough handling of the infant.

      □ Limit-setting should involve redirecting the infant's behaviors to safer activities.

  o Immunizations

    ▪ The Centers for Disease Control and Prevention (CDC) publishes a recommended schedule annually that protects infants and children from 14 diseases by building immunity.

      □ Diphtheria

      □ Hepatitis A

      □ Hepatitis B

      □ Haemophilus influenza type B

      □ Influenza

      □ Measles

      □ Mumps

      □ Pertussis

      □ Meningococcal

      □ Polio

      □ Rubella

      □ Tetanus

      □ Chickenpox

      □ Rotavirus

  o Infant restraints

    ▪ Use a semi-reclining infant car seat that faces the rear until the infant weighs 10 kg (20 lb).

    ▪ Use a seat belt to anchor the car seat.

    ▪ The middle of a car's back seat is the safest area for the infant's car seat to be placed.

    ▪ Infant car seats should not be used in the front seat because of passenger-side airbags.

NOTES

- o Aspiration of foreign objects
  - Common objects include food, buttons from clothing, baby powder, and small toys
  - Emergency measures for an infant who is choking
    - Administer 5 back blows, 5 chest thrusts (repeat until successful).
    - Do not perform a blind finger sweep.
- o Health deviations
  - Accidents are the leading cause of death for infants up to 1 year
    - Falls (depth perception does not develop until 7 to 9 months)
    - Suffocation, aspiration, and drowning
    - Burns
  - Parent education
    - Childproof the environment.
    - Constantly supervise the infant.
    - Provide anticipatory guidance.
      - ‣ Provide an appropriate car seat restraint.
      - ‣ Assess the temperature of the infant's bath water, formula, and food.
      - ‣ Do not prop the bottle during the infant's feedings or at bed time.
      - ‣ Supervise the infant during bath time, changing table, and play time.
      - ‣ Select age-appropriate toys for the infant.
      - ‣ Turn handles of pots/pans away from the infant's reach.
      - ‣ Keep side rails of the infant's crib up during bed time.
- o Sudden Infant Death Syndrome (SIDS)
  - Cause of SIDS is unknown, but contains multiple theories.
  - Infants who are at risk
  - Mostly boys who are ages 2 to 4 months
  - Preterm infants who have apnea problems
  - Multiple births

- Occurs during sleep, usually in winter months
- Parent education
  - The infant should sleep in a supine or side-lying position, not prone.
  - Provide a firm mattress with no pillows. Avoid overheating the infant during sleep.
  - There is a lower incidence of SIDS if the infant is breastfed.

Toddler

AGE	VITAL SIGNS
Toddler – 1 to 3 years	• Temperature – 97.5° to 98.6° auxiliary • Apical heart rate – 180 to 120/min • Respirations – 20 to 30 breaths/min • Blood pressure – 92/55 mm Hg

- Physical characteristics
  - o Large abdomen, long legged, clumsy
  - o Slowing rate of growth for height and weight (adult height – approximately doubles height at 2 years)
  - o Dentition
    - By 2 ½ years – all 20 primary teeth
    - Adult should brush child's teeth by age 2
    - First visit to dentist by age 2
  - o Vital signs
    - Pulse – ranges from 80 to 110/min
    - Respirations – range from 25 to 35/min
    - Blood pressure – average is 100/70 mm Hg
- Nutrition
  - o Growth lag (80 calories/kg)
  - o Expresses independence through food preferences; food fads are common
  - o Wants to feed self; very ritualistic, messy
  - o Space meals with frequent nutritious snacks (cheese, peanut butter and jelly sandwiches)

NOTES

- o Small portions (physiologic anorexia)
- o Fluid requirements – 115 mL/kg/day
  (3 cups whole milk/day)
- Activity/rest
  - o Sleeps 10 to 12 hr with naps
  - o Routines and rituals are reassuring
  - o Nightmares and night terrors are possible
- Motor skills
  - o 13 to 16 months
    - Uses spoon and cup, but will spill
    - Walks without help (since about 13 months)
    - Climbs up and down stairs on buttocks
    - Mimics housework
    - Stacks 2 to 3 blocks (15 months)
    - Throws and drops things (15 months)
    - Loves containers of all kinds
  - o 16 to 18 months
    - Runs clumsily; falls often
    - Throws ball overhand
    - Pulls and pushes toys
    - Uses spoon and cup without spilling
    - Removes clothes (shoes, socks)
    - Jumps in place
    - Kicks small ball
  - o 2 years
    - Walks up and down stairs
    - Runs well
    - Turns knobs to open doors; unscrews lids
    - Dresses self in simple clothing
    - Builds tower of 5 blocks
    - Turns pages of a book
    - Climbs
  - o 2 ½ to 3 years
    - Holds crayon with fingers
    - May have daytime bowel and bladder control
    - Strings beads
- Language development
  - o Ten words by 18 months
  - o May say "no" when agreeing (means "yes")
  - o Uses two-to three-word phrases by 2 years; vocabulary of 300 words; verbalizes needs (toileting, food, drink); uses pronouns
  - o Gives first and last name by 2 ½ years
- Developmental stages
  - o Psychosocial development (Erikson)
    - Autonomy vs. shame and doubt (1 to 3 years)
      - □ Egocentric
      - □ Negativism and temper tantrums
      - □ Uninhibited at showing independence
    - Gains control over bodily functions
  - o Cognitive development (Piaget)
    - Sensorimotor (1 to 2 years)
      - □ Objects are cause of action
      - □ Separation anxiety
    - Preoperational (2 to 4 years)
      - □ Concrete thinking begins
      - □ Egocentric
      - □ Symbolic play
- Play
  - o Parallel play
    - No sharing
    - Ownership determined by possession of object
    - Short attention span
  - o Types of activities
    - Gross motor
      - □ Jungle gym
      - □ Push-pull toys
      - □ Tricycle (2 ½ to 3 years)
    - Fine motor
      - □ Crayons, paints, paper
      - □ Building blocks
      - □ Musical toys
    - Enjoys being read to

NOTES

- Health maintenance
  - Toilet training (18 months to 2 years)
    - Physiologic readiness (sphincter control at approximately 18 months)
    - Imitation; potty chair
    - May not be complete until 4 to 5 years of age (nocturnal control often delayed)
  - Discipline
    - Toddlers are negative and ritualistic
    - Limits must be simple and consistent
  - Safety
    - Precautions
      - Childproof the environment.
      - Supervise at all times.
      - Use child restraining devices (may switch to a forward-facing car seat when the child weighs approximately 10 kg [20 lb]).
    - Immunizations
      - MMR – 15 months
      - HIB – 15 months
      - DTaP, IPV – 18 months
      - Varicella zoster (chickenpox) – after 1 year
- Health deviations
  - Accidents
    - Motor vehicles – passengers, pedestrians
    - Burns
    - Drowning/suffocation/aspiration
    - Falls
    - Ingestions
      - Have phone number for poison control and emergency department readily available.
      - Lock up all medications and potentially toxic substances.
      - Use child resistant caps appropriately.
      - Avoid referring to medication as candy.
      - Avoid transferring potentially toxic solutions from original containers.

  - Anticipatory guidance
    - Supervise the toddler closely near water.
    - Store flammables and lighters out of the toddler's reach.
    - Use child car seats in vehicles.
    - Avoid giving the toddler foods that can easily be aspirated, such as grapes, hot dogs, popcorn, round candy, and nuts.

Preschooler

AGE	VITAL SIGNS
Preschooler – 3 to 6 years	• Temperature – 97.5° to 98.6° auxiliary • Apical heart rate – 70 to 110/min • Respirations – 16 to 22 breaths/min • Blood pressure – 95/57 mm Hg

- Physical characteristics – an average 4-year-old is 101 cm (40 in) tall and weighs 18 kg (40 lb)
- Nutrition
  - Growth lag (70 kcal/kg)
  - Encourage finger foods such as cheese and fruit
  - Food fads are common
- Activity/rest
  - May give up nap, but still needs quiet time
  - Peak time for sleep disturbances
    - Refusal to go to bed
      - Child resists bed time and comes out of room frequently
      - Nursing Interventions
        - Stress the need for a consistent bed time.
        - Help the parents' identify strategies to ignore attention-seeking behaviors.
        - Suggest that parents avoid bringing a child into their bed (consider client's culture).
        - Promote the use of a transitional object such as a blanket or a toy.

NOTES

- Nighttime fears
  - Child resists bed time because of a fear of the dark or monsters.
  - Nursing Interventions
    - Tell the parents to reassure the child in a calm manner.
    - Suggest that parents use a night light for the child.
    - Suggest that parents monitor what the child watches on TV when it is nearing bed time.

- Motor skills
  - 3 years
    - Dresses with supervision, but still needs help with buttons
    - Rides a tricycle
    - Climbs the stairs with alternate feet
    - Pours fluid from a pitcher
  - 4 years
    - Hops and skips on one foot
    - Walks upstairs without using a handrail and alternates feet walking down the stairs
    - Uses scissors
    - Laces shoes, but cannot tie
  - 5 years
    - Hops and skips on alternate feet
    - Walks backward
    - Can master a two-wheel bike or roller skates
    - Uses simple tools and can print name
    - May master tying shoes

- Language development
  - 3 years
    - Vocabulary of 900 words
    - Talks constantly, regardless of whether anyone is listening
    - Talks in complete sentences
  - 4 years
    - Vocabulary of 1,500 words
    - Questions constantly
    - Exaggerates by telling tall tales
    - May stutter and pick up profanity
  - 5 years
    - Vocabulary of 2,000 words
    - Uses all parts of speech
    - Speech is 100% intelligible to others, although some sounds may still be imperfect

- Developmental stages
  - Psychosocial development (Erikson)
    - Initiative vs. guilt (3 to 5 years)
      - Vigorous behavior
      - Limit testing
    - Child develops a conscience
  - Cognitive development (Piaget)
    - Preoperational (2 to 7 years)
      - Egocentric in thought and behavior
      - Concrete, tangible thinking
      - Vivid imagination
        - Magical thinking (thoughts can cause events)
        - Peak age for fears
  - Socialization
    - 3 years
      - May have an imaginary friend
      - Increased ability to separate from parents
    - 4 years
      - May be bossy and impatient
      - Privacy and independence become important
    - 5 years
      - Less rebellious and more responsible
      - Cares for self and hygiene needs with minimal supervision
  - Sexuality
    - Knows own sex and sex of others by 3 years
    - Masturbation is a normal, healthy expression, if it is not excessive
    - Sexual exploration demonstrated in playing doctor
    - Answers questions honestly and simply

NOTES

- Play
  - Cooperative play beginning
    - Enjoys loud, physical activities
    - More socialization during play
    - Self-criticism or boasting becomes evident
  - Purposes of play
    - Increased coordination
    - Decreased tension and anxiety
    - Deal with fantasies
    - Enhanced self-esteem
    - Sense of power and control
    - Increased knowledge of self
  - Materials
    - Physical – bat, ball, sand box, sled, bike, puzzles
    - Dramatic – dress-up clothes, dolls, costumes; imitate adult behavior
    - Creative – pens, paper, crayons, paint, scissors, play dough, chalk
- Health maintenance
  - Safety
    - Car seats
      - Forward-facing car seats for children weighing 40 to 80 lb
      - Parents are encouraged to follow the manufacturer's recommendation for height and weight
    - Maintain the immunization schedule
    - Anticipatory guidance
    - Traffic safety
    - Water safety
      - Personal safety to prevent abduction

School-Age Child

AGE	VITAL SIGNS
School-Age Child – 6 to 12 years	• Temperature – 97.5° to 98.6° auxiliary • Apical heart rate – 70 to 100/min • Respirations – 16 to 20/min • Blood pressure – 107/64 mm Hg

- Physical characteristics
  - Grows 2.5 to 5 cm/year (1 to 2 in/year)
  - Gains 1 to 3 kg/year (3 to 7 lb/year)
  - Pubescent changes may begin to appear
    - Girls – by approximately 10 to 12 years
    - Boys – by approximately 12 to 14 years
  - Vital signs become similar to adults
    - Pulse – ranges from 60 to 80/min
    - Respirations – range from 18 to 20/min
    - Blood pressure – averages 90 to 110/55 to 60 mm Hg
  - Dentition
    - Permanent teeth start showing up at about 6 years
    - 32 permanent teeth by 18 years of age
    - May wear braces (orthodontia)
- Nutrition
  - Food selections are influenced by peers and mass media
  - Junk food and fast food full of empty calories is preferred; encourage nutritious snacks
  - Obesity is possible if there is inadequate exercise
- Activity/rest
  - Sleeps 8 to 10 hr/day with vivid dreams
  - Somnambulism (sleep walking) is common
- Motor skills
  - Gross-motor skills

NOTES

- Roller skates, bicycles, skateboards, scooters
- Competitive sports
- Swimming
  - Fine-motor skills
    - Cursive writing
    - Musical instruments
    - Arts and crafts
    - Keyboarding skills
- Language development
  - Masters all sounds by 7 ½ to 8 years
  - Uses telephone and computer to communicate with peers
  - Reads and writes
- Developmental stages
  - Psychosocial development (Erikson)
    - Industry vs. inferiority (6 to 12 years)
      - Primary tasks relate to learning skills and activities
      - Afraid of failure and gets embarrassed by poor grades
    - Child develops self-esteem
  - Cognitive development (Piaget)
    - Concrete operations (7 to 11 years)
      - Classifies and sorts; enjoys collecting
      - Concrete logic and problem solving
      - Less egocentric
    - Inductive thinking
  - Socialization
    - Prefers peers of same age and sex
    - Responds positively to rewards
    - Belonging is important – enjoys scouts, clubs, team sports; may join a gang
    - Cliques may become evident (9 to 10 years)
    - May be left alone for short periods (10 to 12 years), but that depends on the maturity of the child
  - Sexuality
    - Preadolescents need specific, age-appropriate information about puberty and physical changes (10 to 12 years)

- Answer questions openly and honestly
- Develops interest in opposite sex (10 to 12 years)
- Play
  - Cooperative
  - Characteristics
    - Clubs or gangs (8 to 12 years)
    - Best friends (9 to 10 years)
    - Secrets
  - Suggested play activities
    - Table games
    - Collections
    - Computer or video games
    - Community sports or group activities
    - Creative (dance, art, music)
- Health maintenance
  - Safety
    - Prevention
      - Focus on teaching the child to be safe
      - No longer needs parental supervision at all times
    - Recommended immunizations for 11 to 12 year old
      - Tetanus, diphtheria, pertussis
      - Human papillomavirus
      - Meningococcal
  - Common behavior issues
    - Swearing
    - Lying
    - Cheating
    - Stealing
    - Nail biting
    - Sibling rivalry
      - Often jealous of younger/older sibling
      - Encourage the parent not to become involved except in cases of physical/emotional harm
  - Discipline
    - No punitive measures

NOTES

- Consistency
- Withdrawal of privileges
- Time out
  - Stress and coping
    - School-age children face enormous societal pressures.
    - They do not have cognitive skills to deal with societal pressures.
    - Professionals need to be aware that sleep problems, enuresis, changes in appetite, or behavioral problems may be indicative of inadequate coping.
- Health deviations
  - Accidents
    - Motor vehicles (use seat belts)
    - Fractures due to increased activity (use helmets and other protective gear)
    - Firearms
      - Make sure firearms are always kept locked up and out of reach of children (these accidents are increasing in frequency).
    - Drowning
  - School phobia
    - Fear or dread of school
    - Manifestations
      - Nausea, vomiting, and/or abdominal pain on school mornings
      - Abrupt onset
      - Manifestations subside when child is at home
    - Etiology
      - Teacher/child mismatch
      - Fear of failure
      - Bully
    - Treatment
      - Identify the child's cause for concern
      - Support the child in attending school daily
      - Seek professional (psychiatric) help in severe cases

Adolescent

AGE	VITAL SIGNS
Adolescent – 12 to 20 years	• Temperature – 97.5° to 98.6° auxiliary • Apical heart rate – 55 to 90/min • Respirations – 12 to 20 breaths/min • Blood pressure – 120/70 mm Hg

- Physical characteristics
  - Very individualized
  - By 17 years, 100% of adult stature
  - Vital signs reach adult norms
  - Dentition
    - Third molars (wisdom teeth) develop by approximately 18 years
    - Orthodontia in progress or completed
  - Sexual maturation/puberty
    - Female
      - Breast enlargement (approximately 11 years)
      - Pubic hair
      - Growth spurt
      - Menarche (onset of menstruation)
        - Approximately 11 years of age
        - Ovulation approximately 6 months to 1 year after menarche
    - Male
      - Body hair growth
      - Growth of external genitalia
      - Growth spurts and increased muscle mass
      - Voice changes
      - Ejaculation/nocturnal emission
- Nutrition
  - Growth spurt
  - Increased protein, iron, and calcium needs
- Activity/rest
  - Sleep needs increase due to growth demands

NOTES

- o Tires easily
- Motor skills
  - o Risk takers
  - o Sense of indestructibility
  - o General increase in physical and psychomotor skills enhances the adolescent's self-esteem
- Language development
  - o Sophisticated ability to communicate through verbal and written means
  - o Use of slang is prominent
- Developmental stages
  - o Psychosocial development (Erikson)
    - Identify formation vs. identify diffusion (12 to 18 years)
      - □ Identify future career goals
      - □ Incorporate physical changes into identity
  - o Cognitive development (Piaget)
    - Formal operations (11+ years)
    - Abstract thinking (ability to hypothesize)
  - o Socialization
    - Emancipation from family
    - Peer groups have major influence because of the strong need to belong
    - Employment
    - Less adult supervision
  - o Sexuality
    - Establishes sexual identity and orientation
    - Experiments with intimate relationships
    - Common issues
      - □ Sexually transmitted diseases
      - □ Human immunodeficiency virus (HIV)
      - □ Adolescent pregnancy
- Recreation
  - o Reflects psychosocial needs
  - o Group activities with mixed sexes
  - o May include dating, sports
  - o Suggested recreational activities for adolescent who is hospitalized
    - Computer or video games

- Cards
- Portable CD player
- Health maintenance
  - o Safety
    - Accident prevention
      - □ Focus on educating the adolescent to make safe choices
      - □ Be alert to signs of depression, substance abuse
    - Immunizations
      - □ Tetanus-diphtheria (Td) needed every 10 years
      - □ Hepatitis B series if not previously administered
  - o Discipline
    - Increased independence
    - Consistency
  - o Stress and coping
    - Faced with enormous societal pressures
    - Feels pressure to belong, conform, and achieve
    - Common reactions to stress
      - □ Early adolescent – mood swings and self-focused
      - □ Middle adolescent – increased rebellious behavior
      - □ Later adolescent – better coping skills
    - Common issues
      - □ Runaways
      - □ Eating disorders
      - □ Substance abuse
        - ▸ Nonprescription, illicit, or street drugs
        - ▸ Alcohol
        - ▸ Tobacco
- Health deviations
  - o Crashes
    - Motor vehicles
      - □ Driver's education
      - □ Drunk driving
    - Firearms

NOTES

- Spinal cord injuries
- Drowning
  - o Homicide
  - o Suicide

SECTION 2

THE HOSPITALIZED CHILD

Stress of Hospitalization

- Potential Regression
  - o Children usually adapt well to hospitalization
  - o Respect the child's use of this defense mechanism
  - o Assist the child to achieve past developmental levels
- Child's Reaction to Hospitalization (Age/ Developmental Specific)
  - o Protest – strong, conscious need for a parent; may be confused, frightened, or cry
  - o Despair – mourning period; may be withdrawn and apathetic
  - o Denial – represses true feelings; feels the parent has failed; interested in surroundings, but not the parent
- Developmental Influences on Stress of Hospitalization
  - o Infant: trust vs. mistrust
    - 0 to 6 months – loss of consistent parent
    - 6 to 12 months – strong need for the parent; separation anxiety
  - o Toddler – autonomy vs. shame and doubt
    - Separation anxiety, loss of significant other, inconsistency
    - Loss of mobility due to restraints, crib
  - o Preschooler – initiative vs. guilt
    - Separation anxiety
    - Threats to body integrity may cause increased aggression
  - o Concept of illness
    - Magical thinking (believes that feelings and thoughts can cause the illness)

- May believe the illness or hospitalization is a punishment
- School-age child – industry vs. inferiority
  - o Loss of control
  - o Separation from peers, school, and activities
  - o Concept of illness
    - Perceives an external cause for illness
    - May view the illness as a result of doing something wrong
    - Understands the difference between acute and chronic illness
- Adolescent – identity vs. role diffusion
  - o Threats to body image
  - o Loss of control
  - o Separation from peers, school, and activities
  - o Concept of illness
    - Adolescent believes she is invulnerable
    - Understands the internal cause of her disease
    - Cooperates with treatment plan if she understands the immediate benefits
- Stress of Hospitalization on Family
  - o Shock and Denial
    - Recognize and accept defense mechanisms by allowing the family to verbalize their feelings.
    - Enhance coping strategies.
    - Implement an open visitation policy so the family can stay with child as much as possible.
    - Explain to the family that regressive behavior and separation anxiety is normal and expected.
- Adjustment
  - o Encourage communication between the family and medical personnel.
  - o Encourage the family to participate in decision-making and care giving.
- Reaction to Pain

 Point to Remember – A rule of thumb to assume is that if a procedure would be painful for an adult, it is also painful for a child

---

NOTES

Nursing Interventions – Strategies for pain management

- o Age-appropriate assessment
  - Ask child with age-appropriate language.
  - Use pain-rating tool (Baker-Wong, Faces).
  - Conduct developmental pain assessment.
    - □ Infant
      - ▸ Generalized body response of rigidity, thrashing
      - ▸ Loud crying, facial expression
      - ▸ May sleep to avoid pain experience
    - □ Toddler
      - ▸ Localized response – will withdraw from pain
      - ▸ Physical resistance after painful stimulation
    - □ Preschooler
      - ▸ Verbalizes pain
      - ▸ Attempts to avoid painful stimulus
      - ▸ May view pain as punishment
    - □ School-age child
      - ▸ Verbalizes pain
      - ▸ Stalling behavior; vocal protest
      - ▸ Recognizes physical cause of pain
    - □ Adolescent
      - ▸ Sophisticated, verbal expression of pain
      - ▸ Less resistance offered – still physical, vocal
      - ▸ Understands physical and psychological pain
- o Use of pharmacological control methods
  - Weight-appropriate (kg/lb) dosages
  - Oral and IV routes are preferred over IM because the child will avoid the shot
  - Use conscious sedation for painful procedures – midazolam (Versed), fentanyl citrate (Sublimaze)
  - PCA is appropriate for children who understand the cause and effect (approximately 7 years)
  - Eutectic mixture of local anesthetics (EMLA) cream is a topical anesthetic that can be applied as a thick dollop and covered with a transparent dressing approximately 1 to 2 hr prior to a procedure (venipuncture, injection) to lessen the pain
- o Use of nonpharmacological control methods
  - Distraction
  - Relaxation
  - Kinesthetic (rocking) stimulation
- Strategies for Stress Reduction
  - o Prefacility preparation, preoperative teaching, and tour
  - o Specially trained pediatric staff
  - o Use of outpatient facilities eliminates the need for overnight hospitalization and separation
- Therapeutic play
  - o Purposes
    - Mastery of situation
    - Ego strengthening
    - Deal with fears, anxiety, and the unknown
  - o Nursing Interventions
    - Play with the child based on his developmental level and illness.
    - Allow the child to set the pace of play.
    - Provide a variety of play materials.
    - Reflect back on the child's feelings.
- Communication strategies
  - o Appropriate for the situation
  - o Be clear and consistent
  - o Communicate in an age-appropriate manner with the child
    - Verbal
    - Nonverbal

NOTES

SECTION 3

NURSING CARE OF THE CHILD WITH CONGENITAL ANOMALIES

Congenital Heart Defects

- Hemodynamics of Fetal Circulation
  - Ductus venosus – carries oxygenated blood from placenta to inferior vena cava; partially bypasses liver; closes by approximately 8th week of life
  - Ductus arteriosus – bypasses flow of blood through lungs by shunting oxygenated and unoxygenated blood from pulmonary artery to aorta; closes 7 to 10 days after birth
  - Foramen ovale – connects right and left atria; allows blood to flow from right atrium to left atrium, bypassing the right ventricle and pulmonary circuit; closes in 2 to 3 months
  - Transition to newborn circulation
  - At first breath, lungs expand, which increases blood flow to pulmonary system
  - Pulmonary vascular resistance is decreased and systemic vascular resistance increases
  - These changes lead to the closure of the ductus venosus, ductus arteriosus, and foramen ovale
- Contributing Factors
  - Unknown etiology, but possible genetic factors in addition to intrauterine infection, radiation, or medications.
  - Incidence is 1 in 1,000 live births and accounts for 50% of all deaths in the first year of life. May be associated with other birth defects and syndromes.
  - May not be diagnosed while hospitalized in newborn nursery.
- Clinical Assessments
  - Newborn
    - Cyanosis – especially circumoral and acrocyanosis; cyanosis on exertion (feeding, crying)
    - Dyspnea – especially on exertion
    - Failure to thrive

- Frequent upper respiratory infections
- Feeding difficulty
- Weak or muffled cry
  - Older child
    - Cyanosis and dyspnea (as above)
    - Impaired growth
    - Fatigue
    - Digital clubbing
    - Squatting
    - Polycythemia – increased RBC count to compensate for impaired gas exchange; increases oxygen-carrying capacity of blood
  - Heart failure
    - Tachypnea, dyspnea
    - Exercise intolerance
    - Tachycardia (above 160/min)
    - Diaphoresis
    - Hepatomegaly and edema (late signs)
- Increased risk of bacterial endocarditis
- Diagnosis
  - Cardiac catheterization
  - Echocardiography
  - Nursing Interventions
  - Cardiac Catheterization
    - Consider developmental level of the child when planning teaching strategies.
    - Explain to the parents that the procedure is done under conscious sedation.
    - Be alert to postprocedural concerns (same as adult).
  - Anticoagulant Therapy
    - Explain why this is necessary for children who have prosthetic valves or increased blood viscosity.
    - Instruct parents to be alert for signs of increased bleeding, excessive bruising, epistaxis, hematuria, and bloody stools.
    - Explain the need for bleeding precautions.

NOTES

- o Preoperative Preparation
  - ▪ Promote parental involvement to decrease anxiety.
  - ▪ Include a description of what the child will feel during the procedure or surgery, based on the developmental level.

 Nursing Interventions for diminished cardiac output related to failure of the myocardium to meet the demands of the body

- o Reduce energy expenditures by providing adequate rest periods, planning care to reduce interruptions, and recognizing signs of fatigue.
- o Infant seats are very helpful.
- o Avoid temperature extremes.
- o Administer and monitor medications that promote cardiac function.
  - ▪ Digoxin (Lanoxin) – same as adult except
    - □ Check apical heart rate 1 full min prior to administering – hold digitalis if heart rate is below 100/min for infants, 80/min for toddlers and preschoolers, and 60/min for school-age children and adolescents.
    - □ Administer medication on an empty stomach. Do not give with food or juice and do not repeat dose if child vomits.
    - □ Digoxin therapeutic level is 0.8 to 2 mcg/dL.
  - ▪ Diuretics – furosemide (Lasix), chlorothiazide (Diuril), ethacrynic acid (Edecrin)
    - □ Monitor potassium levels and supplement losses, and observe for hypokalemia and increased risk of digitalis toxicity.
    - □ Include daily weights, I&O, and respiratory assessment in daily care.

 Point to Remember – Cardiac infants usually have a weak suck reflex, become cyanotic during feedings, tire easily, and may fall asleep while feeding

- o Provide small, frequent feedings using a soft nipple with a large hole.
- o Administer 24 kcal/oz formula to increase caloric intake.

- o Limit oral feedings to 20 min; gavage feed the remainder.

 Nursing Interventions for parental coping and support

- o Discipline is the most difficult area of parenting due to feelings of guilt and powerlessness.
- o Parents need help remembering that the child should be treated as normally as possible.
- o Counsel the family regarding the possibility of developmental delays; including infant stimulation in teaching.
- o Assist with grieving over the loss of the perfect infant.

Neurologic Defects

- • Hydrocephalus – imbalance in either absorption or production of cerebrospinal fluid within intracranial cavity
  - o Classification is either congenital or acquired
  - o Usually diagnosed at birth or within 2 to 4 months of life
  - o Often associated with other neural tube defect (myelomeningocele)
- • Contributing Factors
  - o Impaired absorption of cerebrospinal fluid (CSF) within the subarachnoid space
  - o Obstruction to the flow of CSF through the ventricular system
  - o Developmental malformations; neoplasm, infection and trauma
- • Manifestations (categorized by age)
  - o Infant – increased head circumference, tense bulging anterior fontanel, distended scalp veins, high-pitched cry, irritability, feeding problems, discomfort when held
  - o Older child – headache, vomiting (especially in the morning), diplopia, blurred vision, behavioral changes, decreased motor function, decreased level of consciousness, seizures
- • Diagnosis
  - o May be detected on prenatal sonogram

NOTES

- o Clinical signs
  - Increased intracranial pressure
  - Increased head circumference
- o Computed tomography or magnetic resonance imaging scan confirms diagnosis by showing excessive fluid in ventricles
- Medical-Surgical Treatment
  - o Pressure is relieved by surgically inserting a shunting device.
  - o Components of a shunt include a catheter, reservoir, pumping device with one-way valve, and distal tubing with regulator valve.
  - o The most common type of shunt is ventriculoperitoneal.
  - o Complications of the device include shunt failure and infection.
  - o Shunt will require revision (lengthening of tubing) as the child grows.
  - o Early treatment is necessary to prevent progressive mental retardation.
- Nursing Interventions
  - o Preoperatively measure head circumference by obtaining occipitofrontal measurement.
  - o Postoperatively
    - Perform frequent neurologic assessment by measuring head circumference daily.
    - Position on nonoperative site; check anterior fontanel to determine positioning of the head; do not pump shunt without order.
    - Monitor for signs and symptoms of shunt failure – lethargy, vomiting, and irritability.
    - Institute seizure precautions.
  - o Decrease shunt infection
    - Monitor for elevated vital signs, decreased level of consciousness, vomiting, and feeding problems.
    - Assess the incision site frequently for manifestations of inflammation or leakage.
  - o Implement care to meet physiologic and developmental needs.

Myelomeningocele: Most common type of neural tube defect

- Type of spina bifida, a fissure in spinal column leaving meninges and spinal cord exposed
- Contributing Factors – Etiology unknown
  - o Failure of posterior laminae to fuse with herniation of saclike cyst of meninges, cerebrospinal fluid, and spinal nerves
  - o Usually associated with other neurologic defects (hydrocephalus)
  - o May be prevented by folic acid supplementation for women of childbearing age prior to conception and through first trimester
- Manifestations
  - o Partial to complete paralysis determined by location of defect (usually lumbosacral)
  - o Musculoskeletal problems such as clubfoot, scoliosis, congenital hip dysplasia
  - o Sensory disturbances parallel motor dysfunction
  - o Bowel and bladder problems including constipation, incontinence, and neurogenic bladder
- Diagnosis
  - o Amniocentesis – 98% accurate; elevated alpha fetoprotein, confirmed by prenatal sonogram
  - o Apparent at birth – visible sac
- Surgical Treatment
  - o Decision to correct the defect or not is difficult as well as controversial
  - o Early surgical closure is advocated to preserve neural function, reduce risk of infection, and control hydrocephalus
- Nursing Interventions
  - o Prevent infection
    - Preoperatively; priority of care is to preserve integrity of sac
      - □ Keep infant in prone position.
      - □ Cover sac with 4 x 4 gauze moistened with sterile saline.
      - □ Check sac frequently for tears or cracks.

NOTES

- Do not cover sac with clothing or diapers because that places too much pressure on the sac.
- Perform perineal care to prevent contamination of sac.
- Monitor for manifestations of meningitis such as irritability, anorexia, fever, and seizures.

■ Postoperatively; priority of care is to promote healing and preserve neurologic integrity

- Place the infant in a prone position with head slightly lower than body.
- Place a protective barrier across the incision to prevent contamination.
- Be aware of long-term problems of infection related to urinary retention, reflux, and chronic urinary tract infections.
  ▸ Teach parents the Credé maneuver.
  ▸ Encourage independent intermittent self-catheterization, which can be performed as early as 5 to 6 years of age.
  ▸ Stress hydration and early recognition of urinary tract infections.
  ▸ Explain to parents that urinary diversion procedures are often required.

o Perform neurologic checks by measuring head circumference daily.

o Monitor for manifestations of increased intracranial pressure.

o Promote effective parental and familial coping strategies.

 o Point to Remember – Increased risk for latex allergy – recognize that children with neural tube defects are at increased risk for latex allergy to common medical (or other) products containing latex. Vinyl gloves and balloons should be avoided.

Cerebral Palsy

- Group of permanent disorders of movement and posture causing activity limitation, disturbances of sensation, perception, communication, cognition and behavior

- Contributing Factors
  o Causes undetermined; may be related to prenatal, perinatal, or postnatal factors
  o Birth asphyxia
  o Prenatal brain abnormalities
- Diagnosis
  o Classified by nature and distribution of neuromuscular dysfunction
  o May not be diagnosed until child is several months old
  o Confirmed by physical evaluation, or supplemental tests (electroencephalogram test, tomography, or metabolic screening)
- Manifestations (Early)
  o Persistent primitive reflexes
  o Hyper or hypotonicity (stiff or floppy arms and legs)
  o Poor hand control and body control
  o Feeding difficulties
  o Irritability
  o Delayed attainment of developmental milestones
- Treatment (based on degree of disability)
  o Physical therapy (active and passive)
  o Anticonvulsants – phenobarbital or phenytoin (Dilantin)
  o Modified toys or equipment to enhance development
  o Surgery to correct contractures or spastic deformities
- Nursing Interventions
  o Teach the family safe use of adaptive devices.
  o Modify the environment to enhance safety.
  o Institute seizure precautions if appropriate.
  o Encourage physical safety techniques such as aspiration precautions and adequate rest.
  o Encourage self-care activities to foster independence and confidence.
  o Modify the environment, devices to enhance development, enhance safety, and increase functional abilities.

NOTES

REVIEW OF ACYANOTIC CONGENITAL HEART DEFECTS

Anomaly	Hemodynamics	Clinical Manifestations	Treatment
• Patent Ductus Arteriosus o A vascular channel between the left main pulmonary artery and the descending aorta, as a result of failure of the fetal ductus arteriosus to dose	• Shunt of oxygentated blood from the aorta into the pulmonary artery • Increased left ventricular output and work load	• Usually asymptomatic, but frequent impairment of growth or heart failure • "Machinery murmur" • Wide pulse pressure	• Medical – adminstration of indomethacin (Indocin) (prostaglandin inhibitor) is effective in some newborns and premature newborns • Surgical – ligation of patent ductus (in infancy)
• Ventricular Septal Defect o In membranous muscular portion of the ventricular septum; may vary from small to large defect	• Shunt of oxygenated blood from left to right ventricle • Leads to right ventricular hypertrophy • Needs surgical repair • Bidirectional shunting may occur with very large defect (Eisenmenger's complex)	• May be asymptomatic • Heart murmur is heard in first week of life (systolic) • Growth failure, feeding problems during the first year of life; failure to thrive; frequent respiratory infections • Heart failure	• Some small defects may close spontaneously • Open heart – direct closure suturing with plastic prosthesis (usually preschooler; may be done earlier in infancy for large defects)
• Atrial Septal Defect o Malfunctioning foremen ovale; or abnormal opening between the atria	• Shunting of oxygenated blood from the left to right atrium • Increased right ventricular output and work load • May develop pulmonary hypertension in adulthood (if not surgically treated in childhood)	• Acyanotic; asymptomatic • Soft blowing, systolic murmur • Thin and asthenic • Frequent episodes of pulmonary inflammatory diseases • Poor exercise intolerance	• Open heart with direct closure or suturing with plastic prosthesis (usually preschooler)

• Coarctation of aorta:
  o Preductal constriction of the aorta between subdavian artery and ductus arteriosus
  o Postductal constriction of aorta directly beyond the ductus
	• Obstructions of the flow of blood through the constricted segments
	• Increased left ventricular pressure and work load
	• Extensive collateral circulation bypasses coarctated area to supply lower extremities with blood
		• Hypertension in upper extremities with decreased blood pressure in lower extremities
		• Weak or absent pulsations in lower extremities
		• Heart failure
		• May be asymptomatic; occasionally fatigue, headaches, leg cramps, epistaxis
			• Surgical resection of coarctate area with direct anastomosis or use of a graft
			• Correction usually done by 2 years of age to prevent permanent hypertension

---

NOTES

REVIEW OF CYANOTIC CONGENITAL HEART DEFECTS

Anomaly	Hemodynamics	Clinical Manifestations	Treatment

• Tetralogy of Fallot – combination of four defects
  o Pulmonary stenosis
  o Ventricular septal defect (VSD)
  o Overriding aorta
  o Hypertrophy of right ventricle
	• Obstruction to outflow of blood from the right ventricle into pulmonary circuit and increased pressure in the right ventricle leads to right to left shunting of oxygenated blood through the VSD directly into the aorta
	• Severity of defect depends on degree of pulmonary stenosis and size of VSD
		• Acute cyanosis at birth
		• Cyanosis developing during early months that increases with physical exertion
		• Clubbing of fingers and toes
		• Systolic murmur
		• Acute episodes of cyanosis and hypoxia called "tet spells" or hypercyanotic episodes occur if oxygen supply cannot meet demand (crying, exertion, exercise, feeding)
		• Squatting
		• Growth retardation
			• Surgical – Blalock-Taussig procedures; provides blood flow to pulmonary arteries from the left to right subdavian artery
			• Repair – open heart closure of VSD and resection of stenosis. Usually performed in the first 2 years of life.

• Transposition of Great Vessels (TGV)
  o The aorta originates from the right ventricle and the pulmonary artery from the left ventricle
	• Two separate circulations without mixture of oxygenated and unoxygenated blood except through shunts
	• Mixture of blood may occur through one or more septal defects
	  o Ventricular septal defect (VSD)
	  o Atrial septal defect (ASD)
	  o Patent ductus arteriosus (PDA)
		• Usually deep cyanosis shortly after birth or after closing of ductus
		• Early clubbing of toes and fingers
		• Poor growth and development, failure to thrive
		• Rapid respirations; fatigue
		• Heart failure
			• Prostaglandin medications are given to keep ductus arteriosus open until surgery. Prostaglandin inhibitors are given to close duct.
			• Repair – arterial switch treatment of choice; must be done within the first few days of life; great vessels reimplanted under complete circulatory arrest
			• Several other types of repair are all multiple stage approaches

NOTES

- o Refer to occupational and speech therapy for evaluation and development of verbal and nonverbal communication skills.
- o Teach parents alternative communication methods to facilitate positive adjustments of child and family.

Musculoskeletal Defects

Congenital Dysplasia of the Hip

- Imperfect development of the hip to varying degrees
  - o Head of femur is not properly seated within the acetabulum; easily dislocated with movement or positioning
- Contributing factors unknown; familial tendency; females are 8 times more likely to develop
  - o Early detection is critical – if untreated, it will lead to lordosis, scoliosis (duck waddle)
  - o The head of the femur must be properly located within the acetabulum for correct development of the hip joint
  - o As ossification proceeds, correcting the hip defect becomes more difficult
  - o Once the child begins to walk, prognosis becomes questionable
  - o Most common type is subluxation (incomplete dislocation of hip)
- Diagnosis
  - o Assessment techniques with newborn (Ortolani's "click")
  - o X-rays are difficult to read in early infancy because ossification of femoral head does not occur until 3 to 6 months of life
- Manifestations
  - o Shortening of affected leg
  - o Asymmetrical skin folds
  - o Limited abduction
  - o Ortolani's sign (audible "click" as examiner slips femoral head forward)

- Treatment
  - o If diagnosed within first 2 to 3 months of life, the hip joint abduction is maintained through double diapering, Frejka pillow, splint, or Pavlik harness.
  - o Once adductor muscles contract, traction and/or casting may be used; usually by 6 months (once the child is standing and walking) both methods are used in conjunction with surgery (Bryant's traction if below 2 years).
- Nursing Interventions
  - o Conduct frequent neurovascular checks using circulation, motion, sensation.
  - o Provide routine cast care. If hip spica cast is used, teach parents not to use abductor stabilizer bar as a handle when moving the child.
  - o Use Bryant's traction, in which the child's legs are elevated at a 90° angle to the body. The child's weight provides countertraction, and the correct amount of traction is applied until the child's buttocks are elevated slightly above bed.
  - o Maintain skin integrity.
  - o Promote mobility.

Congenital Clubfoot (Talipes Equinovarus)

- Deformity of the ankle and foot in which the foot is pointed downward and inward in varying degrees of severity.
- Contributing Factors
  - o Multifactorial
  - o Attributed to abnormal positioning and restricted movement in utero.
  - o Abnormal embryonic development
- Manifestations
  - o Heel tilted inward (varus), plantar flexion at ankle
- Diagnosis and treatment
  - o Important to differentiate between positional and true clubfoot (true clubfoot cannot be positioned in normal alignment with range of motion)
  - o Apparent at birth; longer treatment postponed, more soft tissue changes occur and correction is more difficult

---

NOTES

- o Serial casting is employed to gradually manipulate the foot into normal position; casts are changed at weekly intervals; as each new cast is applied, the foot is remanipulated and recasted.
- o Dennis-Brown splint may be used to maintain position once casting is completed.

 Nursing Interventions

- o Teach parents range-of-motion exercises and neurovascular assessments.
- o Monitor for infection.
- o Maintain skin integrity around cast edges.
- o Promote developmental activities.

Gastrointestinal Defects

- Cleft Lip
  - o Failure of the maxillary processes to fuse with the nasal processes (may be unilateral or bilateral)
  - o Contributing factors unknown, but there are strong genetic or environmental factors
  - o More common in males
  - o May or may not be accompanied by cleft palate
- Pathology
  - o Prone to ear, nose, and throat infection
  - o Long-term problems include speech, hearing, and dentition problems
- Diagnosis and treatment
  - o Defect apparent at birth
  - o Surgical repair initiated within first 3 months of life
  - o Staggered z-shaped suture line used to minimize scarring

 Nursing Interventions

- o Preoperative nursing care
  - ▪ Follow precautions during feedings.
  - ▪ Assess strength of the sucking reflex.
  - ▪ Encourage the parents to express feelings.
- o Postoperative nursing care
  - ▪ Monitor for respiratory distress.
  - ▪ Maintain suture integrity.

- ▪ Provide age-appropriate activities.
- o Preserve suture line.
- o Restrain elbows.
- o Avoid sucking.
- o Cleanse suture after each feeding.
- o Maintain airway and prevent aspiration.
- o Provide support to the parents.
- Cleft Palate
  - o Congenital anomaly that occurs as a result of the failure of the soft tissue and bony prominences to fuse in the oral cavity
- Contributing Factors
  - o Include genetic, hereditary, and environmental factors
  - o Exposure to radiation or rubella virus
  - o Chromosome abnormalities
  - o May or may not be associated with cleft lip
  - o Ear, nose, and throat infections
- Diagnosis and treatment
  - o Repair usually completed by 12 to 18 months of age to prevent speech problems
  - o Surgery may be performed in stages
- Manifestations
  - o More common among females
  - o Problems associated with feeding; aspiration; swallowing; ear, nose and throat infections

 Nursing Interventions

- o Assess respiratory status and ease of respiratory effort.
- o Assess ability to suck and swallow.
- o Monitor I&O.
- o Weigh daily.
- o Modify feeding techniques utilizing obturators, special nipples, and feeders.
- o Feed in upright position in frequent, small amounts; burp frequently.
- o Keep suction equipment and bulb syringe at bedside.
- o Teach the parents appropriate feeding and prevention interventions prior to discharge.

NOTES

- o Encourage the parents to verbalize feelings and offer emotional support.

SECTION 4

NURSING CARE OF THE CHILD WITH AN ACUTE ILLNESS

Fever

- Characteristics
  - o Classified as temperature in excess of 38° C (100.4° F)
  - o Not always related to severity of illness; varies from child to child
  - o Always consider
    - Age of the child (below 6 months is a more serious concern)
    - If child is immunosuppressed or receiving chemotherapy
  - o Most fevers in children are viral and self-limiting; may play a role in recovery from infection
- Diagnosis
  - o Feeling a child's skin for warmth is not an accurate indicator.
  - o Always investigate family epidemiology and take a careful history for exposure to communicative diseases.
  - o Remember that diet, activity level, and behavioral changes are subtle diagnostic clues.
  - o Laboratory tests may include CBC, urinalysis, chest film, and blood cultures; a "septic workup" includes all of the above with the addition of a lumbar puncture and urine culture.
- Treatment
  - o Fever management is questionable because fever is considered a part of the body's defense mechanism.
  - o Antipyretics, such as acetaminophen (Tylenol) or ibuprofen (Motrin), should be given in weight-appropriate dose.
  - o No aspirin due to the risk of Reye syndrome
- Nursing Interventions
  - o Febrile seizures

- Usually seen in children between 6 months and 3 years old; related to sudden rise of temperature (above 38.9° C [102° F]); child usually has a respiratory or gastrointestinal infection.
- Therapeutic treatment includes diazepam (Valium) and/or antipyretics.
- Provide safe care during febrile seizure.
  - □ Maintain airway.
  - □ Prevent aspiration and injury.
  - □ Observe the seizure.
- o Maintain fluid and electrolyte balance.
  - Assess for signs of dehydration.
  - Provide IV fluids.
  - Monitor renal function.
- o Maintain afebrile status.
  - Frequently assess temperature.
  - Encourage clear liquids.
  - Expose skin and avoid excessive clothing.
- o Knowledge deficit related to home care.
  - Educate parents regarding seizure precautions, methods to control fever, and how to prevent dehydration.
  - Address parental fears about fevers.

Vomiting

- Characteristics
  - o Assessment includes – amount, color, consistency, time of day emesis occurs, and relationship to eating
  - o Vomiting causes a loss of hydrochloric acid, which leads to metabolic alkalosis
- Diagnosis
  - o Child is dehydrated and appears emaciated
  - o Diagnostic procedures for prolonged or unusual emesis may include – upper gastrointestinal series, barium enema, abdominal ultrasound, CT scan of abdomen, pH probe, esophagoscopy

---

NOTES

- o If metabolic alkalosis, may appear lethargic, poorly perfused, hyperventilating
- Treatment
  - o It is essential to correct both the fluid and acid-base imbalance.
  - o If the vomiting is predictable and of brief duration, antiemetics may be prescribed to depress the vomiting center (promethazine HCl [Phenergan], chlorpromazine HCl [Thorazine], metoclopramide HCl [Reglan], trimethobenzamide [Tigan]).
  - o Gastroesophageal reflux is treated with medications that promote gastric mobility and emptying, such as metoclopramide (Reglan) or omeprazole (Prilosec); take gastroesophageal reflux precautions (positioning with the head of the bed elevated, especially after meals or feeding).

 Nursing Interventions

- o Assess for signs of dehydration.
- o Maintain fluid and electrolytes.
- o Adhere to strict I&O and daily weights.
- o Maintain NPO status until asymptomatic.
- o Introduce clear liquids slowly and frequently.
- o Administer antiemetics as prescribed.
- o Monitor for metabolic alkalosis.

Gastroenteritis (Diarrhea)

- An increase in fluid, frequency and volume of stool; usually results from increased rate of peristalsis; stools are watery, acidic, green in color, expelled forcefully; Na+, K+, and bicarbonate are lost via the stool
  - o Diarrhea is serious in young children because
    - The extracellular space is larger, so greater amounts of fluid will be lost
    - Younger children have a greater body surface area and gastrointestinal surface areas in relation to body weight
    - Younger children have a higher basal metabolic rate, so the fluid and electrolyte balance is unstable

- o Weight is a critical indicator of fluid loss in young children; 1 g of weight equals 1 mL of body fluid, a weight loss or gain of 1 kg in a 24 hr period represents a fluid shift of 1,000 mL; the loss of fluid and electrolytes in the diarrhea stool results in dehydration and electrolyte depletion
- o Causative factors – bacteria (salmonella, shigella), viral (rotavirus), allergies, emotional disturbances, dietary and malabsorption problems
- o Chronic nonspecific diarrhea or irritable bowel syndrome is the most common form of chronic diarrhea in children
    - Diarrhea persists longer than 3 weeks
    - Normal growth and development
    - No evidence of enteric pathogens
- Diagnosis
  - o Serum electrolytes, CBC, and blood cultures may be prescribed
  - o Antibiotic therapy is a common cause of diarrhea
  - o Obtain a thorough history including dietary habits, family history, recent travel, or exposures to contagious illness
- Treatment
  - o Mild dehydration (2% to 9%) without hypernatremia; generally treated with oral rehydrating solutions; critical behaviors that demand immediate attention are persistent diarrhea, weight loss, bloody stools, or physiological changes such as deep breathing, listlessness, or reduced urinary output
  - o Secondary lactose intolerance may occur following gastroenteritis; child may be maintained temporarily on a lactose-free diet
  - o Severe dehydration (greater than 10% weight loss) is an acute medical emergency; the child is NPO (12 to 48 hr), parenteral fluids are administered
  - o Nursing Interventions
  - o Assess for signs of dehydration or poor skin turgor.
  - o Maintain fluid and electrolyte balance.
  - o Monitor daily weights and strict I&O.
  - o Apply skin barrier (zinc products).

NOTES

- o Monitor for metabolic acidosis.
- o Maintain NPO status until asymptomatic.
- o Introduce clear liquids slowly and frequently (avoid apple juice).
- o Administer antidiarrheals as prescribed.

Respiratory Infections

- Acute otitis media (most prevalent childhood disease)
  - o Characteristics
    - Middle ear infections are common in children under age 5 – breastfed infants have decreased incidence
      - □ Eustachian tube is shorter, wider, and straighter
      - □ Organisms from nasopharynx have easier access to middle ear
      - □ Tonsils and adenoids are usually enlarged
      - □ Young children have poorly developed immune mechanisms
      - □ Infants and toddlers are supine a large portion of the day
    - Usually follows an upper respiratory infection during which the swollen mucosa close off the eustachian tube; the growth of the organism along with the fluid retention in the ear combine to cause the infection
    - Most frequently seen bacterial infection in young children; most serious long-term problem associated with otitis is conductive hearing loss, tinnitus or vertigo
    - Clinical manifestations – fever; irritability; pulling, tugging or rubbing the affected ear; anorexia; signs of a upper respiratory infection; older children may report earache or pain when chewing or sucking; purulent discharge may be present
- Diagnosis
  - o Otitis media – otoscopy reveals an intact tympanic membrane that appears inflamed, bulging, and without a light reflex

- o Chronic otitis media – otoscopy reveals dull, gray membrane with visible fluid behind eardrum
- Treatment
  - o Oral antibiotics; therapy should last 10 to 14 days.
  - o Oral decongestants such as sympathomimetics (vasoconstriction) or antihistamines (reduce congestion) may be used; analgesics may be prescribed to reduce pain, discomfort.
  - o Following completion of the antibiotic regimen, treatment effectiveness should be evaluated.
  - o Children with recurrent otitis media should be tested for hearing loss.
  - o Myringotomy (surgical incision of the ear drum) and insertion of pressure-equalizing (PE) tubes may be ordered in cases of recurrent chronic otitis media.
- Nursing Interventions
  - o Pain
    - Administer analgesics such as acetaminophen (Tylenol) as needed; apply warm compresses to affected ear; avoid foods that require chewing.
    - Assess for nonverbal signs of discomfort; changes in behavior can be an early indicator of pain; humidity, clear PO fluids may also be helpful.
    - Parent teaching
      - □ Instruct the parents regarding the importance of antibiotic compliance; medication should be taken for 10 to 14 days (even after manifestations have gone away).
      - □ Instruct the parents in feeding techniques to reduce the incidence of ear infection (upright when feeding; breastfeeding offers protection against pathogens).
      - □ Eliminate tobacco smoke and known or potential allergens from environment.

NOTES

- □ Following myringotomy and PE tubes insertion, some drainage from the ears is expected; report obvious bleeding and an abrupt rise in temperature; the ear should be kept dry; avoid activities that require submerging the head in water (use ear plugs for bathing).
- Epiglottitis – acute bacterial infection of the supraglottic structures resulting in obstructive airway problems
  - ○ Seen primarily in children 2 to 8 years of age; considered a medical emergency, immediate treatment must be initiated
  - ○ Most common causative organism – H. influenza, type B
  - ○ Clinical manifestations – abrupt onset with rapid progression to severe respiratory distress, sore throat, stridor, high fever (38.9 to 40° C [102 to 104° F]), drooling, dysphagia, muffled voice; tripod position (sit upright, lean forward with mouth open and tongue protruding)
- Diagnosis
  - ○ Throat is red, inflamed with a cherry-red epiglottis; under no circumstance should an inspection of the throat be initiated unless emergency equipment is available (trach setup, ET tube); do not take a throat culture
  - ○ Lateral neck film (soft-tissue x-ray) reveals swollen epiglottis
- Treatment
  - ○ Must be NPO immediately.
  - ○ Parenteral therapy with IV antibiotics is begun; PO antibiotics for 10 to 14 days following IV therapy
  - ○ Steroid therapy – frequently used for anti-inflammatory effects
  - ○ Intubation or tracheostomy usually necessary to prevent obstruction; extubation may occur within 3 to 4 days
  - ○ Vaccine prevention – H. influenza type B conjugate vaccine effective against H. influenza epiglottitis
- Nursing Interventions
  - ○ Frequently assess for respiratory distress.
  - ○ Available oxygen, suction, emergency.

- ○ Maintain NPO status.
- ○ Do not leave child unattended.
- ○ Give medications as prescribed.
- ○ Humidified oxygen
- ○ Bronchodilators
- ○ Steroids
- ○ Antibiotics
- ○ Antipyretics
- Laryngotracheobronchitis (croup)
  - ○ Characteristics
    - ■ Most common form of croup; peak age is below 5 years; because of smaller airway diameter, child is more prone to significant airway narrowing
    - ■ May begin as an upper respiratory infection that proceeds to lower respiratory structures
    - ■ Most common causative organisms – parainfluenza viruses
    - ■ Clinical manifestations are the result of inflammation and subsequent narrowing of airway – hoarseness, barking or "seal-like" cough, inspiratory stridor, increasing respiratory distress
  - ○ Diagnosis
    - ■ Clinical manifestations are diagnostic
    - ■ Lateral or soft-tissue x-rays of neck may be ordered
  - ○ Treatment
    - ■ Humidity with cool mist provides relief by reducing inflamed mucosa
    - ■ Aerosol epinephrine (Racepinephrine) may also be used if child is hospitalized
    - ■ Corticosteroids may be used for their anti-inflammatory effects
  - ○ Nursing Interventions
    - ■ Monitor the child's respiratory status frequently.
    - ■ Provide humidified oxygen.
    - ■ Encourage fluids.
    - ■ Keep environment quiet and calm.

NOTES

- Have suction and emergency intubation equipment available at the bedside.
- Assess parental anxiety.
- Medications
- Humidified oxygen
- Bronchodilators
- Steroids

- Bronchiolitis
  - Characteristics
    - Acute viral infection that primarily affects bronchioles; most commonly seen in infants between 1 to 18 months; occurs in winter and spring months
    - Respiratory syncytial virus (RSV) is responsible for half of the documented cases of bronchiolitis; mode of transmission is hand to nose, droplet infections; reinfection common in all ages
    - Bronchiolar obstruction leads to hyperinflation and air trapping
    - The younger the child, the greater the chance of severe lower respiratory disease requiring hospitalization; infants at high risk for severe RSV infection include – premature infants, infants with underlying cardiac or respiratory conditions, infants with immune deficit
    - Clinical manifestations – initial manifestations of upper respiratory infection that progress to tachypnea; paroxysmal coughing, increased restlessness; nasal flaring, fever, cyanosis intercostal and substernal retractions, wheezing, and decreased breath sounds indicate severe lower-respiratory tract disease
  - Diagnosis
    - Manifestations are clinically diagnostic
    - RSV is diagnosed using enzyme linked immunosorbent assay (ELIZA) from nasal secretions
    - Chest film will reveal areas of consolidation that are difficult to differentiate from bacterial pneumonia; areas of hyperinflation

  - Treatment
    - Treated symptomatically; humidity, rest, adequate hydration are main therapeutic interventions; can be successfully treated at home in most cases
    - Rationale for hospitalization – tachypnea (> 70 breaths/min), severe retractions, change in behavior, hydration problems; at-risk children with chronic or debilitating diseases should be hospitalized
    - In serious cases, steroids and inhaled bronchodilators will be administered
    - With severe RSV infection, ribavirin (Virazole), an antiviral aerosol, may be administered via oxygen tent or hood; teratogenic effects have been reported, so pregnant caregivers are at-risk, strict guidelines exist for use
    - Palivizumab (Synagis) immunization is given to at-risk infants during their first winter. (This includes infants born at less than 32 weeks gestation, a large number of those born between 32 and 35 weeks gestation, and children with chronic lung or heart disease.)
  - Nursing Interventions
    - Monitor respiratory status frequently.
    - Assess oxygen saturation levels and ABGs.
    - Maintain fluid and electrolyte balance.
    - Maintain isolation precautions.
    - Medications
      - Bronchodilators
      - Steroids
      - Ribavirin (Virazole)
    - Provide teaching for parents.
    - Prevent recurring infection under children who are age 2 with the use of palivizumab (Synagis) or IV immunoglobulin.
    - Use a bulb syringe or humidifier.
    - Wash hands frequently.
    - Observe for signs of dehydration.

NOTES

SECTION 5

NURSING CARE OF THE SURGICAL CHILD

Preoperative Preparation

- Assess parents' and child's level of understanding
- Teach based on developmental level of child
- Involve parents and allow discussion
- Gather baseline data

Common Surgical Problems

- Tonsillectomy and adenoidectomy (T&A)
  - ○ Tonsils help protect body from infections; typically enlarged in children
  - ○ Rationale for surgery
    - Chronic tonsillitis (controversial)
    - Massive hypertrophy that interferes with breathing (obstructive apnea)
  - ○ Preoperative care
    - Assess bleeding and coagulation time
    - Confirm child is free from current infection
    - Prepare the child
  - ○ Nursing Interventions (postoperative)
    - Hemorrhage – greatest risk first 48 hr, then 7 days later; manifestations – frequent swallowing or clearing of throat, bright red emesis, oozing from capillary bed, shock (late sign, indicates significant blood loss); prevention – avoid coughing, sneezing, sucking on straw
    - Avoid red-colored foods. Offer cool fluids; ice pops to decrease edema and to relieve pain. Avoid pretzels, crackers, chips, and dairy products.
    - Pain – administer analgesics regularly first 24 hr – acetaminophen (Tylenol); may require rectal or parenteral route due to throat pain; may return to school in 1 to 2 weeks
- Pyloric stenosis
  - ○ Congenital hypertrophy of pyloric sphincter
  - ○ Clinical manifestations
    - Insidious vomiting occurring 2 to 3 weeks after birth, increasing in intensity until forceful and projectile (no bile) by about 6 weeks of age
    - Small, olive-size mass in right-upper quadrant
    - Weight loss, dehydration
    - Chronic hunger
  - ○ Diagnosis
    - History and physical signs
    - Upper gastrointestinal series
    - Barium swallows under fluoroscopy
  - ○ Treatment
    - Correct dehydration, metabolic alkalosis
    - Pylorus resected
  - ○ Nursing Interventions
    - Preoperative – NPO; daily weights; NG tube for gastric decompression; monitor I&O and specific gravity; monitor emesis
    - Postoperative – position on right side to prevent aspiration; begin oral feedings 4 to 6 hr postoperatively after bowel sounds return; maintain in upright position after feeding in infant seat; start with small, frequent feedings of oral rehydration solution (Pedialyte); monitor for emesis; advance feeding as tolerated
- Appendicitis
  - ○ Inflammation of vermiform appendix
  - ○ Problem in school-age children
  - ○ Characteristics
    - Periumbilical pain radiating to right-lower quadrant; rebound tenderness
    - Low-grade temperature
    - Nausea and vomiting
    - Elevated WBC count – 15,000 to 20,000/mm^3
    - May perforate and lead to peritonitis; sudden relief of pain followed by increased pain and rigid abdomen; high fever
  - ○ Nursing Interventions
    - Preoperative nursing care
      - □ Provide pain relief.

NOTES

- □ Place in right side-lying position.
- □ Perform abdominal assessment frequently.
- □ Maintain NPO status.
- □ Provide fluid and electrolyte balance.
- ■ Postoperative nursing care
  - □ Assess vital signs and perform abdominal assessment frequently.
  - □ Monitor for signs of infection.
  - □ Promote mobility.
  - □ Promote respiratory toileting.
  - □ Provide pain management as ordered.
- Intussusception
  - o Telescoping of the bowel
  - o Characterized by
    - ■ Colicky pain with knees drawn up
    - ■ Currant jelly stools
  - o Treatment
    - ■ Barium enema – diagnostic; may reduce intussusception by hydrostatic pressure
    - ■ Bowel resection if barium enema does not reduce
  - o Nursing Interventions
    - ■ Prepare for procedure.
    - ■ Provide routine postoperative abdominal surgical care.
- Hirschsprung's disease (megacolon)
  - o Congenital absence of parasympathetic ganglion in distal colon
  - o Bowel proximal to a ganglionic section becomes enlarged
  - o Characterized by
    - ■ In newborn – failure to pass meconium within 24 hr after birth
    - ■ In older child – recurrent abdominal distension; chronic constipation with ribbon-like stools; diarrhea; bile-stained emesis
  - o Treatment
    - ■ Cleansing enemas with antibiotics preoperatively
    - ■ Temporary colostomy

- ■ Bowel resection to remove aganglionic portion
- o Nursing Interventions
  - ■ Colostomy care – same as adult
    - □ Check stoma for color.
    - □ Change dressings frequently (abdominal, perineal).
    - □ Monitor accurate I&O.
    - □ Avoid incision irritation (keep diapers low).
  - ■ Parent and child instruction
    - □ Encourage independence based on age of child.
    - □ Discuss diet and hydration.
- Hernias
  - o Most common – inguinal and umbilical
  - o Always consider developmental level (mutilation fears) when preparing child
  - o Usually repaired in ambulatory surgery setting
  - o Nursing Interventions
    - ■ Instruct parents
      - □ Care for surgical site.
      - □ Note manifestations of an infection.

SECTION 6

NURSING CARE FOR CHILDHOOD ACCIDENTS

Ingestions

- General information
  - o Provide emergency care – ABCs.
  - o Identify substance, save evidence of poison.
  - o Call poison control center for treatment advice.
  - o Remove substance.
    - ■ Activated charcoal
    - ■ Gastric lavage
    - ■ Specific antidote
  - o Provide supportive therapy.
  - o Educate parents about childproof environment.
  - o Provide anticipatory guidance.

NOTES

- Infants and toddlers – at risk because everything goes into the mouth
- Adolescents – at risk for intentional ingestion
- Types of ingestions
  - See Overview of Common Accidental Ingestion Table on page 208.

Pediatric Medication Administration

- General information
  - Consider age and developmental level of child
  - Identify any contraindications to oral route (poor swallow, no gag reflex, oral surgery)
  - Evaluate child's ability to cooperate and understand
- Preparation
  - Use caution with calculation and administration; especially IV medications
  - Nearly all medications are administered to children by calculating the desired amount of medication according to the child's weight (mg/kg)
  - Use vastus lateralis for IM injections
  - Place medication in, or on nipple, and allow infants to suck
  - If administering via oral syringe, never squirt directly into back of throat

Burns

- Characteristics of burns in children
  - Due to the difference in proportions of head, trunk and limbs, burn percentages are rated differently for children.
  - Due to the high percentage of extracellular fluids in the child, fluid loss can quickly lead to hypovolemic shock
- Treatment
  - Similar to adult
  - Children are likely to resist eating enough calories to sustain healing and growth needs. Parenteral or enteral feedings are usually necessary
- Rehabilitation
  - Incorporate play into the physical or occupational therapy regimens for improved success

- Consider psychosocial needs of the child
- Adjustment and transition back to school may be very difficult for the child who has sustained a disfiguring burn

Fractures

- Characteristics of fractures in children
  - Due to immaturity of bones and incomplete ossification, greenstick (incomplete) fractures are commonly seen
  - Fractures to the epiphysis (growth plate) are of greater concern as growth in limb can be stunted depending on the amount of injury
- Treatment
  - Similar to adult, although pediatric fractures often have shorter healing times
  - May use cast (plaster or, more commonly, fiberglass) soft splint, traction, or bracing

Child Abuse

- Types
  - Physical neglect – failure to provide necessities of life
  - Physical abuse – deliberate infliction of injury
  - Emotional neglect – failure to provide emotional nurturing
  - Emotional abuse – deliberate assault on child's self-esteem
  - Sexual abuse – use of child to meet adult's sexual needs
  - Munchausen syndrome by proxy (MSBP) – a disorder in which a caregiver (usually parent) falsely reports or intentionally causes symptoms in their own child to seek attention
- Risk factors
  - Parental
    - Poor self-esteem
    - Abused as a child
    - Lack of knowledge
    - Lack of support system, poor coping skills
  - Child
    - Unwanted pregnancy or sex
    - Difficult temperament, hyperactive

NOTES

OVERVIEW OF COMMON ACCIDENTAL INGESTION

Ingestion	Clinical Manifestations	Treatment	Nursing Interventions
Salicylate (Aspirin)	• Tinnitus • Hyperpyrexia • Seizures • Bleeding • Hyperventilation	• Emesis • Hydration • Vitamin K • Activated charcoal	• Anticipatory guidance • Bleeding precautions • Counseling if suicide attempt
Acetaminophen (Tylenol)	• Livery necrosis in 2 to 5 days; nausea; vomiting; pain in right upper quadrant; jaundice; coagulation abnormalities; hepatotoxic	• Emesis • Mucomyst (antidote)	• Counseling if suicide attempt • Liver assessment
Lead (paint, soil near heavily traveled roads, household dust)	• Developmental regression • Impaired growth (encephalopathy) • Irritability • Increased clumsiness	• Chelation therapy – to remove heavy metals • Promote hydration	• Neuro assessment • Diet high in calcium, iron • Educate the parents to wash the child's hands, toys, and to frequently remove lead dust • Lead abatement
Hydrocarbons (kerosene, turpentine, gasoline)	• Burning in the mouth • Choking and gagging • CNS depression	• Do not induce emesis • Activated charcoal • Gastric lavage	• If vomiting, reduce aspiration.
Corrosives (drain or oven cleaner, chlorine bleach, battery acid)	• Burning in the mouth • White, swollen mucus membranes • Violent vomiting	• Do not induce emesis • Dilute toxin with water • Activated charcoal	• Keep warm and inactive.

- ○ Environment
  - ■ Chronic stress
  - ■ Socioeconomic factors
- • Recognition of abuse and neglect
  - ○ Physical neglect
    - ■ Failure to thrive – disruption in maternal-infant bonding; poor feeding behaviors; mother does not respond to infant's cues; weight less than 5th percentile; developmental delay
    - ■ Poor health care, lack of immunizations
    - ■ Failure to meet basic needs – malnutrition, poor hygiene
  - ○ Physical abuse
    - ■ Bruises – not on bony prominences, in varying degrees of healing; with patterns
    - ■ Burns – with immersion lines, in patterns
    - ■ Fractures – spiral, twisting
    - ■ Shaken baby – unconscious infant with retinal hemorrhage and no external signs of trauma
    - ■ Conflicting stories given by parents, child or others
    - ■ History incompatible with physical findings or developmentally improbable
    - ■ Delay in seeking medical attention

NOTES

- ○ Emotional neglect and abuse
  - ▪ Extremes of behavior
  - ▪ Poor self-esteem
- ○ Sexual abuse
  - ▪ Bruising of the genitalia
  - ▪ STD
  - ▪ Sudden change in behavior, regressive behavior
- ○ Munchausen syndrome by proxy
  - ▪ Victims usually under age 6
  - ▪ May have lasting emotional impact
  - ▪ Increased risk for child to develop Munchausen syndrome as adult
  - ▪ Parent well versed in medical knowledge

 Nursing Interventions
- ○ Document suspected findings.
- ○ Do not leave child unattended.
- ○ Refer psychiatric consult.
- ○ Establish trust with child.

SECTION 7

NURSING CARE OF THE CHILD WITH CHRONIC OR LONG-TERM PROBLEMS

Immune Disorders

- Eczema – Inflammation of the skin not due to a specific etiology. Known as atopic dermatitis.
- Contributing Factors
  - ○ Unknown but appears to be related to abnormal function of the skin, including alterations in perspiration, peripheral vascular function, and heat intolerance
  - ○ Family history of eczema, allergy, asthma or allergic rhinitis
- Manifestations
  - ○ Papules are red and oozing; predominantly on face and extensor surfaces in infants, flexural areas in children (knees, wrists, antecubital fossa)
  - ○ Lesions eventually become scaly
  - ○ Pruritus may lead to secondary infection

- Treatment
  - ○ Topical steroids – triamcinolone (Kenalog); avoid chronic use
  - ○ Diphenhydramine HCl (Benadryl) or hydroxyzine HCl (Atarax) – reduces itching
  - ○ Elimination diet (milk, eggs, chocolate, wheat)
  - ○ Antibiotics if secondary infection occurs

 Nursing Interventions
- ○ Maintain skin integrity
  - ▪ Educate parents to control dry skin to minimize itching.
    - □ Use nonsoap cleanser.
    - □ Apply lubricating creams.
  - ▪ Advise parents that the child may be more comfortable in cotton, long-sleeved clothing.
  - ▪ Instruct parents to launder with a nonsoap or hypoallergenic cleanser.
  - ▪ Fingernails and toenails should be kept short to prevent scratching.
- ○ Assess developmental needs.
- ○ Provide a hypoallergenic diet.
- ○ Provide parental support and education.
- Bronchial asthma – Chronic inflammatory disorder of the airways involving mast cells, eosinophils, and T Lymphocytes. Inflammation causes recurrent episodes of wheezing, breathlessness, chest tightness, and cough. Also known as reactive airway disease. A chronic condition with acute exacerbations.
- Contributing Factors
  - ○ In response to allergen or trigger, acute hyperactive changes occur in reactive (lower) airways
    - ▪ Spasm of smooth muscle
    - ▪ Edema of mucous membranes
    - ▪ Thick, tenacious mucus
    - ▪ Severe, sudden dyspnea
  - ○ Potential triggers
    - ▪ Foods
    - ▪ Inhalants (secondhand smoke)
    - ▪ Infection

NOTES

- Vigorous activity
- Stress, anxiety
- Allergens (pet dander, dust)
- Cold air
- Manifestations
  - Paroxysmal, hacking nonproductive cough
  - Prolonged expiratory phase with expiratory wheeze
  - Respiratory distress, anxiety
- Complications
  - Pneumonia
  - Atelectasis
- Treatment
  - Chronic (home) management of child
    - Medications via nebulizer or metered-dose inhaler
      - Bronchodilators – albuterol (Proventil) useful for acute attack; salmeterol (Serevent) for chronic daily use, not for acute attack
      - Inhaled corticosteroids – effective in reducing airway hyper-reactivity; for chronic daily use, not acute attack; avoid chronic oral steroids that can stunt growth
      - Cromolyn sodium (Intal) – mast-cell inhibitor; reduces allergic response; for chronic daily use, not acute attack

 Nursing Interventions

  - Avoid allergens and triggers.
  - Teach correct use of metered-dose inhaler (with spacer device).
  - Plan activities that require stop and start energy.
  - Use of a peak-flow meter to monitor airway compliance.
- Status asthmaticus – severe respiratory distress requiring hospitalization
  - Bronchodilators
    - Epinephrine (Adrenalin) – subcutaneous
    - Aminophylline (Phyllocontin) – IV drip
  - Steroids – IV

- Inhalants – bronchodilators; albuterol (Proventil), metaproterenol (Alupent)
- Antibiotics – prophylactic
- Hydration
  - Oxygen therapy
- Rheumatic fever – an inflammatory disease that involves the joints, skin, brain, serous surfaces, and heart. Cardiac valve damage is the most significant complication. Sequelae includes scarring and damage to mitral valve.
- Contributing Factors
- Usually occurs 2 to 6 weeks after an upper-respiratory infection with group A beta-hemolytic strep
- Diagnosis
  - Elevated or rising antistreptolysin O (ASO) titer with elevated erythrocyte sedimentation rate (ESR)
  - Jones Criteria (presence of two major, or one major and two minor manifestations)
- Manifestations
  - Arthralgia; low grade fever that spikes in the afternoon; hot, red, swollen joints (polyarthritis); tachycardia with precordial friction rub; subcutaneous nodules; truncal rash (erythema marginatum)
  - Chorea
    - Sudden, involuntary movements with involuntary facial grimaces
    - Muscle weakness and speech disturbances
    - Is transitory; reassure parents that chorea will self-resolve
- Treatment
  - Medication therapy (penicillin, salicylates)
  - Bed rest in the acute phase
  - Prophylactic antibiotics with all dental work
 Nursing Interventions
  - Assess vital signs.
  - Control joint pain and inflammation with massage and alternating hot and cold applications.
  - Provide bed rest in acute febrile phase.

NOTES

- ○ Administer antibiotics and anti-inflammatory medications as prescribed.
- ○ Initiate seizure precautions if child experiencing chorea.
- ○ Instruct parents about the importance of followup.
- ○ Instruct parents that the child will require prophylactic antibiotics when at risk for infection.

Musculoskeletal Disorders

- Scoliosis – lateral curvature of the spine
  - ○ Most common form is idiopathic, seen (predominately) in adolescent females; unknown etiology
  - ○ Acquired scoliosis; associated with deformity resulting from other neuromuscular disorders
- Contributing Factors
  - ○ No apparent cause identified
- Diagnosis
  - ○ Screening exam in school – child flexes at waist; one scapula more prominent
  - ○ Spinal x-ray
- Treatment
  - ○ Mild scoliosis (< 20° curvature) – observation, encourage physical exercise
  - ○ Moderate scoliosis (20 to 40 degree curvature) – fitted Milwaukee brace
    - Goal is to prevent worsening of curve
    - Nursing Interventions
      - □ Address developmental needs of client.
      - □ Client teaching; skin care, commitment of therapy, and fashion concerns
  - ○ Severe scoliosis (> 40° curvature) – requires surgery
    - Spinal fusion with instrumentation
    - Requires prolonged immobilization in cast, brace, or body jacket
    - Nursing Interventions
      - □ Postoperative nursing care
      - □ Log roll for first 24 hr.

- □ Perform neurovascular assessments frequently.
- □ Promote pulmonary toileting.
- □ Provide pain management.
- □ Encourage age-appropriate activities.
- Juvenile rheumatoid arthritis (JRA) – autoimmune, inflammatory disease affecting the joints occurring most often in girls
- Contributing Factors unknown
  - ○ Early diagnosis essential due to long-term complications (blindness, contracture); early onset often associated with spontaneous permanent remission
- Classification
  - ○ Systemic (fever, rash, and organomegaly in addition to joint involvement)
  - ○ Polyarticular (many joints)
  - ○ Pauciarticular (few joints)
- Manifestations
  - ○ Swelling, thickening of joint
  - ○ Pain, stiffness, impaired range of motion
  - ○ Lethargy, weight loss
- Treatment
  - ○ Medications
    - NSAIDs
    - Methotrexate
    - Corticosteroids
    - Supportive treatment to maintain joint mobility
- Nursing Interventions
  - ○ Promote mobility and range of motion.
  - ○ Encourage nutritional intake.
  - ○ Provide pain relief (medication, heat, and cold).
  - ○ Monitor for exacerbation of symptoms.

Endocrine Disorders

- Type 1 diabetes mellitus
  - ○ Contributing factors
    - May be autoimmune response to environmental factors

NOTES

RENAL DISORDERS		
	Nephrotic Syndrome	Acute Glomerulonephritis
Other names	Childhood nephrosis	Poststreptococcal glomerulonephritis
Etiology	Cause unknown; likely autoimmune	Antigen – antibody reaction secondary to infection elsewhere in the body; usually a streptococcus ß-hemolytic, Group A of the upper respiratory tract
Incidence	Average age of onset about 2 ½ years; more common in boys	Two thirds of cases are in children who are under 4 to 7 years; more common in boys
Pathology	Increased permeability of the glomerular membrane to protein	Inflammation of the kidneys; damage to the glomeruli allows excretion of RBCs
Clinical Manifestations	Edema – appears insidiously; usually first noticed in the eyes and can advance to the legs, arms, back peritoneal cavity and scrotum; massive proteinuria; anorexia; pallor	Periorbital edema – appears insidiously; tea-colored urine from hematuria; hypertension; oliguria
Blood Pressure	Usually normal; transient elevation may occur early	Varying degrees of hypertension may be present; when blood pressure is elevated, cerebral manifestations may occur as a result of vasospasm; these may include headache, drowsiness, diplopia, vomiting, convulsions
Laboratory Findings	Urine shows heavy hematuria	Urine contains RBCs; has a high specific gravity
Blood	Involves reduction in protein (mainly albumin); gamma globulin is reduced; during the active stages of the disease, the sedimentation rate is greatly increased	BUN value is elevated; anemia (reduction in circulating RBCs, in Hgb or both) tends to develop rapidly
Course and Prognosis	Characterized by remissions and relapses; with protection against infection and suppression of proteinuria by steroid therapy, most children can eventually expect a favorable outcome	Recovery from acute glomerulonephritis is to be expected in nearly all children; mild illnesses last as little as 2 to 3 weeks; in exceptional instances, the disease is progressive and takes on the characteristics of chronic nephritis
Treatments	Prednisone (Deltasone) Furosemide (Lasix) Salt-poor albumin	Antibiotics for strep infection Antihypertensives and diuretics Corticosteroids
Nursing Interventions	Control edema; provide skin care; prevent infection; monitor nutrition: low sodium, high protein, high potassium: monitor urine for proteinuria; monitor for side effects from steroid therapy	Bed rest if hypertensive; restrict fluids; monitor neuro status; monitor blood pressure; provide low potassium diet, no added salt; prevent infection

- Genetic component – inherited tendency, not disease
- School-age child (5 to 7 years or puberty)

o Characteristics
  - Onset – rapid with progression to abrupt ketoacidosis
  - Hypertrophy and hyperplasia of islet cells occur early
  - Remission (honeymoon) phase
  - Insulin replacement (cannot use oral hypoglycemics)
  - Exercise lowers blood glucose
  - Management difficult due to
    □ Immaturity of child
    □ Lack of insight

o Developmental needs
  - Preschooler – biggest issues are the fear of injections and poor appetite (difficult to maintain diet); "free diet"
  - School-age child – how will children maintain their regular activities (birthday parties, pizza after the soccer game)
  - Adolescent – adolescents have difficulty complying; they are not interested in long-term effects; they want to be like their peers

Hematological Disorders

- Hemophilia – group of bleeding disorders which includes a deficiency in one of the factors necessary for coagulation of the blood.
  o Characteristics
    - Deficiency of clotting factors
    - Sex-linked recessive trait more common in males
    - Factor VIII and IX are most common deficiencies
    - Hemarthrosis (bleeding into joint cavities), bruises easily
  o Manifestations
    - Bleeding into subcutaneous and intramuscular tissue

- Hemarthrosis (bleeding into joint space) characterized by swelling, warmth, redness, pain, and loss of movement in joints
- Bruising
- Cryoprecipitate (transfusion that replaces missing clotting factor)
- Supportive therapy

 o Nursing Interventions
  - Control bleeding.
    □ Immobilize joint.
    □ Provide ice packs.
    □ Administer cryoprecipitate.
      ‣ Give prophylactic cryoprecipitate for invasive procedures.
      ‣ Risk for AIDS and/or hepatitis is decreased because of screening, but does still exist.
  - Safety directed toward developmental level to prevent injury, bleeding
    □ Avoid contact sports (difficult for children).
    □ Childproof environment.
    □ Avoid aspirin.
  - Provide parental, education and support.

- Sickle cell anemia – disease in which hemoglobin A is partly replaced by abnormal sickle hemoglobin S. Accounts for elongated shape of RBCs.
  o Contributing Factors
    - Sickling occurs in response to
      □ Infection, stress
      □ Dehydration
      □ Decreased oxygen
      □ High altitude
    - Sickling increases blood viscosity, which causes further sickling and RBC destruction
    - Types of crisis
      □ Vaso-occlusive – "hand-foot syndrome" caused by stasis of blood in capillaries; schema and infarction

---

NOTES

- □ Sequestration – pooling of large amounts of blood in liver, spleen; hypovolemia and shock
  - ■ Manifestations
    - □ Shortness of breath, fatigue
    - □ Tachycardia, pallor, jaundice
    - □ Lethargy, irritability, weakness
    - □ Pain, nausea, vomiting, anorexia
    - □ Swelling, fever
  - o Treatment
    - ■ Eliminate cause of crisis
    - ■ Analgesics
    - ■ Blood transfusions
    - ■ Monitor complications
      - □ Anemia
      - □ Splenic sequestration
      - □ Cerebrovascular accidents
   o Nursing Interventions
    - ■ Provide hydration.
    - ■ Administer analgesics, antibiotics as prescribed.
    - ■ Reduce stress of hospitalization.
    - ■ Provide parental support.

Renal Disorders

- • Glomerulonephritis
- • Nephrotic syndrome
- • See the Renal Disorders table on page 212.

Metabolic Disorders

- • Cystic fibrosis – CF is a genetic disease that affects salt and water movement in and out of body cells. Thick mucus causes blockages of small tubes and ducts in the body. Primarily affects the lungs and digestive system.
  - o Contributing Factors
    - ■ Inherited disease
    - ■ Requires inheritance of two mutated CF genes, one from each parent
  - o Manifestations
    - ■ Chronic respiratory infection

- ■ Accumulation of sticky, thick mucus in the lungs, adventitious or decreased breath sounds, wheezing and chronic cough with blood streaking, changers in color and amount of sputum
- ■ Stools pale or clay colored, foul smelling, float on surface of water
- ■ Weight loss, failure to thrive in infants, abdominal swelling
- ■ Excessive salt in sweat, dehydration
- ■ Abdominal pain, flatulence
- ■ Fatigue
- ■ Clubbing of fingertips
- o Treatment
  - ■ Pulmonary postural drainage, aerosol therapy, and treatment with antibiotics for infection
  - ■ Pancreatic enzymes with meals and supplementation of fat soluble vitamins – A, D, E, K (twice the normal daily age requirement)
  - ■ Free use of salt
  - ■ Possible lung transplantation
 o Nursing Interventions
  - ■ Assess respiratory status; oxygenation, color and amount of sputum.
  - ■ Daily weight, intake and output.
  - ■ Consistent, scheduled chest physiotherapy and postural drainage with cough and deep breathing.
  - ■ Provide small frequent feedings with pancreatic enzymes with each meal.
  - ■ Provide parental education and emotional support.
  - ■ Teach parents how to avoid exposing the child to infection, and to avoid environments containing smoke.
- • Celiac disease – disease of digestive system that damages the small intestine and interferes with the absorption of nutrients and food, particularly gluten products
  - o Contributing Factors

NOTES

- Inborn error of metabolism. Manifestations associated with fat and gluten intolerance.
  - Diagnosis
    - Bowel biopsy
    - Sweat test
  - Manifestations
    - Diarrhea
    - Large bulky stools
    - Anemia
    - Delayed growth and development
    - Frequent infection
    - Malabsorption of vitamin D
   - Nursing Interventions
    - Monitor weight and dietary intake.
    - Provide gluten free diet
    - Supply fat-soluble vitamins A, D, E, and K.
    - Assure the family that the child's lifespan will not be affected as long as the child follows a gluten-free diet.
    - Instruct the parents to avoid giving the child foods made with gluten; also, avoid barley, rye, oats, wheat (BROW diet)
    - Make appropriate referrals.
    - Provide emotional support.

SECTION 8

NURSING CARE OF THE CHILD WITH AN ONCOLOGY DISORDER

Leukemia

- Term for a group of malignancies that affect the bone marrow and lymphatic system. Causes bone marrow dysfunction that leads to anemia and neutropenia. Acute Lymphocytic Leukemia (ALL) is the most common childhood cancer.
  - Contributing factors
    - Unknown. Peak incidence is 2 to 6 years of age and is more common in boys older than one year. Incidence may be related to environmental exposures. Characterized by proliferation of immature WBCs.

- Leukemic infiltrate
    - Limb and joint pain
    - Lymphadenopathy
    - CNS involvement
    - Hepatosplenomegaly/bleeding tendencies
- Classification
  - Acute lymphocytic (ALL)
  - Acute nonlymphoid (ANLL)
  - Acute myelogenous leukemia (AML)
  - Manifestations
    - History of frequent infection and fever
    - Decreased platelet and RBC count
    - Increase immature WBCs
    - Anemia, pallor, and fatigue from decreased RBCs, headache
    - Low grade fever
    - Petechiae and epistaxis from decreased platelets
- Complications (secondary to bone marrow depression)
  - Infection
  - Intracranial hemorrhage
  - Secondary cancer or relapse
- Diagnosis – bone marrow aspiration reveals hypercellular marrow, abnormal cells
- Treatments
  - Lumbar puncture for analysis of CSF
  - Ultrasound for liver and spleen infiltration
  - Baseline liver and kidney function studies
  - Chemotherapy
    - Purine antagonists – 6-mercaptopurine (Purinethol) (may affect kidneys)
    - Alkylating agents – cyclophosphamide (Cytoxan) (causes chemical cystitis)
    - Folic acid antagonists – methotrexate (Folex)
    - Plant alkaloid – vincristine sulfate (Oncovin) (neurotoxic)
    - Steroids – prednisone (Prelone)
    - Enzymes – L-asparaginase (Elspar)

NOTES

o Radiation therapy for CNS involvement

Nursing Interventions

- o Complete history and physical assessment.
- o Monitor for anorexia, headache, and fatigue.
- o Assess vital signs and oxygenation.
- o Monitor CBC, temperature fluctuations.
- o Assess for infection.
- o Weigh daily.
- o Assess intake and output.
- o Provide support care related to chemotherapy.
- o Provide anticipatory guidance to child and family.
- o Provide emotional support and appropriate referrals.
- o Provide instruction for complex home care management.

Nephroblastoma (Wilms' Tumor)

- Type of renal cancer with a peak age of 3 years
  - o Contributing Factors
    - Certain genetic conditions or birth defects can increase risk. Arises from embryonal tissue.
    - Children at risk should be screened for Wilms' tumor every 3 months until age of 8. Most common clinical sign – swelling, mass within the abdomen. May also see – anemia, hypertension, hematuria
- Manifestations
  - o Most common clinical sign is swelling; mass within the abdomen
  - o Anemia, hypertension, hematuria
- Diagnosis
  - o IV pyelogram
  - o Computerized tomography
  - o Bone marrow to rule out metastasis
- Treatment
  - o Nephrectomy and adrenalectomy
  - o Radiation and chemotherapy determined by staging

Nursing Interventions

- o Preoperative care
  - Support parents, and keep explanations simple.
  - Monitor blood pressure due to excess renin production.
  - Prevent rupture of encapsulated tumor.
    - □ Post sign on bed – DO NOT PALPATE ABDOMEN.
    - □ Bathe and handle child gently.
- o Postoperative care
  - Assess vital signs, respiratory and oxygenation status.
  - Monitor blood pressure.
  - Assess dressing for bleeding.
  - Provide pain management.
  - Monitor urinary output and kidney function; dipstick urine for protein or blood.
  - Provide age appropriate developmental support and emotional support to parents.

Neuroblastoma

- Malignancy that occurs in the adrenal gland, sympathetic chain of the retroperitoneal area, head, neck or pelvis area. Most frequently seen in children less than 2 years.
- Contributing Factors
  - o An embryonal malignancy of the sympathetic nervous system arising from neuroblasts (pluripotent sympathetic cells)
  - o Frequently called "silent" tumor because by the time of diagnosis, metastasis has occurred
  - o Manifestations
    - Abdominal mass, urinary retention and frequency, lymphadenopathy, generalized weakness, and malaise
  - o Primary site is abdomen, most often in flank area
- Diagnosis
  - o Computerized tomography
  - o Bone marrow to determine metastasis
  - o Excessive catecholamine production

NOTES

- Treatment
  - Surgery to remove as much of the tumor as possible and determine staging
  - Chemotherapy and radiation determined by staging of tumor
- Nursing Interventions
  - Assess vital signs; height and weight.
  - Monitor intake and output and nutritional status.
  - Administer chemotherapeutic agents as prescribed and according to established protocols.
  - Assess for developmental delays related to illness.
  - Provide education and support to child and family.
  - Make appropriate referrals.
  - Provide age appropriate diversional activities.

Hodgkin's Lymphoma

- Cancer of the lymphatic system primarily affecting adolescents and young adults
- Contributing Factors
  - Originates in the lymphoid system. Metastasis may include spleen, liver, bone marrow, and lungs.
- Diagnosis
  - Computerized axial tomography
  - Lymph node biopsy, exploratory laparotomy (to stage)
- Treatment
  - Radiation and chemotherapy determined by clinical staging
  - Surgical laparotomy
  - Splenectomy
- Nursing Interventions
  - Assess vital signs; height and weight.
  - Monitor intake and output and nutritional status.
  - Administer chemotherapeutic agents as prescribed and according to established protocols.
  - Assess for developmental delays related to illness.

- Provide education and support to child and family with a splenectomy, increased susceptibility to infection and chronic illness.
- Make appropriate referrals.
- Provide age appropriate diversional activities.

SECTION 9

NURSING CARE OF THE CHILD WITH INFECTIOUS DISEASE

Prevention

- Immunizations
  - Schedule recommendations established by CDC and reviewed by American Academy of Pediatrics
  - Contraindication with active illness and fever greater than 40° C (101° F)
  - Precautions
    - Hepatitis B – allergy to baker's yeast, liver disease
    - DTaP – delay 30 days after immunosuppression
    - Hib – delay if child is ill
    - MMR – do not administer if child is allergic to eggs, neomycin, gelatin. Also, do not give to pregnant women or those who expect to get pregnant in 3 months
    - Varicella – do not administer if allergic to neomycin or gelatin
    - Pneumococcal – sensitivity to diphtheria may cause anaphylaxis
    - Influenza – do not administer if child is allergic to eggs; encourage those undergoing immunosuppressive therapy to receive a flu shot
    - Meningococcal – unknown impact on pregnancy
- Communicability
  - Communicable diseases are most contagious prior to the onset of manifestations or rash and in the early prodromal period
  - Most require respiratory isolation if the child requires hospitalization

---

NOTES

- o Most are preventable through immunization or other measures
- Common childhood infections
  - o See Communicable Diseases Guide on page 219.

SECTION 10

CPR GUIDELINES FOR CHILDREN AND INFANTS

- Establish That Victim is Nonresponsive
- Activate
  - o Unwitnessed event – activate the Emergency Response System (EMS) after performing five cycles of CPR
  - o Sudden, witnessed event – activate EMS after verifying that the victim is unresponsive
- Open the Airway
  - o Use head tilt and chin lift unless trauma is suspected; when trauma is suspected, use jaw thrust
- Rescue Breathing
  - o Open the airway, look, listen, and feel for 5 to 10 seconds.
  - o Give 2 breaths, each 1 second long. If unable to get chest to rise and fall, reposition and try again.
  - o If chest still does not rise and fall, suspect obstructed airway and perform back blows and chest thrusts. Do not perform a blind finger sweep of the mouth. Only remove object if it is visible.
- Check Pulse
  - o Child (ages 1 to 8) – carotid pulse; if no pulse or if pulse is less than 60/min with signs of poor perfusion, start CPR
  - o Infant (less than 1 year) – Brachial pulse; if no pulse or if pulse is less than 60/min with signs of poor perfusion, start CPR
- Start CPR
  - o Compression location
    - Child – center of breastbone between nipples
    - Infant – just below nipple line on breastbone
  - o Compression method

- Child – heel of one hand
- Infant – two fingers
- o Compression depth – ½ to 1 inch depth of chest
- o Compression rate – 100/min for infant and child
- o Compression-ventilation ratio
  - 30:2 for single rescuer CPR
- AED
  - o Child – use AED as soon as available; use child pads or a child system for children ages 1 to 8, if available; if child pads are not available, use adult AED and pads
  - o Infant – AED is not recommended for infants less than 1 year of age
- Obstructed Airway
  - o With a responsive victim
    - Infant – use a combination of back blows and chest thrusts.
    - Child and Adolescent – use abdominal thrusts and Heimlich maneuver
  - o Remove large debris in oral cavity
  - o Do not reach into mouth of an infant unless the object is visible.
  - o Place recovered child into recovery position
  - o Use calm approach with victim
  - o Administer oxygen as prescribed

NOTES

COMMUNICABLE DISEASES GUIDE

Transmission	Incubation	Clinical Manifestations	Treatment and Nursing Interventions	Prevention
Meningitis Viral or bacterial (H. influenza – 3 months to 3 years; meningococcal meningitis				
Direct invasion via otitis media, upper respiratory infection, head injury	2 to 10 days	Onset abrupt with fever, headache, irritability, altered level of consciousness, nuchal rigidity, increased intracranial pressure; must do lumbar puncture to isolate organism	Isolate; reduce environmental stimuli; monitor hydration; seizure precautions; IV antibiotcis	(Rifampin); given to contacts of client with meningococcal meningitis as prophylaxis
Mumps Viral paramyxovirus)				
Saliva, direct contact or droplet	14 to 21 days	Prodromal stage – headache, malaise, anorexia, followed by earache; parotitis 3 days later with pain/ tenderness	Symptomatic and supportive; analgesics; antipyretics; hydration	MMR
Pediculosis capitis (head lice) Pediculus humanus capitis				
Sharing of personal items (hair ornaments, caps, hats)	Eggs hatch in 7 to 10 days	Intense itching; can visually see nits attached to base of hair shafts; differentiate from dandruff	Do not share personal items. Shampoo with anti-lice products, wash linens and clothing in hot water	Caution children about sharing hair items
Pertussis (whooping cough) Bordetella pertussis				
Respiratory droplets and direct contact	7 to 21 days	Initially "cold" manifesations; progresses to spasms or paroxysmal coughing (whooping cough)	Antibiotics; corticosteroids; supportive care; isolation; stay with child during coughing spells	DTaP
Rabies Viral				
Contact with saliva of infected animal	1 to 3 months or as short as 10 days	Prodromal – malaise, sore throat followed by hyper-sensitivity, excitation, convulsions, paralysis; high mortality	Irrigate wound; psychologic follow up	Avoid contact with wild animals; rabies shot (given after exposure)

COMMUNICABLE DISEASES GUIDE

Transmission	Incubation	Clinical Manifestations	Treatment and Nursing Interventions	Prevention
Reye syndrome **Viral**				
Unknown – proceeded by viral infection and associated with the use of aspirin	NA	Prodromal – malaise cough, upper respiratory infection; 1 to 3 days after – fever, decreased level of consciousness, hepatic and cerebral dysfunction; high mortality	Monitor live function; peak age 4 to 11 years; neuro assessments; intracranial pressure monitoring	Avoid the use of aspirin in adolescents and children
Rheumatic fever **Group A beta-hemolytic strep**				
Nasopharyngeal secretions; direct contact with infected person or droplet spread	1 to 3 weeks after acute infection, develops inflammatory disease	Carditis, arthritis, chorea (involuntary ataxic movements), subcutaneous nodules, erythema marginatum (rash)	Bed rest in acute phase to decrease cardiac workload; full course of antibiotics (penicillin/erythromycin); high dose of aspirin therapy (monitor for toxicity tinnitus)	Adequate, prompt treatment of strep infection (must finish entire course of therapy)
Roseola (exantehm subitum) **Viral (human herpes virus type 6)**				
Unknown (limited to children 6 months to 2 years of age)	Unknown	Persistent high fever for 3 to 4 days; precipitous drop in fever with appearance of rash (rose-pink maculopapule on trunk, then spreading to neck, face and extremities); lasts 1 to 2 days	Antipyretics to control temperature and prevent febrile seizures; hydrate	None
Rubella (German measles) **Viral (rubella virus)**				
Nasopharyngeal secretions – direct contact, indirect via freshly contaminated nasopharyngeal secretions or urine	14 to 21 days	Prodromal phase; absent in children, present in adults; rash; first face and rapidly spreads downward to neck, arms, trunk, and legs; teratogenic to fetus	No treatment necessary; isolate child from pregnant women; women of childbearing years should have rubella titer down	MMR

COMMUNICABLE DISEASES GUIDE

Transmission	Incubation	Clinical Manifestations	Treatment and Nursing Interventions	Prevention
Rubeola (measles) Viral				
Respiratory-droplets	10 to 21 days	Prodromal stage – fever and malaise, coryza, conjunctivitis, Koplik spots (spots with blue/white center on buccal mucosa opposite molars); rash: starts on the face, spreads downward, may desquamate (peel)	Antipyretics to control temperature and prevent seizures; dim lights if photophobia; respiratory precautions	MMR
Scarlet fever Group A beta-hemolytic strep				
Nasopharyngeal secretions, direct contact with infected person or droplet spread	2 to 4 days	Prodromal stage – abrupt high fever, pulse increased, vomiting, chills, malaise, abdominal pain, enanthema – tonsils enlarged, edematous reddened, covered with patches of exudate; strawberry tongue; exanthema – rash appears 12 hr after prodromal signs	Full course of antibiotics (penicillin/erythromycin); isolate; monitor for rheumatic fever; glomerulonephritis hydrate	Adequte, prompt treatment of strep infection (must finish entire course of therapy)
Tetanus Clostridium tetany				
Deep punture, not contagious, "anerobic"	7 to 14 days	Gradual stiffening of voluntary muscles until rigid (lockjaw, rigid abdomen); sensitive to stimuli; clear sensorium	Eliminate stimuli; monitor respirations, blood gases; muscle relaxants; monitor hydration	DTaP, Td

UNIT SEVEN

PHARMACOLOGY FOR NURSING

SECTION 1

REVIEW OF CALCULATIONS AND CONVERSIONS

Metric System

- 1 kg = 1,000 g
- 1 gm = 1,000 mg
- 1 mg = 1,000 mcg
- 1 L = 1,000 mL
- 1 mL = 1 cc = 1 g
- 1 cm = 10 mm

Apothecary System (rarely used today)

- 1 dram = 60 grains
- 1 oz = 8 drams
- 1 dram = 60 minims
- 1 fluid oz = 8 fluid drams

Household System

- 1 lb = 16 oz
- 1 Tbsp = 3 tsp
- 1 oz = 2 Tbsp
- 1 cup = 8 oz
- 1 pint = 16 oz
- 1 quart = 2 pints
- 1 gallon = 4 quarts

Conversions Between Systems

- 1 grain = 60 mg
- 1 gm = 15 grains
- 1 tsp = 5 mL
- 1 Tbsp = 15 to 16 mL
- 2 Tbsp = 1 oz = 30 to 32 mL
- 1 cup = 8 oz = 240 mL
- 8 oz = 240 to 250 mL
- 2 cups = 1 pint = 500 mL
- 1 inch = 2.54 cm
- 1 kg = 2.2 lb

- 1 lb = 454 gm
- 1 minim = 1 drop
- 1 mL = 15 minims = 15 drops

Temperature Conversions

- 37.0° C = 98.6° F
- C = (F - 32) x 5/9
- F = (C x 9/5) + 32

Calculations for IV Administration

- Number of hours = total volume/mL/hr
- gtts per min = total volume x gtts/mL in administration set/total number of minutes

Calculations for Dosage

- Dosage on hand (H)/mL = Dosage desired (D)/mL

Fill-in-the-Blank question format

- An NCLEX alternate-test item where the answer is placed in the box below a question.

Practice Test Questions (answers on the following page)

1. A client has the following food for lunch: one cup of tea, one cup of coffee, and 240 mL of milk. The client drinks all of the tea and coffee and half of the milk. The total intake for lunch is

2. A client has a prescription for 0.25 mg of lanoxin (Digoxin). There are 0.5 mg tablets of lanoxin on hand. How many tablets should the client receive?

3. A client's IV infusion rate is 75 mL/hr. How many hours will a 500 mL bag of IV fluid last?

4. When the IV rate is 100 mL/hr and the administration set is 15 drops/mL, how many drops per minute should the IV run?

5. A 4-year-old child is prescribed 5 mL of ampicillin (Polycillin Pediatric) for otitis media every 6 hr. When preparing the child for discharge, the nurse should tell the child's mother to give how much ampicillin every 6 hr?

NOTES

6. A client has a prescription for heparin (Heparin Sodium) 7,000 units IV. The vial contains 10,000 units/mL. How many milliliters of heparin should the nurse administer?

7. A nurse is preparing 300,000 units of procaine penicillin (Wycillin). The vial contains 1,500,000 units/2 mL. How many milliliters should the nurse administer?

8. A client weighs 180 lb and has a prescription for 0.5 mL of medication per kilogram of body weight. How many milliliters of medication should the client receive?

9. A client is receiving dextrose 5% in water at 50 mL/hr in one IV and D$_5$W 75 mL/hr in another IV. The client also receives IV piggyback medication every 8 hr prepared in 100 mL of fluid. How much IV fluid will the client receive in 8 hr?

10. When the IV administration set delivers 10 drops/mL, the rate of flow in drops/min for 1,000 mL dextrose 5% in water to infuse in 8 hr is

11. When measuring a client's output, the nurse records 300 mL of urine at 0800, 450 mL of liquid stool at 1130, 225 mL of urine at 1300, and 35 mL of emesis at 1430. What is the client's total output for this shift?

12. A client receiving an IV infusion has a prescription for 1,000 mL in 12 hr. Using a micro-drip system that delivers 60 micro drops/mL, the nurse should adjust the infusion for how many drops per minute?

A. 45

B. 68

C. 83

D. 96

13. A client's temperature is 100° F. What is this temperature in degrees centigrade?

14. A nurse has available meperidine (Demerol) 50 mg/mL. The order is to administer meperidine 35 mg. How many milliliters should the nurse safely administer?

15. A nurse is preparing an IV antibiotic in 100 mL of dextrose 5% in water to infuse over 20 min. The infusion set is calibrated for 10 gtts/mL. What drip rate should the nurse use?

Test Answers:

1. 600

2. 0.5

3. 7

4. 25

5. 1

6. 0.7

7. 0.4

8. 41

9. 1,100

10. 21

11. 1,010

12. 83

13. 37.7

14. 0.7

15. 50

SECTION 2

PHARMACOLOGY

Medication Actions, Interactions, and Reactions

- Medication Properties (pharmacokinetics) – the absorption, distribution, metabolism, and excretion of a medication; describes the onset of action, peak level, duration of action, and bioavailability

- Medication Interaction – when a medication is given with another medication and alters the effect of either or both medications

NOTES

- Adverse Reactions – untoward effects experienced by a client as the result of a specific medication, which may be hazardous, tolerated, or subside with continued use

Pharmacotherapy Across the Lifespan

- Medications and Pregnancy – a majority of medications cross the placental barrier therefore, increasing the risk of teratogenicity; all medications should be given with extreme caution to ensure safety to the developing fetus
- Medications and Breastfeeding
  - Most medications taken by a mother who is breastfeeding appear in breast milk. Medication levels tend to be the highest in the newborn immediately after the medication is administered to the mother. Mothers who are breastfeeding are advised to breastfeed before taking the medication.
- Medication in Children
  - Pharmacokinetics are influenced by a child's age, size, and maturity of targeted organ. To reduce the risk of toxicity, these factors must be considered; safe calculation of the child's dosage mg/kg/day, medication that is age-appropriate, monitoring of IV medications to prevent fluid overload (no more than 2 hr of IV therapy with a fluid-control device), usage of the vastus lateralis site for IM injections in children who are < 2 years of age, and the administration of inhalants using a metered-space device.
- Medication in Older Adults
  - Age-related changes impact therapeutic effects of medications in older adult clients. Older adult clients experience twice as many adverse effects as younger adults due to aging body systems. Confusion, lethargy, falls, and weakness may be mistaken for senility, rather than adverse reactions. If the adverse reaction is not identified, unnecessary medication may be prescribed to treat complications caused by the medication. As the client continues to receive medications, the risk for toxicity increases.
  - Toxicity in older adults – a greater risk when taking diuretics, antihypertensives, digoxin, steroids, anticoagulants, hypnotics, and over-the-counter medications

Safe Medication Administration

- By following the six rights of medication administration (client, medication, dosage, route, time, and documentation), the nurse protects the safety of the client as well her professional licensure.

SECTION 3
ANALGESIC MEDICATIONS

Nonopioid Analgesics

- Acetylsalicylate acid (Aspirin)
  - Indication
    - Mild pain relief or fever, management of transient ischemic attack, prophylactic MI, cerebrovascular accident, angina
  - Action
    - Anti-inflammatory effect by inhibiting prostaglandin
  - Adverse Effects
    - Tinnitus, gastrointestinal bleeding, thrombocytopenia, prolonged bleeding time
   - Nursing Interventions
    - Discard if vinegar odor.
    - Avoid giving to children.
    - Assess for occult stool.
- Acetaminophen (Tylenol)
  - Indication
    - Mild pain or fever
  - Action
    - Inhibits prostaglandin
  - Adverse Effects
    - Rash, jaundice, hypoglycemia
   - Nursing Interventions
    - The maximum adult dose in a 24-hr period is 4 g; may provide a false drop in blood glucose levels.
    - Monitor for hepatotoxicity.
    - Instruct the client to avoid alcohol.

NOTES

- Ibuprofen (Advil)
  - o Indication
    - ■ Mild to moderate pain, arthritis, fever, dysmenorrhea
  - o Action
    - ■ Inhibits prostaglandin, antipyretic
  - o Adverse Effects
    - ■ Headache, nausea, gastrointestinal bleeding, tinnitus
  - o Nursing Interventions
    - ■ It may increase the risk of MI, stroke, thrombotic events, or gastrointestinal bleed.
    - ■ Have the client take the medication with meals or milk.
    - ■ Instruct the client to wear sunscreen.

Opioid Analgesics

- Codeine (Codeine)
- Hydromorphone HCl (Dilaudid)
  - o Indication
    - ■ Moderate to severe pain, nonproductive cough
  - o Action
    - ■ Alters the perception of pain, suppresses cough reflex
  - o Adverse Effects
    - ■ Sedation, respiratory depression, constipation, orthostatic hypotension
  - o Nursing Interventions
    - ■ Avoid use if the client's respirations are < 12.
    - ■ Encourage slow postural changes.
    - ■ Instruct the client to avoid alcohol and monitor for constipation.
    - ■ Take with meals or milk.
- Meperidine (Demerol)
- Methadone HCl (Methadone)
- Morphine (MS Contin)
- Oxycodone (OxyContin, Percodan, Percocet)

- o Indication
  - ■ Moderate to severe pain
- o Action
  - ■ Alters perception of pain
- o Adverse Effects
  - ■ Euphoria, bradycardia, heart failure, dry mouth, hypokalemia, respiratory depression
- o Nursing Intervention
  - ■ Monitor for respiratory depression, because naloxone HCl (Narcan) is an antagonist.

SECTION 4

ANTI-INFECTIVE MEDICATIONS

Antifungals

- Fluconazole (Diflucan)
  - o Indication
    - ■ Treats candidiasis infection
  - o Action
    - ■ Binds to fungal cell membranes and causes death of fungal growth
  - o Adverse Effects
    - ■ Headache, alters taste, diarrhea
  - o Nursing Interventions
    - ■ Prothrombin time is increased with warfarin (Coumadin); therefore, it decreases the metabolism of the oral hypoglycemic agents glyburide and glipizide.
    - ■ Monitor glucose levels closely.

Antimalarials

- Hydroxychloroquine (Plaquenil)
- Quinine sulfate (Quinine)
  - o Indication
    - ■ Prevent malarial attacks, rheumatoid arthritis, systemic lupus
  - o Action
    - ■ Binds with DNA of organisms to alter mutation

NOTES

- o Adverse Effects
  - Blurred vision, headache, anorexia, alopecia

- o Nursing Interventions
  - Take the medication at the same time daily to maintain therapeutic level.
  - Toxicity signs include drowsiness, seizure, and cardiovascular collapse.

Antiprotozoals

- Metronidazole (Flagyl)
  - o Indication
    - Treatment of trichomoniasis and giardiasis, postoperative infection in contaminated colorectal surgery, *Clostridium difficile*, pelvic inflammatory disease, vaginosis
  - o Action
    - Cell death to microorganism
  - o Adverse Effects
    - Metallic taste, headache, red-brown urine, joint pain, vomiting, decreased libido

  - o Nursing Interventions
    - Instruct the client to avoid alcohol (disulfiram affects gastrointestinal system), edema secondary to sodium retention.
    - Treat both partners for trichomoniasis.

Antituberculars

- Isoniazid (INH)
- Rifampin (Rifadin)
  - o Indication
    - Prevention and treatment of acute tuberculosis
  - o Action
    - Inhibits *mycobacterium tuberculosis*
    - Adverse Reaction
      - □ Peripheral neuropathy and hepatotoxicity with isoniazid
      - □ Epigastric pain, flatulence, and red-orange color to bodily fluids with rifampin.

- o Nursing Interventions
  - Encourage the client to consume foods containing vitamin B_6.
  - When taking isoniazid (INH), avoid foods containing tyramine.
  - Contact the provider if jaundice is present.

Aminoglycosides

- Vancocin (Vancomycin)
- Gentamicin sulfate (Gentamicin)
  - o Indications
    - Septicemia infection, meningitis, staphylococcus, klebsiella pneumoniae, serious infections
  - o Action
    - Inhibits bacterial growth
  - o Adverse Reactions
    - Ototoxicity, nephrotoxicity, anemia, headache

  - o Nursing Interventions
    - Monitor the client for signs of tinnitus.
    - Monitor creatinine and BUN levels.
    - For gentamicin sulfate, maintain peak levels at 4 to 12 mcg/dL and trough levels at 1 to 2 mcg/dL.
    - For vancocin, maintain peak levels at 20 to 40 mcg/dL and trough level at 5 to 15 mcg/dL

Antiretrovirals

- Acyclovir (Zovirax)
- Valacyclovir HCl (Valtrex)
- Zidovudine (AZT, Retrovir)
- Indications
  - o Treatment of genital herpes with acyclovir; treatment of genital herpes and shingles with valacyclovir HCl ; prevention and management of HIV with zidovudine
  - o Action
    - Inhibits DNA growth

NOTES

- Adverse Reactions
  - Headache, loss of appetite, fatigue, weakness, insomnia, fever, seizures

- Nursing Interventions
  - Instruct the client not to skip doses and to increase fluids.
  - For acyclovir and valacyclovir HCl, take with food.
  - For zidovudine, take on an empty stomach while sitting upright to avoid esophageal irritation.

Cephalosporins

- Cephalexin (Keflex) 1st generation
- Cefaclor (Ceclor) 2nd generation
- Cefotaxime (Claforan) 3rd generation
  - Indications
    - Upper respiratory, skin, urinary tract infections and postoperative infections
    - First generation is often administered preoperative as a prophylactic
  - Action
    - Similar to penicillin; cephalosporin causes rapid bacterial cell wall destruction
  - Adverse Reactions
    - Abdominal pain, fever, hypersensitivity, *Clostridium difficile.*

- Nursing Interventions
  - There is a cross-sensitivity with penicillin.
  - Use cautiously in clients who have renal/hepatic failure.

Fluoroquinolones

- Ciprofloxacin (Cipro)
- Levofloxacin (Levaquin)
  - Indications
    - Bronchitis, Chlamydia, gonorrhea, pelvic inflammatory disease, pneumonias, prostatitis, sinusitis, urinary tract infection, septicemia
  - Action
    - Destroys the bacterial agent

- Adverse Reactions
  - Agitation, hallucinations, hepatotoxicity, colitis, headache, dizziness

- Nursing Intervention
  - Use cautiously in clients who have hepatic disease, renal insufficiency, or seizure disorders.

Macrolides

- Azithromycin (Zithromax, Z-pack)
- Clarithromycin (Biaxin)
  - Indications
    - Various infections in upper respiratory/sinus systems
  - Action
    - Inhibits RNA protein synthesis
  - Adverse Reaction
    - Diarrhea, palpitations, vaginal candidiasis, dizziness, photosensitivity, metallic taste with clarithromycin

- Nursing Intervention
  - Instruct the client to complete the entire course of the medication, increase fluids, and avoid long exposure to sunshine.

Penicillins

- Amoxicillin (Amoxil)
- Ampicillin
  - Indications
    - Pneumonia, upper respiratory infections, septicemia, endocarditis, rheumatic fever, gynecologic infections
  - Action
    - Bacteriocidal causing rapid cell destruction
  - Adverse Reactions
    - Hypersensitivity that includes rash, fever, and in severe cases, anaphylaxis

NOTES

o Nursing Interventions

- There is a cross sensitivity with cephalosporin.
- Instruct the client to complete the medication, even if symptoms disappear within initial doses.

Sulfonamides

- Trimethoprim-sulfamethoxazole (Bactrim, Septra)
  - o Indications
    - Urinary tract infections, bronchitis, otitis media
  - o Action
    - Inhibits bacterial growth
  - o Adverse Reactions
    - Oliguria, uric crystals, photosensitivity
  - o Nursing Interventions
    - Instruct the client to increase daily fluid intake to 3,000 mL.
    - Instruct the client to use a back-up contraceptive if taking an oral contraceptive.
    - Avoid prolonged sun exposure.

Tetracyclines

- Doxycycline calcium (Vibramycin)
- Tetracycline HCl (Tetracycline)
  - o Indications
    - Fungal, bacterial, protozoal, rickettsia infections
  - o Action
    - Inhibits infectious growth
  - o Adverse Effects
    - Extreme gastrointestinal distress, *Clostridium difficile*, decreased urinary output, photosensitivity
  - o Nursing Interventions
    - Encourage the client to increase his daily fluid intake.
    - Avoid prolonged sun exposure.
    - Advise the client of permanent tooth discoloration if administered to children younger than 8 years of age.

ACE Inhibitors

- Captopril (Capoten)
- Enalapril maleate (Vasotec)
- Lisinopril (Zestril)
  - o Indication
    - Hypertension, management of heart failure
  - o Action
    - Prevents productions of angiotensin II causing systemic vasodilation
  - o Adverse Effects
    - Dry cough, dizziness, decreased blood pressure 3 hr after first dose
  - o Nursing Interventions
    - Encourage slow postural changes.
    - Monitor daily weight.
    - Monitor for signs of heart failure.

Antianginal

- Nitroglycerine (NitroTab)
  - o Indication
    - Angina management
  - o Action
    - Dilate coronary arteries, decreases cardiac workload
  - o Adverse Effects
    - Headache, tachycardia, palpitations
  - o Nursing Interventions
    - Protect the medication from sunlight, moisture and heat.
    - Give a sublingual dose every 5 min, with no more than three pills during an acute angina episode.
    - Access emergency medical care if no relief after three doses.
    - Wear gloves when applying topical medication.

NOTES

Antiarrhythmics

- Amiodarone HCl (Cordarone)
- Lidocaine HCl (Xylocaine)
  - Indication
    - Ventricular arrhythmias
  - Action
    - Reduces ventricular irritability
  - Adverse Action
    - Bradycardia, heart block and heart failure with amiodarone HCl
    - Tachycardia, bradycardia, and hypotension with lidocaine HCl
  - Nursing Interventions
    - Remain with the client during infusion.
    - Closely monitor the client with ECG and frequent vital sign checks.

Antihypertensives

- Clonidine (Catapres)
- Hydralazine (Apresoline)
  - Indication
    - Hypertension, heart failure
  - Action
    - Relaxes smooth cardiac muscle
  - Adverse Action
    - Tachycardia, palpitations, weight gain, dizziness, diarrhea
  - Nursing Interventions
    - Obtain the client's daily weight.
    - Assess the need for a diuretic.
    - Compliance with medication is an issue, as side effects are severe. Hydralazine is the medication of choice for clients diagnosed with pregnancy-induced hypertension.

Antilipidemics

- Atorvastatin calcium (Lipitor)
- Simvastatin (Zocor)
- Niacin (Niaspan)
  - Indication
    - Hyperlipidemia
  - Action
    - Decreases total cholesterol and lowers LDL
  - Adverse Effects
    - Headache, insomnia, constipation, abdominal distention
  - Nursing Interventions
    - Avoid taking with grapefruit; enzyme inhibits absorption of the medication.
    - Administer in the evening.
    - Increase fluid, fiber, and activity, and select a low-cholesterol diet.

Beta Blockers

- Atenolol (Tenormin)
- Propranolol (Inderal)
- Metoprolol succinate (Toprol)
  - Indication
    - Hypertension, anxiety
  - Action
    - Nonselective beta blocker, decreased blood pressure
  - Adverse Effects
    - Bradycardia, dry mouth, sedation
  - Nursing Interventions
    - Monitor heart rate and blood pressure.
    - Increase fluid intake.
    - Contraindicated with pulmonary hypertension due to blocking beta 2 receptors causing bronchial constriction.

Calcium-Channel Blockers

- Amlodipine besylate (Norvasc)
- Diltiazem HCl (Cardizem)
- Verapamil HCl (Calan)
  - Indication
    - Hypertension, angina

NOTES

- Action
  - Blocks calcium across the cardiac cell membrane, decreasing oxygen demands, leading to a drop in blood pressure and dilation of the arteries
- Adverse Effects
  - Bradycardia, peripheral edema
- Nursing Interventions
  - Teach the client to monitor pulse for bradycardia.
  - Observe for peripheral edema.

Digitalis Glycosides

- Digoxin (Lanoxin)
  - Indication
    - Heart failure
  - Action
    - Increases force of cardiac contractions and decreases heart rate
  - Adverse Effects
    - Bradycardia, muscle weakness, hallucinations
  - Nursing Interventions
    - Monitor the client for signs of toxicity; early signs are bradycardia, nausea, and vomiting; late signs are diplopia and green-yellow halos.
    - Monitor the client's potassium levels and digoxin level. Therapeutic digoxin level is 0.8 to 2 ng/mL.
    - Assess the client's apical pulse for a full minute; hold if < 60 in adult, < 80 in child, < 100 in infant.

Loop Diuretics

- Bumetanide (Bumex)
- Furosemide (Lasix)
  - Indication
    - Pulmonary/generalized edema
  - Action
    - Inhibits sodium and chloride reabsorption in the kidneys
    - Increases excretion of sodium and water

- Adverse Effects
  - Decreased potassium, calcium, sodium, chloride
  - Dehydration, hypotension
- Nursing Interventions
  - Verify the client's potassium level and renal function prior to administration.
  - Increase potassium-rich foods.
  - Observe the client for hypokalemia; muscle weakness/cramps.
  - There is a risk for digitalis toxicity due to hypokalemia.

Platelet Aggregation Inhibitors

- Clopidogrel bisulfate (Plavix)
- Ticlopidine HCl (Ticlid)
  - Indication
    - Prevents clot formation in clients who have unstable angina or recent a MI
  - Action
    - Inhibits platelet aggregation and prevents clot formation
  - Adverse Effects
    - Bleeding, bruising, gastric ulcers, liver disease
  - Nursing Interventions
    - Monitor the client for gastrointestinal bleeding, liver disease, and implement bleeding precautions.
    - Avoid giving the client aspirin.

Potassium-Sparing Diuretics

- Spironolactone (Aldactone)
  - Indication
    - Hypertension, edema
  - Action
    - It is a diuretic that reduces potassium excretion
  - Adverse Effects
    - Hyperkalemia

NOTES

---

o Nursing Interventions

- Monitor the client's serum potassium level and for signs of hyperkalemia.

- Obtain the client's daily weight.

- Instruct the client to avoid high-potassium foods.

Thiazide Diuretics

- Hydrochlorothiazide (Hydrodiuril)
- Indapamide (Lozol)
  - o Indication
    - Hypertension, edema
  - o Action
    - It is a diuretic that increases the excretion of sodium and water
  - o Adverse Effects
    - Hypokalemia, alters glucose metabolism
 o Nursing Interventions
    - Monitor the client for hypokalemia and hyperglycemia.
    - There is a risk for digitalis toxicity due to potassium depletion.

Vasopressors

- Dobutamine HCl (Dobutamine)
- Dopamine HCl (Dopamine)
- Epinephrine sulfate (Epinephrine)
- Norepinephrine bitrate (Norepinephrine)
  - o Indication
    - Increases cardiac output during heart failure (dobutamine HCl)
    - Treats shock and enhances blood to vital organs; increases cardiac output (dopamine HCl)
    - Restores blood pressure during MI (epinephrine sulfate, norepinephrine bitrate)
  - o Action
    - Vasoconstriction and cardiac stimulation
  - o Adverse Effects
    - Headache, restlessness, cardiac arrhythmias, tachycardia, tachypnea, discomfort at IV site

 o Nursing Intervention

- Frequently monitor the client's cardiac stability and urinary output.

SECTION 6
ENDOCRINE SYSTEM

Antidiabetic

- Glipizide (Glucotrol)
- Glyburide (DiaBeta)
- Rosiglitazone maleate (Avandia)
  - o Indication
    - Lowers glucose levels in type 2 diabetes mellitus
  - o Action
    - Reduces glucose metabolism by the hepatic system
  - o Adverse Effects
    - Flatulence, constipation, hypoglycemia, rhinitis, photosensitivity
 o Nursing Interventions
    - Adhere to therapeutic regimen of diet and exercise.
    - Teach the client to monitor for signs of hypoglycemia and to carry candy.
    - Avoid alcohol, which lowers glucose levels.

Insulins

- Insulin glargine (Lantus)
- Insulin isophane suspension (NPH)
- Insulin lispro (Humalog)
- Insulin Regular (Novolin R)
- Combination 70/30 (70% NPH; 30% Regular)
  - o Indication
    - Insulin-dependent diabetes mellitus
  - o Action
    - Lowers glucose levels, transports glucose into cells
  - o Adverse Effects
    - Hypoglycemia, hyperglycemia

NOTES

- o Nursing Interventions
  - Monitor the client's glucose levels frequently.
  - Do not mix other insulins with lispro, glargine, or combination 70/30.

Glucagon

- Glucagon (Glucagon)
  - o Indication
    - Severe hypoglycemia
  - o Action
    - Increases glucose levels
  - o Adverse Effects
    - Hypotension, bronchospasm
  - o Nursing Interventions
    - Monitor the client's glucose levels before, during, and after administration.
    - Give the client additional carbohydrates following alertness to prevent a second episode.

Pituitary Hormones

- Vasopressin (Pitressin)
  - o Indication
    - Diabetes insipidus, gastrointestinal bleeding
  - o Action
    - Promotes reabsorption of water, causing vasoconstriction
  - o Adverse Effects
    - Cardiac arrhythmias, abdominal cramps, diaphoresis, water intoxication
  - o Nursing Interventions
    - Monitor the client's urine specific gravity, blood pressure, and urinary output.
    - Instruct the client to avoid alcohol.

Steroidal Anti-inflammatory

- Dexamethasone (Decadron)
- Hydrocortisone (Solu-Cortef)
- Prednisone (Meticorten)

- o Indication
  - Adrenal insufficiency, inflammation, cerebral edema, bacterial meningitis
- o Action
  - Anti-inflammatory suppresses immune response
- o Adverse Effects
  - Insomnia, euphoria, increased appetite, hypokalemia, hypertension, hyperglycemia, hypocalcemia
  - Cushingoid symptoms, such as weight gain and moon face
- o Nursing Interventions
  - Monitor the client's electrolytes.
  - Encourage the client to consume a high-protein/high potassium diet.
  - Monitor glucose levels in clients who have diabetes mellitus.
  - Reduce a client's doses slowly.

Thyroid Hormones

- Levothyroxine/T4 (Synthroid)
  - o Indication
    - Hypothyroidism
  - o Action
    - Stimulates metabolism of all body systems by accelerating the rate of cellular oxygenation
  - o Adverse Effects
    - Tachycardia, restlessness, diarrhea, weight loss, decreased bone density, heat intolerance
  - o Nursing Interventions
    - Monitor the client's cardiac system.
    - Start by giving the client low doses. Then, advance to higher dosages, while monitoring laboratory values.

NOTES

SECTION 7

GASTROINTESTINAL SYSTEM

Antacids

- Aluminum hydroxide (Amphojel)
- Calcium carbonate
  - Indication
    - Antacid
  - Action
    - Reduces acid in gastrointestinal tract
  - Adverse Effects
    - Constipation, intestinal obstruction, electrolyte imbalance
   Nursing Intervention
    - Monitor for the relief of symptoms.

Antidiarrheals

- Diphenoxylate HCl (Lomotil)
- Loperamide HCl (Imodium)
  - Indication
    - Diarrhea
  - Action
    - Inhibits motility
  - Adverse Effects
    - Sedation, dry mouth, urinary retention, respiratory depression, physical dependence with long-term use
   Nursing Intervention
    - Monitor the client's fluids/electrolytes. If symptoms do not improve after 48 hr, have the client seek medical advice.

Antiemetics

- Meclizine HCl (Antivert)
- Metoclopramide (Reglan)
- Odansetron HCl (Zofran)
  - Indication
    - Nausea, vomiting

  - Action
    - Blocks parasympathetic nervous system
  - Adverse Effects
    - Sedation, constipation, diarrhea, decreased appetite, hypoxia, rash
   Nursing Interventions
    - Monitor liver function in clients who have liver impairment.
    - Assess compatibility with other medications when preparing to administer odansetron HCl .

Antisecretory

- Cimetidine (Tagamet)
- Ranitidine (Zantac)
  - Indication
    - GERD, eliminate *Helicobacter pylori*
  - Action
    - Reduces gastric secretion
  - Adverse Effects
    - Headache, flatulence, dry mouth
   Nursing Interventions
    - Instruct the client not to skip a dose.
    - Take in morning 1 hr before a meal.
    - Avoid crushing tablets.
    - Avoid trigger foods; chocolate, spice, caffeine, nicotine, acid, and mint.

Antiulcer

- Esomeprazole mg (Nexium)
- Omeprazole (Prilosec)
- Lansoprazole (Prevacid)
  - Indication
    - Peptic ulcer disease and GERD
  - Action
    - Inhibits gastric secretions and decreases gastric acidity
  - Adverse Effects
    - Diarrhea, constipation

NOTES

○ Nursing Interventions

- Take medication 30 min before a meal.
- Avoid a double dose.
- Avoid selection of over-the-counter antiulcer medications without an accurate diagnosis. Ranitidine interacts with Dilantin. Do not take together.

SECTION 8

GENITOURINARY SYSTEM

Benign Prostatic Hyperplasia (BPH)

- Dutasteride (Avodart)
- Finasteride (Proscar)
- Tamsulosin HCl (Flomax)
  - ○ Indication
    - Decreases symptoms of BPH
  - ○ Action
    - Decreases inflammation of the prostate gland
  - ○ Adverse Effects
    - Impotence, decreased libido, gynecomastia

 ○ Nursing Interventions

- Inform the client that ejaculate volume decreases.
- Monitor prostate-specific antigen levels (medication may lower level).

Erectile Dysfunction Agents

- Sildenafil citrate (Viagra)
- Tadalafil (Cialis)
- Vardenafil (Levitra)
  - ○ Indication
    - Erectile dysfunction
  - ○ Action
    - Relaxes smooth muscle to enhance blood flow to tissue
  - ○ Adverse Effects
    - Headache, MI, transient ischemic attack, hypotension, retinal bleeding, increased intraocular pressure

 ○ Nursing Interventions

- It is contraindicated with nitrate therapy.
- Seek help if erection lasts longer than 4 hr or priapism lasts longer than 6 hr. Take medication 30 min to 2 hr prior to sexual activity.

Incontinence Agents

- Oxybutynin chloride (Ditropan)
- Tolterodine tartrate (Detrol)
  - ○ Indication
    - Overactive bladder with symptoms of urinary frequency, urgency, or urge incontinence
  - ○ Action
    - Relaxes the smooth muscles of the bladder
  - ○ Adverse Effects
    - Dry mouth, weight gain, headache

 ○ Nursing Intervention

- Contraindicated in clients who have glaucoma, liver, or renal impairment.

SECTION 9

HEMATOLOGIC

Antianemics

- Epoetin alfa (Epogen)
  - ○ Indication
    - Anemia secondary to renal failure, chemotherapy and AZT therapy in clients who are HIV positive
  - ○ Action
    - Mimics erythropoietin; enhances RBC production
  - ○ Adverse Effects
    - Fatigue, hypertension, hyperkalemia, fever, rash

 ○ Nursing Interventions

- Monitor the client's blood pressure, potassium, Hgb level, and temperature.
- Inform the client of potential joint pain and fatigue following injection.

NOTES

- Ferrous sulfate (Slow Fe)
  - Indication
    - Iron-deficiency anemia
  - Action
    - Assists the body in replacing iron stores
  - Adverse Effects
    - Constipation, tarry stools
   Nursing Interventions
    - Administer with orange juice if in pill form.
    - Administer using a straw if elixir.
    - Administer into dorsal gluteus site using the Z-track method if IM.

Anticoagulants

- Heparin sodium (Heparin)
- Enoxaparin (Lovenox)
  - Indication
    - Thrombosis, pulmonary embolism, MI, to maintain patency of central lines
  - Action
    - Prevents conversion of fibrinogen to fibrin and prothrombin to thrombin
  - Adverse Effects
    - Hemorrhage
   Nursing Interventions
    - Monitor prothrombin time (PT) for heparin. Therapeutic PT is 1.5 to 2.0 times control value.
    - Assess the client for bleeding gums, bruises, nosebleeds and petechiae. Protamine sulfate is the antidote.
    - Avoid giving aspirin and NSAIDs.
- Warfarin (Coumadin)
  - Indication
    - Thrombosis, MI, heart valve damage
  - Action
    - Prevents prothrombin formation
  - Adverse Effects
    - Hemorrhage, diarrhea, rash

 Nursing Interventions
  - Monitor PT/INR; therapeutic INR is 2.0 to 3.0.
  - Assess the client for signs of bleeding. Vitamin K is the antidote.
  - Do not interchange brands, and avoid aspirin and NSAIDs.

Neutropenia Medications

- Filgrastim (Neupogen)
  - Indication
    - Neutropenia; decreases infection in clients who are receiving myelosuppressive chemotherapy
  - Action
    - Stimulates growth of neutrophils
  - Adverse Effects
    - Fever, hypotension, bone pain, alopecia, dyspnea
   Nursing Interventions
    - Obtain the client's baseline vital signs prior to therapy.
    - Instruct the client that each vial is only to be used once. Administer the medication subcutaneously.

Platelet Medications

- Oprelvekin (Neumega)
  - Indication
    - To prevent severe thrombocytopenia in clients receiving myelosuppressive chemotherapy
  - Action
    - Stimulates growth of stem cells and platelets
  - Adverse Effects
    - Fever, syncope, tachycardia, thrush, dehydration, elevate calcium, Hgb/Hct levels
   Nursing Intervention
    - Closely monitor the client's fluids/electrolytes and RBC. Administer subcutaneously.

NOTES

Thrombolytic Enzymes

- Tissue plasminogen activator/TPA (Activase)
- Streptokinase (Streptase)
  - Indication
    - Lysis of thrombi obstructing coronary arteries in acute MI
    - Re-establishes patency of occluded central line; indicated for pulmonary embolism and deep vein/arterial thrombosis
  - Action
    - Converts plasminogen to plasmin, causing fibrinolysis
  - Adverse Effects
    - Hypotension, arrhythmias, bleeding, pulmonary edema
  - Nursing Interventions
    - For acute MI, it must be administered within 6 hr of the event; for stroke, must be administered within 3 hr of the event to reduce mortality.
    - For pulmonary embolism or deep vein thrombosis, it must be administered within 7 days.

SECTION 10

HERB/BOTANICAL THERAPY

- Aloe Vera
  - Indications
    - Burns and skin irritation, topically; cathartic, orally
  - Nursing Interventions
    - Has cathartic effect; observe the client for diarrhea.
    - Monitor for dehydration
    - Contraindicated with diuretic, digoxin, and corticosteroid
- Chamomile
  - Indications
    - Gastrointestinal distress, motion sickness, cystitis, sedation, skin inflammation

 Nursing Interventions
- It can cause an anaphylactic reaction when taken by a client who has a history of ragweed, pollen, seasonal allergies, hay fever, or asthma.
- Increases anticoagulant therapy.

- Cranberry
  - Indications
    - Asthma, fever, kidney stones, prevents urinary tract infection (UTI)
  - Nursing Interventions
    - Instruct the client to take on a regular basis to prevent bacterial growth along the bladder wall.
    - Only unsweetened/unprocessed cranberries are effective (prophylactic) in preventing a UTI. Seek pharmacotherapy treatment with the presence of UTI symptoms.
- Black Cohosh
  - Indications
    - Symptoms of menopause, such as hot flashes, vaginal dryness, night sweats, mood swings
  - Nursing Intervention
    - It is contraindicated with the use of oral contraceptives, hormone replacement therapy, antihypertensive, and CNS depressants.
- Echinacea
  - Indications
    - Eczema stimulates the immune system, prevents common colds, upper respiratory infections
  - Nursing Intervention
    - Echinacea should not be used in place of an antibiotic. Prolonged use may overstimulate the immune system and possibly cause immune suppression. Do not use longer than 14 days.
- Feverfew
  - Indications
    - Menstrual cramps, migraine, psoriasis, rheumatoid arthritis, tranquilizer.

NOTES

- Nursing Interventions
  - Monitor the client's INR and prothrombin time if receiving anticoagulant therapy; may enhance bleeding.
  - It must be tapered off to avoid post feverfew syndrome: headaches, insomnia, joint stiffness, and/or lethargy.
- Flax Seed
  - Indications
    - Diverticulitis, constipation, irritable bowel syndrome, decreases total cholesterol levels
    - Increases bleeding time

  - Nursing Intervention
    - Instruct the client to increase his fluid intake, and monitor cholesterol and bleeding time.
- Garlic
  - Indications
    - Decreases cholesterol, HDL and triglyceride levels
    - Prevents gastrointestinal cancer, MI, stroke, and atherosclerosis

  - Nursing Interventions
    - Advise the client to consume garlic in moderate amounts.
    - Instruct the client to stop taking before surgery. Not advised if the client is taking an anticoagulant.
- Ginger
  - Indications
    - Antiemetic, anti-inflammatory, antispasmodic

  - Nursing Intervention
    - Monitor bleeding time.
- Ginkgo Biloba
  - Indications
    - Enhances cerebral circulation
    - Decreases vertigo, tinnitus, and headaches
    - Manages macular degeneration and diabetic retinopathy
    - Used as an adjunct for schizophrenia and pancreatic cancer

- Nursing Intervention
  - Intended for short-term therapy due to toxicity. Treatment is limited to 6 to 8 weeks and no longer than 3 months.
- Ginseng
  - Indications
    - Fatigue, atherosclerosis, diabetes mellitus, bleeding disorders, strength recovery after illness

  - Nursing Intervention
    - Not recommended for use more than 3 months due to hypertension, edema, and insomnia.
- Green Tea
  - Indications
    - Prevents hyperlipidemia and cancer
    - Acts as a mild diuretic and antibacterial

  - Nursing Intervention
    - Advise the client not to drink more than five cups per day. Signs of toxicity include vomiting and abdominal spasms. Interferes with the absorption of multivitamins and supplements.
- Kava
  - Indications
    - Reduces anxiety and used for cystitis, menstrual cramps, and the common cold

  - Nursing Intervention
    - Do not use with MAOIs or levodopa. Intended for short-term use, because longer than 3 months will cause CNS depression and hepatotoxicity.
- Melatonin
  - Indications
    - Insomnia, jet lag, shift-worker disorder, depression, and benzodiazepine withdrawal

  - Nursing Interventions
    - May increase growth hormone levels.
    - Because sedation occurs, be sure that safety precautions are in place.

NOTES

- Milk Thistle
  - Indications
    - Detoxification of liver (cirrhosis, chronic anticonvulsant medication)
  - Nursing Intervention
    - Contraindicated if the client is allergic to ragweed, magnolias, daisies, and chrysanthemums.
- Saw Palmetto
  - Indications
    - Benign prostatic hyperplasia, bronchitis, asthma
  - Nursing Intervention
    - Monitor the client's prostate-specific antigen (PSA) values prior to starting the herb; may cause false negative PSA level.
- St John's Wort
  - Indications
    - Mild to moderate level depression, sciatica, enuresis, gout, viral infections
  - Nursing Intervention
    - Allow 4 to 6 weeks for effect to impact depression.
- Valerian Root
  - Indications
    - Insomnia, sedation
  - Nursing Intervention
    - Take when in bed, as onset is rapid.

SECTION 11

MUSCULOSKELETAL SYSTEM

Antigout

- Allopurinol (Zyloprim)
- Colchicine (Colsalide)
  - Indication
    - Management of gouty arthritis; colchicine is used to slow deterioration in clients who have multiple sclerosis

- Action
  - Reduces uric-acid production
- Adverse Effects
  - Nausea, diarrhea, altered taste, hepatomegaly, rash, fever
- Nursing Interventions
  - Allopurinol is used for chronic gout and prevents acute attacks.
  - Colchicine is administered during acute attacks.
  - Avoid purine foods, such as aged cheeses, wine, and red meats to reduce acute attacks; increase fluids.

Antireabsorptives

- Alendronate (Fosamax)
- Ibandronate (Boniva)
- Zoledronic acid (Reclast)
  - Indication
    - Osteoporosis in women who are postmenopausal or with glucocorticoid-induced osteoporosis
  - Action
    - Suppresses osteoclast activity to preserve bone density
  - Adverse Effects
    - Flatulence, acid reflux, esophageal ulcer, dysphagia
  - Nursing Interventions
    - Alendronate is administered once a week by mouth.
    - Ibandronate is administered once a month by mouth.
    - Zoledronic acid is administered once a year by IV. Administer an oral dose in the morning on an empty stomach. Sit upright for 30 min to avoid esophageal excoriation.

Antirheumatics

- Adalimumab (Humira)
- Auranofin (Ridaura)

NOTES

- o Indication
  - ■ Rheumatoid arthritis
- o Action
  - ■ Suppresses phagocytic activity
- o Adverse Effects
  - ■ Metallic taste, proteinuria, anemia, dermatitis, thrombocytopenia

- o Nursing Intervention
  - ■ Monitor platelets and proteinuria. Therapeutic effects are achieved after 3 months of therapy.

Skeletal Muscle Relaxants

- Succinylcholine chloride (Anectine)
- Baclofen (Lioresal)
  - o Indication
    - ■ Muscle spasms in multiple sclerosis, spinal-cord injury; to relax muscles prior to electroconvulsive therapy
  - o Action
    - ■ Reduces muscle impulse transmission
  - o Adverse Effects
    - ■ Dizziness, hypotension, hypertension, urinary frequency, hyperglycemia

  - o Nursing Interventions
    - ■ Avoid alcohol and antihistamines; may increase CNS depression.
    - ■ Because sedation occurs, be sure that safety precautions are in place.
- Carisoprodol (Soma)
  - o Indication
    - ■ Acute musculoskeletal pain
  - o Action
    - ■ Muscle relaxant
  - o Adverse Effects
    - ■ Dizziness, orthostatic hypotension, hiccups, depressive reaction

  - o Nursing Interventions
    - ■ Avoid alcohol and antihistamines.
    - ■ Encourage slow postural changes.

- ■ Take medication with food.
- ■ Withdraw therapy slowly to avoid insomnia or abdominal cramps.
- ■ Medication may be habit forming.
- Cyclobenzaprine (Flexeril)
  - o Indication
    - ■ Relieves skeletal muscle spasms from acute conditions
  - o Action
    - ■ Reduction of tonic muscle activity at the brain stem
  - o Adverse Effects
    - ■ Tremors, insomnia, headaches, arrhythmias, blurred vision, dry mouth, and urine retention

  - o Nursing Intervention
    - ■ Hypertensive crisis may occur with tricyclic and MAOI antidepressant use. Intended for short-term adjunctive therapy for pain management.

SECTION 12

MATERNAL HEALTH SYSTEM

Antineoplastics

- Methotrexate sodium (Methotrexate, Trexall)
  - o Indication
    - ■ Hydatidiform mole, nonruptured ectopic pregnancy
  - o Action
    - ■ Stops growth of cells; embryonic fetus, early placenta
- Adverse Effects
  - o Abdominal cramps, spotting, fatigue, photosensitivity, immune suppression

- Nursing Intervention
  - o Avoid gas-producing foods and exposure to sunlight. It is contraindicated if the client is receiving immunosuppressant therapy.

NOTES

Contraceptives, Systemic

- Ethinyl Estradiol Norethindrone (Ortho-Novum 7/7/7)
- Mestranol/Norethindrone (Norinyl)
  - Indication
    - Prevention of pregnancy, endometriosis, hypermenorrhea
  - Action
    - Reduces release of follicle-stimulating and luteinizing hormone from pituitary gland
  - Adverse Effects
    - Nausea, headache, spotting
  - Nursing Interventions
    - The client should contact the primary care provider if he experiences a persistent headache, leg or chest pain, double vision, and/or excessive bleeding. Contraindicated for clients who smoke, are older than 35, and/or have a history of cardiac disease or thrombus.
    - Use alternate contraception during antibiotic therapy.
- Medroxyprogesterone Acetate (Depo-Provera)
  - Indication
    - Prevention of pregnancy, endometrial cancer, endometriosis
  - Action
    - Progestin hormone that suppresses ovulation and causes endometrial thinning
  - Adverse Effects
    - Nausea, pulmonary embolism, breakthrough bleeding, weight changes
  - Nursing Interventions
    - It may cause significant loss of bone density
    - An IM injection must be given every 3 months to maintain effective contraception.
    - Amenorrhea can occur with prolonged use.

- Estrogens
- Estradiol (Estrace)
  - Indication
    - Menopausal symptoms, palliative care for breast cancer, osteoporosis
  - Action
    - Hormone replacement
  - Adverse Effects
    - Nausea, intolerance of contact lens, aggravates astigmatism, breakthrough bleeding, hypothyroidism, and dermatitis
  - Nursing Interventions
    - It can be administered orally, topically or transdermally.
    - Instruct the client to take it orally with milk or food to decrease gastrointestinal upset.
    - It is contraindicated in clients who have a history of cardiac disease or cancer (other than inoperable breast cancer).

Fertility Medications

- Clomiphene citrate (Clomid)
- Menotropin (Repronex)
  - Indication
    - Controlled ovarian stimulation for conception
  - Action
    - Stimulates ovulation and development of corpus luteum
  - Adverse Effects
    - Nausea, headache, depression, weight gain, alopecia, hot flashes, irritability
  - Nursing Intervention
    - Discuss the possibility of multiple births. Daily intercourse is encouraged.

Oxytocics

- Dinoprostone (Cervidil)
  - Indication
    - Ripens cervix

NOTES

- Action
  - Produces strong uterine contractions
- Adverse Effects
  - Headache, hot flashes, arrhythmias, vaginal pain
- Nursing Interventions
  - Monitor the client's cardiac functions, increase her fluids, and avoid giving aspirin.
  - The client will need to be hospitalized during use.

- Methylergonovine maleate (Methergine)
  - Indication
    - Prevents postpartum hemorrhage
  - Action
    - Increases uterine stimulation to prevent hemorrhage
  - Adverse Effects
    - Seizures, headaches, nausea, leg cramps, hypotension, hypertension, diaphoresis
  - Nursing Intervention
    - Monitor the client's blood pressure, heart rate, and firmness of the fundus.

- Oxytocin (Pitocin)
  - Indication
    - Induce or stimulate labor contraction pattern, reduce postpartum hemorrhage, incomplete abortion
  - Action
    - Causes intense contraction of the smooth muscle of the uterus and mammary glands
  - Adverse Effects
    - Arrhythmias, abruptio placenta, uterine rupture, water intoxication, hypertension, and tachycardia
  - Nursing Interventions
    - Monitor the client's I&O. Antidiuretic effect may lead to water intoxication (seizures, coma, and death).
    - Monitor the client's vital signs every 15 min. Turn oxytocin off if contractions last longer than 90 seconds and/or fetal bradycardia occurs.

- It is contraindicated in clients who have placenta previa. Keep magnesium sulfate available to relax a uterus that is hypertonic.

Preterm Labor Medications

- Tocolytics
- Magnesium sulfate
  - Indication
    - Stop premature labor
  - Action
    - Relaxes smooth muscle of uterus
  - Adverse Effects
    - Hot flashes, hypocalcemia, decreased respirations, hypotension, decreased urine output, fetal bradycardia
  - Nursing Interventions
    - It has a therapeutic range between 4 to 7 mEq/L. Calcium gluconate is the antidote for magnesium toxicity.
    - Monitor the client's vital signs every 15 min and urine output every hour.
    - Constantly monitor the client's deep tendon reflexes; if reflexes diminish or are absent, administer antidote immediately.

- Ritodrine (Yutopar)
- Terbutaline sulfate (Brethine)
  - Indication
    - Stops premature labor
  - Action
    - Relaxes smooth muscle of uterus and bronchial passage
  - Adverse Effects
    - Tachycardia, dyspnea, nervousness, hypokalemia, decreased urine output, muscle weakness
  - Nursing Interventions
    - Monitor the client's cardiac function and electrolytes.
    - It is administered to stop contractions between 20 and 35 weeks of gestation.

NOTES

- Discontinue use if maternal heart rate is > 120, if there are signs of pulmonary edema, and/or the fetal heart rate is >180. Propranolol (Inderal) reverses cardiovascular adverse effects.

Antenatal Corticosteroid Therapy

- Betamethasone dipropionate (Diprolene, Celestone)
  - ○ Indication
    - ■ Prevents respiratory distress syndrome in infants who are preterm
  - ○ Action
    - ■ Stimulates maturity of the fetus' lungs to release lung surfactant
- Adverse Effects
  - ○ Maternal pulmonary edema, hyperglycemia, and hypertension

 Nursing Interventions

- ○ Two doses are given IM 12 hr apart.
- ○ Teach the client to report respiratory difficulties or pulmonary edema.

SECTION 13

MENTAL HEALTH SYSTEM

Antianxiety Agents (Benzodiazepines)

- Alprazolam (Xanax)
- Diazepam (Valium)
- Lorazepam (Ativan)
  - ○ Indication
    - ■ Generalized anxiety disorders, panic disorders, substance abuse withdrawal
  - ○ Action
    - ■ Depresses CNS
  - ○ Adverse Effects
    - ■ Sedation, hypotension, dry mouth, urinary retention, blurred vision, tremors, sexual dysfunction, dyspnea, habit forming

 ○ Nursing Interventions

- ■ Instruct the client to avoid alcohol.

- Inform the client not to stop medications suddenly; the provider must decrease the medication slowly to minimize rebound symptoms or seizures. Flumazenil (Romazicon) is the antidote for benzodiazepine overdose.

Attention-Deficit Disorder Agents

- Atomoxetine HCl (Strattera)
- Methylphenidate HCl (Concerta)
- Methylphenidate (Ritalin)
- Dextroamphetamine (Adderall)
  - ○ Indication
    - ■ ADHD
  - ○ Action
    - ■ Releases norepinephrine
  - ○ Adverse Effects
    - ■ Nervousness, insomnia, weight loss, anorexia, dermatitis, rash, tachycardia, arrhythmias

 ○ Nursing Interventions

- ■ Monitor the client's height and weight.
- ■ Give the client his last daily dose 6 hr prior to bedtime and after meals to avoid anorexia.
- ■ Instruct him to avoid caffeinated beverages.

Antidepressants, Tricyclic

- Amitriptyline (Elavil)
- Nortriptyline (Pamelor)
  - ○ Indication
    - ■ Depressive disorder
  - ○ Action
    - ■ Increases norepinephrine and serotonin
  - ○ Adverse Effects
    - ■ Anticholinergic effects, hypotension, fluid retention, photosensitivity, tremors, diaphoresis

 ○ Nursing Intervention

- ■ Interacts with MAOIs, increasing the risk of hypertensive crisis. Use comfort measures to minimize anticholinergic effects. Monitor cardiac function due to fluid retention.

NOTES

Antidepressants, SSRIs

- Citalopram (Celexa)
- Escitalopram (Lexapro)
- Paroxetine HCl (Paxil)
- Sertraline (Zoloft)
  - Indication
    - Major depressive disorder
  - Action
    - Inhibit reuptake of serotonin
  - Adverse Effects
    - Increased appetite, decreased libido, elevated glucose levels with escitalopram
   Nursing Interventions
    - Paroxetine HCl is effective with obsessive compulsive disorder, social anxiety disorder, posttraumatic stress disorder, and panic disorder.
    - SSRIs have fewer adverse effects and can be used safely in older adults. Instruct the client to take it at the same time every day and allow up to 4 weeks for therapeutic effect.
    - Teach the client to avoid alcohol and other CNS depressants.

Antidepressants, Other

- Bupropion HCl (Zyban/Wellbutrin)
- Duloxetine (Cymbalta)
- Trazodone (Desyrel)
  - Indication
    - Depressive disorder, seasonal affective disorder, smoking cessation (Wellbutrin)
  - Action
    - Inhibits norepinephrine, serotonin uptake and dopamine
  - Adverse Effects
    - Dry mouth, tremors, agitation, headache, constipation
   Nursing Interventions
    - Instruct the client not to skip a dose when depression subsides.

- Monitor suicide ideation in the client who is under 24.
- Increase the client's fluids and monitor her blood pressure.

Antipsychotics

- Aripiprazole (Abilify)
- Clozapine (Clozaril)
- Haloperidol (Haldol)
- Olanzapine (Zyprexa)
  - Indication
    - Schizophrenia, acute manic disorder, agitation
  - Action
    - Binds to dopamine receptors
  - Adverse Effects
    - Extrapyramidal symptoms (greatest risk with haloperidol), sedation, dystonia, akathisia, tardive dyskinesia, neuroleptic malignant syndrome, photosensitivity, anticholinergic effect, increased glucose levels and weight gain (highest in olanzapine), agranulocytosis with clozapine
   Nursing Interventions
    - Benztropine mesylate (Cogentin) is given with haloperidol to diminish extrapyramidal symptoms associated with Parkinson's disease.
    - Clients who are taking clozapine should have their WBCs checked weekly.
    - Antacids inhibit absorption.
    - Encourage the client to increase fluids and monitor her for tardive dyskinesia and neuroleptic malignant syndrome.

Bipolar Agents

- Lithium carbonate (Lithobid)
  - Indication
    - Prevent or control mania
  - Action
    - Alters CNS receptors and replaces sodium ions

NOTES

- Adverse Effects
  - Dizziness, fine tremors, signs of intoxication with lithium

- Nursing Interventions
  - Lithium has a narrow therapeutic level (0.8 to 1.2 mg/dL) and increases the risk of toxicity.
  - Monitor the client for early signs of toxicity, which include diarrhea, vomiting, drowsiness, slurred speech, tremors, and seizures.
  - Depakote is a safer choice, but the nurse must monitor the client's liver function during therapy.
  - Encourage the client to increase her fluid intake and obtain adequate amounts of sodium.
  - Instruct her to avoid caffeine and excessive perspiration.

Hypnotics

- Temazepam (Restoril)
- Zolpidem tartrate (Ambien)
  - Indication
    - Insomnia
  - Action
    - Sedative
  - Adverse Effects
    - Drowsiness, flu-like symptoms, nausea

- Nursing Interventions
  - It is beneficial for older adults.
  - Its onset is rapid, so encourage the client to be in bed prior to administration.
  - Instruct the client to avoid alcohol and that it is habit forming.

SECTION 14

NEUROLOGICAL SYSTEM

Alzheimer Disease Agents

- Donepezil HCl (Aricept)
- Tacrine HCl (Cognex)

- Indication
  - Mild to severe Alzheimer's dementia
- Action
  - Increase acetylcholine levels
- Adverse Effects
  - Insomnia, diarrhea, seizures

- Nursing Interventions
  - The medication does not cure dementia, but stabilizes or relieves symptoms.
  - Instruct the client to take the medication with meals to decrease gastrointestinal distress.

Anticonvulsants

- Carbamazepine (Tegretol)
  - Indication
    - Tonic-clonic seizures, bipolar I episodes, restless leg syndrome
  - Action
    - Limits seizure activity by managing sodium across cell membrane of motor cortex
  - Adverse Effects
    - Dizziness, diplopia, photosensitivity, nystagmus, agranulocytosis

- Nursing Interventions
  - Monitor the client's WBC levels.
  - Encourage the client to obtain regular eye exams.
  - Instruct the client to take the medication with food. It may turn urine pink to brown.
  - Instruct the client to avoid alcohol.
- Divalproex sodium (Depakote)
  - Indication
    - Complex seizures, mania, migraine headaches
  - Action
    - Increases levels of aminobutyric acid in the brain, which decreases seizure activity

NOTES

- Adverse Effects
  - Prolonged bleeding time, elevated liver enzymes, sedation, constipation, thrombocytopenia

- Nursing Interventions
  - Discontinue therapy slowly to avoid seizures.
  - Monitor liver enzymes, and platelets.
- Gabapentin (Neurontin)
  - Indication
    - Management of seizures and shingles pain
  - Action
    - Unknown, but thought to increase seizure threshold
  - Adverse Effects
    - Drowsiness, diplopia, rhinitis, constipation

  - Nursing Intervention
    - Avoid abruptly discontinuing therapy.
- Phenobarbital (Luminal)
  - Indication
    - Anticonvulsant, febrile seizures, status epilepticus, sedation
  - Action
    - Depresses CNS
  - Adverse Effects
    - Bradycardia, respiratory depression, apnea, somnolence, Stevens-Johnson syndrome

  - Nursing Interventions
    - Monitor the client's therapeutic level (15 to 40 mcg/mL).
    - Paradoxical excitement in older adults decreases the effectiveness of oral contraceptive.
- Phenytoin (Dilantin)
  - Indication
    - Management of seizures, status epilepticus
  - Action
    - Manages sodium across membranes across cell membrane of motor cortex

- Adverse Effects
  - Gingival hypertrophy, diplopia, drowsiness, hirsutism, Stevens-Johnson syndrome, agranulocytosis, changes urine pink, red or brown

- Nursing Interventions
  - Monitor the client's therapeutic level (10 to 20 mcg/dL).
  - Instruct the client not to change brands once stabilized.
  - Instruct the client to avoid alcohol, maintain regular oral hygiene.
  - Zantac interrupts phenytoin therapy.

Antiparkinsonian

- Carbidopa/levodopa (Sinemet)
- Levodopa (Dopar)
  - Indication
    - Parkinson's disease
- Action
  - Increases dopamine to minimize parkinsonian symptoms
- Adverse Effects
  - Twitching, headache, dizziness, arrhythmias, dark urine, agitation, confusion

Nursing Interventions
  - Encourage the client to changes positions slowly.
  - Vitamin B$_6$ foods interfere with the therapeutic effect of the medication (avoid liver, pork, chicken, eggs, sweet potatoes, wheat germ).
  - The therapeutic effect achieved in 4 to 6 weeks. Avoid abrupt discontinuance to avoid parkinsonian crisis.

SECTION 15
ONCOLOGY

Alkylating Agents

- Cyclophosphamide (Cytoxan)
- Cisplatin (Platinol)

NOTES

- o Indication
  - ▪ Treatment of leukemia, ovarian, and breast cancer
- o Action
  - ▪ Interferes with RNA growth
- o Adverse Effects
  - ▪ Decreases WBC, RBC, and platelets
  - ▪ Nausea, anorexia, alopecia, amenorrhea, bladder irritation, and metallic taste

- o Nursing Interventions
  - ▪ Implement measures to prevent infection.
  - ▪ Promote nutrition and hydration.
  - ▪ Report any hematuria or mouth blisters.

Antibiotic Antineoplastics

- • Doxorubicin HCl (Adriamycin)
  - o Indication
    - ▪ Cancers, Kaposi's sarcoma, non-Hodgkin's and Hodgkin's lymphoma, leukemia, Wilms' tumor
  - o Action
    - ▪ Interferes with RNA synthesis
  - o Adverse Effects
    - ▪ Hair loss, thrush, decreased RBC, WBC, and platelets, anorexia, amenorrhea, decreased libido, left-ventricular failure, irreversible cardiomyopathy

  - o Nursing Interventions
    - ▪ Monitor the client's cardiac function.
    - ▪ Premedicate the client with an antiemetic to decrease nausea.
    - ▪ Promote hydration, nutrition, mouth care and prevent infection.
    - ▪ Tell the client that his urine will be red-orange the first 2 days of therapy.
    - ▪ Hair regrowth can be expected 2 to 5 months following the final dose of therapy.

Hormone Altering Antineoplastics

- • Tamoxifen citrate (Nolvadex)
  - o Indication
    - ▪ Advanced breast cancer and prophylaxis for women at high risk
  - o Action
    - ▪ Estrogen antagonist
  - o Adverse Effects
    - ▪ Hot flashes, nausea/vomiting, rash, bone pain

  - o Nursing Interventions
    - ▪ Instruct the client to take an antacid prior to taking the medication to manage gastrointestinal distress.
    - ▪ Provide comfort measures when the client experiences a hot flash.

SECTION 16
OPHTHALMIC

Antiglaucoma/Beta Blockers Topical

- • Levobunolol (Betagan)
- • Timolol maleate (Timoptic)
  - o Indication
    - ▪ Treatment of glaucoma
  - o Action
    - ▪ Reduces intraocular pressure and ocular hypertension
  - o Adverse Effects
    - ▪ Fatigue, weakness, hypotension

  - o Nursing Interventions
    - ▪ Monitor the client's heart rate and blood pressure.
    - ▪ Teach the client aseptic technique and to apply gentle pressure on tear ducts for 1 min after administering eye drops.

Miotics

- • Atropine sulfate (Atropine)
  - o Indication
    - ▪ Dilates pupil for eye exam, eye surgery

NOTES

- Reduces inflammation in the iris
  - Action
    - Anticholinergic action blocks muscarine receptors to dilate pupils
  - Adverse Effects
    - Photophobia, tachycardia, blurred vision, increased intraocular pressure, no accommodating for near vision, conjunctivitis

  - Nursing Intervention
    - It is contraindicated in glaucoma.

Mydriatics

- Pilocarpine HCl (Pilocar)
  - Indication
    - Relieves symptoms of glaucoma
  - Action
    - Constricts pupils to reduce intraocular pressure
  - Adverse Effects
    - Blurred vision, eye redness/irritation, tearing

  - Nursing Interventions
    - Follow specific directions for use to avoid incorrect dosage.
    - Follow aseptic technique with eye drop technique to prevent infection.

SECTION 17

RESPIRATORY SYSTEM

- Antiasthma
- Cromolyn Sodium Inhaler Intal
- Montelukast Singulair

Antihistamines

- Cetirizine HCl (Zyrtec)
- Loratadine (Claritin)
- Fexofenadine HCl (Allegra)
  - Indication
    - Seasonal allergic rhinitis and hives

- Action
  - Blocks histamine to reduce symptoms of sneezing, nasal congestion, and eye irritation
- Adverse Effects
  - Drowsiness, dry mouth, diarrhea.

- Nursing Interventions
  - Avoid taking with medications that depress the CNS.
  - Instruct the client to avoid alcohol.
  - Promote safety practices.
  - Instruct the client not to drive or operate machinery.
  - Instruct the client to increase her fluids.

Antitussives

- Hydrocodone (Hycodan)
- Hydrocodone with acetaminophen (Vicodin)
  - Indication
    - Relieves cough
  - Action
    - Decreases cough reflex in CNS
  - Adverse Effects
    - Drowsiness, dry mouth, urine retention, constipation

  - Nursing Interventions
    - Avoid taking with medications that depress the CNS.
    - Encourage safety precautions.

Bronchodilators

- Albuterol sulfate (Proventil)
- Ipratropium bromide (Atrovent)
- Levalbuterol HCl (Xopenex)
- Theophylline (Theo-Dur)
  - Indication
    - Bronchospasm, status asthmaticus
  - Action
    - Relaxes smooth muscles of bronchial passage

NOTES

- Adverse Effects
  - Tachycardia, restlessness, insomnia, palpitations, anxiety

- Nursing Interventions
  - Instruct the client to avoid alcohol, caffeine, chocolate, nicotine, and medications containing ephedra.
  - Therapeutic levels are monitored with Theo-Dur (10 to 20 mcg/dL).

Expectorants

- Benzonatate (Tessalon Perles)
- Guaifenesin (Robitussin, Mucinex)
  - Indication
    - Expectorant
  - Action
    - Liquifies thick, tenacious mucus
  - Adverse Effects
    - Dizziness, nausea, rash, headache

  - Nursing Interventions
    - Understand that certain medications contain alcohol.
    - Increase the client's fluid intake, and encourage activities that promote air exchange: deep breathing exercises; increased ambulation; and turning, coughing, and deep breathing.

Miscellaneous

- Acetylcysteine (Mucomyst)
  - Indication
    - Thickened pulmonary secretions, acetaminophen toxicity
  - Action
    - Reduces viscosity of respiratory secretions
    - Restores liver in acetaminophen toxicity
  - Adverse Effects
    - Stomatitis, nausea, flushing, fever, drowsiness

  - Nursing Interventions
    - Monitor the client for bronchospasm if medication is administered via the trachea.

- Activated charcoal impairs the effectiveness of acetylcysteine with acetaminophen overdose.

SECTION 18

THERAPEUTIC MEDICATION MONITORING

- Clozapine (Clozaril) – Monitor WBC differential weekly.
- Digoxin (Lanoxin) – 0.8 to 2 ng/mL therapeutic range
- Erythropoietin (Epogen) – Hct for women is 36 to 48%, and for men it is 42 to 52%
- Gentamicin – Peak is 4 to 12 mcg/mL, and trough is < 2 mcg/mL
- Heparin – Partial prothrombin time is 1.5 to 2.5 times control
- Insulin – Fasting glucose is 70 to 110 mg/dL, and HgbA1c is 6 to 7%
- Lithium – 0.8 to 1.2 mg/dL therapeutic range
- Methotrexate – 0.6 to 1.3 mg/dL therapeutic range
- Phenytoin (Dilantin) – 10 to 20 mcg/mL therapeutic range
- Phenobarbital – 10 to 30 mcg/mL therapeutic range
- Theophylline – 10 to 20 mcg/mL therapeutic range
- Valproate sodium (Depakote) – 50 to 100 mcg/mL
- Vancomycin – Peak 20 to 40 mcg/mL, and trough is 5 to 15 mcg/mL
- Warfarin (Coumadin) – The therapeutic range for INR is 2 to 3; for mechanical mitral valve, the therapeutic range for INR is 3 to 4.5

SECTION 19

ANTAGONISTS/ANTIDOTES

- Activated Charcoal (Charcoal Plus)
  - Indications
    - Poisoning
  - Action
    - Inhibits absorption from gastrointestinal tract
  - Adverse Effects
    - Black stools, obstruction, constipation

NOTES

- Nursing Intervention
  - Prevent aspiration and maintain fluids and electrolytes.
- Digoxin Immune Fab (Digibind)
  - Indications
    - Digoxin toxicity
  - Action
    - Binds digoxin to decrease toxicity
  - Adverse Effects
    - Heart failure, low cardiac output, tachycardia
  - Nursing Intervention
    - Monitor the client's potassium level and cardiac function during administration.
- Disulfiram (Antabuse)
  - Indications
    - Management of alcohol abstinence
  - Action
    - Produces a severe and life-threatening reaction when used with any form of alcohol
    - Used as aversion therapy
  - Adverse Effects
    - Psychosis, metallic or garlic taste, impotence
    - Symptoms disappear after 2 weeks of therapy
  - Nursing Interventions
    - When disulfiram is used with alcohol, side effects include flushing, dyspnea, vomiting, hyperventilation, chest pain, hypotension, blurred vision, and/or anxiety.
    - Instruct the client to start the medication 12 hr after last alcoholic drink.
    - The medication may be taken for 6 months to 1 year until alcohol abstinence is under control.
- Flumazenil (Romazicon)
  - Indication
    - Benzodiazepine overdose
  - Action
    - Reverses sedative effects of benzodiazepines

- Adverse Effects
  - Seizures, arrhythmias, nausea/vomiting, diaphoresis
- Nursing Interventions
  - Instruct the client to avoid alcohol.
  - Avoid CNS depressants and over-the-counter medications for 24 hr.
  - Resedation may occur after the medication is excreted.
- Naloxone HCl (Narcan)
  - Indication
    - Opioid-induced respiratory depression
  - Action
    - Displaces opioid from receptors
  - Adverse Effects
    - Ventricular fibrillation, tachycardia, hypertension, pulmonary edema
  - Nursing Intervention
    - Respiratory rate should increase within 1 to 2 min. Monitor respiratory system; provide oxygen and ventilation until full recovery.
- Protamine sulfate
  - Indications
    - Heparin overdose
  - Action
    - Forms an inert complex with heparin
  - Adverse Effects
    - Bradycardia, circulatory collapse, pulmonary edema/hypertension
  - Nursing Interventions
    - Repeat prothrombin time 15 min following administration.
    - Continuously monitor the client's cardiopulmonary system.
- Sodium polystyrene sulfonate (Kayexalate)
  - Indication
    - Hyperkalemia
  - Action
    - Exchanges sodium for potassium ions in the intestine

NOTES

- Adverse Effects
  - Diarrhea, anorexia, hypokalemia, hypocalcaemia
- Nursing Intervention
  - Monitor the client's fluid and electrolytes.
- Succimer (Chemet)
  - Indication
    - Lead poisoning
  - Action
    - Chelating medication binds to lead and excretes it
  - Adverse Effects
    - Sleepiness, paresthesia, arrhythmias, metallic taste, leg pain, flulike symptoms
  - Nursing Intervention
    - Encourage fluids and monitor lead levels.

SECTION 20

ELECTROLYTE BALANCING MEDICATIONS

Calcium

- Calcium gluconate
  - Indication
    - Hypocalcaemia, magnesium toxicity, hyperphosphatemia
  - Action
    - Elevates calcium levels
  - Adverse Effects
    - Bradycardia, constipation, renal calculi
  - Nursing Intervention
    - Maintain the client's calcium levels and monitor him for signs of hypocalcaemia (confusion, delirium, coma).

Magnesium

- Magnesium sulfate
  - Indication
    - Hypomagnesemia, seizures

- Action
  - Replaces magnesium and acts as an anticonvulsant
- Adverse Effects
  - Hold magnesium if the client's respirations are less than 12/min.
  - Monitor the client's laboratory levels.

Potassium

- Potassium chloride
  - Indication
    - Prevents and treats hypokalemia
  - Action
    - Potassium replacement
  - Adverse Effects
    - Arrhythmias, cardiac arrest, ECG changes, hypotension, hyperkalemia
  - Nursing Interventions
    - Understand that the client is at risk for hyperkalemia, as the medication interacts with ACE inhibitors, digoxin, and aldactone.
    - Maintain therapeutic level.
    - Follow safety measures when administering the medication via an IV infusion; 10 mEq/L in 100 mL of sodium chloride solution over 1 hr via an infusion pump device.
      - Each 10 mEq/L dose will increase the client's laboratory value by 0.1.

Sodium

- Sodium chloride
  - Indication
    - Prevents and treats hyponatremia
  - Action
    - Sodium replacement, isotonic solution
  - Adverse Effects
    - Edema, pulmonary edema, hypernatremia
  - Nursing Intervention
    - Obtain the client's daily weight and assess her for edema and respiratory exchange.

NOTES

UNIT EIGHT

NURSING LEADERSHIP AND MANAGEMENT

SECTION 1

MANAGEMENT

- Concepts of Management
  - ○ Leadership – A way of behaving that influences others to respond, not because they have to, but because they want to. Leaders help others to identify and focus on goals and the achievement of them. Leadership is a personal interaction that focuses on the personal development of the members of the group.
    - ■ Essential components of leadership
      - □ Knowledge
      - □ Self-awareness
      - □ Communication
      - □ Energy
      - □ Goals
      - □ Action
    - ■ Nursing Intervention
      - □ All nurses will need leadership skills to manage other nurses, assistive personnel, and clients. It is essential to the nursing role to identify and implement effective leadership practices.
  - ○ Management – A problem-oriented process with a focus on the activities needed to achieve a goal. Supplying the structure, resources, and direction for the activities of the group. Management involves personal interaction, but the focus is on the group's process. The most effective managers are also effective leaders.
    - ■ Phases of the management process
      - □ Planning
      - □ Organizing
      - □ Staffing
      - □ Directing
      - □ Quality control
    - ■ Management styles
      - □ Autocratic
      - □ Laissez-faire
      - □ Democratic

 ■ Nursing Intervention
  - □ All nurses should learn management skills and identify their own personal leadership style. Nurses should know the differences between being an autocratic and democratic leader. The most effective management style in a health care environment is the democratic leader who uses an interdisciplinary approach to encourage open communication and collaboration, which in turn, will promote individual autonomy and accountability.
- ○ Communication – Involves sending, receiving, and interpreting both verbal and nonverbal information between at least two people.
  - ■ Components of communication
    - □ Basic elements of effective communication
    - □ Assertive communication
  - 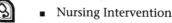 ■ Nursing Intervention
    - □ Effective communication requires commitment, effort, focus, and cooperation, especially when dealing with complex clinical issues and people who have diverse backgrounds and perspectives. It is essential to understand and use effective communication skills to successfully manage others.
- ○ Conflict – Arises when there are two opposing views, feelings, expectations, or other divergent issues. It can occur within an individual, between individuals, or between groups and organizations. Conflict can be managed.
  - ■ Sources of conflict
    - □ Lack of resources and/or economics
    - □ Differences in values
    - □ Struggles for power or influence
    - □ Sexual harassment
  - ■ Process of conflict resolution or negotiation
    - □ Four Steps
      - ▸ Avoidance
      - ▸ Accommodation
      - ▸ Compromise
      - ▸ Competition
      - ▸ Collaboration

NOTES

- Nursing Intervention
  - A nurse manager's role is to identify the source of conflict, understand the issues that have developed, and work toward conflict resolution while maintaining positive regard for each individual. It is essential to address the person with whom there is conflict before going to his superiors (use the chain of command). The most important conflict strategy involves collaboration that results in a win-win solution for everyone.
- Power vs. Influence
  - Power – The ability, strength, and capacity to do something.
  - Influence – Control over people and their actions.
  - Types of power
    - Reward – the ability to control resources
    - Coercive – the ability to inflict aversive outcomes or punishment
    - Legitimate – based on one's position
    - Referent – based on attractive characteristics
    - Expert – based on expertise or knowledge
  - Influence tactics
    - Ingratiation – the ability to manipulate others through flattery and style
    - Conformity pressure – the pressure to conform to the group; this pressure increases as group size increases to greater than six, or as familiarity with the topic decreases
    - Foot-in-the-door – a small request followed by a larger request
    - Door-in-the-face – a large request that is intended to be denied, followed by a smaller request that is intended to be granted
    - Guilt – the practice of inducing guilt before making a request; granting the request reduces the feeling of guilt

  - Nursing Intervention
    - The power of influence is aimed at accomplishing well-defined goals, preferably as a cohesive team.

- Team Building – Activities or efforts intended to unify people into a team to more effectively accomplish the overall objectives and mission of the organization.
  - Components of team building
    - Clear expectations – should be clearly defined and communicated to members of the team
    - Context – members should understand why they are participating on the team
    - Commitment – members should feel valuable, excited, challenged, and be committed to the success of the team
    - Competence – team should feel like it has the resources, strategies, and support it needs to meet its goals
    - Collaboration – rules of conduct should be followed for conflict resolution and cooperative decision-making
    - Communication – there should be a clear, honest, and respectful dialogue between team members
    - Creativity – new and innovative ideas should be encouraged and welcomed
    - Consequences – contributions and success should be recognized and rewarded

  - Nursing Interventions
    - Foster a culture that values collaboration and cooperation.
    - Communicate that teamwork is expected.
    - Publicly celebrate team success.
    - Bring a sense of play and fun to the team.
- Continuity of Care – Focuses on the experience of the client as she moves through the health care system; guiding the client through this experience requires coordination, integration, and facilitation of all the events along the continuum.
- Quality Improvement – A planned process to evaluate the delivery of care and to develop ways to address any problems or difficulties.
  - Continuous vs. total quality improvement
  - Types of quality indicators
    - Structure

NOTES

- ▪ Process
- ▪ Outcome
- ○ Data collection
- Variance/Incidence/Occurrence Reports – A variance or incident is an event that occurs outside the usual expected normal events or activities of the client's stay, unit functioning, or organizational processes.

- ○ Nursing Intervention
  - ▪ Incidence or variance reports are not intended to point blame, just document the facts. Their purpose is to identify situations or system issues that contributed to the occurrence and to engage strategies to prevent reoccurrence or to correct the situation.
- Resource Management
  - ○ Health care delivery
    - ▪ Retrospective vs. prospective payment
    - ▪ Health-maintenance organizations
  - ○ Budgeting
    - ▪ Types of budgets
    - ▪ The budget process
      - ☐ Planning
      - ☐ Preparation
      - ☐ Modification and approval
      - ☐ Monitoring

  - ○ Nursing Intervention
    - ▪ A nurse manager must be aware of economic issues in health care. Budgetary terms are fundamental to understanding the financial management of facilities. The more information available to the nurse, the better the decisions and input into long-range planning for the facility.
- Case Management – Involves the development of a partnership with the client, with the goal of managing changes in health and/or function that are due to serious, acute, or chronic and persistent illness and disability.
  - ○ Types of case management
    - ▪ Independent
    - ▪ Facility based
    - ▪ Provider based

- ▪ Insurance based

- ○ Nursing Intervention
  - ▪ A nurse's role in case management is to arrange services that respond to the hierarchy of client needs. This system provides care that minimizes fragmentation and maximizes holistic individualized client care.
- Consultation and Referral
  - ○ Consultation – To ask for help in solving a problem or meeting a need of an individual or group; this help is then applied and monitored by the nurse; often, it is a request for information from someone who has specialized knowledge, including peers.
  - ○ Referral – A request for assistance from someone who has specialized knowledge or skills to help in the management of the client's problems; most often, it is a request for intervention from another professional who has the needed skills and knowledge; the intervention becomes that specialist's responsibility, but the nurse continues to be responsible for monitoring the client's response and progress.
    - ▪ Common nursing consultation and referral situations
    - ▪ Appropriate use of consultation and referral

    - ▪ Nursing Intervention
    - ▪ The processes of consultation and referral are integral for effective use of services along the continuum. The nurse should support the client/family with appropriate consultation and referral to contacts in the community.

SECTION 2

DELEGATION

- Delegation/Supervision/Accountability
  - ○ Delegation – The act of asking another to do some aspect of care, assignment, or work that needs to be accomplished; can be horizontal to peers, upwardly vertical to management, or downwardly vertical to a subordinate.

NOTES

- Supervision – Monitoring the progress toward completion of delegated tasks; the amount of supervision required depends on the direction of the delegation, the abilities of the person being delegated to, and the location of the ultimate responsibility for outcomes.
- Accountability – Morally responsible for consequences of actions.
- Five rights of delegation
  - Right person
  - Right task
  - Right circumstances
  - Right direction and communication
  - Right supervision and evaluation
- Nursing Intervention
  - It is essential for a nurse manager to understand legal responsibilities when managing and delegating nursing care to a wide variety of health care workers. The nurse manager must delegate activities thoughtfully, taking into account individual job descriptions, knowledge base, and skills demonstrated. Remember, the professional nurse is accountable to determine the extent and complexity of client needs and to assign work that is consistent with the individual's position, description, and duties.

- Roles and Responsibilities for Levels of Staff
  - Assistive personnel (AP)
    - Also referred to as a nursing assistant or patient-service technician
    - Training is often on the job
    - An AP may complete a certification program – Certified Nursing Assistant
    - An AP functions under the direction of the licensed practical nurse (LPN) or RN
    - Skills
      - Basic hygiene care and grooming
      - Reports to the LPN or RN
      - Assistance with ADLs such as nutrition, elimination, and mobility
      - Performing basic skills such as taking vital signs, including pulse oximetry and calculating I&O

- Emphasis is on maintaining a safe environment and recognizing situations to report to their immediate superior
- LPN
  - May also be called a licensed vocational nurse (LVN)
  - Education is approximately 12 to 18 months in an accredited program
  - LPNs must complete and pass the NCLEX-PN exam for licensure
  - Function under the direction of the RN or health care provider
  - Scope of practice is determined by the Nurse Practice Act, which varies from state to state (requirements to maintain an active license are determined by each state)
    - Meet the health needs of clients
    - Care for clients whose condition is considered to be stable and/or chronic
- RN
  - May be diploma, associate degree, baccalaureate degree, or higher
  - Education ranges from 2 to 4 (or more) years
  - RNs must complete and pass the NCLEX-RN exam for licensure
  - Function under the direction of the health care provider
  - Advanced clinical skills in caring for client who is acute and critical; scope of practice determined by the Nurse Practice Act, which varies from state to state (requirements to maintain an active license are determined by each state)
- Advance practice nurses
  - May be nondegree or master's degree (or higher)
  - Education ranges from 18 months to 4 (or more) years (in addition to basic RN program)
  - Must complete and pass a certification exam (in addition to the NCLEX-RN exam) applicable to the specialty and practice (adult nurse practitioner, diabetic educator)

NOTES

- Functions vary according to the state practice act, which may be either autonomously or under the direct or indirect supervision of a provider
- Skills vary according to the state practice act, and may include the ability to prescribe, diagnose, and treat
    - Health care provider
        - May be a provider, provider's assistant, or nurse practitioner
        - In general, only an attending provider has admitting privileges to a facility, although another care provider in the practice may direct the care given to the client

SECTION 3

ETHICAL ISSUES

- Ethical Practice
    - Basic ethical principles
        - Nonmaleficence – the obligation not to harm others (Hippocrates states, "First do no harm.")
        - Beneficence/doing good – the obligation to do good for others
        - Autonomy/self-determination – the right to make one's own decisions
        - Fidelity – the obligation to be faithful to the agreements and responsibilities one has undertaken
        - Justice/treating people fairly – obligation to be fair to all people (when allocating limited resources)
        - Confidentiality/respecting privileged information – obligated to observe the privacy of another and maintain strict confidence
    - Ethical dilemmas
        - An ethical issue for which two opposing viewpoints can each be supported by a sound ethical principle
    - Ethical decision making

- A process in which the nurse, client, the client's family, and the health care team make decisions, taking into consideration personal and philosophical viewpoints, the ANA code for nurses, and ethical principles
    - The American Nurses Association's (ANA)
        - Sets guidelines to use when providing client care; outline the nurse's responsibility to the client, the profession of nursing, and assists the nurse in making ethical decisions
- Organ Donation
    - Determination of death
    - Nursing role
    - Family needs
    - Criteria for donation
    - Nursing Intervention
        - Nurses have an ethical responsibility to participate in the donation process by presenting the option of organ donation to all suitable clients and families. Families in this situation may be receptive to organ donation because they want something positive to come from their loss. The nurse should be comfortable when discussing this and be able to provide appropriate information about it.
- Advance Directives – A document in which a client who is competent is able to express his wishes regarding future acceptable health care (including the desire for extraordinary lifesaving measures including resuscitation, intubation, and artificial hydration and nutrition) and/or designate another person to make decisions for him if he is physically or mentally unable to do so.
    - Legislative action
- Living Will – A declaration of what the client finds acceptable or would refuse under identified situations that may occur in the future.
- Durable Power of Attorney – Designation of another person to make decisions (often financial) for the client when she becomes unable to make decisions independently.

NOTES

o Nursing Intervention

- It is important for a nurse to identify clients who do not have advance directives, to inform them of their rights, and to ensure that clients who have advance directives have copies placed in their charts.

SECTION 4

LEGAL ISSUES

- Informed Consent – Consent given by a client to a surgical/medical procedure or participation in a clinical study after achieving an understanding of the medical facts, risks, and benefits of an offered procedure/service.
  - o Elements of informed consent
  - o Nursing roles and responsibilities
- Client Rights
  - o Client Bill of Rights
  - o Americans with Disabilities Act
  - o Confidentiality – the right to privacy with respect to one's personal medical information
    - Legislation – Health Insurance Portability and Accountability Act (HIPAA) of 1996
      - □ A uniform, federal (national) act that provides privacy protection for health consumers
      - □ State laws that may provide additional protections to consumers are not affected by HIPAA
      - □ Guarantees that clients are able to access their medical records
      - □ Provides clients with control over how their personal health information is used and disclosed
      - □ HIPAA outlines limited circumstances in which a client's personal health information can be disclosed without first obtaining consent of the client or the client's family including:
        - ‣ Suspicion of child abuse.
        - ‣ When otherwise required by law (such as suspicion of criminal activity due to gunshot wounds).

- ‣ Incidences of state agencies or health department requirements; reportable communicable disease.
- Legal Responsibilities
  - o Types of law
  - o Nurse Practice Act
  - o Good Samaritan Law
  - o Mandatory Reporter of Abuse
  - o Malpractice
  - o Negligence
  - o Torts
  - o Breach of duty
  - o Standard of professional practice
- Advocacy – A process by which the nurse assists the client to grow and develop toward self-actualization.

 o Nursing Intervention

- A nurse who is able to recognize the rights and responsibilities in legal matters is better able to protect himself against liability or loss of licensure.

 Point to Remember – A nurse has a duty to intervene when the safety or well being of a client or another person is obviously at risk.

SECTION 5

INFORMATION SYSTEMS AND TECHNOLOGY

- Impact of Technology on the Nursing Profession
  - o Allows candidates to test for nursing licensure (NCLEX) with rapid results
  - o Permits verification of licensure online for nurses and other health care professionals
  - o Improves communication within and between departments through the use of e-mail, Intranet, and the Internet
  - o Eases the retrieval of medical histories to optimize decision making
  - o Automates medication delivery systems to help prevent error
  - o Automates distribution of client-care supplies

NOTES

- o Facilitates client-centered care with portable and wireless terminals, workstations, and laptops
- o Improves and facilitates client education through the use of multimedia software, including graphics, photographs, videos, and 3-D visuals
- o Supports continuing education with distance learning
  - Videoconferencing via satellite
  - Online degrees and certification programs
  - Computer-mediated instruction
- o Increases client monitoring capabilities
- o Decreases deviation from standards of practice
- o Allows electronic documentation
  - Bedside charting
  - Computerized charting
- Future Impact of Technology
  - o Federally mandated electronic transferable medical records
  - o Virtual and augmented reality allowing for simulated client teaching activities
- Data Security
  - o Passwords are necessary to prevent improper access to computers and medication systems.
  - o Only individuals who have a professional relationship with a client may access the client's personal health information, per HIPAA regulations.
  - o Computer terminals must be logged off and locked when not in immediate use.
  - o Monitor screens must be shielded or situated so that unauthorized individuals cannot see the information.

 Point to Remember – A nurse should not share computer passwords with another person, including coworkers and family members.

NOTES

UNIT NINE

COMMUNITY HEALTH NURSING

SECTION 1

RELIGIOUS COMPETENT CARE

- Nursing Process for Spiritually Sensitive Care
  - Assessment
    - What is the client's religion?
    - What is its importance in the client's daily life?
    - What dietary prohibitions does the client follow?
    - Are there rituals or customs that the client may wish to keep, particularly those related to transitions such as birth and death?
    - Is there a spiritual leader that the client wishes to have involved in her care?
    - Is the client using herbal or other traditional remedies?
    - Are there any practices that the client may find that will provide comfort or support?
  - Nursing Interventions
    - Remain sensitive to the client's spiritual beliefs, even if they are in opposition to personal beliefs.
    - Provide a diet that is consistent with the client's customs.
    - Provide the client privacy, as desired, for prayer and other rituals.
    - Allow visits by clergy or supportive members of the client's congregation.
    - Provide the client with a comfortable and supportive atmosphere that is conducive to religious practices.
    - Check the client's herbal and/or alternative methods to make sure they are not interacting poorly with the medications that the facility is providing.
- Buddhism
  - There are many forms of Buddhism; some sects are based on the country of origin
  - Spiritual beliefs
    - Important figure is Siddhartha Gautama
    - Spiritual leaders are priests and monks

- Central focus is enlightenment (Nirvana) and the attainment of a clear and calm state of mind
- Illness is a result of karma (cause and effect) and a consequence of actions in this life, or a previous life
  - Practices associated with life transitions
    - Birth
      - Belief in reincarnation
      - Contraception that prevents conception is acceptable
    - Death
      - The state of mind at the time of death is believed to influence rebirth; therefore, the nurse should ensure a calm, peaceful environment for the client who is dying
      - Organ donation is encouraged as an act of mercy
      - Cremation is common
  - Dietary restrictions
    - A vegetarian diet is practiced by many
  - Healing practices
    - A quiet and peaceful environment is important to allow the client to rest and practice meditation and prayer
- Catholicism
  - A form of Christianity; also known as Roman Catholic
  - Spiritual beliefs
    - Important figures are Jesus Christ, who was born to the Virgin Mary
    - Spiritual leaders are priests, nuns, and deacons
    - God revealed himself to humanity as the Father to Jesus; the Holy Trinity is the Father, the Son, and the Holy Spirit
    - Illness may be God's punishment for sinful thinking or behavior
  - Practices associated with life transitions
    - Birth
      - Contraception, abortion, and sterilization are prohibited

NOTES

- □ Baptism is required if an infant's prognosis is grave. If death of an infant is imminent, a nurse (of any religion) can baptize the infant by pouring a small amount of warm water on the infant's head and saying, "I baptize thee in the name of the Father, and of the Son, and of the Holy Spirit."
  - o Death
    - ▪ If death is imminent, a priest should be called to administer the Sacrament of the Sick, otherwise known as "last rites"
    - ▪ Organ donation is acceptable
    - ▪ Suicide may prevent burial in a Catholic cemetery
  - o Dietary restrictions
    - ▪ Some Catholics may abstain from eating meat on Ash Wednesday and on Fridays during Lent, which is a 40-day period between Ash Wednesday and Easter
  - o Healing practices
    - ▪ Most Catholic clients who are observant will want to see a priest when they are hospitalized
    - ▪ A client may request the Eucharist (communion) and/or the Sacrament of Reconciliation (confession) to aid in healing
    - ▪ A client may wear a cross, medal (symbol of a saint), or scapular (small piece of cloth on a string worn around the neck)
    - ▪ A client may display a statue of Jesus, Mary, or a saint at the bedside, and make use of a rosary (string of prayer beads)
- Christian Scientist
  - o A form of Christianity also known as the Church of Christ, Scientist
  - o Spiritual beliefs
    - ▪ Founder is Mary Baker Eddy
    - ▪ No clergy
    - ▪ Central beliefs consist of God as divine love; God's infinite goodness heals

- ▪ Illness is viewed as a manifestation of human imperfections that can be healed through prayer and spiritual regeneration; no disease is beyond the power of God to heal
  - o Practices associated with life transitions
    - ▪ Birth
      - □ Contraception is an individual decision
      - □ Abortion is prohibited
      - □ A client may choose to give birth at home, aided by a midwife, or to minimize hospitalization by going home the same day of the delivery
    - ▪ Death
      - □ Unlikely to seek medical help to prolong life
      - □ Organ donation discouraged
  - o Dietary restrictions
    - ▪ No requirements, but most abstain from alcohol
  - o Healing practices
    - ▪ Most practitioners rely on spiritual healing, but are not completely opposed to medical providers; individuals are free to make their own decisions in each situation
    - ▪ A client may avoid diagnostic testing to avoid unwanted medical treatment that could violate spiritual beliefs
    - ▪ Medications and blood products are avoided; immunizations are accepted only to comply with the law
    - ▪ Full-time healing ministers (Christian Science Practitioners) practice spiritual healing and do not use medical or psychological techniques; the church maintains a directory of Christian Science nurses available to provide medical care in a spiritual atmosphere
- Hinduism
  - o There are many forms of Hinduism, each with its own practices and customs
  - o Spiritual beliefs

NOTES

- No single founder, universally accepted scripture, or religious hierarchy; may be monotheistic (one god), polytheistic (many gods), or atheistic (no god)
- Spiritual leaders are priests
- Central belief is that spiritual well-being comes from leading a dedicated life based on nonviolence, love, good conduct, and selfless service
- Illness is a result of karma (cause and effect) and a consequence of actions in this life, or a previous, life; illness, accident, or injury may be viewed as a form of purification

o Practices associated with life transitions

- Birth
  - Contraception is acceptable
  - Abortion may be prohibited
  - Noting the exact time of birth is crucial to determining the child's horoscope
  - Males are not circumcised
  - Traditionally, the child is not named until the 10th day of life
- Death
  - Belief in reincarnation, and that the soul will reincarnate until its karma is exhausted
  - Prolonging life artificially is up to the individual, but allowing a natural death is traditional
  - A nurse should ensure a calm, peaceful environment for the client who is dying
  - Organ donation is acceptable
  - Prefer cremation and the casting of ashes in a river

o Dietary restrictions

- A vegetarian diet is encouraged and practiced by many; of those who eat meat, most abstain from beef and pork
- According to traditional dietary law, the right hand is used for eating and the left hand for toileting and hygiene
- There are several days set aside for fasting during a year; vary by sect

o Healing practices

- Personal hygiene is very important and the client may want to bathe daily
- Prayer for health is considered a low form of prayer and therefore, stoicism may be preferred
- Future lives are influenced by how one faces illness, disability, and death

● Islam

o Those who adhere to the Islamic belief are known as Muslims. Sunni Muslims form the worldwide majority and differ from Shi'a Muslims, a worldwide minority, in some matters of faith and practice

o Spiritual beliefs

- Important figure is the Prophet Mohammed
- Spiritual leaders are Imam
- Central beliefs are one God, Allah; holy text, Qur'an; Judgement Day; Final Day of Resurrection
- Illness, pain, and suffering are manifestations of God's will and are necessary to remove sin

o Practices associated with life transitions

- Birth
  - Contraception is acceptable
  - After 130 days of gestation (about 18 weeks), the fetus is considered a full human being
  - Abortion is permitted under certain circumstances (if the mother's life is in danger), but only if the fetus has not attained personhood
  - Circumcision of males is customary
- Death
  - Any attempt to shorten life is prohibited, but prolonging death by means of futile medical interventions is also prohibited
  - The client who is dying may wish to be placed facing Mecca (usually east)
  - Organ donation is acceptable
  - An autopsy is permitted for medical or legal reasons

NOTES

- □ Rituals following death include traditional bathing and burial within 24 hr; cremation is prohibited
  - ○ Dietary restrictions
    - ■ Food must be halal (lawful)
    - ■ Pork, alcohol, and some shellfish are prohibited
    - ■ Ramadan is a period of fasting that occurs from sunrise to sundown during the ninth lunar month (dates vary from year to year); children, pregnant women, and those who are sick are exempt from fasting
  - ○ Healing practices
    - ■ A client may wish to pray five times a day (dawn, midday, midafternoon, sunset, and nightfall) facing Mecca, and may have a prayer rug and Qur'an at the bedside for prayers
    - ■ Privacy during prayer is important
    - ■ Women are very modest and frequently wear clothes that cover their entire body; during treatment and care, the women's modesty should be respected as much as possible
- Jehovah's Witness
  - ○ A form of Christianity; name is derived from the Hebrew name for God
  - ○ Spiritual beliefs
    - ■ Founded in the 1870s as the Watchtower Society
    - ■ Spiritual leaders are older adults
    - ■ Central beliefs include the Bible as the literal word of God, which is historically accurate; all other religions are considered false teachings; conversion of others is important
    - ■ Suffering and illness are permitted by God and results from Satan's influence on the world
  - ○ Practices associated with life transitions
    - ■ Birth
      - □ Contraception is an individual choice
      - □ Abortion is prohibited
      - □ Infants are not baptized
    - ■ Death
      - □ Organ donation is permitted

- □ An autopsy is permitted if it is legally required
  - ○ Dietary restrictions
    - ■ Moderate use of alcohol is permitted, but drunkenness is a sin
  - ○ Healing practices
    - ■ Strongly opposed to blood products for transfusion and will refuse even if refusal means death
      - □ Volume expanders permitted if not derived from blood
      - □ Organ transplantation is permitted if all of the blood is drained from the organ or tissue before being transplanted
      - □ Advocate for a surgery that is bloodless
      - □ Courts have ordered transfusions for very young children; in other cases, they have respected the declared choice of an under-age minor that is able to defend his beliefs to the court in a manner that reflects a mature understanding without undue influence from his parents
    - ■ The reading of scriptures is believed to comfort the client and leads to mental and spiritual healing
- Judaism
  - ○ Predates Christianity and there are several major divisions with different customs and practices
  - ○ Spiritual beliefs
    - ■ Spiritual leaders are rabbis
    - ■ Central beliefs include one God; a holy text, the Torah (the Old Testament of the Bible); the Messiah has yet to come
    - ■ Illness and suffering are not judgements from God, since everyone is mortal
  - ○ Practices associated with life transitions
    - ■ Birth
      - □ Contraception is considered an individual choice
      - □ Abortion is permitted under certain circumstances
      - □ Ritual circumcision of males is called a Bris, which is performed on the eighth day of life

---

NOTES

- Death
  - An autopsy is discouraged, but not prohibited
  - Organ donation is permitted
  - Rituals following death include traditional bathing and burial within 24 hr; cremation is prohibited
  - Bereavement does not begin until after burial
- Dietary restrictions
  - Orthodox and observant Jews will observe dietary laws requiring food to be kosher (properly prepared) and may request a kosher food tray
    - Complex rules regarding food preparation includes a blessing when meat is slaughtered
    - Milk and meat cannot be served at the same meal
    - Pork and shellfish are prohibited
  - Fasting is required on Yom Kippur, the Day of Atonement (in fall, exact date is determined by the Jewish calendar); children, pregnant women, and those who are sick are exempt from fasting
  - Lactose intolerance is common among Jews of European origin
- Healing practices
  - Jewish law places the life of the person above all else
    - Saving a life overrides nearly all religious obligations
    - It is considered to be one of the highest commandments to tend to the sick or dying
    - In case of illness, medical care is obligated and health care providers are seen as instruments of God
  - Prayers for the well-being of the sick may be said
  - Anything that can be done to ease the client's suffering is encouraged

- Males who strictly practice their religion will wear a yarmulke (skull cap) at all times; very observant females may dress modestly and cover their heads at all times
- Church of Jesus Christ of Latter-Day Saints
  - Members refer to selves as belonging to The Church or Mormon faith
  - Spiritual beliefs
    - Founded by the Prophet Joseph Smith
    - Spiritual leaders are priests and older adults
    - Central beliefs – God revealed himself to humanity as the Father of Jesus; the Holy Trinity is the Father, the Son, and the Holy Spirit; the holy text is the Book of Mormon
    - The body is a gift from God and to help keep bodies and minds healthy and strong, God gave a law of health; illness, trials, and adversity are a part of life
  - Practices associated with life transitions
    - Birth
      - Contraception and abortion are forbidden
      - Infants are not baptized
    - Death
      - Organ donation is permitted
      - An autopsy is permitted
      - Life continues beyond death
  - Dietary restrictions
    - Alcohol, coffee, and tea are prohibited (some may drink caffeinated soft drinks or herbal teas)
    - Fasting is required once a month; children, pregnant women, and those who are sick are exempt from fasting
  - Healing practices
    - Medical intervention is God's way of using humans to heal
    - May want to use herbal remedies in addition to medical care
    - When blessing the sick, a person is anointed with oil by two older adults
- Seventh Day Adventist
  - A form of Christianity also known as Adventist

NOTES

- o Spiritual beliefs
    - Central belief includes the Bible as the literal word of God
    - Religious leaders are pastors and older adults
    - The body is the temple of the Holy Spirit (God) and must be kept healthy
- o Practices associated with life transitions
    - Birth
        - □ Contraception is an individual choice
        - □ Abortion is acceptable in cases of rape, incest, or if the mother's life is at risk
        - □ Opposed to infant baptism; adults are baptized by total immersion
    - Death
        - □ An autopsy is acceptable
        - □ Organ donation is acceptable
- o Dietary restrictions
    - A vegetarian diet is encouraged
    - Alcohol, coffee, and tea are prohibited
- o Healing practices
    - Healing can be accomplished both through medical intervention and divine healing
    - Prayer and anointing with oil may be performed for a person who is sick

SECTION 2

CULTURALLY COMPETENT CARE

- Nursing Process for Culturally Sensitive Care
    - o Assessment
        - What is the client's ethnic affiliation?
        - What is its importance in the client's daily life?
        - How well does the client speak, write, read, and understand English?
        - What dietary preferences or prohibitions does the client follow?
        - Are there rituals or customs that the client wishes to keep related to transitions such as birth and death?
    - Does the client want or need to have family involved in his care?
    - Is the client using herbal or other traditional remedies?

 o Nursing Interventions
    - Remain sensitive to the client's spiritual beliefs, even if they are in opposition to personal beliefs.
    - Provide a trained, bilingual interpreter if necessary.
    - Provide a diet that is consistent with the client's customs.
    - Allow family to be involved in the client's care, if desired.
    - Be respectful of the client's cultural preferences for personal space.
    - Be aware of the meaning of eye contact in the client's culture.
    - Check the client's herbal and/or alternative methods to make sure they are not interacting poorly with the medications that the facility is providing.
- African American
    - o African Americans comprise a very diverse population that varies considerably by geographic region, age, and socioeconomic status.
    - o Spiritual beliefs
        - Church and religious life are typically very important
        - Primary religious/spiritual affiliation – most are Christian, primarily Baptist; from other Protestant sects; or Muslim
        - Illness may have both natural and supernatural causes
            - □ Mental illness may be viewed as a lack of spiritual balance
            - □ Some chronic or congenital illnesses may be considered God's will
    - o Practices associated with life transitions
        - Birth
            - □ May give child a name of African origin, or one that is unique

NOTES

- Death
  - The deceased are highly respected
  - Cremation is avoided
  - Organ donation is unusual except in the case of an immediate family member
- Dietary preferences
  - May prefer cooked and fried foods
  - Traditional southern cooking may include cooked greens (collard, mustard, turnip) or yams
- Cultural variations
  - Language – English with traditional dialects is spoken in Louisiana (Creole) and many parts of the south; "Black" English is often spoken in urban areas, primarily inner cities, and is a distinct, expressive dialect with its own rules of grammar and slang
  - Eye contact – viewed as a sign of respect and trust
  - Time orientation – primarily focused on the present with a flexible time frame
  - Personal space – affection is shown by touching, hugging, and being close
  - Family – nuclear, extended, frequently matriarchal (women head the household); grandparents often involved in the care and raising of children
  - Sick role – attention from family and relatives is expected
- Healing practices
  - Home and folk remedies are often used first; usually it is the role of the mother or wife to obtain the remedy from a knowledgeable person
  - Prayer and visits from a minister may be important
  - There may be some mistrust of the medical establishment
- Health risks
  - Hypertension
  - Coronary artery disease
  - Sickle-cell anemia
  - Diabetes mellitus

- Prostate, breast, colorectal cancer
- Renal disease
- Asian American
  - Asian Americans comprise a very diverse population including ethnic groups of Pacific Islanders, Southeast Asians, Chinese, Japanese, Koreans, and others, each of which have their own customs and practices.
  - Spiritual beliefs
    - Primary religious or spiritual affiliations – Buddhism, Christianity, and Hindu
    - View of illness
      - Chinese traditionally believe that illnesses are caused by imbalances in the yin and yang
      - External influences block the circulation of vital energy, or chi
  - Practices associated with life transitions
    - Birth
      - May want female kin at bedside during labor
      - Breastfeeding is the norm
      - Genetic defects may be blamed on something the mother did during pregnancy
      - A new mother may be expected to eat a special diet and remain at home to recuperate for several weeks
      - Circumcision is a decision that depends on religious and ethnic practice
    - Death
      - Organ donation is uncommon
      - An autopsy is discouraged
  - Dietary preferences
    - Depending on the individual ethnic group, food may be considered important in maintaining a healthy balance, and the client may believe that certain foods are "hot" or "cold"
    - Chinese traditionally believe that food is critical to maintaining the balance of yin (cold) and yang (hot) in the body

---

NOTES

- o Cultural variation
  - ▪ Language – many different dialects exist for most major Asian languages, and English competence varies considerably; use a trained, bilingual interpreter if the client has limited English skills
  - ▪ Eye contact – avoided with authority figures as a sign of respect
  - ▪ Time orientation – present oriented; punctuality is not a traditional value, except in Japanese culture where promptness is important
  - ▪ Personal space – client may be very modest and public display of affection (physical touching) is not typical; the head may be considered to be sacred and therefore, touching someone on the head may be disrespectful
  - ▪ Family – patriarchal, extended families are common; wife may become a part of husband's family; filial piety (duty and obedience to one's parents and ancestors) is expected
  - ▪ Sick role – people who are sick usually assume a passive role; the client may not ask questions, as this is seen as disrespectful; however, she may nod politely at everything that is said; the client may be stoic in regards to pain
- o Healing practices
  - ▪ May want to use traditional and herbal remedies in addition to medical care
  - ▪ Older adult immigrants may have a strong belief in traditional folk medicine, while second-generation Asian Americans are often more oriented toward Western medicine
  - ▪ Chinese traditionally believe that health is achieved by restoring balance between yin and yang
  - ▪ Other specific health practices may depend on religion or ethnicity
- o Health risks
  - ▪ Hypertension
  - ▪ Stomach, cervical, liver cancer
  - ▪ Osteoporosis

- ▪ Thalassemia anemia
- ▪ Tuberculosis
- ● Hispanic
  - o Also known as Latino; comprised of a very diverse population including individuals of Mexican, Cuban, Central-American, South-American, Spanish, and Puerto-Rican heritage
  - o Spiritual beliefs
    - ▪ Latinos are traditionally very religious
    - ▪ Primary religious/spiritual affiliation is Catholic/Christian
    - ▪ Traditional belief is that health is controlled by fate, environment, and the will of God
  - o Practices associated with life transitions
    - ▪ Birth
      - □ May want female kin present for labor
      - □ Most breastfeed
      - □ New mother may be expected to eat a special diet and remain at home to recuperate for several weeks
      - □ Circumcision is not the traditional practice
    - ▪ Death
      - □ Extended family may want to tend to the sick and dying
      - □ The body is respected and organ donation is discouraged
      - □ An autopsy is discouraged
      - □ Women who are pregnant may be excluded from attending a funeral
  - o Dietary preferences
    - ▪ Traditional diet contains fresh ingredients; processed foods may be distrusted
  - o Cultural variation
    - ▪ Language – majority are bilingual Spanish/English, although English competence varies significantly; use a trained, bilingual interpreter if the client's English skills are limited; considered respectful to address individuals formally until a rapport has been established
    - ▪ Eye contact – direct eye contact is avoided with authority figures

---

NOTES

- Time orientation – primarily oriented in the present with a flexible time frame

- Personal space – handshaking is considered polite, but other touching by a stranger is generally considered inappropriate; embracing is common among family and friends

- Family – family is believed to come first, and members are expected to have a strong sense of family loyalty; most live in nuclear families with extended families and godparents

- Sick role – clients will often assume a passive role, and may be stoic with regard to pain

  o Healing practices

  - Soup and herbal teas may be thought to speed healing process

  - Siesta is a traditional period of rest after the midday meal thought to be important for maintaining health

  - The client may seek medical care for severe symptoms while using traditional folk healing measures for chronic or "folk" illnesses

  o Health Risks

  - Diabetes mellitus

  - Childhood obesity

  - Hypertension

  - Vitamin B_{12} deficiency anemia

- Native American

  o There are 300 or more different Native-American tribal groups, each with its own culture, beliefs, and practices

  o Spiritual beliefs

  - Belief in the Creator; sacred myths and legends provide spiritual guidance

  - Primary religious/spiritual affiliation – specific tribes follow rituals referred to in a general way by the tribal name; for example, the Navajo Indians follow "The Navajo Way"

  - Illness results from not living in harmony, or being out of balance with nature

  o Practices associated with life transitions

  - Birth

    □ May desire female kin to be present at birth

    □ No circumcision

  - Death

    □ Organ donation usually not desired

    □ An autopsy is usually not desired

    □ Some tribes avoid contact with a person who is dying (a hospital is preferable to home)

  o Dietary preference

  - May vary with tribal affiliation, although most are assimilated to U.S.-style diet

  o Cultural variation

  - Language – most speak English

  - Eye contact – respect is communicated by avoiding eye contact

  - Time orientation – primarily oriented in the present with a flexible time frame; rushing a client is considered rude and disrespectful

  - Personal space – keep a respectful distance

  - Family – some tribes are matrilineal, meaning they trace ancestral descent through the mother's line instead of the father's line; the mother may be the head of the family or clan

  - Sick role – usually quiet and stoic

  o Healing practices

  - A person who is ill may seek both modern medical attention and the services of a traditional medicine man/woman

  - Home and herbal remedies may be used

  - A medicine bag is a leather pouch that is worn around the neck, and the contents of it are considered sacred; it is improper to ask about the contents of the bag, and every effort should be made not to remove it

  - Health practices are intertwined with religious and cultural beliefs

  o Health Risks

  - Alcoholism

  - Gall bladder disease

  - Diabetes mellitus

  - Coronary artery disease

NOTES

- Tuberculosis
- Maternal-infant mortality
- Obesity
- Hypertension

SECTION 3

DISASTER PLANNING

- Disaster – A serious disruption of the functioning of a community that causes widespread human, material, economic, or environmental losses that exceed the ability of the affected community or society to cope with using its own resources.
  - o Internal disasters are events in the health care facility that threaten to disrupt the care environment
    - Structural (fire, loss of power)
    - Personnel related (strike, high absenteeism)
  - o External disasters may be man-made or natural
    - Man-made disasters
      - □ Transportation-related incidents, including car, train, plane, and subway crashes
      - □ Terrorist attacks
        - ▸ Bombs, including suicide bombs and dirty bombs
        - ▸ Bioterrorism
      - □ Industrial accidents
      - □ Chemical spills or toxic gas leaks
      - □ Structural fires
    - Natural disasters
      - □ Extreme weather conditions, including blizzards, ice storms, hurricanes, tornadoes, and floods
      - □ Ecological disasters, including earthquakes, landslides, tsunamis, volcanoes, and forest fires
      - □ Microbial disasters such as epidemics and pandemics

  - o A combined internal/external disaster situation can arise when an external disaster, such as a severe weather condition, both causes mass casualties and prevents health care providers from getting to the facility, perhaps due to traffic or road conditions.

- Disaster Planning
  - o Interagency cooperation within the community is essential in a disaster and requires:
    - Community-wide planning for emergencies and/or hazards that may affect the local area.
    - Coordination between community emergency system and health care facilities.
    - Developing a local emergency communications plan and/or network.
    - Identification of potential emergency public shelters
  - o Role of the nurse
    - In the health care facility
      - □ Joint Commission on Accreditation of Healthcare Organizations (JCAHO) mandates specific standards for hospital preparedness
        - ▸ Disaster plans
        - ▸ Disaster drills
    - In the community
      - □ Education provided to families about disaster planning
        - ▸ A family disaster plan should include:
          - ▹ What to do in an evacuation.
          - ▹ Plans for family pets.
          - ▹ Where to meet in case of an emergency.
        - ▸ A family disaster kit should include:
          - ▹ A flashlight with extra batteries.
          - ▹ A battery-powered radio.
          - ▹ Nonperishable food that requires no cooking (along with a nonelectric can opener).
          - ▹ One gallon of water per person.
          - ▹ Basic first-aid supplies.

NOTES

- Disaster Management
  - Emergency management system
    - Provides public access to immediate health care (911)
    - Dispatch communication center
    - Trained first responders – emergency medical technicians
    - Transportation to medical resources – ground (ambulance) and/or air (helicopter)
  - Declaration of a disaster
    - Disaster area – local officials request that the governor of the state take appropriate action under state law and the state's emergency plan and declare a disaster area
    - Federal disaster area – the governor of the affected state requests declaration of a disaster area by the president to qualify the affected area for federal disaster relief
    - Internal disaster – the nursing or administrative supervisor may declare an internal disaster in case of a facility-related issue
  - Disaster relief organizations
    - Federal Emergency Management Agency (FEMA)
      - FEMA is part of the U.S. Department of Homeland Security
        - Manages federal response and recovery efforts
    - American Red Cross
      - Not a government agency, but authorized by the government to provide disaster relief
      - The American Red Cross provides:
        - Shelter and food to address basic human needs.
        - Health and mental services.
        - Food to emergency and relief workers.
        - Blood and blood products to disaster victims.

- The American Red Cross also handles inquiries from concerned family members outside the disaster area
  - Hazardous material response team (HAZMAT)
    - Hazardous materials may be radioactive, flammable, explosive, toxic, corrosive, biohazardous, or may have other characteristics that make them hazardous in specific circumstances
    - HAZMAT team members are specially trained to respond to these situations and wear protective equipment
    - In a toxic exposure disaster, HAZMAT will coordinate the decontamination effort
  - Role of the nurse
    - Triage – process of prioritizing which clients must receive care first
      - Nonmass casualty situation – the nurse prioritizes client care so that clients with conditions of the highest acuity are evaluated and treated first
      - Mass casualty triage – consists of three levels; emergency services are presented with a large number of casualties; however, they are still functional and able to provide care to victims on all levels
        - Slightly injured – also called nonurgent
        - Seriously injured – also called urgent
        - Critically injured – also called emergent
      - Disaster triage – four levels; emergency services are presented with a number of casualties and/or ground conditions and are unable to treat everyone; therefore, they must provide the greatest good for the greatest number
        - Black tag – allowed to die, prepare for morgue
        - Red tag – critically injured, do not delay treatment
        - Yellow tag – seriously injured, can delay treatment for 1 to 2 hr
        - Green tag – slightly injured, can delay treatment for 2 to 4 hr

---

NOTES

- Health care facility disaster plan
  - A nursing or administrative supervisor may implement the disaster plan due to extreme weather conditions or an anticipation of mass casualties
  - Plans to implement
    - Establishment of an incident command center
    - Premature discharge of clients who are stable from the facility
    - Transfer of clients who are stable from the intensive care unit
    - Postponement of scheduled admissions and elective operations
    - Mobilization of personnel (call in off-duty individuals)
    - Protection of personnel and visitors
    - Evacuation plan
  - Role of the charge nurse during a disaster
    - Preparation of a discharge list that features clients who can safely and quickly be discharged
    - Personnel sent to the command center, if required
    - Off-duty personnel called in, if requested
    - Disaster victims are prepared for admittance
- Psychosocial Aftermath of a Disaster
  - Crisis intervention
    - Mental health response team employs advanced crisis intervention techniques to help victims, survivors, and their families better handle the powerful emotional reactions associated with crises and disasters
    - Goals
      - Reduces the intensity of an individual's emotional reaction
      - Assists individuals in recovering from the crisis
      - Helps to prevent serious long-term problems from developing

- Posttraumatic stress disorder (PTSD) – a mental health condition that can develop following any traumatic or catastrophic life experience
  - PTSD symptoms can develop in survivors of a disaster weeks, months, or even years following the catastrophic event
- Critical incident stress debriefing
  - Health care providers who respond to a highly stressful event that is extremely traumatic or overwhelming may experience significant stress reactions
  - The critical incident stress debriefing process is designed to prevent the development of posttraumatic stress among first responders and health care professionals
    - Defusing – discussion of feelings shortly after the disaster/critical incident (such as at the end of a shift)
    - Formal debriefing – discussion some hours or days after the disaster/critical incident, in a large group setting, with mental-health teams of peer support personnel serving as the leaders

SECTION 4

ALTERNATIVE AND COMPLEMENTARY THERAPIES

- Herbal Medications and Supplements
  - Safety and efficacy
    - The Dietary Supplement Health and Education Act limits the U.S. Food and Drug Administration's (FDA) control over dietary supplements
    - Many herbal drug companies make claims based on their own studies, indicating health benefits from using herbal drugs
      - Studies are not approved by the FDA
      - Labels on the herbal medications must include a disclaimer, stating that the FDA has not approved the product for safety and effectiveness
    - Herbal medications may interact with other medicines, and therefore produce serious side effects

---

NOTES

- o Common supplements
  - Saw palmetto (Serenoa repens)
    - Purported use – treats and prevents benign prostatic hypertrophy (BPH)
    - Side effects – prolonged bleeding time and altered platelet function
    - Herb/medication interactions – additive effect with anticoagulants
    - Studies – several well-conducted studies support the use of saw palmetto for reducing symptoms of BPH
    - Nursing considerations
      - ▸ Allow 4 to 6 weeks to see effects.
      - ▸ Discontinue use prior to surgery.
  - Valerian root
    - Purported uses – insomnia, migraines, and menstrual cramps
    - Side effects – drowsiness, anxiety, hepatotoxicity (long-term use)
    - Herb/medication interactions – additive effect with barbiturates and benzodiazepines
    - Studies – several studies support the use of valerian for mild to moderate sleep disorders and mild anxiety
    - Nursing considerations
      - ▸ Advise the client against driving or operating machinery.
      - ▸ Advise the client against long-term use.
      - ▸ Discontinue valerian at least 1 week prior to surgery.
  - St. John's wort (Hypericum perforatum)
    - Purported uses – depression, seasonal affective disorder, and anxiety
    - Side effects – headache, sleep disturbances, hepatotoxicity (long-term use), and constipation
    - Herb/medication interactions – may reduce the effects of many medications
    - Theophylline (Theo-Dur)
    - HIV protease inhibitors and nonnucleoside reverse transcriptase inhibitors
      - ▸ Cyclosporine (Neoral)
      - ▸ Diltiazem (Cardizem) and nifedipine (Procardia)
    - Studies – several well-conducted studies support the use of St. John's Wort for mild to moderate depression
    - Nursing considerations
      - ▸ St. John's wort has many medication interactions and should not be taken with other medications.
      - ▸ St. John's wort should not be used to treat severe depression.
      - ▸ St. John's wort should only be used with medical guidance.
  - Echinacea (Echinacea purpurea)
    - Purported uses
      - ▸ Prevents and treats the common cold
      - ▸ Stimulates the immune system
      - ▸ Promotes wound healing
    - Side effects – headache, epigastric pain, and constipation
    - Herb/medication interactions
      - ▸ May reduce the effects of immunosuppressants
      - ▸ May increase serum levels of alprazolam (Xanax), calcium-channel blockers, and protease inhibitors
    - Studies – well-conducted studies have conflicted as to the effectiveness of echinacea in the treatment of the common cold
    - Nursing considerations
      - ▸ Long-term use may cause immunosuppression.
  - Ginkgo (Gingko biloba)
    - Purported uses – improves cerebral circulation to treat dementia and memory loss
    - Side effects – dizziness and palpitations
    - Herb/medication interactions
      - ▸ May increase the effects of MAOIs, anticoagulants, and antiplatelet aggregates

---

NOTES

- ▸ May reduce the effectiveness of insulin
  - ☐ Studies – studies conflict as to the effectiveness of gingko in all purported uses
  - ☐ Nursing considerations
    - ▸ Discontinue 2 weeks prior to surgery.
    - ▸ Keep out of the reach of children. It may cause seizures with overdose.
- ■ Ginseng (Panax Quinquefolius)
  - ☐ Purported uses – improves strength and stamina and prevents and treats cancer and diabetes mellitus
  - ☐ Side effects – insomnia and nervousness
  - ☐ Herb/medication interactions
    - ▸ May decrease the effectiveness of anticoagulants and antiplatelet aggregates
    - ▸ May increase the effectiveness of antidiabetic agents and insulin
  - ☐ Studies – conflict as to the effectiveness of ginseng in all purported uses
  - ☐ Nursing considerations
    - ▸ Ginseng is contraindicated for women who are pregnant and/or lactating.
- ■ Glucosamine (2-Amino-2-deoxyglucose)
  - ☐ Purported uses – osteoarthritis and promotes joint health
  - ☐ Side effects – itching, edema, and headache
  - ☐ Herb/medication interactions – may increase resistance to antidiabetic agents and insulin
  - ☐ Studies – several studies support the use of glucosamine in reducing the symptoms of osteoarthritis in the knees
  - ☐ Nursing considerations
    - ▸ Use glucosamine with caution in clients who have a shellfish allergy.
    - ▸ Monitor glucose frequently in clients who have diabetes mellitus.
    - ▸ Allow extended time to see the effects of glucosamine.

- ▸ Use it often in combination with chondroitin.
- ■ Chondroitin sulfate
  - ☐ Purported uses – osteoarthritis
  - ☐ Side effects – headache, hives, photosensitivity, hypertension, and constipation
  - ☐ Herb/medication interactions – may increase the effects of anticoagulants
  - ☐ Studies – several studies support the use of chondroitin sulfate in reducing the symptoms of osteoarthritis in the knees
  - ☐ Nursing considerations
    - ▸ Do not give chondroitin sulfate to women who are pregnant or breastfeeding.
    - ▸ It is often used in combination with glucosamine.
    - ▸ Allow extended time to see its effects.
- ■ Omega-3 fatty acids
  - ☐ Purported uses – hypertriglyceridemia, and helps to maintain cardiac health
  - ☐ Side effects – nausea, diarrhea, hypotension
  - ☐ Herb/medication interactions – may increase the risk of vitamin A or D overdose
  - ☐ Studies – several well-conducted studies support the use of omega-3 fatty acids in reducing blood triglyceride levels, preventing cardiovascular disease in clients with a history of a heart attack, and slightly reducing blood pressure
  - ☐ Nursing Interventions
    - ▸ Omega-3 fatty acids are found in fish oils, nuts, and vegetable oils.
    - ▸ Some fish contain methylmercury and polychlorinated biphenyls (PCBs) that can be harmful in large amounts, especially in women who are pregnant or nursing.

NOTES

- o Nursing assessments for herbal medications
    - Ask the client specifically about herbal medications, vitamins, or other supplements during the client interview.
        - □ Over-the-counter medications are often not considered medications by the client.

- o Nursing Interventions
    - Instruct the client that herbal medications and supplements are not regulated by the FDA, often interact with other medications, and may cause serious side effects.
    - Instruct the client that it is important for him to use herbal medications and supplements cautiously and with medical supervision.

- Alternative and Complementary Therapies
    - o Nonbiomedical therapy
        - Covers a wide range of healing practices and philosophies that mainstream Western medicine (biomedical model) does not commonly use, study, or advocate
        - While some scientific evidence exists regarding some of these therapies, for most, there are key questions that are yet to be answered through well-designed scientific studies; such as whether they are safe and whether they work for the diseases or medical conditions for which they are used
        - Studies show that up to 50% of Americans include alternative and complementary therapies in maintaining their health
        - Nonbiomedical therapies are usually not covered by health insurance
        - Practitioners may not be licensed or regulated
    - o Common alternative therapies
        - Mind-body medicine uses a variety of techniques designed to enhance the mind's capacity to affect bodily function and symptoms
            - □ Prayer
            - □ Meditation – focusing the mind upon a sound, phrase, object, or visualized image to promote relaxation
            - □ Yoga – a form of exercise that emphasizes specific postures in combination with controlled breathing

- □ Biofeedback – a method of treatment that uses monitors to feed back to clients physiological information of which they are normally unaware; by watching a monitor, clients can learn by trial and error to adjust their mental processes to control involuntary bodily processes such as heart rate
    - Biologically based therapies use substances such as herbs, foods, vitamins, and other natural, but as yet unproven, substances
        - □ Aromatherapy
            - ▸ Ancient therapy that uses plant and essential oils
            - ▸ May be inhaled, placed in compresses, or applied to the skin
        - □ Special diets – macrobiotic, vegan
        - □ Herbal supplements
    - Manipulative methods use manipulation and/or movement of one or more parts of the body
        - □ Chiropractic – manipulation of the vertebrae to relieve pressure on the nerves and return the body to balance
        - □ Therapeutic massage – a range of therapeutic approaches involving the practice of kneading or manipulating an individual's muscles and soft tissues
        - □ Hydrotherapy – practice of physiotherapy in a pool (typically heated)
        - □ Tai Chi – an ancient Chinese practice designed to exercise body, mind, and spirit, improving the flow of chi, the vital life energy that sustains health and calms the mind
            - ▸ Described as meditation in motion; participants perform a defined series of postures or movements in a slow, graceful manner
            - ▸ Scientific studies have shown that Tai Chi:
                - ▹ Improves muscle flexibility and builds muscle strength.
                - ▹ Reduces falls in older adults and those with balance disorders.

NOTES

- Energy therapies that involve the use of energy fields; their existence has not been scientifically proven
  - Reiki – a Japanese technique for stress reduction and relaxation
    - Administered by the laying on of hands
    - Based on the idea that an unseen life-force energy flows through us and is what causes us to be alive
  - Therapeutic touch
  - Electromagnetic fields
- Traditional or folk medicine
  - Traditional Chinese therapies
    - Acupressure – placing physical pressure by hand or elbow onto certain points of the body (acupoints) to stimulate the flow of chi, the vital life energy
    - Acupuncture – placing very thin needles into certain points of the body (acupoints) to stimulate the flow of chi, the vital life energy; often used to eliminate or reduce pain
    - Herbs (ginger, green tea)
  - Native-American therapies
  - Various cultural folk remedies
- Nursing assessments
  - Ask the client about the use of alternative, complementary, or folk remedies.
 - Nursing Interventions
  - Assist the client with using the chosen therapy appropriately.
  - Provide client teaching, which includes safety and contraindications of complimentary therapies.
  - Refrain from endorsing products.

NOTES

Hockenberry, M. J., Wilson, D., & Winkelstein, M. L. (2009). Wong's Essentials of Pediatric Nursing (8th ed.). St. Louis, MO: Mosby.

Ignatavicius, D. D., & Workman, M. L. (2006). Medical-Surgical Nursing (6th ed.). St. Louis, MO: Saunders.

Kozier, B., Erb, G., Berman, A. J., & Burke, K. (2008). Fundamentals of Nursing (8th ed.). Upper Saddle River, NJ: Prentice Hall.

Lehne, R. A. (2007). Pharmacology for Nursing Care (6th ed.). St. Louis, MO: Saunders.

LeMone, P., Burke, K., & Mohn-Brown, L. (2006). Medical-Surgical Nursing Care. Upper Saddle River, NJ: Prentice Hall.

Lowdermilk, D. L., & Perry, S. E. (2007). Maternity & Women's Health Care (9th ed.). St. Louis, MO: Mosby.

Marquis, B. L., Huston, Carol J. (2009). Leadership Roles and Management Functions in Nursing (6th ed.). Philadelphia: Lippincott, Williams & Wilkins.

(2010). Nursing 2010 Drug Handbook (30th ed.). Philadelphia: Lippincott Williams & Wilkins.

Potter, P. A., & Perry, A. G. (2007). Fundamentals of Nursing (7th ed.). St. Louis, MO: Mosby.

Smeltzer, S. C., Bare, B. G., Hinkle, J. L., & Cheever, K. H. (2008). Brunner and Suddarth's

Textbook of Medical-Surgical Nursing (11th ed.). Philadelphia: Lippincott Williams & Wilkins.

Townsend, M. C. (2008). Essentials of Psychiatric Mental Health Nursing: Concepts of Care in Evidence-Based Practice (4th ed.). Philadelphia: F. A. Davis.

Varcarolis, E. M., Carson, V. B., & Shoemaker, N. C. (2006). Foundations of Psychiatric Mental Health Nursing: A Clinical Approach (5th ed.). St. Louis, MO: Elsevier.

Wilson, B. A., Shannon, M. T., & Shields, K. M. (2010). Pearson Nurse's Drug Guide 2010. Upper Saddle River, NJ: Prentice Hall.